PREFACE

IT IS IMPORTANT TO NOTE at the outset that this book is incompletely described by its title. Inclusion in the title of all the appropriate qualifications and elaborations would not only have horrified our publisher but would have presented the book designer with an almost impossible task in fitting the title onto the cover. As the reader will discover, the "race differences" we discuss are largely differences between various racial-ethnic groups in the United States, and "intelligence" mostly refers to performance on conventional intelligence tests. Furthermore, our discussion of this topic is chiefly focused on the question of the relative influences of the genes and the environment on such differences, and on some of the social implications of different answers to this question. We have, however, included in appendices some material that extends the discussion beyond the limited focus of the text.

One might well wonder why any behavioral scientist of good sense would willingly, or even reluctantly, become involved in the tangled morass of data, methods, ideologies, and emotions that currently surrounds the question of the relative importance of genetic and environmental variations in accounting for racial-ethnic IQ differences. In this case, it was not one behavioral scientist but three, all of whom generally consider themselves rational. Partly in defense of our reasonableness, but primarily to keep the historical record complete, we think it appropriate to recount some of the events that led us to embark on this project, as well as to outline the manner in which we attempted to carry it out.

In an important sense, this book may be considered a lineal descendant of Robert Sessions Woodworth's 1941 monograph *Heredity and Environment: A Critical Survey of Recently Published Material on Twins and Foster Children*. Not only were both books prepared under the auspices of the Social Science Research Council, but both deal with heredity and environment in relation to intellectual performance. However, this book had its own particular history. At the time this project was conceived, the National Academy of Sciences was finding the topic of race differences a rather slippery one and had rejected a recommendation from one of its own committees that some sort of review of the subject be prepared. A member of that committee, Ernest R. Hilgard, discussed with O. Meredith Wilson the possibility of the Center for Advanced Study in the Behavioral Sciences serving as the host for a small group of invited scientists who would do the task that the Academy had declined. The plan was eventually proposed to one of us (Lindzey) who was active in the affairs of the Social Science Research Council. The question was subsequently brought before the Committee on Problems and Policy of SSRC, where the general importance of a factual and objective survey of existing evidence bearing on the issue was agreed on, and a decision made to refer the matter to the Committee on Biological Bases of Behavior, as the existing SSRC committee that was best qualified to make further recommendations. Lindzey was currently a member of this committee and both he and Spuhler had served on an earlier version of the committee, known as the Committee on Genetics and Behavior.

The Committee on Biological Bases of Behavior agreed that the project was worthwhile and should be pursued if appropriate scholars could be found to prepare the report. Lindzey had planned to take a leave of absence the following year and he agreed to participate in

Race
Differences
in
Intelligence

Race
Differences
in
Intelligence

John C. Loehlin UNIVERSITY OF TEXAS

Gardner Lindzey UNIVERSITY OF TEXAS

J. N. Spuhler UNIVERSITY OF NEW MEXICO

Prepared under the auspices of
the Social Science Research Council's
Committee on Biological Bases of Social Behavior

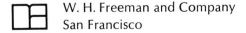 W. H. Freeman and Company
San Francisco

Library of Congress Cataloging in Publication Data

Loehlin, John C
  Race differences in intelligence.

  Bibliography: p.
  Includes index.
  1. Intelligence levels—United States. 2. Race. 3. Ethnic types.
4. Nature and nurture.
I. Lindzey, Gardner, joint author. II. Spuhler, James N., joint author.
III. Title.
BF432.A1L6   155.8′2   75–1081
ISBN 0–7167–0754–3
ISBN 0–7167–0753–5 pbk.

Printed in the United States of America

9 8 7 6 5 4 3 2 1

CONTENTS

Appendices

the project if suitable collaborators could be located. He and Spuhler had previously collaborated on an essay on racial differences in behavior, and Spuhler's background in physical anthropology and human biology provided essential additional competence. Loehlin and Lindzey had been colleagues at the University of Texas for a number of years, and although both were psychologists interested in behavior genetics, their backgrounds were distinctively different, with Loehlin possessing quantitative skills very much needed for the proposed study. It was finally agreed that the project would be undertaken under the auspices of SSRC's Committee on Biological Bases of Social Behavior with the primary participation of Spuhler, Loehlin, and Lindzey, assuming that adequate funding could be found to provide the three authors with some released time from academic responsibilities. Given this plan, the Center for Advanced Study in the Behavioral Sciences generously extended an invitation to the three participants to spend the 1971–72 academic year at the Center.

At this point, Henry W. Riecken (who was then President of the Social Science Research Council) and Lindzey set out upon a search for project funds that, rather to their surprise (given the manifest current interest in the problem and the frequent professions of the need for an objective analysis of the relevant data), proved to be quite elusive. There seemed to be little or no interest in the proposal on the part of federal agencies (not altogether surprising) or private foundations (somewhat more surprising). Some even suggested they would only be interested if we were willing to specify in advance just what the conclusions of the study would be! The one exception to this rather dreary set of interactions was the U.S. Office of Child Development and, specifically, Professor Edward F. Zigler of Yale University, who was then Director of the Office. He was consistently encouraging, and his agency eventually provided major support for the project. Additional financial aid was provided by the University of Texas, and by the National Science Foundation, through its support of the Project on Science, Technology and Society that was administered by the Center for Advanced Study in the Behavioral Sciences.

During the year at the Center our first step was to arrange for an Advisory Board that included representatives of relevant scientific specialties, representatives of the minority groups covered by the study, and persons who were familiar with public policy decisions and the role that scientific data might play in such decisions. This Board consisted of Anne Anastasi, Judge David L. Bazelon, William

Bevan, Marvin Bressler, James E. Cheek, Kenneth B. Clark, Carleton
S. Coon, James F. Crow, Theodosius Dobzhansky, Richard A.
Goldsby, Roger W. Heyns, Ernest R. Hilgard, C. C. Li, Alfonso
Ortiz, Manuel Ramirez III, Curt Stern, Charles W. Thomas, John
W. Tukey, Sherwood L. Washburn, and Dael Wolfle.

The members of the Advisory Board were informed of our general
plan for the monograph, its outline, and the steps we planned to take
in preparing it, and were invited to respond to this information in
any manner they chose: later, they were sent the draft manuscript
for their comments and criticism. We are deeply grateful to all the
members of the Board for their support and cooperation and we
would like to express particular gratitude to Professors Anastasi,
Bevan, Crow, Dobzhansky, Hilgard, Ramirez, Stern, Tukey, and
Wolfle whose detailed and specific comments on the manuscript were
extremely helpful to us in arriving at a final version.

In addition to arranging for the Advisory Board, we were especially
fortunate, early in our planning and study, in being able to meet
personally and consult with a number of social scientists who in
addition to their professional and academic credentials possessed the
unique perspective gained from being members of U.S. minorities.
These consultants included Edward J. Casavantes, then with the
United States Commission on Civil Rights and now at California
State University, Sacramento; William Hayes and William D. Pierce,
West Side Mental Health Center, San Francisco; Frank L. Morris,
the Russell Sage Foundation; Walter L. Wallace, Princeton University; and Robert L. Williams, Washington University. In recognizing here their helpful contributions to our own education, we do
not, of course, mean to imply an endorsement on their part of either
our project or its final product, this book. With each of these individuals we discussed our general plans, the proposed chapter outline
of the book, and various sources of data that might be important to
consider. We also reviewed a list of what we considered to be major
issues in the area and even discussed whether the project should be
pursued further at all—our consultants, like potential funding sources,
were by no means of one mind on this question. Each of the consultants was also later sent a draft of the manuscript and invited to make
suggestions for revision.

Not only were we aided by a Board of Advisors and a series of
consultants but we also attempted to capitalize on the unusual and
diverse talents of our fellow Fellows at the Center. There were some

general seminars early in the year in which we discussed key issues with our interdisciplinary colleagues, and later a number of smaller meetings and informal discussions with Fellows who were particularly interested in one aspect or another of the project. This provided a valuable opportunity for interacting with highly trained scholars whose disciplines ranged from the humanities to the biophysical sciences, although the majority were from the behavioral sciences. Among the Fellows we are particularly indebted to for helpful discussions concerning the project were Lee Cronbach, David Danelski, Nathan Glazer, Robert Hodge, George Lakoff, Joshua Lederberg, Robert LeVine, Robert Nozick, Henry W. Riecken, and David Wiley. We are particularly grateful to O. Meredith Wilson and his staff at the Center for having provided advice as well as a remarkably attractive and stimulating setting for our work.

Finally, we sent the draft manuscript, in two installments, to some fifty additional colleagues in the biological and behavioral sciences, inviting their comments and criticisms. Quite a few responded with extended critiques and suggestions. Others commented more briefly on matters of special interest to them. In a few cases we were fortunate in being able to discuss the manuscript directly with these persons. Among those to whom we are particularly grateful for helpful suggestions are Joan and Stephen S. Baratz, Ned Block, Philip K. Bock, Jack Bresler, Jan Bruell, Luigi Cavalli-Sforza, Raymond B. Cattell, Bernard Davis, Ralph Mason Dreger, Otis D. Duncan, Hans J. Eysenck, Stanley M. Garn, Perry Gluckman, Irving I. Gottesman, Henry Harpending, Richard J. Herrnstein, Joseph Horn, Christopher Jencks, David Jenness, Arthur R. Jensen, Ashley Montagu, R. Travis Osborne, T. Edward Reed, Sherman Ross, H. Eldon Sutton, William Shockley, Steven G. Vandenberg, and Lee Willerman.

In identifying these various distinguished scientists and scholars, we do not, of course, mean to imply or suggest their endorsement of this book. We sent them a draft—in which all of them found at least some room for improvement. Their suggestions were of help to us in putting the draft into its final form. We do want to acknowledge that assistance, plus the encouragement that many of them provided us, but we do not wish to have them saddled with any of our views that they do not share.

In short, we wish to be quite explicit concerning the responsibility for what is contained in this volume. The statements and conclusions in the book have benefited from the wise advice and support of many individuals and agencies, but we, the authors, are solely responsible for what is said.

We are grateful to Noel Dunivant, Jr., for his conscientious help in checking references.

The royalties from this book have been assigned to the University of Texas, the University of New Mexico, and the Center for Advanced Study in the Behavioral Sciences, to provide financial assistance for minority-group students and scholars.

December 1974   John C. Loehlin
                                                 Gardner Lindzey
                                                 J. N. Spuhler

Race
Differences
in
Intelligence

PART I

ISSUES
AND
CONCEPTS

CHAPTER 1

The Problem and Its Context

IT MAY BE THAT WHILE SPECIALISTS in the physical and natural sciences have been embroiled in debates over arms control, atomic energy, atmospheric and water pollution, supersonic transportation, and organ transplants, social scientists have had less than their share of the problems associated with the intersection of science, technology, and public policy. If so, this disparity is fast being removed by the recent eruption of scientific and public concern about individual and group differences in intelligence, their determinants, and the implications of all of this for social and political decisions. Questions concerning the meaningfulness and predictive utility of any estimates of general intelligence, the stability of such estimates, and the relative contributions of genetic and environmental factors to intelligence have remained among the most difficult and emotionally charged issues within the social sciences for more than five decades. When these questions are reexamined in the context of racial and social class differences in a society ridden with unresolved tensions in these areas, it is not surprising that the result should be a massive polemic in which personal conviction and emotional commitment often have been more prominent than evidence or careful reasoning.

The goal of this book is to provide a sober, balanced, and scholarly examination of the evidence that bears upon the role of genetic and environmental factors in the determination of group differences in ability in the United States. Although the focus of our effort will be upon the existing evidence that bears significantly upon this question, we will also be concerned with the policy implications, if any, that such evidence may have, and also with the extent to which further research in this area should be given priority, and what varieties of such research may be most promising in terms of providing significant and clear-cut evidence.

THE GENERAL QUESTION

There is no issue in the history of the social sciences that has proved to be quite so persistently intrusive as the question of assessing *the relative importance of biological and environmental determinants of behavior*. Indeed, an interest in the contribution of what is given as opposed to what is learned far predates the emergence of the biological and social sciences. The modern versions of the question began to emerge following the formulations of Galton and Darwin in the nineteenth century and became more sophisticated early in the twentieth, after the development of the discipline of genetics from Mendel's discoveries and the appearance of a variety of techniques for measuring aspects of behavior quantitatively.

The initial presentations of the major ideas of Darwin, Galton, and Mendel occurred in the span of a few years even though it was to be many decades before all of these ideas were brought together and integrated. Darwin's *Origin of Species*, in which he developed his theory of evolution and particularly his view of the importance of natural selection, was published in 1859. His emphasis upon the continuous and orderly development of new forms of life from other forms and the decisive role played by fitness, or reproductive advantage, was from the beginning linked to behavioral as well as physical attributes and thus directly relevant to social scientists. Galton's concern with the importance of inheritance in determining high levels of achievement was clearly influenced by the ideas of his cousin

Darwin. Galton's studies, published under the title *Hereditary Genius* in 1869, can be seen as an application of Darwin's concepts to an area of human behavior of unusual interest. Galton was able to show that among persons judged to be outstanding in their achievements the number that had biological relatives who were also judged to be outstanding vastly exceeded the number expected on the basis of chance. Galton also introduced the study of twins as a method of providing evidence concerning the relative contributions of heredity and environment. Altogether independent of the work of Darwin and Galton was the plant research of Mendel, first published in 1866, that provided the basis for the laws of segregation and independent assortment of inherited traits. But it was not until the turn of the century that the importance of Mendel's work was recognized and his two laws were suitably elaborated to serve as the foundation for the discipline of genetics. Shortly thereafter the term "gene" was applied to the basic unit that produced the regularities in inheritance that Mendel had noted. At almost the same time the label "genetics" was applied to this field of inquiry and the distinction was made between the *genotype*, the underlying biological makeup of an organism, and the *phenotype*, the external and observable aspect of the organism. What began as the study by a few persons of simple characters or attributes rapidly changed into an entire discipline that was concerned with simple and complex characters and their analysis at many different levels, ranging from molecular processes to the quantitative analysis of polygenic characters in large populations.

It was also around the turn of the century that psychologists began to show serious interest in individual differences and their measurement. The term "mental test," which was first suggested by J. McKeen Cattell (1890), provided a label for a set of diverse activities all of which were intended to identify and measure dimensions of variation among individuals that would be useful in predicting significant aspects of behavior. Initially most of these measures assessed simple sensory or sensory-motor components of behavior, but from almost the beginning of these developments there were psychologists who believed that complex and not simple processes would prove to be the key to predicting "intelligent behavior." It was this perspective that eventually led Binet and Simon, in an attempt to predict the probability of educational success, to develop the Binet-Simon Scale (1908) that in the revision by Lewis Terman (1916) became the Stanford-Binet, the most famous of all tests of intelligence. This instrument, with its associated concept of the intelligence quotient or "IQ," pointed the way to the development of group testing of intelligence and other special abilities or aptitudes during World War I, and all of this signalled the onset of the Mental Testing Movement. The movement was marked by the vigorous development and application of a wide variety of tests in an extraordinarily diverse number of settings. Although psychological tests have not been without their detractors, even at the outset of the movement, there is little doubt that such tests represent one of the most significant technological accomplishments of the social sciences.

While mental tests were emerging and the discipline of genetics was developing, the social sciences were struggling also with the question of how to deal with the relation between genetic variation and behavior. Although social scientists had early contact with ideas of biological determination, particularly in the writings of Galton and Spencer, the social sciences as they developed in the United States demonstrated a very strong preference for formulations and findings that emphasized environmental control of behavior. A clear illustration of this is provided by the reactions to the writings of William McDougall and those of John B. Watson.

McDougall's instinct-based psychology emphasized the biological inheritance of mental characteristics:

> It will help to make clear the influence of innate qualities, if, by effort of imagination, we suppose every English child to have been exchanged at birth for an infant of some other nation (say the French) during some fifty years. At the end of that period the English nation would be composed of individuals of purely French origin or blood. . . . What would be the effect? . . . gradually, we must suppose, certain changes would appear; in the course of perhaps a century there would be an appreciable assimilation of English institutions to those of France at the present day, for example, the Roman Catholic religion would gain in strength at the cost of the Protestant. (1920, p. 165)

Watson, on the other hand, strongly influenced by Pavlov's findings and theories concerning the conditioned response, took a radically environmentalist position:

> Give me a dozen healthy infants, well-formed, and my own specified world to bring them up in and I'll guarantee to take any one at random and train him to become any type of specialist I might select—a doctor, lawyer, artist, merchant-chief and, yes,

even into beggar-man and thief, regardless of his talents, penchants, tendencies, abilities, vocations and race of his ancestors. (1926, p. 10)

McDougall's views, after some modest contemporary popularity in the United States, ebbed rapidly in influence. By contrast, Watson's Behaviorism captured the main body of American psychology with a grip that has only begun to be loosened by the cognitive psychologies of the last decade or two and by the emergence of behavior genetics and psychobiology as interdisciplinary specialties.

Of course, most social scientists most of the time have taken positions somewhere between the hereditarian and environmentalist extremes, accepting the reality that both the genotype and the environment contribute significantly to behavioral variation, but differing in the relative weights to be assigned to the two in accounting for particular aspects of behavior. It was only in the heat of polemic, or in the hands of enterprising journalists, that the joint importance of these two factors was ever denied. Even McDougall saw the changes in England as taking place "gradually," and Watson, in the sentence immediately following the passage quoted above, hedged: "I am going beyond my facts and I admit it . . ." Nonetheless, the consensus position of American social science has always been much closer to Watson than to McDougall.

A MORE FOCUSED QUESTION

Given the rapid development of tests of mental ability in the early part of this century and the obvious significance of mental ability for the individual and society, it is not surprising that discussions of the impact of hereditary and environmental factors upon behavior came to center on intelligence. Thus, during the 1920's and 1930's one of the most active areas of investigation in the social sciences was *nature versus nurture in relation to the IQ*. Questions concerning the relative stability of a person's IQ over time, the extent to which it may be modified through environmental manipulation, and its usefulness in predicting significant performance provided the nucleus for a series of investigations that united certain investigators (and universities) and sharply divided them from others. Many of these studies were based on twins and adopted children and this research was surrounded by acrimonious disputes that led to an influential monograph by the psychologist Robert S. Woodworth (1941), which provided a scholarly and dispassionate discussion of the existing evidence and a clear statement of many of the underlying issues.

In recent decades, the nature-nurture issue with respect to intelligence has mostly lain quiescent, until its dramatic resurgence in 1969 in the form of the so-called "Jensen controversy." All along, a scattering of investigators in the emerging interdiscipline of behavior genetics have been addressing themselves to research on the genetic basis of human abilities. Examples of work in this country may be found in two volumes edited by Vandenberg (1965, 1968), and there has also been a vigorous tradition abroad, as exemplified by the work of Burt (1966) in Great Britain, Husén (1959) in Sweden, and others. Meanwhile, genetically oriented workers in the field of mental retardation made steady progress and even some fairly spectacular advances, as in the successful treatment of phenylketonuria (PKU), and the discovery of the chromosomal basis of Down's syndrome (formerly called "mongolism"). In general, research on abilities during this period tended to focus on individual variation rather than social class or racial differences; the authors were wary of drawing strong implications for education or other matters of pressing social concern; and for the most part little public excitement ensued. There were a few minor flurries following the publication by Audrey Shuey (1958, 1966) of a book reviewing studies of black and white differences on IQ tests in which hereditarian conclusions were reached, but the evidence was indirect, and in any case reviews with very different conclusions were available (Klineberg, 1944; Pettigrew, 1964; Dreger and Miller, 1960, 1968). So Shuey's volume on the whole did not generate a great deal of excitement. Shortly, however, the picture was to change profoundly.

THE CONTROVERSIAL CONTEMPORARY QUESTION

It seems unlikely that there has ever been a controversy that has involved a more complex tangle of ethical, public-policy, emotional, measurement, design, and inference issues than the attempt to determine the relative contribution of genetic and environmental variation to group differences in intellectual performance. Since publication of the controversial monograph by Arthur R. Jensen (1969) the debate has been carried on in speeches, interviews, and technical journals as well as in the mass media. Far from identifying areas of clear agreement and resolvable differences, these discussions have for the most part led to further polarization of positions and could probably be assessed fairly as not having offered much enlightenment to the genuinely interested but uncommitted observer. Those concerned with related public-policy issues have found little to guide or instruct them in making wise decisions. For every expert witness it seems possible to find another purporting to be equally expert who provides contrary advice.

Jensen's lengthy article was published by the *Harvard Educational Review* in 1969. The publication was titled "How much can we boost IQ and scholastic achievement?" and defended three major theses: (1) IQ tests measure a general-ability dimension of great social relevance; (2) individual differences on this dimension have a high degree of genetic determination (about 80 percent); and (3) educational programs have proved generally ineffective in changing the relative status of individuals and groups on this dimension. Jensen also took up Burt's (1961) suggestion that because social mobility is linked to ability, social-class differences in IQ probably have an appreciable genetic component.

All of this would undoubtedly have produced some concern and response from environmentalists, particularly those actually involved in programs of compensatory education. This potential response, however, was enormously magnified by a very small portion of the article dealing with racial differences in intelligence and concluding with the statement:

> So all we are left with are various lines of evidence, no one of which is definitive alone, but which, viewed all together, make it a not unreasonable hypothesis that genetic factors are strongly implicated in the average Negro-white intelligence difference. The preponderance of the evidence is, in my opinion, less consistent with a strictly environmental hypothesis than with a genetic hypothesis, which, of course, does not exclude the influence of environment or its interaction with genetic factors. (p. 82)

Although this statement is considerably more cautious and carefully qualified than many generalizations encountered in the social science literature, the sociopolitical climate of the times in the United States was such that the remark led to a storm of protest. The *Harvard Educational Review* alone published at least a dozen rejoinders, most of them highly critical, as well as a reply by Jensen. Critical commentaries have since appeared in dozens of other publications ranging from the technical journals to mass media; among the early sharp criticisms were articles by Hirsch (1970) and Lewontin (1970). Many of Jensen's critics questioned or denied the validity of IQ tests; some of them disputed the evidence for the high heritability of intelligence; a number pointed out the logical hazards of arguing from individual to group differences on any trait; and almost all found flaws in many of the studies cited by Jensen. In a recent book-length statement (1973a) Jensen has defended and extended his position on racial differences.

As the controversy widened, Jensen became the target of a variety of political and personal abuse, from both outside and within the academic community. A sobering account of this period is presented by Jensen in the preface to his collected writings on the topics of genetics and education (Jensen, 1972a). An article by Herrnstein (1971) dealing with genetic variation, social class, and intelligence also aroused a storm of controversy even though it said virtually nothing on the topic of racial-ethnic differences in intelligence. An expanded treatment of this topic (Herrnstein, 1973) also includes a full discussion of the personal consequences of the controversy for the author.

Soon the debate about race and IQ was taken up in Great Britain, stimulated by the publication of a book by H. J. Eysenck (1971), a distinguished British psychologist not noted for reluctance to engage in controversy. Eysenck's position in the book generally agreed with Jensen's, but Eysenck took on additional targets as well (such as the Irish). The book provoked a flurry of commentary in the British communications media, and led to a physical assault upon Eysenck as he was attempting to deliver a talk at the London School of Economics.

Predating the Jensen controversy, but to a considerable extent brought into public prominence by it, was a running argument in the United States between the Nobel laureate physicist William Shockley and his fellow members of the National Academy of Sciences. Shockley urged the Academy to take vigorous and positive action to investigate racial differences in IQ, and in particular, the possible dysgenic effect of the reproductive patterns of the black population of the United States. The Academy appointed several committees to consider Shockley's proposals and their work led to two reports (National Academy of Science, 1968, 1972) that, although acknowledging the legitimacy of research in this area, declined to consider it of special scientific urgency. A number of Shockley's attempts to present his views in public have also been associated with disruptions or threats of disruption leading to the cancellation or termination of the speeches.

Another major debate running through this period and interweaving with the others was that emanating from the survey, published under the title *Equality of Educational Opportunity*, that had been commissioned by the Department of Health, Education, and Welfare and conducted by a team of distinguished social scientists, headed by the sociologist James Coleman. This massive study, published in 1966 and popularly referred to as the "Coleman Report," indicated that at the time of the survey systematic differences in funding and facilities between U.S. schools serving predominantly black and predominantly white populations had virtually disappeared—except for the fact of segregation itself; that average black and white differences in academic performance remained large and persistent; and that measurable characteristics of the schools appeared to have remarkably little effect on the academic performance of the students attending them. The observed differences in academic achievement between schools seemed largely to reflect differences in the attributes of the students entering them, rather than differences in the pupils' experience in the schools.

This too aroused much controversy. The Coleman Report findings were given a key role by Jensen in his argument for the importance of genetic influences in scholastic achievement. A considerable amount of debate and discussion, and reanalyses of the Coleman data—most of which tended to support the original findings—are presented in a recent volume edited by Mosteller and Moynihan (1972), and the political and social implications of the findings of the Coleman study and other related investigations are discussed at length by Christopher Jencks in his recent book, *Inequality* (1972), which seems certain to keep the argument alive.

TECHNOLOGY ASSESSMENT
AND PSYCHOLOGICAL TESTING

In recent years influential persons in both political and scientific circles have come to view assessing the broad implications for our society of technological changes as one of the most significant of all contemporary problems (National Academy of Sciences, 1969; Brooks and Bowers, 1970). Although discussions of technology assessment generally have centered on the natural sciences and engineering, there has been occasional recognition of the potential importance of the behavioral sciences in any systematic attempt to understand fully the broad effects of new technological and scientific developments. In a few instances, such as the controversy in regard to the supersonic transport, studies have been conducted that have been aimed directly at an understanding of the psychological or behavioral consequences of introducing a technological change.

Less clearly understood has been the fact that psychology is already embarked upon a large-scale assessment of an important part of its own technology—the intelligence test. Current concern with racial-ethnic differences in measured intelligence and the relative contributions of genetic and environmental components to the observed differences is to a considerable degree rooted in an interest in the social consequences of classification and prediction on the basis of psychological tests. The attempt to understand these consequences and to control them in a socially desirable manner represents a clear example of technology assessment, and such a view of the process may serve to lessen somewhat the extremes of emotion often associated with this issue. It may be argued that even those who stand in direct opposition to each other in their interpretation of the basis for group differences in intelligence can share an interest in seeing that psychological tests are used in a more useful and sensible manner than is now often the case.

A series of legal suits brought against school boards and employers charging that psychological tests have served to discriminate against minorities or culturally deprived groups has placed the whole issue quite clearly in an assessment framework. Moreover, a Supreme Court decision (*Griggs et al.* v. *Duke Power Company;* see also *United States* v. *Georgia Power Company*) has placed definite limits on the circumstances under which psychological tests may be used appropriately and legally, and comparable questions are being raised in a variety of educational, legislative, and judicial settings throughout our nation. Indeed, the future of large-scale intelligence testing within our society remains at this juncture quite unclear.

SOME CENTRAL AND COMPLICATING CONSIDERATIONS

The paragraphs that follow include discussion of some persistent misconceptions that have beclouded attempts to understand the roles of heredity and environment in influencing group differences in behavior, as well as some matters of fact and definition central to such an analysis.

"Genetic" does not mean "unchangeable." There is a general confusion between the immutability, or lack of environmental responsiveness, of a trait and its degree of genetic determination. There has been a tendency among many social scientists as well as the general public to believe that when a trait is strongly influenced by genetic factors there necessarily is little possibility for environmental influence. In fact, the ability to manipulate a trait by environmental means may be greatly facilitated by understanding its genetic basis. A classic example is the low intelligence resulting from the gene-based metabolic disease phenylketonuria (PKU). If infants having the genetic constitution for the disease are fed a special diet low in the amino acid phenylalanine, the accumulation in the brain of toxic metabolic products is prevented, and their intelligence develops to a fairly normal level. Throughout this volume we will seek to remind the reader that a high level of heritability for a given trait or character is not to be automatically equated with a low level of modifiability.

Equality is not identity. Many believe that provision for social equity or "equal treatment" is inconsistent with accepting the existence of biological and psychological individuality. This view appears to derive from a failure to distinguish between "equal" and "identical." It is indeed the case that if two persons who differ in relevant biological or psychological properties are accorded *identical* treatment, identical outcomes would not be expected as the result. But this does not mean that there couldn't be different treatments that are *equal* in terms of some appropriate social metric (say, cost) that would when applied to these two persons yield outcomes that are equal in terms of some other appropriate social metric (prestige, say, or income). If not— if equal inputs cannot be found that yield equal outcomes—the question of whether social equity should be defined in terms of inputs or outcomes becomes moot.

General intelligence or special abilities? There is no broad consensus about the utility of the concept of general intelligence and, more specifically, the merit of employing one indicator of intelligence, rather than several. This topic will be explored at some length in Chapter 3 of this book. In general, we will take the position that both the view of intelligence as a unitary dimension and as a composite of special abilities have value in appropriate contexts. We would only add here our belief that any very narrow approach to how "intelligence" (or any other trait) is to be indexed or measured, although not without certain practical advantages, can have unfortunate long-term scientific and social consequences.

Different meanings of "race." The concept of race is used quite differently in the biological and social sciences generally, as well as in varying senses by individual scientists. In the biological sciences, races are customarily considered as biological subspecies, defined by gene frequencies, while in demography and related fields race customarily refers to ethnic identification. An individual's race, for purposes of the U.S. Census, may be quite different from a biological classification of him. Obviously, no discipline has an inherent right to the word, but use of it in different senses can lead to misunderstanding and confusion, especially if one discipline perceives another as clumsily or maliciously misusing "its" term. In this book, to avoid ambuigity, we will usually employ "race" or "racial differences" in the sense of the biologist, as elaborated in some detail in the next chapter. For the demographer's sense of "race," we will prefer the cultural anthropologist's term "ethnic group." In neutral or ambiguous cases we will often use the hybrid term "racial-ethnic group." We do not expect to be entirely consistent in our use of the term "race"; sometimes precedence will be taken by idiomatic usage. Our title is a case in point: logically it should be "racial-ethnic differences in intelligence" but this just seemed too cumbersome.

Disagreements about "heritability." There are several different formal definitions of heritability, and a good deal of ambiguity concerning the extent to which heritability estimates can be generalized from one set of conditions to others. In addition, there is disagreement about whether information concerning the heritability of a given character or trait *within* one or more groups provides any information about the likelihood that genetic variation plays a role in determining differences *between* two or more groups. These topics will be discussed in Chapter 4.

Gene-environment interactions and correlations. There are many different types of gene-environment interactions and correlations that often are not recognized conceptually; none have been empirically explored at all adequately. We would, however, caution against a growing tendency to place a kind of mystical aura around these concepts. Although they are of considerable theoretical interest, it remains an empirical question whether they do in fact account for a significant part of the observed variation of a trait in a particular instance, and there are some techniques available for exploring this question.

Intelligence and natural selection.   It is by no means a matter of general agreement whether intelligence is a trait upon which positive natural selection has operated in recent human evolutionary history, and if so, whether to the same degree in various human groups. From the standpoint of evolutionary theory this is one of the more interesting questions posed by our general topic. We will be pursuing some of its implications in Chapter 2.

Intelligence and socioeconomic status.   The well known differences between racial-ethnic groups in socioeconomic status, combined with evidence that there are marked differences in average IQ between different social classes, has suggested to some observers that whatever intellectual differences are found between different racial-ethnic groups may be attributed to socioeconomic differences. It is clear that social status and ethnicity are correlated variables and that it is not easy to disentangle them. A good deal of attention will be paid to this problem in Chapter 7. It should be noted here that we do not consider it an impossible analytic task to make empirical and theoretical distinctions between these two broad variables.

Intelligence and nutrition.   A further factor that may enter into the relationship between ethnicity, socioeconomic status, and intelligence is nutrition. Not only are there racial-ethnic and socioeconomic correlations with both nutrition and IQ, but it is well established that under certain circumstances nutrition can play a significant role in influencing intellectual functioning. Thus it has seemed to some investigators that nutrition may be the factor that is responsible for the other observed relationships. We will consider this variable in relation to IQ and to ethnicity in Chapter 8.

The probabilistic nature of scientific knowledge.   A few persons who have written about race and intelligence appear to reject the probabilistic nature of empirical science by assuming that all alternative hypotheses must be completely ruled out, and all extraneous variables perfectly controlled, before any inferences or generalizations can be made. It is customary in the behavioral sciences, as well as in the biological and physical sciences, to employ generalizations that are stated in probabilistic terms; recognizing the fact that future investigation and new data may alter or falsify the generalizations. With the topic of racial differences in abilities, however, it seems sometimes to be assumed that we may only make statements when truth is completely revealed and the phenomena understood in every particular. Since such a state is never achieved in empirical science, this view if pursued to its extreme would imply that nothing could ever be stated (no matter how carefully qualified) concerning the sources of racial-ethnic differences in behavior. Needless to say, we do not subscribe to this view.

Between- and within-group differences.   Finally, different observers vary considerably in the emphasis they place on average differences between groups compared with variation within groups. The same data, given first one and then the other of these emphases, may appear strikingly different in implication. This is an issue that will frequently recur throughout this volume.

THE ORGANIZATION OF THIS BOOK

In this first chapter we have attempted to provide something of the background and recent history of the concern with racial-ethnic differences in intellectual performance in the United States, and to introduce some of the theoretical questions with which we will be concerned in the rest of the volume. The three chapters that complete the first part of the book are intended to clarify some of the issues of definition and measurement surrounding three of the key concepts on which the controversy focuses: the concepts of race, intelligence, and heritability.

Following this, the four chapters in the second part of the book review the body of evidence relevant to the major empirical question with which we are concerned: What are the relative roles of the genes and the environment in accounting for differences in average performance of different U.S. racial-ethnic groups on tasks purporting to measure intellectual capacity?

In the concluding section, we attempt to draw whatever theoretical conclusions appear to be justified by the data, and to spell out what appear to be—and not to be—legitimate implications of these conclusions for the formulation of social policy. And finally, we consider what lines of further investigation seem to offer the most promise of shedding light on the scientific questions of interest in this area, and what research (if any) could be undertaken that might assist social decision-making in the many areas touched by the reverberations of this controversy.

Following the text proper are a number of appendices. These fall into several categories. Appendices A, B, and C provide aids to the reader in the form of glossaries of genetic and statistical terms used in the book, and brief descriptions of intelligence tests cited. Some of the remaining appendices, such as D, G, J, K, L, and O, serve primarily as technical supplements that provide detail on matters treated more briefly in the main text. Others, such as E, F, M, and N extend the discussion beyond the main focus of the book to studies carried out in societies other than our own. Finally, Appendices H and I examine in some detail two recent critiques of the evidence concerning the heritability of intelligence.

CHAPTER 2

Race as a Biological Concept

NO DISCUSSION OF RACE DIFFERENCES can proceed unless at least passing attention is given to present usage and the past painful history of the concept of "race" (Spuhler and Lindzey, 1967). The necessity of such attention is underlined by the sizable number of contemporary scientists who are convinced that the concept of race has no legitimate place in the social or biological sciences. Scholars as diverse professionally as Barnicot (1969), Brace (1969), Klineberg (1954), Livingstone (1962), Montagu (1969), and Penrose (1952) argue that the concept only misleads and confuses and serves no legitimate scientific purpose. Alland (1971) claims that the concept is justifiable in sociology but not in biology. Although representatives of almost every social and biological science at one time or another have deplored the use of this concept, it has displayed a tough viability, both as a popular and as a scientific term. Simpson has nicely caught the ambivalence surrounding the concept of race: "It is a fact of biology that human races exist; it is a fact of life that their existence involves not only biology, but also psychology, sociology, economics, politics, theology, and plain old-fashioned hysterics" (1969, p. 98).

The associative link between "race" and *racism* is strong enough in our society to account for a good deal of the discomfort that many scientists display in the presence of the term "race." By racism, we mean the belief that most or all members of one race are innately, biologically superior in socially important ways to most or all members of another race.

Montagu (1964, p. 24) makes a clear distinction between racism and the biological study of race: "The myth of 'race' refers not to the fact that physically distinguishable populations of man exist. Such populations are often called races. Distinctive populations of this kind are not myths, but neither are they races in the sense in which the term is usually employed. That sense is the myth, the myth of 'race,' the belief that physical and mental traits are linked, that the physical differences are associated with rather pronounced differences in mental capacities, and that these differences are measurable by IQ tests and the cultural achievements of these populations." As to whether "the myth of 'race'" in Montagu's sense is *entirely* a myth, we will have more to say in subsequent chapters. But it is clear that the mythological component has often loomed large, and that it has usually been strongly slanted in favor of the in-group.

Ethnocentrism, which Murdock (1949, p. 83) defines as "the tendency to exalt the in-group and to depreciate other groups," is characteristic of all human societies known to ethnography and to history. Of course, as Murdock notes, "ethnocentrism" is a blanket category covering items ranging from local pride, college spirit, and business *esprit de corps*, to religious intolerance, race prejudice, class struggle, and international conflict. Such items share likenesses rather than identities. Nonetheless the tradition of being prejudiced against outgroups appears to be universal in human societies from the most civilized to the most primitive; in many cases it goes so far as to limit membership in the category "man" to the in-group, with members of out-groups being considered nonhuman (Sumner, 1906, p. 13f).

Kroeber (1948) cited the reaction of western white readers to Galton's conclusions in his book *Hereditary Genius* (1869 and later editions) as an example of ethnocentric bias. In this work, Galton rated the biological worth of different races according to the number of their geniuses. Galton concluded that the Negro race ranked two grades below the Anglo-Saxon, on a total scale of sixteen ranks, and the Anglo-Saxon race two lower than the Greeks of fifth century Athens. Many of Galton's Anglo-Saxon readers found the first conclusion much more convincing than the second.

Galton made an impressive contribution to the science of his day by providing evidence that the laws of genetics apply to the mind and behavior as well as to the body, a conclusion directly in conflict with then-current theological views on the independence of the soul and mind from the body. However, Galton's ranking of the biological worth of races according to the number of their geniuses rests on a false assumption—that all geniuses born are recognized as such and historically recorded. For a person to be productive in such a way as to be recognized as a genius requires a genotype of genius and also a favorable environment, such as may be provided by a great culture. Genotypes of genius that occur in primitive environments are less likely to be expressed, and if expressed, less likely to be recorded. Thus it is a fallacy to assume that the relative biological worth of people from different cultural environments can be assessed from the historical record—even apart from possible ethnocentric bias in deciding what counts as a work of genius.

The point is that many of the same persons who were dubious of the validity of Galton's conclusions that nineteenth century Englishmen were inferior to fifth century Athenian Greeks were quite willing to rank the Negro below Anglo-Saxons. As Kroeber (1948, p. 204) concluded: "In short, it is a difficult task to establish any race as either superior or inferior to another, but relatively easy to prove that we entertain a strong prejudice in favor of our own racial superiority."

Thus it is probably inevitable that whenever mankind is classified into races, some persons will immediately construe this in terms of an order of quality, or merit. It seems equally evident that dictators, demagogues, and elitists will employ such classificatory concepts for their own purposes without regard for their technical meaning and validity. However, one may question whether the misuse of the race concept by racists is a compelling argument against the concept if it serves a useful purpose within an empirical discipline, any more than the abuse of genetic concepts by these same individuals should lead to an abandonment of these concepts in theoretical biology (Spuhler and Lindzey, 1967).

In considering the biological concept of race in this chapter, we will focus our attention on its empirical and theoretical significance within the behavioral and biological sciences and deal only in passing with the social and political impact of the term. In other contexts this order of priority might, of course, be reversed.

GENETICS AND THE BIOLOGY OF RACE

Since its beginning in about 1900 genetics has made two major contributions to a theoretical understanding of the biology of race. The first contribution was the particulate, or Mendelian, theory of inheritance, which replaced the earlier blending theory of inheritance. The second contribution of genetics placed the study of race in the perspective of a general theory of biological evolution. This interpretation of the biology of race is based on, or developed from, the mathematical papers on population genetics by Fisher (1930), Haldane (1932), and Wright (1931, 1968, 1969), and has been applied to concrete examples by many biologists, for example, Dobzhansky (1962, 1970), Mayr (1963a), and Simpson (1953, 1961, 1969).

Some of the fundamental processes basic to the biological concept of race are bisexual reproduction, the origin of new genetic variation by mutation, the balance between relative reproductive isolation of local populations and gene flow between such populations, adaptation to the local habitat through natural selection, and some random fluctuation of gene frequencies within local populations by the process of genetic drift.

Because a fallacious theory of heredity was accepted until 1900, nearly all the writing on races and racial taxonomy of man and other species published before then is misleading or wrong. The same can be said of many works published between then and the early 1930's, when population genetics became well established, and of many anthropological works published up to about 1950, when anthropologists seriously began to replace typological approaches to race with a population-genetical point of view.

Typology and "Race"

Nearly all of the recent arguments for the nonexistence of human races are in fact sound arguments against the typological notion of race, which long antedates modern biology.

Before the effective beginning of genetics around 1900, biologists considered hereditary material to be a homogeneous substance that could be mixed or diluted but that was identical in all members of a "pure" race. If two individuals were alike in one hereditary aspect, they would be alike in all others. Within a "pure," that is, unmixed, race, all variation was thought to be due to environmental effects. Just as copper and tin are different elements so two races were thought to have different kinds of hereditary material. As atoms of copper and tin join to make bronze, so, it was thought, two "pure" races might join to make a mixed race, in the manner of formation of a metallic alloy. It was possible to think of individuals of mixed races as being "mostly white" or "mostly black," in the same way it was possible to think of bronze as being 8 parts copper to 1 part tin. Or using an analogy from ceramics, certain anthropologists as late as the 1940's spoke of race X having a "wash" of race Y. Such beliefs are refuted by the identification of identical genes in different races, the genetic heterogeneity of all races, and the fact that individual genes, not total genotypes and certainly not phenotypes, are inherited.

If the hereditary materials were blended like wine in water, or more generally like solutes in solvents (as nineteenth century biologists assumed), the members of a breeding population would soon reach hereditary uniformity (the genetic variation being reduced by one-half in each generation), and, excepting the action of recurrent mutation or gene flow, a "pure" race would be established in the locality occupied by each breeding population. The genetic material would become unique to each local breeding population, and the genetic makeup of offspring would necessarily be a midway blend of those of their parents. But, in fact, the genetic variation is not reduced by one-half each generation; rather it fluctuates over a small range, on the average remaining fairly steady, as Galton (1889) noted for the proportions of eye color over four generations of an English population, and as many later geneticists have observed for various genes. Thus "pure" races do not form.

Typological thinking in racial classification derives at least from the time of Plato and Aristotle. Plato distinguished the eternal and changeless ideal essences or archetypes of plants and animals from the transient, variable, individual plants and animals we observe. Aristotle departed from Plato in considering that the archetype was actual in the individual plants and animals we perceive. The essence of races and species is still debated by some philosophers. Realists assert the reality of universal archetypes of man and other species. Nominalists deny the reality of archetypes and affirm that only individuals are real.

As started by Linnaeus, biological classification was based on Aristotelian realism. Biological species were taken to be real, immutable entities, all directly created at the beginning, and varieties and the diversity of individuals within a species were taken to be imperfections in the expression of the archetype. Most modern biologists disagree with Linnaeus, and hold that taxonomic classifications do not reflect archetypical individual ancestors, but are to be explained by the evolution of breeding populations with genetic modification.

The following statement by Hooton (1926, p. 79) is an example of typological thinking about race: "One must conceive of race not as the combination of features which gives to each person his individual appearance, but rather as a vague physical background, usually more or less obscured or overlaid by individual variations in single subjects, and realized best in a composite picture."

The older typological approach to racial anthropology used at least three different concepts of "types." All are unacceptable to modern genetics, each for a different reason.

1. The *average type* of a population is defined by a set of traits used to identify members of the "pure" race. Thus Nordics are characterized by tall stature, long heads, blond hair, and blue eyes. From the genetic point of view there is an essential difficulty in this typological approach to race: only a small fraction of the members of any local breeding population in fact possess the full set of traits used to define the average type; thus the vast amount of genetic variability known to be present in all sexually reproduced populations is not recognized. For example, Retzius and Fürst found only 10.1 percent of a large sample of Swedish conscripts had all four of the above type-diagnostic traits for Nordics (Dahlberg, 1942a). It is in this sense misleading to pick out a typical (average) member of any natural race; race is a population concept and must account for a diversity of individual members.

2. The concept of *morphological type* is similar, but allows for variation within a race. A morphological type is defined by a cluster of phenotypes that are assumed to occur together in "pure" members of the type. The morphological type differs from the average type in that a race is always polytypic. The number of morphological types recognized in most published studies of human races usually lies be-

tween 2 and 10, although some typologists have employed 16 or more morphological types.

The morphological type approach is rarely used for simple anatomical description of a population sample. Rather it is generally employed to reconstruct racial history over a few hundreds or thousands of years. First the morphological types are chosen. For example, Hooton (1930) in a well known study of the skulls of Pecos Pueblo, New Mexico, sorted out eight types: Basket Makers, Pseudo-Negroid, Pseudo-Australoid, Plains Indian, Long-faced European, Pseudo-Alpine, Large Hybrid, and, of course, "Residual." Then the history of the local group is explained by the migration and intermixture of individuals belonging to the several morphological types, all assumed to be stable over time and to represent pure ancestral stocks.

3. According to the Czekanowski group of Polish anthropologists, an *individual type* is defined by "racial elements," that is, a cluster of traits assumed to be controlled by one or several closely linked genes. These genes are assumed to affect simultaneously the set of type-defining traits. This typology would be compatible with Mendelian genetics if the observed frequencies of the "racial elements" were the same as the frequencies of the genes held to be responsible, a possibility that has not, however, received much support from empirical studies (Bielicki, 1965).

In brief, the observed facts and genetic theory argue strongly that *typological* "races" do not exist.

Race as a Concept in Population Biology

Dobzhansky has written, "Members of the same species who inhabit different parts of the world are often visibly and genetically different. This, in the simplest terms possible, is what race is as a biological phenomenon" (1970, p. 269).

A "race" is a category more inclusive than the "individual" and less inclusive than the "species." Most contemporary biologists equate the anthropological concept of race with the zoological concept of subspecies, except that races usually are not given Latin scientific names. Mayr (1963a), Simpson (1969), and Dobzhansky (1970) give excellent survey statements on the population biology of races and subspecies.

A species of sexual organisms is a population or group of populations maintaining genetic continuity and unity over time by interbreeding among themselves and maintaining genetic identity by relative or absolute absence of interbreeding with members of other species (Simpson, 1969).

Assignment of all living human beings to one species implies neither that they are all the same nor that their differences are negligible. A similar conclusion holds for assignment of individuals to a race or subspecies. At no degree of differentiation within the species are individual differences negligible, not even at the level of the mating pair, which represents the smallest subgrouping.

A race or subspecies is a genetically distinguishable subgrouping of a species distributed within a more or less localized territory that interbreeds with other subgroups of the species in areas of overlap or when brought into contact with them. The frequency of gene exchange between races is highest in the overlap zone and decreases away from it.

Thus the genetic characteristics of a species are not uniform over the full distribution of the species in space at a particular time. Given the raw materials of inherited variability, the genetic structure of a species depends largely on local selection intensities on the one hand, and gene flow between different local areas on the other. If there is much gene flow, the species will tend to remain genetically uniform; if there is less, clines may form; if still less, local races may differentiate. When the genetic characteristics are not uniform over an area occupied by a species, it is sometimes useful to recognize and name races or subspecies within the species.

In the absence of massive geographical barriers such as mountain ranges or oceans, changes in gene frequency are gradual, and any attempt to separate populations into races sharply distinguished by different gene frequencies is arbitrary. A classification of populations based on one set of genes will often differ from a classification based on another set of genes.

Even so, we cannot understand fully the evolutionary history of mankind either in terms of individuals alone, or in terms of the species as a whole, because individuals do not evolve, and the details of the evolutionary process are not necessarily the same for all regional and other subdivisions of the species. This is why it is of theoretical importance to recognize races or subspecies in evolutionary biology whether or not they are considered descriptively important.

The attributes or characteristics observed in the study of races are called *morphs*. Black or yellow spots in lady beetles and human eye and skin color are examples of morphs. A breeding population with two or more different morphs is said to be *polymorphic*. Often the different morphs known in a given species do not occur with equal frequency in every part of the area occupied by the species. Such a differential distribution of morphs provides the basis for dividing a species population into geographical races or subspecies.

Note that a set of individuals with a given morph do not as such constitute a race or subspecies. Rather such a group within a species whose members share one or more distinctive morphs is a *variety*. Varieties as such are neither biological populations, nor units of racial classification, nor units of evolution. They are merely distinctive phenotypes within a race or species, for example, the variety of red-haired people or of yellow-spotted lady beetles. In the dynamics of population biology, varieties do not perform the same role as races or subspecies; they are not breeding populations. Before modern genetics, confusion of variety and race was long a source of serious misunderstanding in the study of species and races.

The degrees of racial differentiation within species may vary greatly, both within living species at a given moment of time, and within species over time. Some living species are monotypic; they have no races. During the course of time a species may start in a monotypic state, diversify into a polytypic, and then become monotypic again. Monotypic species tend to have a restricted geographical distribution and a uniform ecological setting. Some monotypic breeding populations may represent the surviving members of a former polytypic species that had a wide geographical distribution in the past. Geographically separate populations or races are sufficiently distinct in about one-half of North American mammals to have been designated as subspecies (Mayr, 1963a).

The degree of racial differentiation may vary greatly from one species to another in the same genus. In the fruit fly *Drosophila melanogaster*, a favorite organism for genetical study, geographical variation is detectable only by refined biometric measurement, and the relative frequencies of the morphs are only slightly different throughout the wide area occupied by the species. Another species of the same genus, *D. polymorpha*, shows conspicuous variation and is classified into several sharply defined races.

In extreme cases of race differentiation, nearly 100 percent of the members of one race may exhibit certain morphs almost totally absent from the other races of the species.

In most vertebrate species, races are allopatric: different races live in different territories. Modern man, cultivated plants, and domestic animals are exceptional in being sympatric: different races share the same territory, their continued separation as races or breeds depending on control of their reproduction.

Clones of asexual and some parthenogenic species are "pure races" with numerous, often millions, of individuals that have identical genotypes. These, of course, are produced directly by equational cell division, and not by the sexual process of gamete formation and fertilization. In general, populations of a sexually reproducing species have a genetic structure that excludes the possibility that more than a few individuals will have identical genotypes (the exceptions being the individuals produced in monozygous multiple births). Thus, "pure" races in the sense of possessing complete genetic uniformity do not exist and have never existed in the human species. Races in sexually reproducing species intergrade, or overlap, in biological makeup because of sexual reproduction and gene exchange.

Races differ from species in the extent of reproductive isolation. Species are highly, if not absolutely, isolated reproductively. Races are not isolated reproductively from other races of the same species; in zones of contact races interbreed intermittently or regularly, according to local mating rules, customs, or opportunities.

Some biologists believe that races and subspecies should be defined differently, with subspecies being more distinct in gene frequencies, more uniform, and more widespread than races. However, the only really consistent difference in practice is in nomenclature. Subspecies are systematic categories with trinomial Latin designations, such as *Homo sapiens afer*. Races, on the other hand, have common names, such as Chinese, Khoisan, or American Indian, such a name being used to set apart any local within-species breeding population that is distinguished for purposes of study.

Races of House Sparrows in North America

Since emotional overtones nearly always accompany a discussion of the races of man, it may be useful to examine the races of a nonhuman animal. Racial variation in color patterns and body size of the house sparrow (*Passer domesticus*) is a good example of racial variation in

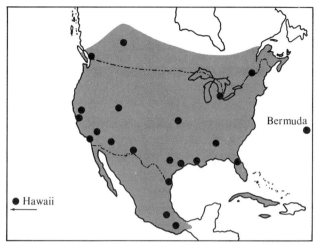

FIGURE 2.1
Map of North America showing distribution of house sparrows (shaded area) and localities where specimens were taken (dots). (From Johnston and Selander, 1964. Copyright 1964 by the American Association for the Advancement of Science.)

general (Johnston and Selander, 1964). Race formation in this species in North America is of special interest because it has taken place during an accurately known period of time.

The house sparrow was introduced into the United States from England and Germany in 1852. There were, at most, 111 generations during the interval between their introduction and the termination of the extensive study by Johnston and Selander in 1962–1963. Much of the observed racial differentiation in the North American populations of house sparrows must have occurred during the present century because house sparrows did not reach Mexico City until 1933, were not present in Death Valley, California, before 1914, nor in Vancouver, British Columbia, before 1900. They were introduced to the Hawaiian Islands in 1870 or 1871.

Johnston and Selander collected 100–250 house sparrows in fresh plumage during October and November in each of some two dozen localities in North America, the Hawaiian Islands, Bermuda, England, and Germany. They found pervasive geographical variation in a large number of characters.

The sparrows in each population sample were different to a greater or lesser degree from sparrows in other North American localities

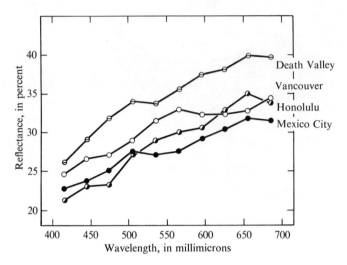

FIGURE 2.2

Spectral reflectance curves for the breast of female house sparrows from four localities. The sample size is 3 for each locality. (From Johnston and Selander, 1964. Copyright 1964 by the American Association for the Advancement of Science.)

and from those in England and Germany. Regional variation is especially pronounced in the color of the plumage. The overall geographical pattern of variation in color conforms with Gloger's rule, which relates pigmentation to regional variation in temperature and humidity. The amount of black pigment is reduced in warm dry areas, and of brown pigment in cold humid areas. For instance, house sparrows from northern and Pacific coastal areas are darkly pigmented, those from Vancouver, British Columbia, being especially dark, and sparrows from southern California east to central and southern Texas are pale in color, those from Death Valley, California, and Phoenix, Arizona, being the lightest. Samples from Salt Lake City and from Lawrence, Kansas, are of intermediate pigmentation. The Hawaiian house sparrows are most distinctive in color; probably because of geographical isolation they differ in this respect from all members of the species living elsewhere. They have less dark markings on the plumage, absence of fine streaks on the underparts, an overall rufous-buff color, and pale buff rather than dark brown legs and feet.

Johnston and Selander emphasize that the variation in plumage color of North American house sparrows is marked and consistent; in many cases pigmentation alone may serve as a criterion for correct

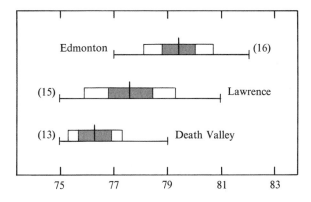

FIGURE 2.3
Individual and geographic variation in wing length (mm) from three local-
ities. The vertical lines represent the means, the horizontal distances the
observed ranges. The solid rectangle represents one standard deviation and
the open rectangles two standard deviations on either side of the mean.
(From Johnston and Selander, 1964. Copyright 1964 by the American
Association for the Advancement of Science.)

sorting of 100 percent of the specimens from two localities. Geographical variation in the color of the breast in female house sparrows
from Death Valley, Vancouver, Mexico City, and Honolulu is shown
in Figure 2.2 where the percentage of reflectance is plotted against the
wavelength. Reflectance refers to the percentage of light that is reflected (not absorbed) by the feathers at each wavelength, and is
greatest for the lighter colored birds from Death Valley. The difference is most marked at the longer (red) wavelengths, with the lighter,
browner birds from Death Valley having a reflectance about one-
fourth greater than the darker birds from Mexico City.

The house sparrows of North America also vary considerably in
size of the body and its parts. The variation in size, just as in plumage
color, parallels what is observed among races of many native species.
When evaluated by size, the sparrows form a cline with the largest
individuals living in the more northern localities, the smallest in the
desert southwest, and the birds from localities between these two
regions being intermediate in size.

The geographical variation in wing length of adult male house
sparrows from three populations is shown in Figure 2.3. On the
average, sparrows living in the cold climate of Edmonton, Canada,
have wings about 3 millimeters longer than sparrows living in the

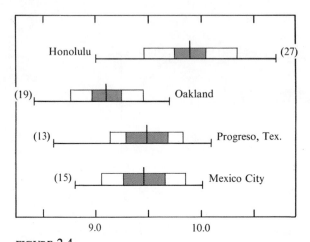

FIGURE 2.4

Individual and geographic variation in bill length (from nostril to tip) in adult male house sparrows from four localities. The means, ranges, and standard deviations are represented as in Figure 2.3 (From Johnston and Selander, 1964. Copyright 1964 by the American Association for the Advancement of Science.)

warm climate of Death Valley, California. Variation in bill length in birds from four localities is shown in Figure 2.4. Although there is a tendency for bill length to be shorter in birds living in colder climates, the size of the bill in sparrows is more highly correlated with the type of food taken than with temperature.

Body weight is a good index of total body size in birds, provided that the relative amounts of body fat on specimens being compared are similar. The samples collected by Johnston and Selander are comparable in this respect since all birds taken had just completed the annual molt, a time when sparrows have uniformly moderate degrees of subcutaneous fat deposition. In Figure 2.5 the mean body weight of adult males from 17 localities in North America is plotted against the isophanes of the locations. An "isophane" is a line plotted on a map through points presenting similar climatic factors. Isophanes are calculated from the latitude, longitude, and altitude for the localities and thus reflect regional variation in climate. Samples from the 14 localities north of southern Texas show a close relationship between body weight and climate. Larger sparrows are found where winters are severe, and smaller ones where winters are mild but summers may be extremely hot. For the 14 localities, 93 percent of the variation in average body size between populations is

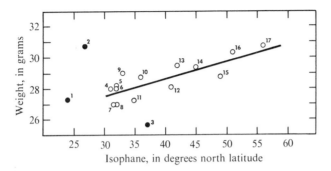

Mean body weights of adult house sparrows plotted against isophanes (see text for explanation). Localities: 1. Oaxaca City, Mexico; 2. Progreso, Tex.; 3. Mexico City, Mexico; 4. Houston, Tex.; 5. Los Angeles, Calif.; 6. Austin, Tex.; 7. Death Valley, Calif.; 11. Oakland, Calif.; 12. Las Cruces, N.M.; 13. Lawrence, Kan.; 14. Vancouver, B.C.; 15. Salt Lake City, Utah; 16. Montreal, Quebec; 17. Edmonton, Alberta. The regression line is based on data from localities 4 to 17 and has the equation $Y = 24.1 + 0.12 X$. (From Johnston and Selander, 1964. Copyright 1964 by the American Association for the Advancement of Science.)

attributable to the linear regression effect. The adaptive trend in body size is related to the physiology of metabolic heat production and body temperature control. The observed relationship is called Bergmann's rule, which records the tendency for the smaller sized races to occupy the warmer parts of the species range and the larger sized races the colder parts. A similar relation between body size and climate is found in many species of birds and mammals native to North America, and among American Indian populations.

Current classificatory practice in ornithology recognizes formal scientific names at the subspecific level for biologically definable geographic races. The level of racial differentiation achieved by the house sparrows introduced in the Hawaiian Islands and a number of areas in continental North America are fully equivalent to those shown by many species of birds with formally recognized and named subspecies. Because Johnston and Selander are more interested in the evolutionary dynamics of race formation than in formal classification, and because their observations represent a patently dynamic system, they have not introduced new subspecific names.

The house sparrows of North America exhibit conspicuous adaptive, racial differentiation in color and size. The patterns of variation parallel those shown by the native polytypic species of birds and conform with Gloger's and Bergmann's ecological rules relating variation in color and size with climatic variation. The racial differentiation of house sparrows entering a new and wide ecological niche may require no more than 50 generations.

Racial Classification

Classification and naming are aids to memory and communication. A racial classification allows a student to become familiar with the superficial physical characteristics of three billion living members of the human species in a short period of study.

Classification is an essential part of science. When we want to refer quickly to great and broad scientific achievements we point to classifications, for example, the Periodic Table of Elements, or the Sequential Table of Geological Ages. Both are compact classificatory schemes, the former having about 100 elements, and the latter about 16 periods. On a more complex level, the classification used for organic chemical compounds is a thing of elegance in which the individual names give considerable information on the structure and other properties of millions of carbon compounds. And, of course, the hierarchical classification of species, genera, and higher taxa is to some an elegant scientific product, which, while not compact, allows us to judge certain properties, including phylogenetic relationships, of millions of plant and animal species according to their place in the classification. Even imperfect classifications may be highly useful —the alphabet we use in writing English is not a particularly "good" classification of English phonemes. Classifications of the living varieties of man, although not as elegant as some, can nonetheless be useful.

Any racial classification is to a degree arbitrary. Initially, "racial differences" are those genetic differences that are used to define "races." It does not automatically follow that the geographic distribution of other genetic traits will be concordant with that of the selected set of morphs used to define the racial groupings. But as Simpson (1961, p. 175), in commenting on misapprehensions about subspecies, wrote: "subspecies do not express the geographic variation of the characters of a species and are only partially descriptive of that variation. They are formal taxonomic population units, usually arbitrary, and cannot express or fully describe the variation in those populations any more than classification in general can express or fully describe phylogeny. They are not, for all that, any less useful in discussing variation."

In an earlier section we gave reasons why there is no definite, correct number of races of mankind or any other sexual species. Any two breeding populations of a species, even adjacent ones, will be found to differ significantly if enough measurements are taken to enough decimal places on enough individuals.

The total number of contemporary, local breeding populations (demes) in the human species is not known, but something of the order of one million, that is, an average population number per deme of 3500, is probably reasonable. Thus one million might be taken as a maximum value for the number of races in our species.

By the time Darwin wrote his *Descent of Man* (1871) the following numbers of races had been proposed by various authors: Virey, 2; Jacquinot, 3; Kant, 4; Blumenbach, 5; Buffon, 6; Hunter, 7; Agassiz, 8; Pickering, 11; Bory St. Vincent, 15; Desmoulins, 16; Morton, 22; Crawford, 60; and Burke, 63. Perhaps Quatrefages (1861, p. 366) holds the record with 150 named races. The *Dictionary of Races and Peoples*, by Folkmar and Folkmar (1911) has 562 entries.

A recent and reasonable approach to racial classification is that of Garn (1971), who recognizes nine major geographical races of contemporary mankind:

1. Amerindian
2. Polynesian
3. Micronesian
4. Melanesian-Papuan
5. Australian
6. Asiatic
7. Indian
8. European
9. African

PREHISTORY OF RACE FORMATION IN MAN

Because the rates of evolutionary diversification are fairly similar among closely related animals, and fairly constant over geologically short periods of time, it is clear that information on the time of the original diversification of the human races is important in assessing the extent of genetic differences between the modern races of man.

Recognition of racial variation in man based on differences in morphology and pigmentation is as old as recorded history. Haddon (1910) notes that the Egyptians of the Nineteenth Dynasty (before 1200 B.C.) painted polychromic human figures on the walls of their royal tombs showing peoples of different skin color and hair form: red (Egyptian), yellow (Asiatic or Semitic), black (southern African), and white (western and northern European, also shown with blue eyes and blond beards). Also, the distinction between Bushman and Negro was made in prehistoric Bushman rock drawings.

However, it is interesting that human racial distinctions are not manifest in the otherwise beautifully representative polychromic cave art of the Upper Paleolithic in western Europe, dating from 35,000 to 15,000 B.P. (before the present) (Ucko and Rosenfeld, 1967).

Recognition of the differences between the local in- and out-groups is universal in known human society and is, with little doubt, geologically old in primate social tradition. It is not clear when in the history of modern man the differences between local breeding populations began to be considered in morphological or hereditary terms. For a long time in- and out-group distinctions appear largely to have been based on cultural differences, rather than on some ancient equivalent of the genotype. The specific modern idea of racism, the belief that biologically inherited physical differences are associated with differences in mental capacity and cultural achievement, is for the most part a product of the last couple of centuries (Gossett, 1963; Montagu, 1965).

Statements about the existence of human races prior to historical records or datable prehistoric drawings are based on the examination of skeletal remains, especially skulls. Accurate assignment of living individuals to racial categories is sometimes difficult; it is always difficult with skeletal material. Authorities disagree on the reliability of racial identifications of hominid skulls (see Krogman, 1962, for an optimistic evaluation and Le Gros Clark, 1964, for a skeptical one). The best methods use multivariate statistical analyses. In a discriminant-function analysis using 7 anthropometric measurements on 408 skulls of known race (Negro and white) from dissecting room collections, Giles and Elliot (see Krogman, 1962) correctly classified 90.9 percent of the skulls by race.

Most anthropologists (but not all, as will be discussed) assume that the races of modern man date back no farther than the formation of *Homo sapiens* as a species distinct from *Homo erectus*. The age of *H. sapiens* is in some dispute, however. As there is general agreement that all hominids associated with Upper Paleolithic and later cultural materials belong to *H. sapiens*, the species is at least 30,000–35,000 years old. There is not general agreement on the time of the earliest appearance of *H. sapiens* in the Pleistocene Period. Le Gros Clark (1964) states several hominid skeletons of Pleistocene age are not distinguishable in total morphology from modern *H. sapiens*; other workers prefer to classify these same specimens as pre-sapiens (Vallois, 1954) or early Neanderthaloid (for a recent discussion see Howells, 1973). The oldest of these specimens assigned to *H. sapiens* by Le Gros Clark include the Swanscombe skull bones dating from about 250,000 B.P. from Kent, England, and the Steinheim skull dating from about 200,000 B.P. from near Stuttgart, Germany. If the identification of these Pleistocene hominids as *H. sapiens* is correct, modern man has existed as a species for at least 250,000 years.

Campbell (1972), a leading authority on hominid nomenclature and classification, divides *H. sapiens* into two sets of chronological subspecies with a 50,000 B.P. time-line separating the living geographical subspecies from the four fossil subspecies *neanderthalensis* (Europe), *rhodesiensis* (Africa), *palestinus* (western Asia), and *soloensis* (eastern Asia), all of which are separated from the late subspecies of *H. erectus* by a 300,000 B.P. time boundary.

The best established cases for racial differentiation of fossil *H. sapiens* are from western Europe and from Indonesia and Australia.

All five Cro-Magnon skeletons recovered in 1868 from a rock shelter near Les Eyzies in Dordogne, south-central France, dating from 20,000–30,000 B.P., as well as skeletal material from more than a dozen other sites of like age in western Europe, share a number of distinctive and easily recognizable anatomical features. Soon after their discovery, E. T. Hamy (1873) pointed out the close anatomical resemblance between one of these Cro-Magnon skulls and recent skulls from Dalarna, now the province of Kopparbert, Sweden, and from Teneriffe, Canary Islands. Affinities between Cro-Magnon skulls and recent skulls from various other European sites have also been noted. Individuals anatomically similar to the Cro-Magnons are reported from several living populations of the Caucasoid race, including the residents of Dordogne itself, the Kabyles of North Africa, and especially the Guanches of the Canary Islands (Baker, 1968). The Cro-Magnon remains provide extensive evidence that the Caucasoid race has existed in western Europe for some 20,000–30,000 years.

The skulls of the native Australian race are as distinctive in structure as those of the Cro-Magnons. Weidenreich (1946) asserts that
there is an affinity between skulls of the present-day Australoids and a
number of fossil skulls from Australia, New Guinea, and Java. These
fossil specimens give evidence that the Australoid race has existed
in Indonesia and Australia for at least some 6000–12,000 years.

Other claims for racial identification of fossil *H. sapiens* specimens are less convincing. The Grimaldi IV skeletons, from near the
Mediterranean coast of Italy, dating from about 17,000–20,000 B.P.
are classified as Negroid by some authorities, and as representing the
Mediterranean division of the Caucasoid race by others. Authorities
disagree on the placement of the Rhodesian skull from Broken Hill,
northern Rhodesia, dating from about 30,000 B.P., both as to species
(*H. erectus* versus *H. sapiens*) and race (Negroid or not). The skulls
of western Eskimos are more distinctive in structure than those of
most other groups of modern man. Some anthropologists classify
the Chancelade skull, from the Chancelade Rock Shelter, Dordogne,
France, 12,000–17,000 B.P., with the Eskimo, while others are convinced it is Cro-Magnon (Le Gros Clark, 1964).

One anthropologist, Carleton Coon, has proposed that human races
may predate *H. sapiens*. Coon (1962) proposes that five major races
of modern man—Australoid, Capoid (Bushmen and Hottentot),
Congoid (Negroid), Caucasoid, and Mongoloid—developed independently and at different times from corresponding races of *H.
erectus* during the period from about 30,000 to 250,000 years ago.
Coon thus proposes that the major races of man may have existed
for as long as 500,000 or more years, and that *H. erectus* evolved
into *H. sapiens* "not once but five times, as each subspecies, living in
its own territory, passed a critical threshold from a more brutal to a
more *sapient* state" (Coon, 1962, p. 657).

Now, in general, by definition and in empirical fact, there is some
gene flow between the races or subspecies of a given species. Coon's
thesis assumes that the rate of gene flow between hominid subspecies,
what he calls "peripheral gene flow," for both pithecanthropine and
sapient men during a period of nearly 500,000 years (say 20,000
generations) was so small as to allow five subspecies of one species to
evolve independently and in parallel into exactly the same five de-
scendent subspecies of a new species. There is no well-documented
case from vertebrate paleontology that such subspecific-parallel evolu-

tion has occurred. There is no absolute theoretical reason why it could not have occurred in hominid evolution (Mayr, 1963b), but if it did, then the mating behavior of early hominids in its degree of reproductive isolation between adjacent subspecies was remarkably different from all known reproductive behavior between races of modern man from Ainus to Zulus, not to mention the higher non-human primates.

In summary, history establishes that some of the major races of modern mankind have existed for some 6000 years, prehistoric archeology suggests that they have existed for some 30,000 years, and paleontology allows, but does not establish, that they may have existed for up to 250,000 years. Coon (1962) is nearly alone in claiming that five contemporary major races may have existed for as long as 500,000 years.

How Different Genetically Are Modern Races?

A great deal of information has been accumulated in the last few decades concerning variation among human populations in the frequencies of gene-based diseases (Damon, 1969) and of various blood-group and protein genes. Such data suggest that for the majority of genes the differences among racially differing populations are relatively small but for some genes they are quite large. Two gene loci showing fairly typical between-race variation, the loci for the ABO and MNS blood groups, are shown in Table 2.1, along with two blood-group loci that show marked between-race differences.

On the whole, most loci are like those for ABO and MNS; i.e., there is only modest variation in average gene frequencies from race to race. Lewontin (1972), on the basis of a survey of published frequency data for 17 polymorphic genes, estimated that only about 6 percent of the genetic diversity in the total human population of the earth is accounted for by racial membership. (Genetic differences between local populations within races accounted for about 8 percent more, but by far the largest portion of the genetic variation, more than 85 percent, represented differences between individuals within populations.) Nei and Roychoudhury (1972, 1974) studied 62 protein and 34 blood-group loci in Caucasoids and Negroids. From their data one can calculate that on the average, two randomly chosen genes at a given protein locus would be the same 89.6 percent of the time if they were both drawn from within the white population, 90.8 percent of the time if they were both drawn from within the black popu-

TABLE 2.1. *Some gene-frequency differences between racial groups.*

Blood-group System	Allele[a]	Gene Frequencies[b]		
		Caucasoid	Negroid	Mongoloid
ABO	A_1	.21	.10	.19
	A_2	.07	.08	.00
	B	.06	.11	.17
	O	.66	.71	.64
MNS	MS	.24	.09	.04
	Ms	.31	.49	.57
	NS	.07	.04	.01
	Ns	.39	.38	.38
Rhesus	R_0	.02	.74	.04
	R_1	.40	.03	.76
	R_2	.17	.04	.20
	r	.38	.12	.00
	r'	.00	.07	.00
P	P_1	.52	.89	.17
	P_2	.48	.11	.83

Source: Data from Cavalli-Sforza and Bodmer, 1971, Table 11.7, p. 724f.
[a] Rare alleles omitted.
[b] Based on largest available sample within each racial group.

lation, and 89.2 percent of the time if one were drawn from each population. The corresponding figures for the blood-group loci were 80.3 percent, 83.8 percent, and 80.8 percent. Thus the cross-race comparisons yielded only a slightly lower probability of allelic identity than did the average of the within-race comparisons. The genetic variability that existed was predominantly within rather than between populations, at most of these loci. And yet at some blood-group loci, and presumably at loci affecting skin color, physical appearance, and a number of other biological characteristics, these populations have strikingly different distributions of allelic frequencies. (For a review of some biological differences between U.S. blacks and whites, see Malina, 1973).

Do the genes that influence intelligence fall into the major category —in which there are only small differences in frequencies between races—or the minor category—in which differences in frequencies may be quite large? This is one way of putting the central question of this book. We will have more to say later in this chapter about the processes that might lead to gene-frequency differences between populations, and more to say in the next couple of chapters on the question of how much influence genes have on intelligence. But first we wish to examine an attempt to infer the past history of races from current genetic differences among them.

Estimating Racial History from Gene Frequencies

Cavalli-Sforza and Bodmer (1971) use a model of evolution based on a uniform rate of genetic drift, a measure of genetic distance based on differences in gene frequencies, and the observed gene frequencies for 16 polymorphic blood-group systems, to estimate the times when the human population separated into the three major races.

The statistical details of the evolutionary model and of the measure of genetic distance are beyond the scope of this chapter. The essential points are that a measure of genetic distance, $\bar{f}$, combines genefrequency information from a number of loci, and that change in the value of a logarithmic function of $\bar{f}$ is assumed to be proportional to the time since separation of the ancestral populations.

The genetic distances between the three pairs of major races, in terms of $\bar{f}$ values based on 16 blood-group systems, are:

Negroid/Mongoloid	0.416 ± 0.140
Negroid/Caucasoid	0.352 ± 0.078
Mongoloid/Caucasoid	0.242 ± 0.062

To convert these genetic distances into time periods, Cavalli-Sforza and Bodmer make use of the genetic distance between American Indians and certain native populations of Australia and New Guinea, which they calculate to be 0.176 ± 0.053. Because, as is known from archeological evidence, human migration to the North American continent took place 15,000 or more years ago, it may be assumed that the two groups under comparison have been separated for at least 15,000 years. On the assumptions of the model, this implies separation of the pairs of major races for at least:

Negroid/Mongoloid	41,000 years
Negroid/Caucasoid	33,000 years
Mongoloid/Caucasoid	21,000 years

with large standard errors.

If the baseline estimate for separation of the American Indian from the Australian and Indonesian peoples is too small—for example, if these groups had been separated for a considerable period prior to the inhabitation of North America—the absolute time periods given here are too short, but the relative intervals between the separations would remain the same.

Nei and Roychoudhury (1974), using data on proteins and rather different theoretical assumptions, arrive at estimates of 120,000 years, 115,000 years, and 55,000 years for the three separations—i.e., the sequence is the same, but times are longer by a factor of about 3. In their data Negroids are rather more different from Mongoloids and Caucasoids than the latter are from each other. In both analyses the Caucasoids are intermediate between the other two races.

PROCESSES LEADING TO GENETIC
DIFFERENCES BETWEEN POPULATIONS

Given existing knowledge of genetics, is it plausible that there might be significant differences between different racial groups in the frequencies of one or more of the genes affecting intellectual performance? And if so, is it reasonable that such genetic differences could add up to a substantial effect on general intellectual levels? For the most part, our discussion will be indifferent to the *direction* of differences between particular racial-ethnic groups. For example, we will be just as concerned with the plausibility of the argument that U.S. blacks might have an advantage over U.S. whites in the genes influencing intellectual development, as the reverse. What we wish to examine is the question of whether there is a reasonable basis for *any* such group differences, given known evolutionary mechanisms and the probable time spans involved.

From the standpoint of population genetics, there are four principal evolutionary mechanisms to consider: mutation, drift, migration, and natural selection. The first two of these, mutation and drift, are essentially random processes. In the present context, this means that we are asking whether substantial racial differences in frequencies of genes relevant to intellectual performance are likely to have resulted from the operation of chance alone. Let us consider this possibility first, before moving on to consider the more directed processes of migration and selection.

Mutation

Mutation refers to apparently random errors in the duplication of DNA. We are interested here only in mutations that affect the genetic material transmitted to offspring. Such errors are individually rare events. Average mutation rates on the order of 10^{-5}–10^{-7} per locus per generation are typically quoted (see, e.g., Cavalli-Sforza and Bodmer, 1971, pp. 102–110). This means that on the average only one child in a hundred thousand or more will have a particular mutant gene that his parents did not carry. In a small primitive tribe having a breeding population of a few dozen pairs, a particular mutation might well never occur in a thousand generations. In a large modern population with an annual birthrate in the millions, it might occur several times in a given year.

What then, are the odds that two modern races might differ in genes related to intellectual development sheerly by virtue of there having been chance mutational events in one race that did not occur in the other?

In the very early history of mankind, when populations were small, the effect of chance mutational events on between-population differences may well have been appreciable. During the last 10,000 years or so, however, the population of each of the major races has been large enough that it is likely that every mutation of a gene that affects intellectual development has occurred repeatedly in every race. Moreover, for a trait influenced by many genes, as general intellectual capacity probably is, even an initial large genetic divergence due to chance is unlikely, since favorable mutations at some loci in one population would likely be offset by favorable mutations at other loci in the second population.

Drift

Genetic drift refers to the random variation of gene frequencies from generation to generation in small populations, caused by the fact that each offspring's genes are a random sample from those of his two parents. In a large population, drift is negligible, since individual sampling variations average out, and in the absence of selective factors each generation *in toto* closely reproduces the genotypic proportions of the last. But in small populations drift may lead to appreciable changes in gene frequencies.

In order to assign a substantial role to drift in accounting for gene-frequency differences among modern major racial groups, one would need to assume that these groups originated at some past time from small populations, which developed distinctive patterns of gene frequencies due to drift, and which then expanded to distribute their characteristic patterns of gene frequencies across wide sections of the globe. Subdivisions may have developed repeatedly within these populations, and the gene frequencies again may have drifted to some degree in these subdivisions, but with enough gene interchange among them to keep them recognizably similar to each other and to the ancestral pattern.

A characteristic feature of differences between populations due to drift is that such differences tend to occur at all loci for which the populations show genetic variance, rather than at just one or two loci, as is often true, for example, of gene-frequency changes due to selection. As we have seen in an earlier section of this chapter (pp. 37–39), most genetic loci show rather modest differences between races, but a few genes display markedly larger differences. It is tempting to attribute the smaller differences to drift and the larger ones to differential selection, but in the absence of direct evidence, this must remain speculative. In theory, drift can sometimes produce large differences, and selection may act to stabilize as well as diversify gene frequencies. Good direct evidence distinguishing between the effects of differential selection and drift is not easy to obtain for human populations (cf. Adams and Ward, 1973), although it is available from experimental studies of animal populations, especially *Drosophila* flies of several species.

The above considerations are based on single genes. What about polygenic traits, as general intelligence is thought to be? Here one would expect any differences due to drift to be even smaller. The larger the number of loci involved, the less likely it is that chance factors would all happen to act in the same direction, and hence the less probable it is that a large genetic difference between populations could result from the operation of drift.

Migration

It is possible that, even if there were no important differences in gene frequencies between the major racial groups, there could be such differences between subpopulations in the United States derived from these groups if the original immigrants constituted biased samples of the populations from which they were drawn. (It is also possible, of course, that a genetic difference between the parent populations could be diminished, eliminated, or even reversed in the corresponding populations in the United States by appropriate selection of migrants.) There has been considerable speculation about the possibility that the Africans who were imported to slavery in the United States might have differed in average intelligence from the African population at large; Eysenck (1971) in particular has emphasized this possibility. This possibility in reference to Americans of Oriental origins has been less discussed, at least in recent years, but clearly the Chinese brought in to build the railroads of the West may not have constituted a random sample of the Chinese population of the time. And for that matter, the immigrants from European populations were not necessarily a random sample of their respective gene pools, either (see, e.g., Franzblau, 1935). Even the original natives, the American Indians, were themselves immigrants some 15,000 years earlier, but here it can of course be only the sheerest speculation as to how, if at all, they might have differed in intellectual skills from the Mongoloid peoples who stayed behind.

The effects of migration, like those of genetic selection, which we will consider in the next section, differ from those of mutation and drift with respect to the distinction between single gene and polygenic traits. Whereas mutation and drift are more likely to cause large effects on single-gene traits, because of the improbability of chance events simultaneously affecting a number of genes in the same direction, this need not hold for selective migration and natural selection. For these latter mechanisms, the critical factors are the intensity of the selection and the heritability of the trait, not the number of genes involved. In fact, since the genetic influences on many socially conspicuous traits, such as height, physical strength, general health, intelligence, and skin color, appear to be polygenic, it is perhaps even more likely that (say) migration will be selective for a polygenic trait than for a monogenic one. Selection for a polygenic trait will tend to affect individual gene frequencies less than will an equal degree of selection for a monogenic trait, since no single gene is as closely correlated with the phenotype, but given equal degrees of heritability and selection the net amount of genetic change will be the same in both cases.

Thus migration cannot be dismissed as a possible factor leading to differences among U.S. subpopulations in the frequencies of genes that affect intellectual traits. However, if *large* average genetic differences are attributed to selective migration, extremely severe selection must be postulated. To produce a genetic difference of one standard deviation by selecting individuals from a normal IQ distribution, all migrants would have to be selected from only the 15 percent of the population at one extreme. This assumes a fairly high heritability of IQ; if the heritability is lower, the selection must be even more extreme. (The method of calculation is given in Appendix D.) It is not too easy to imagine social mechanisms that would work this selectively for IQ—the emigration of Jewish intellectuals from Hitler's Germany in the 1930's comes to mind, but even here many persons of only average intelligence emigrated. Certainly it seems implausible that this degree of selectivity on intellectual traits would have been achieved by the machinery of the slave trade, or by the processes that brought any of the other major racial-ethnic subpopulations to the United States. The relevant social factors determining which persons migrate—being rich or poor, winning or losing wars, living in Place A rather than Place B, being in or out of political favor—just don't have *high* correlations with IQ, although on occasion low or moderate correlations might exist.

We may approach the question from the other direction. Suppose that migrants were only moderately selected for IQ, that they were, say, 25 percent more likely to be derived from the bottom than from the top half of the IQ distribution, or vice versa—what average genetic difference would this produce? By the same general methods (see Appendix D) we can calculate the average expected genetic difference to be about 0.05 σ, or the equivalent of less than one IQ point.

In brief, while it seems plausible that selective factors in migration have produced *some* average differences among racial-ethnic subpopulations in the United States in the genes that influence intelligence, and while one cannot exclude the possibility that in narrowly defined groups such differences might be of appreciable magnitude, it seems unlikely that for broad racial groups the degree of selectivity could have been sufficiently great to have produced anything like the large between-group differences that are currently observed.

Natural Selection

The fourth mechanism, natural selection, depends upon the reproductive advantage of individuals carrying a certain gene, which leads to the increase in frequency of that gene in the population in succeeding generations. Such a reproductive advantage may stem from many sources—a greater likelihood of the individual's surviving until reproductive age, a greater probability of his mating and reproducing, a larger number of offspring, an earlier age at reproduction, and so on.

Natural selection, like selective migration, is as effective with polygenic traits as with monogenic ones. Unlike mutation and drift, it can be as potent a factor in large populations as in small ones. And finally, unlike a one-time migration, very small degrees of natural selection, acting over many generations, can produce very large genetic effects.

Let us consider what could happen to gene frequencies in two major races that have been separate for some 25,000 years, or about 1000 generations. Suppose that at the beginning of this period a given gene of intermediate dominance is at low frequency in both populations, say .01. In one population the gene remains at this frequency, but in the other there is a selection in its favor of .01, that is, possessors of the gene have a 1 percent reproductive advantage over nonpossessors. At the end of 1000 generations, the frequencies of the gene in the two populations will be .01 and more than .99 (see Appendix D for the method of making this calculation). Thus selective advantages on the order of .01 or less would easily be capable of producing even the largest of the between-race differences in gene frequencies that were noted in Table 2.1. As Cavalli-Sforza and Bodmer remark: "No published study is available that has been done with enough people to detect selective differences on the order of one percent. . . . It is a paradox of evolutionary theory that the small differences that may be so effective in molding the future of a species are so difficult to measure directly" (1971, p. 314f).

Now in real life, probably nothing stays constant over 1000 generations. Selective advantages no doubt shift with changes in environmental and cultural conditions, and may vary with the frequency of the gene itself in some instances. Thus exact quantitative predictions over long time spans should not be taken too seriously. Nevertheless, it is quite clear that even small average selective advantages, operating over many generations, can have large genetic effects.

The same applies to small *differences* in selective advantages. It has sometimes been proposed that intelligence is at a selective advantage in all human populations and that therefore racial differences in the genetic basis of general intelligence are unlikely to exist. If intelligence is at a selective advantage in all human populations, all populations will gradually get more intelligent, to be sure, at least until all the relevant genetic variation is exhausted. But unless intelligence is at an exactly *equal* selective advantage in all populations, in some the genes relevant to intelligence will increase more rapidly than in others, and if these differences prevail over sufficiently long periods of time, the genetic divergence between populations may become considerable.

Let us again look at a hypothetical numerical example. Suppose that at some point IQ is a normally distributed trait with a mean of 100 and standard deviation of 15 in each of two populations, and that it has the same moderately high heritability in each. Suppose that IQ is at a slight selective advantage in both populations, due entirely to a single mechanism: a reproductive disadvantage among individuals at the very bottom of the IQ distribution. That is, there is some mental level below which individuals are unable to perform the minimal intellectual functions necessary to survive until adulthood, to attract a mate, or to rear competent offspring. We will not assume an absolute all-or-none threshold, but rather a distribution such that as intelligence decreases there is some point at which there is only a slight reproductive disadvantage, and another at which the disadvantage is almost total, with a range of intermediate values in between. In assuming a normal distribution of IQ, we are in effect ignoring the excess cases, found at the bottom of real IQ distributions, of birth accidents, chromosomal aberrations, intrauterine infections, head injuries, and other accidental events that can severely depress IQ. We are only concerned here with the intellectual deficiency that forms the lower end of the distribution of normal intelligence.

We will assume that there is one important difference between our two hypothetical populations, namely, that because of their cultural values and traditions or the rigors of their natural environments selection against the individuals of low intelligence is somewhat more severe in one population than in the other. We will assume that in Population A, the point at which an individual incurs a $2\frac{1}{2}$ percent reproductive disadvantage corresponds to his having an IQ of about 60, and the point at which the disadvantage is $97\frac{1}{2}$ percent to an IQ of about 40; in Population B the corresponding points are equivalent to IQs of 65 and 45. In other words, conditions in Population B are just a bit harsher for an individual of low intelligence, and we come to persons at a reproductive disadvantage about 5 points sooner as we move down the IQ scale.

The consequences of this differential selection are that the next generation of Population A will show an increase in average IQ level of approximately 0.024 IQ points, and that of Population B an increase of 0.064 IQ points. (The details of the calculation are given in Appendix D.) The increases, as well as the difference between them, would be essentially undetectable in a single generation. But in 100 generations, assuming the relative degree of selection remained the same, there would be the equivalent of 4 IQ points' difference between the population averages, and in 1000 generations, 40 IQ points. Of course by this time it is unlikely that conditions would remain the same, but nevertheless, the point should be clear. A small degree of differential natural selection, such as might reasonably be produced by moderate ecological or cultural differences between populations, if continued over a sufficiently long span of time could plausibly result in large differences between the populations in the genes influencing intelligence.

The preceding illustration used differential selection at the low end of the intelligence distribution, but mechanisms operating at the high end of the distribution will work as well. If in one cultural tradition the most intelligent men become chiefs and receive extra wives, while in another the most intelligent men become celibate priests, the same sort of result could ensue. It may be debatable whether cultural arrangements of this kind would persist over the necessary time span, but it should be kept in mind that for most of the time period of human evolution, the human population consisted of preliterate hunting and gathering peoples, among whom cultural change may be presumed to have been extremely slow by modern standards. Also, it is not necessary that selection be absolutely constant. A degree of selection fluctuating around a low average level will have much the same effect. Or for that matter, a higher level of selection operating for a shorter period of time could produce an equivalent result. If Population A is exposed for a few dozen generations to a situation making moderately increased demands on intelligence for survival—say, a climatic change or a major migration—and Population B is not, an appreciable genetic difference could emerge between them. If agriculture places slightly more of a premium on intelligence than hunting and gathering—or if it places slightly less—groups whose times of transition from hunting and gathering to agriculture differ by thousands of years can be expected to differ in genes related

to intelligence. And the effects do not have to be very large per generation for the accumulated difference to be considerable.

In short, the mechanism of differential selection, much more
plausibly than the mechanisms of mutation, migration, and drift,
could result in substantial differences between large human populations in the distribution of the genes underlying general intelligence.
Whether this mechanism has in fact produced such differences between particular human groups is, of course, a quite separate question,
which will be our concern in later chapters.

CHAPTER 3

Intelligence and Its Measurement

A PERSON WALKS INTO A SITUATION in which others are floundering, appraises it, and selects an effective course of action. If he does such a thing only once, we may say he is lucky. If he can do it only in particular kinds of situations, we may say he has a special knack or talent. But if he does it over and over again, in a wide variety of situations with which his prior familiarity is no greater than yours or mine, we say he is intelligent.

This seems to be the core, commonsense meaning of the term *intelligence*. We may paraphrase it as "general problem-solving ability," if we recognize that the "problems" comprise a very wide range of situations, and that abilities can be recognized only by their fruits in word or deed.

In brief, then, we consider an act to be intelligent if it reflects a grasp of the essential features of an obscure or complex situation; we consider a person to be intelligent if he characteristically performs intelligent acts; and we consider intelligence (if we elect this degree of abstraction) to be the attribute of the person that enables him to behave in this fashion.

A number of the conditions are relative, of course. Obscurity and complexity obviously admit of degrees, and there can be no satisfactory *general* rule for how many exceptions negate the claim that a person "characteristically" does so and so, since "it all depends"— classifications are rooted in purpose. But commonsense usage is relative, too: an "intelligent" move for a beginner at chess need not be the same one a grandmaster would choose, and, clearly, people differ in the breadth with which they apply a term such as intelligence —because indeed "it all depends."

For the better part of a century, psychologists have been trying to give theoretical and empirical definition to this commonsense notion, by devising "intelligence tests," and by linking performance on these tests to theories of intellectual ability. This is not the place to review this history, which the reader may pursue in other places (e.g., Guilford, 1967; Peterson, 1925). We propose, in fact, to confine ourselves in this section to brief comment on three central questions— one primarily methodological, one primarily theoretical, and one primarily empirical. Our three questions are: How can one measure intelligence? Is intelligence unitary, or composed of a number of specialized component abilities? And, is intelligence innate or acquired?

How Can One Measure Intelligence?

The general strategy is simple: (1) Confront the person in question with a number of situations, each so designed that if he comprehends the essential features of the situation he is likely to do one thing, and if he doesn't he is likely to do something else. (2) Assign the person an intelligence score based on the proportion of situations in which he selects intelligent acts, the promptness with which he performs them, or some other suitable criterion.

Let us consider these two steps in turn. The selected situations in step (1) are ordinarily referred to as intelligence-test *items*. They may be of many kinds: solving puzzles, defining words, doing arithmetic problems, discovering analogies, classifying letters or figures, deducing the rule underlying a sequence, detecting similarities and differences. They may be presented visually or aurally (or indeed to touch or other senses); they may require a verbal response or the pointing of a finger, or they may entail the active manipulation of blocks, beads, or other objects or apparatus. Now successful performance on any *one* intelligence-test item might reflect merely a lucky guess, or a specialized knack, or some fortuitous fragment of knowledge. Thus a number of items of different types are used in general-purpose intelligence tests such as the *Stanford-Binet,** on the assumption that any special factors affecting a person's performance one way or the other on particular items will tend to average out over the whole set of items, and allow his general level of ability to show clearly through. We will have more to say on this point in our next section.

Sometimes, however, tests used as measures of intelligence do *not* employ a variety of item types. A popular test of this kind is Raven's *Progressive Matrices*, in which all of the items take the form of two-way sequence-completions. Vocabulary tests are also sometimes used as intelligence measures (for example, the *Peabody Picture Vocabulary Test*). The justification for using any such specialized test as a measure of general intelligence is, simply, that for the population in question it does in fact predict general good performance on intellectual tasks. Indeed, this is the justification for using *any* test to measure intelligence—there is no *logical* necessity that someone who displays intelligent performance in the contrived situations of an "intelligence test" will also be able to do so in other contexts. There is, of course, much *empirical* evidence of human consistency on this point. On the average, the person who performs well on one intelligence test does well on others, and also performs well in school, achieves high occupational status, is judged by teachers and peers as bright, and so on. The extent of this consistency, as measured by the correlation between test performance and some real-life indicator of intelligence, is technically called the *validity* of the test.

An important point to keep in mind here is that the validity of an intelligence test is not an inherent property of the test, but rather depends on the population in which it is used (and other factors as well). Knowledge of how many nickels there are in a quarter may have some validity as a predictor of the general intellectual competence of

---

*Brief descriptions of most of the intelligence tests referred to in this book may be found in Appendix C.

a young child in the United States but very little as a predictor of the intellectual competence of a young Chinese child—or a U.S. college student. We will return to this theme later, in discussing intelligence-test comparisons across different subcultural groups.

The second step in the measurement process, assigning a score based on the person's performance on the test items, is also an important one. A simple count of number of items correct could be used as an intelligence score, but such a measure suffers from at least two shortcomings: first, it is meaningful only for comparisons of results on tests of identical length and difficulty, and second, numbers obtained in this way will often have peculiar properties as a measurement scale. For example, in a test with three very easy items and a dozen of moderate difficulty, the difference between the intellectual level of someone who gets three right and someone who gets four right might be much greater than the difference between someone who gets four right and someone who gets ten right.

One answer to these problems is to calibrate the obtained test scores against a known metric, and the commonest means of doing this in intelligence testing with children is to use the average performance of children of different ages as the reference scale. This procedure gives rise to the "intelligence quotient," or IQ, which as traditionally calculated is the ratio of the age level at which the child performs intellectually, to his actual age. A child who performs on the test in question at the level of the average 5-year-old, but who is actually only 4, will have an IQ of $5/4 \times 100$, or 125. By definition, the average child of any age in the population will have an IQ of 100, and empirically it turns out that the standard deviation of IQ scores tends to run around 15 or 16, that is, in a normally distributed population, about two-thirds of the individuals will have IQs within 15 or 16 points of 100, either way.

Because empirical standard deviations obtained in this fashion tend to vary somewhat at different ages and with different tests, and because the logic of the traditional method breaks down with adults, among whom the change of intelligence with age is much more gradual, IQs are obtained from most modern tests by means of tables that convert raw scores to IQs in such a way that the resulting score distributions have a uniform mean of 100 and standard deviation of 15 (or 16), at any given age. These tables (sometimes referred to as tables of *norms*) are based on the actual test performances of a *stand-*

ardization sample, which is—or should be—a representative sampling of the population at the given ages.

It is this standardization sample that provides the reference base that gives meaning to IQs. A 4-year-old child has an IQ above 100 if he performs better on the test than the average child of his age in the standardization sample—and by inference, in the population from which that sample was drawn. He has an IQ of 130 (or 132) if he performs just two standard deviations above the standardization sample mean for 4-year-olds, a level of achievement expected in only about 2 or 3 percent of persons in a normally distributed population. (Empirical population IQ distributions are usually fairly close to, though not exactly, normal in form.) And this IQ of 130 will also mean, because of the rough equivalence to the traditional IQ, that this 4-year-old will be performing a little better than the average 5-year-old on intellectual tasks.

Thus the IQ is a relative measure, a measure that expresses performance on intellectual tasks relative to a standardization population. If a particular test were standardized on the U.S. white population (as were the Stanford-Binet and the Wechsler Intelligence Scale for Children) and you were to test a black child with it and obtain an IQ, this would tell you how his performance compares with the performances of U.S. white children of his age on these tasks at the time and under the conditions of the standardization of the test. This may be what you want to know, or it may not be, but clearly it is important to be aware that this is what the score means.

One or Many?

The second central issue on which we wish to comment briefly is the theoretical question of whether intelligence is best viewed as a single general intellectual capacity that expresses itself in a variety of different ways, or as a series of special abilities that tend to be positively intercorrelated in the general population.

Does it matter? Much of the time, in fact, it doesn't. Much of the time we will treat these two descriptions as alternative ways of talking about the same data, the one more useful in certain contexts, the other in others, analogous to the physicist's wave and particle theories of light. Often we will speak of "general intelligence," reflecting the fact that the majority of the data we will be discussing have been gathered by general-purpose IQ tests. On other occasions, however, we will speak of more specific abilities: verbal comprehension, numerical facility, the ability to visualize spatial relationships, and the like, as measured by tests designed to assess these specific competences. From this point of view, "general intelligence" is an average level of performance on a series of measures of special abilities, which have arbitrarily been mixed together in an "IQ test."

Nor, in general, will we wish to take a stand on how many of such special abilities there might be—the five to nine "Primary Mental Abilities" defined by Thurstone (1938), the twenty or so intellectual dimensions described in French's (1951) survey, or the 120 factors in Guilford's "Structure of Intellect" (1967). Indeed we will take the position that one can define as many abilities as he pleases, simply by being increasingly specific on the items he combines into a test: thus one could devise a test of "memory" with varied content, or a test of "auditory memory," or a test of "short-term memory for spoken digits." Sometimes one wants to make very fine distinctions, sometimes one doesn't. In this book, on the occasions when we do subdivide "general intelligence," we will usually find it useful to deal with a fairly small number of broad abilities, and thus we will more often operate at a Thurstonian than at a Guilfordian level of differentiation; we will, however, take this to be merely a matter of convenience, not of basic theoretical commitment.

Two other classifications of ability, on a somewhat different basis, will be relevant to our discussions later on, and so will be briefly mentioned here. One is Jensen's (1969, 1970a) hierarchical classification of Level I and Level II abilities. The other is Cattell's (1943, 1971) distinction between fluid and crystallized abilities. In Jensen's classification, Level I includes certain basic learning and memory capacities, which are held to be necessary for the later development of Level II abilities. The latter include the capacities for problem solving and conceptual thinking that most immediately underlie good performance on intelligence tests and success in traditional academic curricula.

Cattell's classification also involves two sequentially related kinds of ability. He discriminates between the ability to make original adaptations in novel situations, which he calls fluid ability, and the ability to reinstate earlier adaptations on later occasions, which he calls crystallized ability. The ability to form a new concept would be an example of the former. The ability to use that concept effectively later would be an example of the latter. Crystallized abilities imply that there was a corresponding level of fluid abilities in the past, but not necessarily that there is such a correspondence with current fluid abilities. For example, a person might preserve a high crystallized verbal ability into old age despite a considerable deterioration in his fluid ability. Neither Cattell's nor Jensen's classification coincides with the heredity-environment distinction—in both it is assumed that genes and environment influence both kinds of ability. Cattell does suggest, however, that fluid abilities should show somewhat higher heritability than crystallized abilities.

Earlier in this section, we remarked that much of the time the distinction between intelligence as a single general ability and as a number of correlated special abilities could be treated as arbitrary, with the choice being made in a particular context for the sake of convenience. We said much of the time, not all of the time. When not? One time is when we are pursuing explicit hypotheses concerning the genetic basis of performance on intellectual tasks. It makes a difference whether the hypothesis has separate genes underlying each special ability, with the separate abilities brought into correlation by such broad environmental factors as a favorable intellectual climate in the home, or whether the hypothesis specifies a gene-based general competence that is differentiated into special abilities by specific environmental encounters. (The possibilities are of course not limited to these two.)

Recent evidence in fact suggests that one of the capacities involved in performance on many IQ tests, namely the ability to visualize spatial relationships, may be rather substantially under the influence of a single recessive gene on the X-chromosome (Stafford, 1961; Hartlage, 1970; Insel, 1971; Bock and Kolakowski, 1973). There is also an intriguing report that persons blinded by retinoblastoma (an eye tumor that can be caused by a dominant autosomal gene) seem to show an exceptionally high level of verbal intelligence (Williams, 1968; Levitt et al., 1972). Further findings along these lines could render far less arbitrary our choices of how we describe the structure of mental ability. For the present, however, we will freely exercise our option to speak either of general intelligence or of special abilities, depending on the circumstances.

Innate or Acquired?

As mentioned in the introductory chapter, much of the history of the intermittent skirmish known as the nature-nature controversy has focused on the trait of intelligence, as measured by such tests as the

Stanford-Binet. In the next chapter we will discuss how one actually estimates the extent to which differences in IQ scores tend in a particular population to vary with the genetic or with the environmental variation in that population. Here we merely wish to emphasize that whether it is the genes or the environment that regulate the process, intelligence is clearly not innate, it is *developed*. In a normal human being, the ability to comprehend complex situations increases more or less steadily from the day he is born until senility sets in, although the ability to perform certain kinds of intellectual tasks, especially those involving speed and novelty, may begin to show a gradual decline after the late teens. That a person's IQ remains relatively constant does not mean that he doesn't grow intellectually, but rather that his course of intellectual growth is such as to hold stable his standing among his fellows. Although each individual's intellectual development may show some sort of approximation to the traditional growth curve of diminishing returns, the spread of IQs indicates that some individuals develop faster and rise further in their course of intellectual growth than others do.

We do not wish to give an exaggerated impression of the regularity of individual intellectual development. Especially in the early years, there may be considerable fluctuations in a child's measured IQ. Ordinarily, after the initial school years IQ can be expected to be reasonably stable, but many exceptions occur, and shifts of 5–10 IQ points are quite common. The relatively large changes in measured IQ that are typical during the very early years of life probably reflect more than just the lability of the developing intellect, however. They very likely result in part from the differing sets of abilities measured by the tests at early ages. Before a child learns language, he may be tested mostly on his perceptual capabilities or his motor coordinations. A child with good verbal but poor motor capacity may test as dull at one year of age and bright at three years, not because his abilities have changed, but because what is measured is different.

One theory of intelligence which focuses on its developmental aspects, and which has become increasingly influential among psychologists in recent years, is that of Jean Piaget (e.g., 1950). Piaget believes that the course of development of a child's intellectual capacity can be most clearly traced in his progressive comprehension of certain basic properties of the physical and social world: that objects maintain a separate and permanent existence; that certain characteristics of substances, such as volume and mass, endure through superficial changes of shape or appearance; that other persons have motives and values independent of one's own, and so on. The theory specifies the sequence in which these properties of the world are comprehended, and Piaget and his followers have developed a variety of tasks intended to assess the stage of development that a particular child has reached. Since the basic properties of the world are presumably observable in all human environments, Piagetian tasks have been widely used in cross-cultural research on intelligence. Studies in the United States that have used adaptations of the Piagetian procedures (e.g., Tuddenham, 1970) suggest that performance on these tasks tends to correlate fairly highly with performance on more traditional nonverbal IQ tests. Since the Piagetian tests tend to be rather cumbersome to administer and score, it seems unlikely that they will replace conventional intelligence tests for routine applications, but they continue to be of interest in connection with cognitive theory, and in cross-cultural research. Some examples of Piagetian cross-cultural research are reviewed in Appendix F.

INTELLIGENCE AND STATURE—
AN ILLUSTRATIVE PARALLEL

We wish in this section to explore some analogies between the trait of intelligence and the trait of stature. Since the latter trait is well studied, relatively easy to measure, and less subject to polarized emotional attitudes than is intelligence, it offers certain advantages as an illustrative parallel. Most discussions of the inheritance of intelligence and stature agree on the mode of inheritance of both as polygenic, although there are differences of opinion concerning the *degree* of heritability of intelligence, as we shall see in the next chapter.

Both intelligence and stature are quantitative characteristics, rather than discrete ones—that is, there is a range of expression of the characteristic rather than simply presence or absence of it. In this respect, stature and intelligence are like many other characteristics—structural and behavioral—for example, weight, skin color, extroversion, anxiety proneness, and muscular strength. Stature (along with weight) is one of the commonly used measurements of size or the accumulative effects of growth. Height is perhaps the most striking feature of physical growth and one of the most conspicuous differences between people. Stature, like quantitative measurements of intelligence, differs both within and between human groups. And like intelligence, stature starts small (the fertilized human egg has a diameter of about 140 microns, that is, about 1/12,000 of adult body height), grows rapidly before birth and thereafter until reaching a maximum around age 20 years or so, stays fairly constant through middle age, and declines somewhat in old age.

It is a common observation that heredity is important in determining body size in man and farm animals. Large animals tend to have large offspring, in both family lines and whole populations. Human males tend to be larger than females, a difference that evolved in our ancient primate ancestors perhaps because it conferred adaptive value in sexual selection and in protection against predators. It is also a common observation that certain environmental factors, especially nutrition, are important determinants of body size. Teenage British and American males are about half a foot taller today on the average than were their predecessors of a century ago; the gain is due in part to earlier maturation since the difference is less for adults. (See Tanner, 1962; Thieme, 1954. Such temporal trends in growth are discussed in more detail in the next chapter.) Family resemblances exist for intelligence as well, and in Chapter 4 we will review evidence suggesting that both heredity and environment are important in accounting for such resemblances. In Chapter 6 we will review the evidence concerning temporal trends in intelligence.

The Evolution of Human Stature

The early history of stature in the human evolutionary line is not well known because few full skeletons of ancestral forms have been recovered. Of course the early history of intelligence in the human line is even less well known. However, it seems likely that modern man became as tall as he is before he became as intelligent as he is; the evidence for this conclusion is that remains of the pithecanthropine men of Java who lived about 500,000 years ago suggest that their average height was about 5 feet 8 inches, but their brain volume was only about two-thirds that of modern man.

The development of upright, bipedal locomotion with an erect standing posture was a key event in the evolution of the human body and behavior. Bipedal locomotion freed the hands from their early function as feet, and in the primate line that led to man, hands remained unspecialized, five-digited, with thumb opposable to the fingers. Permanently free from locomotor duties, the hominid hand became available for both powerful holds and skilled manipulation—

a new level of tool use and manufacture. These changes in the function of the forelimb were concomitant with changes in the visual system and in brain size. There was increased coordination of the hand and eye and increased skill in fine manipulation.

The evolution of cranial capacity lagged somewhat behind that of stature, as noted, but at least by the time of Neanderthal man, some 50,000 years ago, human brain size approximated that of contemporary man.

World Distribution of Stature

Although the world range in stature of human populations has changed very little during the past 30,000 years, the world distribution of stature has changed, especially since the agricultural and industrial revolutions, toward a small increase in average height. The normal extremes of shortness and tallness seemingly were about the same among peoples living in Late Paleolithic times (up to 30,000 years ago) as they are today. But today a greater proportion of the people in a given population are taller, so that the average stature of the total world population has increased. Frasetto (1927, cited in Martin and Saller, 1958) estimated the mean stature of the living varieties of man, regardless of sex, to be 160 cm. Using samples from 386 populations, Martin and Saller (1958, vol. 2, p. 777) estimated the average stature of the adult male world population as 165 cm in the year 1920 and as 168–170 cm in 1958.

The distribution of average stature in samples of adult males from 855 populations is shown in Figure 3.1. The range in average height is from 138 to 185 cm, with a mean of 164.4 and a standard deviation of 6.84. The distribution is skewed toward the short end. It is presumed that the minor irregularities at the low end of the distribution merely reflect sampling errors between populations. As will be discussed later, major genes that result in pathologically short or tall stature are well known, but the frequency of these genes is very small in all known populations. The genetic control of stature is predominantly polygenic in short, medium, and tall populations.

Negroid population samples represent 259 out of the total of 855 shown in Figure 3.1. The Negroid samples are shaded in the diagram. The range of stature for Negroid samples is seen to be equal to the world range, with no non-Negroid groups being taller on the average than the tallest Negroid group. But 9 of the 259 Negroid samples have an average stature shorter than 144 cm, the shortest average

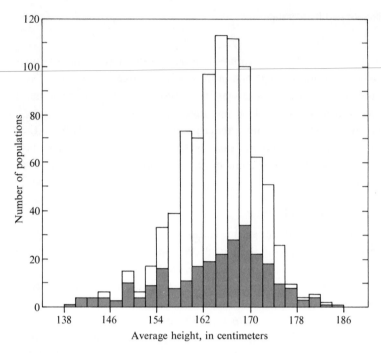

World distribution of average stature in adult males as determined in samples from 855 populations. The class intervals in the graph are 2 centimeters. Negroid samples are shaded. (Data from Sullivan, 1919, and various later sources.)

height of the non-Negroid samples represented in the diagram. These short Negroid populations are adapted for life as hunters and gatherers in the tropical rain forest where small size presumably has an overall selective advantage.

The world distribution of intelligence is much less well understood, in large part due to the great difficulty of obtaining comparable measures in different populations. Based on the analogy with stature, a crucial question relative to between-group variation would concern the possibility that intelligence might in the past have been selected to different degrees in the differing environments in which human populations live (cf. pp. 45–48).

Growth of Stature

There are two ways of studying growth. One is the longitudinal method, in which the stature or other body measurement of the same person is recorded at intervals from birth to maturity, or better, over the full life cycle. Since human beings require more than twenty years to reach maximum stature, longitudinal studies of large samples over the full growth period are obviously expensive and time consuming. In long-term growth studies conducted at a single center there is nearly always serious attrition in the sample as persons move away, die, or stop cooperating with the investigators.

The other method is called the cross-sectional approach. A cross section of the population is measured, which gives data on the size of different persons at different ages (but successive measurements are not made on the same person). This is an economical method, the only one that is practical for very large samples such as a military population, the principal source of information on the size of young men and women.

Perhaps the best all-purpose design for a growth study is a combination of the longitudinal and cross-sectional methods, that is, a semilongitudinal study in which persons grouped into age cohorts, say, five years apart, are each measured at successive intervals over a five-year period.

All three methods of measuring growth can be applied, and have been applied, to the growth of intelligence as well as stature.

As Boveri showed around the turn of the century (see Wilson, 1928), the body cells of both giants and midgets are nearly the same size as those of normal persons. The difference in body size lies primarily in different numbers of cells, as a result of differing amounts of growth. A person's stature comprises many parts with different growth patterns, patterns that may differ between individuals and populations. A glance at the human skeleton shows some major components that affect stature. When we measure total body height we add up the heights of at least some parts of the calcaneus, talus, tibia, femur, ischium, pubis, ilium, usually 5 sacral, 5 lumbar, 12 thoracic, and 7 cervical vertebrae, and basioccipital, temporal, and parietal bones, a total of 39 bones (counting paired bones only once). These bones each have two to five ossification centers, so that increase in height involves well over 100 different growth centers. The total height of a person is influenced by many different physiological processes, including the amount of pituitary growth hormone, the efficiency of the stomach and the small intestine, and the rates of ossification of the bones of the axial skeleton. Each of these is controlled by many distinct enzymes; the production of each enzyme is, in turn, regulated by one or more pairs of genes. As gene expression may vary independently at nearly all of the relevant loci, it is clear that any reasonably complete analysis of growth in stature must be very complex.

This complexity has not been fully explored (Tanner, 1962). We will not pursue it further here, except to note that the mode of inheritance of stature must, in the light of the facts just mentioned, be polygenic.

Intellectual growth may well share this very differentiated character. Certainly it appears to do so phenotypically, since the score on a standard intelligence test is a composite of performance scores on tasks influenced by many separate skills that can develop somewhat independently of one another. But as we know so much less about the physiological basis of intellectual development than that of stature, we can only presume that the genetic complexity underlying development is comparable in the two cases.

INTELLIGENCE AND CULTURE

The Definition of Culture

Just as biologists disagree on the definition of "life," psychologists on the definition of "mind" and "intelligence," so anthropologists fail to reach consensus on the definition of "culture."

The most quoted definition is the original one by E. B. Tylor (1871, p. 1) in his *Primitive Culture:* "Culture or Civilization . . . is that complex whole which includes knowledge, belief, art, morals, law, custom, and any other capabilities and habits acquired by man as a member of society."

Probably the most compact definition of culture is by Bain (1942, p. 87): "Culture is all behavior mediated by social symbols." Definitions that place emphasis on symbols are increasingly popular, for example, White (1949, p. 15): "The cultural category, or order, of phenomena is made up of events that are dependent upon a faculty peculiar to the human species, namely, the ability to use symbols. These events are the ideas, beliefs, languages, tools, utensils, customs, sentiments, and institutions that make up the civilization—or *culture,* to use the anthropological term—of any people, regardless of time, place, or degree of development."

Kroeber and Kluckhohn (1952, p. 357) concluded that the central idea of culture is formulated by most social scientists approximately as follows: "Culture consists of patterns, explicit and implicit, of and for behavior acquired and transmitted by symbols, constituting the distinctive achievement of human groups, including their embodiments in artifacts; the essential core of culture consists in traditional (i.e., historically derived and selected) ideas and especially their attached values; culture systems may, on the one hand, be considered as products of action, on the other as conditioning elements of further action."

Anthropological Views Concerning
Cross-cultural Comparisons of Intelligence

In this section we present some views of cultural and social anthropologists on the problem of racial or gene-based differences in intelligence between populations. Anthropologists are by no means in complete agreement on the problem, but the majority of contemporary cultural anthropologists defend a strongly environmental position.

At one extreme, many would agree with Boas (1938) that, given the normal range of human biological variation, differences in genotype are never *important* variables in the explanation of differences between groups in intellectual behavior or, for that matter, in any cultural behavior.

Some other anthropologists' views admit a limited but somewhat greater scope for genetic differences, like the following expressed by Kroeber (1948, p. 204):

> As a matter of fact, the anatomical differences between races would appear to render it likely that at least some corresponding congenital differences of psychological quality exist. These differences might not be profound, compared with the sum total of common human faculties, much as the physical variations of mankind fall within the limits of a single species. Yet they would preclude identity. As for the vexed question of superiority, lack of identity would involve at least some degree of greater power in certain respects in some races. These pre-eminences might be rather evenly distributed, so that no one race would notably excel the others in the sum total or average of its capacities; or they might show some minor tendency to cluster on one rather than on another race. In either event, however, race difference, moderate or minimal, qualitative if not quantitative, would remain as something that could perhaps be ultimately determined.

> But it is one thing to admit this theoretical probability and then stop through ignorance of what the differences are, and another to construe the admission as justification of mental attitudes that may be well grounded in historical conditioning but are in considerable measure unfounded objectively.

A few anthropologists follow Lévy-Bruhl (1922) in making the "primitive mind" (which, for Lévy-Bruhl, included the mind of many of the world's darkly pigmented peoples) differ in kind from the mind of civilized man. Lowie (1937, p. 218) gives a compact summary of Lévy-Bruhl's view: "Primitive people perceive nothing as we do, conceive nothing as we do, dispense with the principles of contradiction and of casuality. Their thinking is prelogical, though not on principle antilogical, in that it is a matter of indifference whether the law of contradiction holds or not. In other words, the primitive mentality makes an inseparable jumble of logical and nonlogical procedures." Among social anthropologists, Evans-Pritchard (1966), who made extensive field studies of African cultures, recently affirmed a qualified acceptance of the Lévy-Bruhl position. But the majority of cultural anthropologists who have long field contact with, and a deep knowledge of, a "savage" culture, and especially, intimate acquaintance with its language, do not find such differences between the primitive's mode of thinking and ours, and conclude that primitive people on the whole think as rationally as we do. Indeed, Lévy-Bruhl himself considerably modified his earlier views on this matter (Lévy-Bruhl, 1949).

The cultural anthropologists' view that between-group performance differences primarily stem from between-group cultural differences has been highly influential in psychology, and doubtless continues to be the majority view among psychologists concerning subpopulation differences within western societies (e.g., Baratz and Baratz, 1970; Cole and Bruner, 1971; Sarason, 1973).

Cultural Bias in Intelligence Tests

Logically, performance on a conventional IQ test can be a function of many factors besides sheer mental competence. A person cannot do his best on an IQ test if he isn't sufficiently motivated—nor can he do his best if he is too anxious that he do well, and is more concerned over his performance than with the materials of the test itself. Many tests include items that assume certain specific prior learning— vocabulary items are a case in point. A person whose experience has simply not included exposure to the relevant words will not score well on such items, no matter how intellectually capable he may be otherwise.

Matters of this kind have been of concern to intelligence testers since the beginning of intelligence testing. In the training of psychologists to administer individual intelligence tests, great emphasis is placed on developing and maintaining good rapport with the testee, and on taking the testee's background into account in the choice of tests—as by using appropriate nonverbal tests with persons whose language backgrounds might handicap them on standard tests, and so on.

These issues come particularly into prominence when persons of different cultural or subcultural backgrounds are to be compared. Obviously, the comparison of the intellectual competence of, say, a member of a nonliterate Amazon Indian tribe with that of a middle-class suburban New Yorker presents very great difficulties, and despite many ingenious efforts to devise tasks and testing conditions under which this sort of comparison can validly be made, it is probably fair to say that the majority of psychologists and anthropologists remain skeptical concerning the outcome of such efforts. Culture is so pervasive in human behavior that many anthropologists would insist that, except for behavior traits controlled by certain chromosomal abnormalities (e.g., Down's syndrome) or major genes (red-green color perception), no psychological test of sense perception, motor performance, or intellectual ability is either *culture free* or, when applied transculturally, *culture fair*. Indeed some would require that the criterion for a culture-fair test would be that scores on the test show no significant variation in central tendency or distribution when applied across culturally differing groups (again, with exceptions for known genetic effects). Because such a criterion begs the question to which this book is addressed, we cannot ourselves take so extreme a view. It does, however, serve to emphasize the difficulties inherent in cross-cultural comparison, particularly when the cultural disparities are great. As an illustration of how difficult are the problems of attaining cross-cultural comparability of psychological measurements, a number of cross-cultural studies of sense perception are reviewed in Appendix E. Even in this apparently simple realm, questions about the effects of culture on measurement continually arise.

On almost any measure, the cultural distance between the New York ghetto and the New York suburb is small compared to the distance between either one and the Amazon jungle, but it is clear that the cultural distance between suburb and ghetto is not zero. Consequently, many of the same issues may arise when comparisons of intelligence-test performance are made between different racial-ethnic subpopulations in the United States, or other westernized countries.

Attempts to Reverse Culture Bias

If ability tests or achievement tests can be biased by selection of test items or procedures to favor one culture or subculture over another, it should be possible to devise a test with reverse bias by selection of test items or procedures to favor the other culture. This has been done in several cases, and the resulting tests have given the expected results when administered to members of the two cultures.

It is obvious that all verbal information tests involve language comprehension and information and that both of these differ between cultures. To give an obvious example:

Can you answer the following questions?

1. ཁྱེད་རང་གི་མིང་ལ་ག་རེ་ཟེར་གྱི་ཡོད། །

2. आप का नाम क्या है?

3. 貴姓

4. オ名前 ハ 何 ト オッシヤイマス カ。

5. What is your name?

6. ཝཱ ཨིཟ ཡུཨར་ ནེའིམ།

The questions ask "What is your name," in (1) Tibetan, (2) Hindi, (3) Chinese, (4) Japanese, (5) English, and (6) English written in Tibetan script.

It would, of course, be fairly easy to select deliberately items for intelligence, information, or performance tests that would be so distributed between cultures or other groups as to insure that any desired group would repeatedly test inferior on one set of questions, or superior on another set. Indeed, many cultural anthropologists believe that it is in practice virtually impossible to avoid some such bias.

Yet many of the intelligence, information, and performance tests that have been interpreted to show that in the United States black, American Indian, rural, and foreign-born children are inferior to urban white children were in fact developed and standardized using urban white children. For example, as mentioned earlier, the widely used Stanford-Binet intelligence test was standardized only on white children.

A pioneering study of test-bias reversal was carried out by Myra Shimberg (1929) on urban and rural children in the state of New York. She standardized an "Information Test A" on 6,477 urban school children in a city of 47,876 inhabitants and an "Information Test B" on 4,875 rural school children from eight school districts in New York state. Each test had 25 questions, examples of which are given in the following two lists along with the percentages of correct answers given by the original standardization populations.

Information Test A

Question   1.   What are the colors in the American flag?   (99.0)

        5.   Who is President of the United States?   (94.1)

     10.   What is the largest river in the United States?   (79.3)

     15.   How can banks afford to pay interest on the money you deposit?   (48.0)

     20.   What is the freezing point of water?   (23.4)

     25.   What is a referendum in government?   (1.3)

Information Test B

Question   1.   Of what is butter made?   (98.3)

        5.   Name a vegetable that grows above ground.   (90.5)

     10.   Why does seasoned wood burn more easily than green wood?   (80.2)

     15.   About how often do we have a full moon?   (60.6)

     20.   Who was President of the U. S. during the World War?   (43.3)

     25.   How can you locate the Pole star?   (11.4)

The results of the two tests administered to children in rural and and urban schools are given in Tables 3.1 and 3.2.

On Test A the results of rural children in grades 4, 5, and 7 were significantly inferior to urban children. On Test B the situation was entirely reversed, the results of both rural boys and girls being significantly superior to those of urban boys and girls in each of the grades 4–7.

TABLE 3.1.   *Comparison of results of rural and urban school children on Test A.*

	Rural			Urban		
Grade	No.	Mean	σ	No.	Mean	σ
4	127	36.3	6.8	970	40.7	9.0
5	125	44.6	7.3	988	47.8	9.0
6	116	50.1	6.3	955	50.2	9.0
7	96	53.3	5.5	932	54.7	8.1

Source: Shimberg, 1929, p. 45.

Note: Difference between means is significant in Grades 4 and 5 at $p < 0.01$, in Grade 7 at $p < 0.05$, is not significant in Grade 6.

Shimberg's analysis of the answers of urban and rural children on Test B, and of overlapping questions in preliminary versions of Tests A and B, led her to conclude that Test B was no more specialized or biased in favor of rural children than Test A (or perhaps any test developed and standardized in city schools) was specialized or biased in favor of urban children. She also found that 14 rural school superintendents could not designate correctly in almost 20 percent of the cases which questions would be found to favor the rural children. This suggests that test items culturally "fair" to a certain group may not always be identifiable a priori.

Prior to Shimberg's investigation some seventeen studies had found that urban, English-speaking school children in the United States and Great Britain scored appreciably above their rural counterparts on tests of intelligence and school achievement. Since many IQ tests include some information items, and since biases may affect other types of items also, Shimberg's results suggest that the differences found between urban and rural children in earlier studies were in part a function of the tools of measurement rather than of genuine intellectual differences, although they do not, of course, rule out the possible operation of other factors.

DuBois (1939) standardized a Draw-a-Horse Test on Pueblo Indian children in New Mexico, following the same general method Goodenough (1926) used to standardize her Draw-a-Man Test on white children. The 955 Indian children were students at 26 United Pueblo

TABLE 3.2. *Comparison of results of rural and urban school children on Test B.*

Grade	Sex	Rural			Urban		
		No.	Mean	σ	No.	Mean	σ
4	Boys	436	11.02	4.1	136	8.74	3.9
	Girls	448	10.32	3.8	161	7.94	2.9
5	Boys	444	14.24	3.1	119	10.42	4.0
	Girls	397	13.36	3.6	114	9.44	3.8
6	Boys	402	16.32	3.4	151	13.46	4.0
	Girls	402	15.42	2.0	125	11.72	3.8
7	Boys	392	17.76	3.2	79	13.84	3.6
	Girls	353	17.42	2.9	77	13.38	3.6

Source: Shimberg, 1929, pp. 49–50.
Note: Difference between means is significant for both sexes in all grades at $p < 0.01$.

Agency day schools, most of which were in the middle Rio Grande Valley. The horse drawings were scored on a scale of 60 points, in analogy with the man-drawing test. The test-retest reliability for the Draw-a-Horse Test administered to Pueblo Indian children ranged from .64 for the four-year-olds to .90 for the children of age nine. DuBois administered the test to eleven-year-old white boys in the Albuquerque Public Schools and found that on the average they obtained an IQ of 74—that is, 26 IQ points below the average for the Pueblo Indian children (Norman, 1963).

Williams (1972) devised a BITCH Test purposely biased to favor American blacks over American whites; the acronym refers to *B*lack *I*ntelligence *T*est of *C*ultural *H*omogeneity. It is a multiple-choice vocabulary test based on words and phrases distinctive to the black culture. Blacks, on the average, score much higher than whites on the test. Williams has suggested that such a test may have value for identifying capable black children who, because of their limited exposure to white culture, are seriously underestimated by conventional tests. Research to test this hypothesis is under way, but results have not yet been reported.

Since the three preceding studies were all done with U.S. subpopulations, they clearly demonstrate that differences in test performance among such groups *can* be produced by cultural bias in the tests. In these studies the test content was more or less deliberately selected to make this point, so they do not provide a basis for estimating what proportion of the between-group differences on typical IQ tests stem from this source. They do, however, make plausible the argument that *some* such bias probably contributes to observed group differences.

The Assessment of Culture Bias

It is important to be cautious in making the leap from the conclusion that an influence probably exists to the assumption that that influence alone is responsible for whatever effects are observed.

Black English provides a case in point. In recent years, such linguists as Labov (1970) and Stewart (1970) have emphasized that most U.S. blacks speak a grammatically coherent dialect that differs in many ways from Standard English, and it has very plausibly been argued that a lack of appreciation of this fact can lead to serious educational problems in ghetto schools. It has also been suggested that since IQ tests are administered in Standard English, some or even most of the observed average handicap of blacks on these tests might be due to this dialectical difference. At least one direct test of this hypothesis has been carried out—and its results were essentially negative. Quay (1971) had the Stanford-Binet translated into Black English. Black examiners gave IQ tests to 100 inner-city black 3-, 4-, and 5-year-olds who were in a Philadelphia Head Start program. Half of the children, selected at random, were tested with the dialect version of the Stanford-Binet, the other half were tested with the regular version. There turned out to be an insignificant difference in performance (less than half an IQ point) in favor of the group tested with the dialect version. A comparison of more and less verbal test items did not reveal any important difference between the two versions; on the whole it appeared that both groups performed better on more verbal items than on less verbal items.

After the fact, one can suggest reasons for such an outcome. Urban black children, by virtue of extensive exposure to television, have had considerable practice in understanding Standard English, even though they may speak only the dialect. Also, the instructions on the Stanford-Binet are designed to be at a low level of language difficulty, so that a child can understand the tasks required of him at an age well below that at which he is expected to be able to perform them.

Obviously the results of this one study should not be generalized too far. Linguistic biases may be more important for other IQ tests. Other groups, such as rural Southern blacks, or members of minorities that do not have English as a native language, may face more serious dialectic or linguistic difficulties with standard tests. The Quay study did not manipulate nonlinguistic cultural factors, and these may be playing an important role (Cohen, 1969). Equally obviously, well designed empirical studies analogous to Quay's could go a long way toward removing some of these matters from the realm of speculation, as well as further clarifying the role of black dialect (e.g., Baratz, 1973; Hall and Freedle, 1973).

One empirical approach to assessing cultural bias in intelligence tests is exemplified by recent work of Jensen (1973b, in press), who has proposed that different patterns of test or item difficulty or item intercorrelation in different groups could be taken as evidence of different cultural influences on test performance. He has in fact found such differential patterns for British as compared to U.S. school children, for U.S. Mexican Americans compared to whites, and for females compared to males. He does not find such evidence of culture bias in comparisons of U.S. urban blacks and whites, however.

All in all, while the existence of some amount of cultural bias in some IQ tests for some intergroup comparisons can hardly be doubted, we are a long way from being able to assess with confidence the precise importance of such biases for particular group comparisons.

Bias in Predictions from Tests

Quite apart from possible biases in the tests themselves, problems may arise when the tests are used in the selection of applicants for jobs, admission of students to higher education, and the like (Cleary, 1968; Darlington, 1971; Thorndike, 1971; Humphreys, 1973a,b; Murray et al., 1973). As discussions by Flaugher (1974) and Schmidt and Hunter (1974) have recently emphasized, there is a basic dilemma in defining the predictive "fairness" of tests for members of different groups. A procedure that is "fair" and unbiased at the individual level—i.e., that maximizes accuracy for individuals and does not systematically over- or under-predict the performance of persons who are members of any particular group—will tend to select a smaller proportion of members of the lower scoring groups than are in fact capable of competing successfully at school or on the job, and thus be "unfair" at the group level. Conversely a test that selects applicants from various groups in proportion to the number of competent individuals actually in each group will select some persons who have a relatively lower probability of success while rejecting some others who have a relatively higher probability of success, and in general make more errors of prediction for individuals and select a less qualified group of applicants. Essentially, this situation comes about because predicting individual success is more difficult in a group in which fewer succeed—any chance factors work more strongly against correct prediction.

This dilemma cannot be avoided by shifting to other means of selection, such as ratings or interviews, because the same difficulties obtain there. Indeed, such a shift would probably make things worse, since the lower the validity of the selection device, the more serious the problem, and ratings and interviews tend in practice to have lower validities than tests for most kinds of selection.

Improving the validity of tests provides a way out—a test that predicts job success perfectly will be "fair" in both of the senses described above (it will be biased only if job success itself is biased). In the meantime, we should recognize that either form of "fairness" may come at some social cost.

CHAPTER 4

Heritability

Is INTELLIGENCE HERITABLE? How heritable? What bearing does this have (if any) on differences in IQ-test performance in different racial or cultural groups?

All of these questions are central to the general purpose of this book, and thus full discussion of them, in some sense, constitutes the entire book. We will, however, in this chapter attempt to clarify just what it is that these questions *mean*, and to review certain lines of evidence having primarily to do with the heritability of IQ *within* racial-ethnic subpopulations.

First, let us consider *heritability*. This variously used word will be employed in this book to refer to a technical concept from population genetics, a concept that has three essential features: (1) it refers to a particular trait, as measured in individuals (e.g., IQ test scores); (2) it refers to the variation—differences from person to person—of that trait in some specified population (e.g., IQ differences among U. S. elementary-school children); and (3) it describes what proportion of the variation of this trait in this population is genetic (i.e., is attributable to the genetic differences among individuals in that population).

In short, if we say that the heritability of Stanford-Binet IQ among U.S. elementary-school children is .70 we mean that 70 percent of the IQ-test-score variation we observe among elementary-school children is attributable to genetic differences among them, and that 30 percent of the observed variation is attributable to other sources (environment, errors of measurement, etc.). Some further necessary qualifications will be introduced later, but this is the basic sense in which we will use the term heritability: the proportion of the variation of a trait in population that is attributable to genetic variation in that population.

We can now return to the three questions with which we began. First, is intelligence heritable? Clearly, as stated this is too general a question to answer, but if we understand it to refer to some particular population (e.g., the children currently attending U.S. public elementary schools), and some particular set of measurements (e.g., score on IQ tests appropriate to this population), and if we understand "heritable" to mean "having some value of heritability greater than zero," we can answer this question. In this case, we can confidently answer "yes, intelligence is at least somewhat heritable" —indeed we probably can give this answer with some assurance for *any* behavioral trait, because the determination of behavior is inherently complex, and it is almost inconceivable that *some* aspect of the multiple processes governing any behavior would not be influenced to *some* degree by some gene with respect to which some persons in the population differ from others.

The interesting question then is not "Is intelligence heritable," but rather our second question "How heritable?" The answer ".01" has very different theoretical and practical implications from the answer ".99." We will be pursuing some of these implications in subsequent chapters, and later in the present chapter we will consider some answers to the question of how heritable IQ is in the United States and western Europe. But before we do, let us glance briefly at our third question: "What value does an estimate of the heritability of IQ have in explaining differences in IQ-test performance between different racial or cultural groups?"

A general answer can be given quite briefly: Within-population heritability estimates *may*, but *need not* have value for interpreting between-population differences on a trait. It all depends on how the relevant genetic and environmental differences are distributed within and between the populations. Let us be more concrete. Suppose that two populations have exactly the same frequencies for each of the genotypes affecting some trait. Then any average differences on this trait between the two populations must be entirely attributable to environmental factors, whether the heritability of the trait within the populations is high, low, or intermediate. Conversely, if the two populations differ genetically but are subject to exactly the same distribution of environmental influences, then any between-population difference in the trait must be wholly genetic, again irrespective of the heritability of the trait within the populations. However, when there are the same kinds of genetic and environmental differences between populations as within them, within-population heritability may be of some use in interpreting between-population differences—although even then it is likely to be quantitatively a rather rough index, since rarely are within- and between-population differences exactly proportionate. For the reader who wishes to explore in more detail the relation of within- to between-population heritability, some relevant equations based on the work of DeFries are presented in Appendix G.

Heritability and Developmental Genetics*

As indicated earlier, heritability is a population concept, referring to the manner in which genetic differences are related to differences in a trait among a population of individuals. The heritability of a trait depends on (but is not directly deducible from) the machinery by which genetic information regulates the development of the individuals in that population.

The spectacular advances of molecular biology in recent years have greatly clarified how the genetic information is actually represented in the long chain of the molecule of DNA (deoxyribonucleic acid). Although from a functional standpoint, the concept of the gene as a hereditary particle is still valid, we can no longer point to a well defined material entity as a gene, in the sense that it has been visualized in "beads-on-a-string" models. Instead we must think of the

---

*We thank Joshua Lederberg for contributing the original version of the material incorporated in this section.

genetic information as being encoded in the sequence of symbols (nucleotide pairs) that extend uninterruptedly for lengths of millions of units in the giant DNA molecule. A precise analogy can be drawn with a computer tape, which, from a physical standpoint is a homogeneous strip; yet, upon it can be written discrete numbers, letters, words, sentences, paragraphs, etc. The meaning of these units depends on the electronic devices that decode the tape. Likewise, the meaning of the genetic message depends on the decoding of the DNA by the protein-synthesizing machinery of the cell—the messenger RNA, the ribosomes, and the series of enzymes that transfers information from one format to another. Factors in the biochemical environment can influence the decoding machinery, and of course there are still untold complexities between the production of specific proteins and the eventual regulation of the entire organism.

A number of disparate definitions have been offered for the functional unit, or gene. The most appropriate for present purposes is to define a gene in the sense that (historically) corresponds to the term "cistron"—that is, a stretch of DNA that codes for a specific protein (or more precisely a single polypeptide unit of a protein). The actual span of the cistron depends on the message itself, for certain words (strings of unit symbols) are interpreted "start a protein" and others, "stop." This interval from "start" to "stop" is characteristically 500–1000 nucleotides long.

Despite this complexity, the genes can still be regarded as functional particles, since the formal behavior of the DNA sequences corresponds precisely to the particle model in most general considerations of inheritance, and in any evident application of genetic theory to problems of race biology. The complexity of gene action at the molecular level does require that we give careful attention, however, to such questions as the finality with which the genetic information determines traits of the most urgent human interest; certainly molecular genetics, even as it has clarified the precision of gene action, shows innumerable ways in which environmental influences may play upon genetic determination. Estimates of heritability constitute a way of quantifying one aspect of this interplay: the extent to which differences among the individuals in a population tend to be associated with differences in the patterns of information in their DNA molecules, as compared to differences in the pattern of environmental influences that have acted upon them from the moment of conception until the moment of our observation.

Variance Components

In discussions of genetic and environmental influences on differences among the individuals in a population, trait variation is ordinarily described in terms of a statistical concept, the *variance*. So expressed, the variation may be divided into additive components that sum to the whole. In the simplest case, the variance may be divided into two components: that part which is associated with genetic differences within the population; and that part which is not, but which reflects influences of the environment on the development of the trait and errors of measurement. Often one may wish to go further than this and subdivide the major components. For example, one may wish to divide the genetic variance into that part due to the additive effect of the genes, that part due to the effects of genetic dominance, and that part due to epistatic effects (see p. 79 for a discussion of these concepts). Or one might divide the nongenetic variance component into portions representing environmental variation occurring within families, environmental differences between families, and measurement error.

Any such subdivision is arbitrary, and may be chosen to suit the circumstances. Thus sometimes one might wish to divide genetic or environmental variance into a component reflecting differences between different social classes or ethnic groups within a population, and a component reflecting differences among individuals within such groups. Another common partition of variance is into a component reflecting stable individual differences in the trait in question, and a component reflecting the accidents and errors accompanying any actual set of measurements of the trait. Or one may wish to specify components of variance associated with particular environmental factors—such as the conditions common to pupils in a particular elementary school, or to a particular classroom in that school, or to sitting in the front rows versus the back rows of that classroom. Sometimes one may wish to nest classifications: for example, one might isolate variance associated with races, social classes within races, families within social classes, stable individual differences within families, and error of measurement. The general approach is clearly a very flexible one.

Covariance and Interaction

Sometimes the division of variance into components is not quite so simple. For example, suppose that intelligent parents tend to provide their children with genes conducive to the development of high intelligence, but also tend to provide them with environments favorable to the development of this trait, such as good schools, intellectual stimulation at home, and so forth. We may need to divide the observed variance among individuals in a population into a component that is associated with genetic endowment, when intellectual stimulation is held constant, a component that is associated with environmental stimulation, with genetic potential constant, and a third component associated with the covariance of heredity and environment, that is, with how the first two components vary relative to each other. If the genes and environment are positively associated, as in the example cited, this will cause an increase in the total variance, since there will be an increase in the likelihood of children receiving highly favorable or highly unfavorable gene-environment combinations. The added component of variance cannot logically be assigned to either the genes or the environment: it is a result of the association of their separate effects. Furthermore, the possibility of predicting intelligence from information about either the genes or the environment is enhanced by virtue of the overlap: each predicts some of the influence of the other.

Negative covariance of genes and environment, that is, the effect resulting when unfavorable genes for a trait tend systematically to be exposed to favorable environments, or favorable genes to unfavorable environments, probably seldom obtains for intelligence, although tendencies in this direction may be implicit in compensatory educational philosophies that concentrate educational attention on backward children. Negative covariance decreases total variance, and decreases the possibility of predicting the trait from information about either the genes or the environment.

We may note one further complication. There may be a component of the observed variation that cannot be predicted from *either* genetic or environmental influences alone, but that can be predicted from the two considered jointly. Thus certain combinations of genes and environments may have disproportionately favorable or unfavorable effects upon a trait, effects quite out of line with the usual influences of these genes or environments on the trait in question. In this case we may speak of a gene-environment *interaction*, and can specify a part of the total variance that is due to the effect of the particular combinations, over and above what might be predicted for the components separately.

Because of frequent misunderstandings on this point, it is important to make clear that the interaction referred to here is a statistical interaction based on the relationship between genotypes and environments in a whole population—and has nothing immediately to do with how genes interact with each other and their biochemical environment in the course of the physiological development of an individual, or with how a child interacts with his teacher in a classroom. Fortunately, relationships at the population level may often be additive, or nearly so, over the ranges of genetic and environmental variation found in natural situations, even though the underlying biochemical and behavioral processes are highly complex and nonlinear.

It is also perhaps worth pointing out that the presence of an interaction component of variance does not in itself indicate the nature of the interaction. Certain genes may be ineffective when an environmental effect is lower than some threshold level, but sensitive to environmental variation above that level. Certain environmental effects may be positive for some genotypes, but negative for others. Some genes and environments may multiply, rather than add, in their effects upon a trait. A wide variety of such possible sources of interaction exists, and all that a significant interaction component indicates is that one or more of them is present. (For an extensive discussion of gene-environment interaction, see Erlenmeyer-Kimling, 1972.)

Components of the Genetic Variance

As indicated in a preceding section, the effect of the genes on the variance in a quantitative trait may be broken down into three components: additive, dominance, and epistatic. The first of these is the average effects of individual genes on the trait, irrespective of their genetic context. The second is the genetic interaction at single chromosomal loci—since if dominance exists, the effects of a gene may depend on what other allele is present at that locus. Finally, epistasis is interactions among genes at different loci; the effect of a particular gene may depend on what other genes are simultaneously present. In practice, because dominance and epistatic effects on trait variance tend generally to be similar in character, and thus difficult to discriminate except in rather large and precise experiments, these two components are often treated together as a nonadditive variance component. Alternatively, the effect of epistasis may be assumed to be negligible, and the nonadditive genetic variance simply referred to as the dominance component.

The presence of nonadditive genetic variance in a trait may be of considerable theoretical interest in providing clues to the evolutionary history of that trait. Natural or artificial selection tends to reduce additive genetic variance. Hence a trait that has been subject to strong selective pressures in the past may have a relatively large proportion of its genetic variance nonadditive. In addition, directional selection of a trait (i.e., selection in one direction, as for tall stature or high intelligence) may tend to capitalize on dominance effects, so that the alleles which tend to favor the trait at various relevant loci will tend to be dominant alleles. This may be detectable by so-called "inbreeding depression," or lowered values of the trait in the offspring from matings of closely related individuals; or conversely, by "heterosis," or increased values of the trait in the offspring from matings of members of a previously inbred population with outsiders. These concepts will be further discussed with specific reference to the traits of stature and intelligence in a later section of this chapter.

Also of genetic relevance is *assortative mating*, the mating with each other of individuals who tend to be similar in the trait in question. This tends to increase the amount of additive genetic variance of the trait over that which would be expected if mating were at random. Thus selection and assortative mating tend to have opposing effects on the additive genetic variance of a trait, assortative mating increasing it and selection decreasing it. Assortative mating by itself will not, however, affect the average level of scores on a trait in a population, while selection may.

Heritability Coefficients

As we indicated earlier, a *heritability coefficient* is simply a proportion: the proportion of the observed variance of a trait that is genetic. We will find it useful to distinguish two such coefficients: the so-called "broad" and "narrow" heritabilities. Broad heritability, which we will symbolize as h_B^2, refers to all the genetic variance. Narrow heritability, h_N^2, refers to just the additive part of the genetic variance. If nearly all the genetic variance of a trait is additive, these two heritabilities will be approximately the same, and a choice between them is not critical. But a trait whose expression involves a great deal of dominance and epistasis could have a high h_B^2 and a low h_N^2. Which one of these coefficients is best to use depends on the circumstances.

If we are concerned with the extent to which differences in scholastic achievement in some population are associated with genetic differences among the individuals in that population, then the broad heritability is the figure of interest. On the other hand, if we are assessing the impact of reproductive patterns on the IQ of the next generation, then h_N^2 is what is wanted, since that includes just that portion of the genetic variance that predicts average effects across generations.

The broad and narrow senses of the term heritability are not always distinguished in discussions of the heritability of intelligence, and sometimes one finds estimates of h_B^2 used in contexts where h_N^2 would clearly be more appropriate. As a rule of thumb, when education is at issue, h_B^2 is usually the more relevant coefficient, and when eugenics and dysgenics are being discussed, h_N^2 is ordinarily what is called for. Methods of heritability estimation relying on twins usually yield some sort of approximation to h_B^2, while those using parents and offspring usually estimate h_N^2. A number of technical details related to various methods of subdividing variance and calculating heritability coefficients are treated in Appendix G. However, one general theoretical point and one important methodological issue need to be made explicit here.

The theoretical point is that a heritability coefficient refers to a particular trait in a particular population. In other populations, or in the same population at other times, the variation of genes or environments may be different, and if so, the heritability of the trait will be different. This does not mean that if one finds a given trait to be highly heritable in one human population, he should be astonished to find it also highly heritable in another. After all, humans share a common gene pool and many common social and environmental features. It does mean, however, that if a heritability coefficient is derived in one population and used in another, it is important to note possible relevant differences between the two populations, since the greater these are, the riskier the generalization will be. In a later chapter we will be examining these risks in a concrete case, in comparing the heritability of IQ test scores in different U.S. subpopulations.

The methodological issue that should be mentioned is the influence of heredity-environment covariance and interaction on heritability estimates. Many methods of calculating heritability coefficients make fairly arbitrary allocations of these components. The reader should

TABLE 4.1. *Median values of intelligence-test-score correlations obtained in 56 studies conducted between 1911 and 1962.*

Number of Samples	Biological Relationship	Condition of Rearing	Median Correlation
15	One-egg twins	Same family	.88
4	One-egg twins	Separate families	.75
21	Two-egg twins	Same family	.53
39	Siblings	Same family	.49
3	Siblings	Separate families	.46
7	Unrelated	Same family	.17

Source: Estimated from Figure 3 of Jarvik and Erlenmeyer-Kimling, 1967.

be aware, for example, that a number of methods of estimating heritabilities from empirical data lump the covariance component with genetic variance: thus "heritability" may in practice sometimes designate the proportion of variance that is genetic *or* results from environmental factors that happen to be correlated with genetic variation. On the other hand, many of these methods lump the variance due to gene-environment interaction with the environmental component. Thus some of the "environmental" part of the variance is no more environmental than it is genetic: it is predictable only jointly.

This too is a topic to which we will return.

The Heritability of IQ in Caucasian Populations

Various lines of evidence suggest that much of the variation in intelligence-test scores among members of Caucasian populations in the United States and western Europe is associated with genetic differences among the individuals in these populations. Since this evidence has been reviewed and discussed extensively in several places recently (e.g., Anderson, 1974; Broadhurst et al., 1974; Burt, 1966, 1972; Jarvik and Erlenmeyer-Kimling, 1967; Jencks, 1972; Jensen, 1967, 1969, 1970b; Lindzey et al., 1971; Vandenberg, 1971) we will not attempt more here than a brief summary of the evidence, and a comment or two on its implications.

Essentially, inferences about trait heritability are based on the resemblances found among persons of differing degrees of genetic relationship and similarity of environmental backgrounds. Thus if biological brothers who are reared together in the same family, who attend the same schools, who interact with the same neighborhood peer groups, and so on, turn out to be much more alike on a trait

TABLE 4.2. *Estimates of variance components in intelligence-test scores.*

Component	Proportion
Genetic	
Additive	.52
Assortative mating	.12
Dominance	.11
Total genetic	.75
Environmental	
Within families (including error)	.12
Between families	.13
Total environmental	.25

than biological brothers who because of adoption are reared in different families, there are grounds for attributing a substantial effect to the environmental factors associated with family, school, and neighborhood. Or conversely, to the extent that biologically related persons exposed to quite different environments continue to resemble each other, there are grounds for giving weight to genetic factors.

Table 4.1 gives average resemblances in IQ for persons of various genetic relationships and different conditions of rearing, based on a compilation of studies from the literature (Jarvik and Erlenmeyer-Kimling, 1967). The original studies were conducted over a 50-year span, and used a variety of intelligence tests. All but one or two were based on largely Caucasian populations in the U.S. and western Europe; omission of the exceptions would not substantially change the figures given.

It is clear in Table 4.1 that resemblance in intelligence-test scores reflects both closeness of biological relationship and the similarity of conditions of rearing; it is equally clear that the former is much more predictive than the latter. Thus persons reared together in the same family may vary in resemblance from an average correlation of .17 to one of .88, depending on their biological relationship, but persons of a given degree of genetic relationship (siblings) vary only from an average correlation of .46 to one of .53, for environmental relationships ranging from being reared in separate families to being reared together as twins.

Starting from the correlations, one may divide the observed variance in intelligence-test scores into various components. Table 4.2 shows such an analysis, following a model presented by Fulker

(1973). In addition to the correlations of Table 4.1, this particular analysis requires a correlation for spouses and one for parents and offspring. The former is not provided in Jarvik and Erlenmeyer-Kimling's survey, and their value for the latter is not usable here, being based on an unspecified mixture of single and midparent data. Therefore we have taken median values of .52 and .48 for these correlations from the U.S. studies listed in Jencks's tabulations (1972, pp. 272, 274). Since meaningful standard error estimates are not readily derivable for the median correlations, we have used a simple unweighted least-squares solution (see Jinks and Fulker, 1970) rather than the more elaborate maximum likelihood procedure employed by Fulker.

The estimate of broad heritability yielded by these data is the sum of all the genetic components in Table 4.2, or .75. The estimate of narrow heritability in this population (assuming equilibrium under a constant level of assortative mating) is the sum of the additive and assortative mating components, or .64. It will be noted that the environmental variance is divided about equally within and between families. However, since the within family component is inflated by errors of measurement (probably somewhere between 5 and 10 percent of the total variance), these data suggest that environmental factors common to family members outweigh those for which family members differ.

The reader is cautioned not to take these numerical estimates too literally. The genetic model employed is oversimplified; for example, it does not explicitly take into account gene-environment covariance and interaction. In addition, the empirical correlations used represent averages that in some cases are based on limited and conflicting data. Various adjustments of the raw correlations for restrictions of range, measurement errors, or other sources of possible bias can shift the obtained values materially upward or downward, according to the proclivities of the adjuster.

Fortunately, none of the conclusions to be drawn in the present book depend very heavily on exact figures for the heritability of IQ, provided only that its heritability is appreciable. Whether the true figure for h_B^2 is closer to .40, .60, .75, or .90 might sometimes affect matters of emphasis, but rarely matters of substance. Most quantitative estimates in the literature derived from either or both of the two major sources of evidence—twin studies and adoptions—have yielded estimates of the broad heritability of IQ in the range .60 to .85, although critics can certainly be found who offer arguments as to why such estimates might run a bit high (e.g., Morton, 1972). Recently, however, one writer, after making a serious effort at reviewing the evidence (Jencks, 1972) arrived at a broad heritability of .45, another critic (Layzer, 1974) suggested a figure between .00 and .50, and still another (Kamin, 1973) went so far as to assert that "a critical review of the literature produces no evidence which would convince a reasonably prudent man to reject the hypothesis that intelligence test scores have zero heritability."

While Jencks's estimate of .45 for broad-sense heritability presents no serious difficulties for the general arguments of this volume, the discrepancy between it and the estimates of other investigators relying on essentially the same evidence has led us to scrutinize it with some care, and in Appendix I we suggest that correction of a technical difficulty in Jencks's treatment of selective placement, plus some reasonable alternative decisions at one or two other points, would yield a figure rather more in line with those obtained by others, as well as fitting some data that cause difficulties in Jencks's analysis.

Layzer's analysis, like Jencks's, places great emphasis on gene-environment covariance, which indeed is of considerable theoretical interest. But the contact with empirical data is weak, since Layzer relies rather heavily on only one subset of the IQ evidence, and a rather internally inconsistent one—IQ correlations among adopted siblings. He also cites in support of his argument some studies of the heritability of commercially important traits in dairy cattle (Donald, 1969). This is probably an unfortunate choice, as these are traits undergoing artificial selection, which could markedly affect the heritabilities. In addition, Layzer may have misunderstood the conditions of the experiments themselves as being more closely analogous to the human studies than they in fact were in regard to rearing together and apart, and the like.

Kamin's more radical assertion of zero heritability, if substantiated, might not render the present book entirely meaningless, but it would certainly require a considerable revision of its language and point of view. In Appendix H we have taken a second look in the light of Kamin's critique at some of the data that provide the main focus for his misgivings, namely the studies of adoptive families and separated identical twins. We do not find these data to be quite as fragile as does Kamin, and we find Kamin's analysis to suffer from a number of statistical and logical problems; our conclusion is that a reasonable person with environmentalist preferences could very well emerge from an appraisal of these data with a lower figure for the broad heritability of IQ than, say, Jensen's estimate of .80 (Jensen, 1967) or Burt's of .87 (Burt, 1972), but we do not believe that that figure would be anywhere in the neighborhood of zero. Essentially similar conclusions would hold for another recent paper in the spirit of Kamin's, by Schwartz and Schwartz (1974).

Covariance and Interaction: More

We do need, however, to examine more closely the matter of gene-environment interaction and covariance.

As far as gene-environment interaction is concerned, some part of the 25 percent of the variance in intelligence-test scores in largely Caucasian populations that is classified as "environmental" may well stem from this source. In an analysis in which direct measures of environmental variables are not included, there is inevitably confounding of variation due to differences in environmental input with variation due to differences in responsiveness to that input. Complete unconfounding requires independent control over both genotypes and environmental treatments, a condition that is approximated in some research with lower animals, but is not technically feasible in most research with human populations. Thus a dedicated hereditarian can always assert that some part of what the environmentalists claim is rightfully as much his as theirs.

There is, however, one test available that is capable of detecting some kinds of genotype-environment interaction (Jinks and Fulker, 1970). If, for example, individuals with the sorts of genotypes that tend to lead to high IQs are more sensitive to environmental inputs than individuals with the sorts of genotypes that tend to lead to low IQs, then one might expect a given environmental difference to have a larger effect for an identical twin pair with high IQs than for a pair with low IQs. Such an interaction effect could be detected in the form of a correlation between pair means and within-pair differences, in a sample of identical twin pairs. Such a test has been applied to existing IQ data by Jinks and Fulker (1970; Fulker, 1973) and Jensen (1970b). Little evidence of interaction was found. However, it should be noted that this method will only detect interaction effects that are linked in a fairly simple way to levels of the trait in question. If one kind of genotype (scattered throughout the IQ range) is much more sensitive to environmental effects on IQ than another, this is an instance of genotype-environment interaction, but it will not be detected by this procedure.

What about gene-environment covariance? One source of such covariance, which we have previously discussed, is that due to the fact that parents having certain genotypes may influence their offspring both through direct genetic transmission and through environmental inputs. This is the covariance Jencks estimates (see Appendix I). The effects of this kind of covariance can be evaluated by using adoption studies, studies of half-siblings, and the like. There is, however, another kind of gene-environment covariance that may develop due to the interplay of organism and environment. If, for example, persons having genotypes predisposing them to high intelligence tend to seek out intellectually stimulating environments, or if the values of the society are such that budding talent tends to be encouraged wherever it is observed, then we have a potential correlation between genes and environmental input that is tied to the individual himself, and escapes our experimental control by moving with him into an adoptive family. Note that the development of such a correlation does imply some degree of involvement of the genes, since without genetic variation it could not occur; however, such genetic involvement could conceivably be irrelevant to the trait in any direct biological sense.

One can imagine hypothetical cases in which the entire "genetic" component of a trait could be due to such a mechanism. Let us suppose that there is a society in which the belief is strongly held that the number of books a person should read is strictly proportional to the lightness of his eye-color. Let us also suppose that the level of intelligence-test performance in this population is determined solely by an environmental variable—the number of books read. Finally, let us suppose that lightness of eye-color is highly heritable. The result would be that a conventional study of the heritability of intelligence in this population would show it to be highly "heritable"— since identical twins would be more alike in intelligence than fraternal twins, siblings reared apart would continue to resemble one another in IQ, and so on. But the "genetic" component of the variation in IQ would be entirely the function of a gene-environment correlation. Obviously, one can still predict IQ from a knowledge of genotype in this population, and in that sense it is not entirely incorrect to speak of a high heritability of this trait. But equally obviously, the knowledge that this prediction depends on a feedback loop in which the immediate causal factors lie in the environment is of great practical importance to someone interested in changing IQ in this population or in predicting the distribution of intelligence in another population known to be genetically similar to this one but to have strongly egalitarian reading habits.

How can one assess the role that feedback-based gene-environment correlations might play in inflating the "heritability" of intelligence in real populations? One possibility is to find subgroups within the population in which such feedbacks can reasonably be postulated to be more or less strongly operative, and compare heritability estimates in these groups. Suppose, for example, that with respect to IQ there were a strong positive heredity-environment correlation of this kind among U.S. whites, but a much lower one among U.S. blacks. A heritability estimate that included variance due to gene-environment correlation along with variance attributable to the genes should then be substantially higher for the white than for the black population. Some writers (e.g., Jensen, 1968; Scarr-Salapatek, 1971a) have suggested that IQ heritabilities might be lower in socially disadvantaged U.S. groups, such as blacks or lower-income whites, by virtue of restricted or suppressive environments in such groups. This can be interpreted as postulating lower (or even negative) gene-environment correlations in such disadvantaged groups, relative to the U.S. population as a whole. Such a mechanism should tend to produce lower heritability estimates in the disadvantaged groups, as well as a lower total variance, since the total is increased by a positive covariance component.

But other possibilities exist. To the extent that socially disadvantaged groups are exposed to a social and cultural environment that is arbitrarily limited in various ways relevant to intellectual development (as measured by intelligence tests), the component of intelligence-test-score variance that is due to environment could also be diminished in such groups. This would again have the effect of decreasing total IQ variance, but it would have the opposite effect on heritability: by decreasing the environmental component, the genetic component should increase relative to the total, and heritability estimates should rise.

In addition, we need to consider the effect on heritability estimates of a third mechanism, which will be discussed in more detail in Chapter 7, namely intergenerational social mobility. This presumably operates to a considerable extent across social class lines in the U.S., but to only a very slight extent across racial lines. To the extent that social-class groups are constituted on the basis of variables correlated with intelligence such as education or occupation, the variance in IQ within such groups will be less than in the total population. Whether the heritability of IQ within such groups will go up, down, or remain the same depends on whether the selection is stronger relative to those aspects of intelligence-test performance that are more influenced by environment, or to those aspects that are more influenced by genotype. If one assumes that the social-class environment tends to be conservative in its effects, and that those individuals changing social class are most likely to be those receiving exceptionally propitious or exceptionally unfortunate selections from the parental gene-pool, then one would predict that within-class genetic variance would tend to be decreased, and heritability measured within such groups would be lowered. But one would not expect within-*race* variance to be materially affected by this mechanism.

In summary, then, one might reasonably predict lower heritabilities in socially disadvantaged groups, higher heritabilities in socially disadvantaged groups, or lower heritabilities in social-class but not racial groups, depending on which of the above mechanisms one chose to emphasize.

To add one final complication, some methods of estimating heritability are differently sensitive to environmental variance within and between families, a fact that must be kept in mind in evaluating particular findings.

In short, while the presence of differential heritabilities of a trait in different social groups might well be relevant to assessing the significance of gene-environment covariance for that trait, the prediction of the consequences of such covariance is by no means simple, since a number of mechanisms may operate jointly, with differing effects. Thus the detailed pattern of observed heritabilities and variances is likely to be more instructive than any particular single comparison between groups.

In Chapter 5 we will examine existing studies that offer empirical evidence on the relative heritability of intelligence in U.S. black and white subpopulations, and (to a very limited extent) in different social-class groups.

The Distribution of a Quantitative Trait

We will briefly consider in this section the implications of different sorts of environmental and genetic influences on the population distribution of a quantitative trait. We will take the trait of stature by way of concrete example, but the comments would be equally applicable to other continuously distributed traits, such as IQ.

Let us first consider environmental effects. If all members of a population had identical genotypes for stature, all variation in height within the population would be caused by environmental differences. If there were only two alternative classes of environments, one increasing and the other decreasing stature, only two phenotypical classes, one shorter and the other taller, would exist. If the environmental agency were equally likely to be present or absent during the growth of all persons, the two phenotypes would occur in the ratio 1:1. Given two such environmental factors affecting stature, with equal and cumulative actions, three phenotypes for height would exist according to whether neither, one or the other, or both factors were active during the growth of an individual, and the frequencies of the phenotypes would be in the ratio of 1:2:1. With six such factors, 7 different genotypic classes are possible

$$+++++, +++++-, ++++--, +++---,$$

$$++----, +-----, ------$$

and the ratio 1:6:15:20:15:6:1 for these is predictable from the binomial expansion $(\frac{1}{2} + \frac{1}{2})^6$. As is generally true of binomial distributions, the greater the number of such environmental factors affecting stature, the closer would the frequency distribution of phenotypes approach the normal distribution.

The same would hold true for a simple polygenic model. In the simplest case, in which the alleles are equal in effect, cumulative in action, and each have a frequency of $\frac{1}{2}$, the normal distribution is quite well approximated with five or six gene loci. With unequal gene frequencies or gene effects, or the presence of dominance or epistasis, a larger number of loci are required to approach normality, but provided these conditions are not too correlated or too extreme, the deviation from normality will be slight if, say, a dozen loci or so are involved in the genetic influence on the trait.

One can obtain equally good fits to the observed distribution of stature in human populations by assuming either relatively few loci with multiple alleles at each locus, or relatively many loci with only two alleles at each locus. However, a model with multiple alleles (say, $A^1, A^2, A^3, \ldots, A^n$) at a *single* locus cannot explain the observed wide range of stature observed in some large families. Two parents have, at a single locus, no more than four different alleles, say $A^1A^2 \times A^3A^4$, and, therefore, their offspring may have a maximum of only four different genotypes (A^1A^3, A^1A^4, A^2A^3, and A^2A^4) based on multiple allelism at a single locus. But the children in large families that have one tall and one short parent may vary in adult stature over a wide range, indicating that more than four different degrees of genetically controlled phenotypes may occur (Stern, 1973). This is not to suggest that multiple allelism does not occur at the loci controlling stature in human populations; rather it is to suggest that we must postulate more than a single locus for stature.

Correlation of Relatives, Assortative Mating, Dominance, and the Inheritance of Stature and Intelligence

Perhaps the best single illustration of the importance of dominance and nonrandom mating for the inheritance of quantitative traits such as stature or measured intelligence comes from comparisons of the expected and observed correlations between certain biological relatives when differing amounts of positive assortative mating and of dominance are assumed.

A satisfactory statistical fit between expected and observed phenotypic correlations of both lineal and collateral biological relatives is, in fact, obtained with models of quantitative inheritance that assume partial positive assortative mating and partial dominance. The observed fit is not satisfactory with models assuming random mating and either complete dominance or no dominance. These conclusions were first empirically supported for stature by Fisher (1918) and for measured intelligence by Burt and Howard (1956). These results provide perhaps the best available evidence on the nature of quantitative inheritance with respect to continuous morphological and behavioral traits in human populations.

The essentials of this illustration are given in Table 4.3, which is reassembled from Burt and Howard (1956). The observed correlations for stature (column 4) in parent-offspring and sibling pairs are based on a sample of more than 2000 pairs reported by Pearson and Lee (1903). The other three correlations in column 4 are based on samples collected by Burt and Howard (1956) of, from top to bottom, 263,

TABLE 4.3.   *Expected and observed correlations among relatives for stature and intelligence in the English population under various models of quantitative inheritance differing in the degree of positive assortative mating and dominance.*

	Stature						Intelligence		
	Expected						Expected		
	Random Mating		Assortive Mating, Partial			Assortive Mating, Partial	
Relationship	Complete Dominance (1)	No Dominance (2)	Dominance (3)	Observed (4)	Dominance (5)	Observed (6)
Lineal						
Parent-offspring	.333	.500	[.507]	.507	[.495]	.489
Grandparent-offspring	.167	.250	.301	.322	.311	.335
Collateral						
Sibling-sibling	.417	.500	.536	.543	[.514]	.507
Uncle/aunt-nephew/niece	.167	.250	.301	.287	.309	.354
Single first cousins	.083	.125	.181	.236	.215	.289

Source: Burt and Howard, 1956.

615, and 584 pairs, respectively. Both sets of samples were collected from families of the British university-student class.

The theoretical values in column (1) were first derived by Pearson (1904), those in column (2) by Yule (1906), and those in column (3) by Fisher (1918).

In column (3) the first value of .507, given in square brackets, is the empirical correlation obtained by Pearson and Lee, and the rest were calculated by Burt and Howard from this value and the observed marital correlation of .280 for stature, from the same study.

A similar calculation for measured IQ was carried out by Burt and Howard, as shown in column 5 of Table 4.3. The theoretical values in square brackets were calculated from the observed spouse correlation of .386 and some rough estimates of genetic parameters; the corresponding empirical values were then employed to obtain refined estimates of the parameters for use in calculating the rest of the expected values (for details, see Burt and Howard, 1956).

As can be observed from Table 4.3, the empirical correlations for both stature and intelligence appear to fit a model based on assortative mating and partial dominance considerably better than they fit either of the alternative models presented. The different analysis reported earlier in this chapter (Table 4.2, p. 83) led to similar conclusions for intelligence.

Secular Increase and Heterosis

There is an extensive literature on the increase in average stature during the last 150 years in the United States, western Europe, and Japan. The data show that there has been a general increase of about 1 cm per decade (or 1 inch per generation) over the last five or six generations (Genovés, 1970). The increase may be greater in certain subpopulations, for example, Newman (1963) reported an increase of about one-half inch in height between the military populations of World War II and the Korean War, at corresponding ages. This is equivalent to a rate of increase of about 1.4 cm per decade. Rapid changes have also been reported for U.S. 14- and 15-year-olds. Thieme (1954) observed that 14-year-old white boys measured in 1954 in the Detroit, Michigan, area averaged 5.9 inches (15 cm) taller than boys of the same age measured in Boston in 1877, and that 15-year-old Michigan boys were 2.6 inches ($6\frac{1}{2}$ cm) taller than those from Hagerstown, Maryland, measured in 1937. These are differences in the range of 2–4 cm per decade. Girls in the southeastern Michigan sample

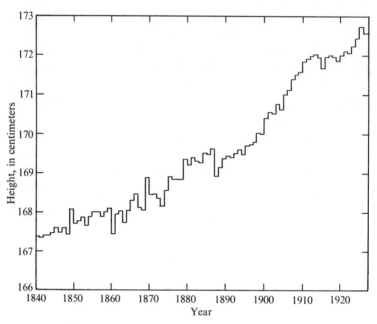

FIGURE 4.1
Secular increase in mean stature of Swedish recruits, 1840–1926. (Data from Hultkrantz, 1927.)

were correspondingly taller than girls of earlier generations. These and Newman's findings presumably reflect changes in the timing of growth, in addition to changes in the eventual height attained. More typical values for stature change are reported by Kimura (1967), who estimated that the Japanese population at age 20 has increased in height by about 6 cm among males and about 5 cm among females during the first 50 years of this century. One of the most extensive bodies of data on the secular increase in stature was collected by Hultkrantz (1927) on Swedish recruits, measured at age 21 from 1840 to 1914 and at age 20 from 1914 to 1926. A plot of the Swedish results is given in Figure 4.1. Since 1890 the increase has been at a rate of 1 cm per decade, before that it was slightly less.

There is also some evidence, although it is considerably more ambiguous, to suggest an increase in average intelligence-test performance in some populations during the last half-century—evidence that we will examine in more detail in Chapter 6. Because there might well be some parallels in the genetic and environmental mechanisms involved in the two cases, we will explore the case of stature further in the present section.

Two differing explanations are commonly given for the observed secular increase in stature: one environmental, the other genetic. The environmental explanation relates the increase to changes in nutrition, sanitation, medical care, or psychophysiological factors. The genetic explanation stresses heterosis consequent upon isolate breaking, that is, a decrease in inbreeding and increase in outbreeding (see, for example, Broman, Dahlberg and Lichtenstein, 1942). The two explanations need not, of course, be mutually exclusive.

The environmental arguments are probably straightforward enough to require no further elaboration here. The genetic hypothesis may, however, be less familiar to some readers.

Heterosis is a well recognized phenomenon in plants and animals. Work on maize hybrids from 1880 through the 1920s provided extensive information on heterosis. Two observations resulting from the maize research were made prior to the rediscovery of Mendel's laws around 1900: (1) Differences in growth rates between hybrid and nonhybrid populations are greater than the final size differences attained; (2) Hybrid vigor in the offspring of the second generation diminishes but does not disappear. These results are relevant to the evaluation of recent studies on heterosis in human populations.

Two supplementary theories were advanced to explain heterosis. Davenport (1908) introduced the "dominance" theory, which held that heterosis could be explained by favorable dominant alleles masking the effects of deleterious recessives. The competing "overdominance" theory, introduced by East (1907) and Shull (1908), held that something about heterozygosity as such gives the heterozygotes greater fitness or luxuriance of growth than the homozygotes. Crow (1952) presents a succinct account of these two theories.

Before discussing the evidence for heterosis as an explanation of the secular increase in stature in human populations some conceptual and terminological clarification is in order. Fitness heterosis differs from metric heterosis. Fitness heterosis (named euheterosis by Dobzhansky, 1952) refers to an increase in Darwinian fitness (measured by relative mortality and fertility) with increase in heterozygosity. Metric heterosis (sometimes called luxuriance) refers to an increase in the measure of a trait resulting from altered growth rates with increase in heterozygosity. The existence of metric heterosis is widely confirmed in plants and animals other than man. Many examples of fitness heterosis may also be considered examples of metric heterosis: milk yield, egg yield, litter size, etc. However, increases in traits such as these do not always lead to an overall increase in population fitness (Cody, 1966).

We need also to distinguish between monogenic (single locus) heterosis and polygenic heterosis. Monogenic heterosis implies over-dominance at the relevant chromosomal locus; i.e., the heterozygote exceeds both homozygotes on the fitness or metric trait. In man the best known case of monogenic heterosis is the fitness heterosis in the hemoglobin AS (sickle-cell) heterozygotes. Polygenic heterosis may, however, occur in the absence of overdominance at individual loci. Dahlberg (1948, 1942b) used a formulation by Wahlund (1928), of the effect of isolates on the distribution of genotype frequencies in the general population, to argue that secular change in stature may be due to increased heterozygosity as a result of the outbreeding of formerly inbred isolates. If σ_q^2 is the between-isolate variance in gene frequency, following isolate breakdown the frequency of each homo-zygous class will be decreased by an amount equal to σ_q^2, and the heterozygous class increased by $2\,\sigma_q^2$, relative to the frequencies before breakdown. More generally, this argument predicts that if there is dominance, a change in the system of mating can change the mean or the variance of a polygenic trait, or both. Hybridization due to isolate breakdown or to race mixture is a dramatic change in a system of mating.

Anthropologists were interested in race mixture before the begin-ning of modern genetics in 1900. Boas (1894) studied the offspring of French Canadian and Ojibwa Indian marriages and compared them to Indian and white controls assumed to represent the unob-served parental populations. He found the hybrid offspring mothers had more children (mean of 7.9 compared to 5.9) than Indian mothers living in the same social conditions. The height of the hybrid offspring exceeded that of the Indians and presumably that of the white parents, since on the average French Canadians were shorter than adult Ojibwa males. Boas concluded that the greater height of the hybrid offspring was due to more rapid growth during adolescence.

Subsequent workers have sometimes found similar results, and sometimes not, and their conclusions often seem to have been heavily influenced by current political and social attitudes (Provine, 1973). Trevor (1953) summarizes the results of 9 race-mixture studies carried out in human populations in the first half of this century; American Negroes, Jamaican Negroes, European-Sioux Indian, European-Ojibwa Indian, Spanish-Maya Indian, European-Hottentot, European-Kisar Islanders, English-Tahiti Islanders, and English-Asian Indians. On the whole, he concludes that the 9 studies yielded little overall support for the existence of heterosis for stature in hybrid populations. Most of the studies suffered from more-or-less severe defects in sampling, whose effects are difficult to evaluate.

Several investigators have studied the offspring of endogamous versus exogamous matings with the community unit being the village, county, or ethnic group. Beckman (1962), from a study of army conscripts in Sweden, found that the effect of exogamy upon stature was different in different places. In the northern county of Norrbotten there was a positive effect of exogamy, that is, offspring of exogamous matings were taller than those of endogamous matings. In the central county of Kopparberg there was a negative effect. In the southern county of Malmöhus no significant effect was detected. There is a cline in stature in Sweden increasing from north to south. Beckman assumed that differences in the stature of native and inmarrying individuals were responsible for the results found.

Damon (1965) observed a positive heterotic effect on the stature of Italian-Americans of Neapolitan ancestry. Ferák et al. (1968) found that the offspring of exogamous matings in the villages of eastern Czechoslovakia were not significantly taller in a sample of 6–13 year olds but were in a sample of 17–20 year olds. Saldanha (1962) concluded that dominance effects account for the observation that the mean stature of Brazilian-Italian hybrids is closer to the mean of the taller Italian than to that of the Brazilian population. And Hulse (1969) found that offspring of exogamous marriages between persons in isolated Swiss villages were taller than offspring of within-village marriages.

In general, then, though there is some support for the notion that an increase in outbreeding may sometimes have a heterotic effect on stature, the evidence is far from univocal, and it would seem doubtful that this particular mechanism can serve as a sole explanation for the observed strong secular trend for this trait, although it may well be a minor contributing factor.

A number of studies on the intelligence of racial hybrids have also been carried out, and will be reviewed in Chapter 5. These studies tend to suffer from sampling difficulties at least as severe as those in studies of stature, and are faced with serious measurement problems as well. Perhaps the best evidence for heterotic effects on the trait of intelligence is provided by the converse phenomenon, inbreeding depression, in a study in Japan by Schull and Neel (1965). In that study, 865 offspring of marriages of related persons (first to second cousins) in the city of Hiroshima were compared with 989 offspring of marriages of unrelated persons. The children of unrelated persons averaged about 5 IQ points higher than children of first cousins on a Japanese version of the Wechsler Intelligence Scale for Children, and were also superior in school performance. The latter finding was replicated for a second sample in Nagasaki, which did not receive the IQ test.

A problem in interpretation was presented by the fact that the married cousins in this study tended to be somewhat lower in socio-economic status than the unrelated partners, and IQ score was related to measures of socioeconomic status. A statistical control using a composite measure of socioeconomic status based on education, occupation, and housing reduced the group difference by about 20 percent but did not eliminate it, so the authors concluded that there was a genuine inbreeding effect. Since there must always be some doubt as to whether the socioeconomic measure optimally indexed the environmental differences relevant to intellectual development, the possibility of undercorrection can always be raised, and hence there must remain a degree of uncertainty concerning the magnitude of the inbreeding effect. It does not seem likely that it would vanish altogether under some more appropriate adjustment for environmental differences, although this possibility cannot be completely excluded.

Heritability and Social Policy

Recent papers by the population geneticists Morton (1974) and Lewontin (1974), appearing in the same issue of the *American Journal of Human Genetics*, comment on the concept of the heritability, including its implication, or lack of implication, as a guide to social policy. Both authors argue that the concept has limited value, since high heritability of a trait need not counterindicate environmental change as a means of modifying the trait. In addition, Morton emphasizes the difficulties in obtaining good heritability estimates in human populations. In a succeeding article (Rao, Morton and Yee, 1974) he and his associates develop a fairly elaborate method for the analysis of genetic and environmental components of trait variation using path coefficients, the details of which are beyond the scope of our discussion here.

Lewontin's more radical critique of the concept of heritability focuses on its local and descriptive nature. He provides a number of hypothetical examples to show that genetic and environmental variance components estimated under a particular set of environmental conditions may not be at all predictive for a different environment (many of his more dramatic examples, it should be noted, involve shifts to environments completely outside the range of those in which heritability was originally estimated).

One may subscribe to Lewontin's wish for more powerful and extensive descriptions of how genotypes and environments combine to produce phenotypes, without dismissing altogether the value of estimating genetic and environmental variance components of particular traits in existing environments. For one thing, we are nowhere close to having the full descriptions (for polygenic human traits of interest), although we can estimate heritabilities to some degree. But more important, the great majority of immediate policy decisions revolve around just that set of environments for which heritability estimates have the most relevance: the existing set. Most proposed policy changes involve minor redistributions of environments within the existing range, and it is precisely regarding such changes that a heritability estimate has its maximum predictive value. For instance, one message that a high heritability coefficient can convey is that minor fiddling around with environmental factors that already vary widely within the population has poor odds of paying off in phenotypic change—and thus new ideas about environments need to be tried. Surely this is a message of enough social and practical implication to justify continued interest in heritability and its estimation.

PART II

THE EMPIRICAL
EVIDENCE

CHAPTER 5

Genetic Designs

IN THIS AND THE FOLLOWING THREE CHAPTERS, we will review some of the principal lines of evidence concerning the origins of racial-ethnic differences in abilities. Our aim is to scrutinize the types of data most often cited in recent discussions of this topic, and to arrive at some judgments concerning the main trends in the empirical evidence, and how they bear on the question with which we are centrally concerned: the relative contribution of genetic and environmental factors to the observed differences in ability between U.S. racial-ethnic groups.

We will begin in this chapter with a consideration of studies that confront the heredity-environment issue directly, by attempting specific control of genetic and environmental variation through the use of traditional genetic designs: twin studies, adoptions, studies of racial mixture, and so forth. We will find the evidence in many cases to be limited, conflicting, or methodologically unsatisfactory, but nonetheless it is clearly important to examine such data as exist.

The studies to be reported deal mostly with U.S. blacks and whites, as socially defined. This social definition of the groups means that there will be some persons who identify themselves as "blacks" who do not differ appreciably in their ancestry from some persons who identify themselves as "whites," and thus that the genetic differences between the two groups will be less than if some more biologically oriented racial classification were employed. But since the social and public-policy issues primarily concern differences between the existing socially defined groups, the social definition would seem to be the most relevant one for our purpose.

The reader should be cautioned that many of the studies to be discussed use samples that are much too small for accurate estimation of genetic and environmental parameters (Eaves, 1972). Nevertheless we will be interested in observing any consistent trends among studies. Successful replication can powerfully increase confidence in statistically weak results.

TWIN AND SIBLING STUDIES

It has sometimes been suggested that an ideal design for studying black-white differences would involve separated pairs of identical twins, with one member of each pair white and one black. Needless to say, we will not be reporting any such studies (although, given a social definition of race, they would not be *logically* impossible). We will, however, be examing studies in which comparable estimates for blacks and for whites of the heritability of intellectual measures are derived from samples of twin or sibling pairs. We have been unable to find any studies in which parent-child correlations have been reported in black samples, or studies obtaining heritability estimates in U.S. racial-ethnic groups other than blacks and whites.

As was indicated in our earlier discussion of heritability (pp. 88–89), the comparison of U.S. black and white IQ heritabilities is interesting on several grounds, even if it is not decisive on the question of whether the average difference *between* the two groups is genetic or environmental in origin. Within-group heritability could in theory be raised by restriction of the range of environments, or lowered by a lack of positive environmental feedback. Or heritabilities might differ as a result of differences in genetic variation between the groups concerned.

Three recent investigations have compared heritabilities in U.S. black and white twin samples; one of them provides extensive sibling data as well. The three studies are by Osborne and Vandenberg, on a sample of twins from Louisville and Atlanta, by P. L. Nichols, with twin and sibling data from the U.S. Collaborative Study, and by Scarr-Salapatek, with twins from the Philadelphia public schools. A fourth study, by Jensen, provides black and white sibling correlations for a California school population.

The Vandenberg-Osborne Studies

In the course of a series of twin studies at Louisville, Kentucky, in the mid-1960s, Vandenberg presented to 137 identical and 99 same-sex fraternal pairs a battery of cognitive tests—mainly focused on spatial abilities, but also containing a number of tests of verbal, perceptual, and numerical abilities (Vandenberg, 1969). Jointly and simultaneously, R. T. Osborne presented the same test battery to a smaller sample—33 identical and 12 same-sex fraternal pairs in Atlanta, Georgia (Osborne, Gregor, and Miele, 1968, and other papers cited therein). The combined Vandenberg and Osborne samples contained 32 black identical and 11 black fraternal pairs, about half from Kentucky and half from Georgia. Later, both authors independently published papers based on the combined samples, in which they compared the heritabilities of the measured abilities in the black and white subsamples (Osborne and Gregor, 1968; Osborne and Miele, 1969; Vandenberg, 1970). They arrived at strikingly different conclusions:

Vandenberg: "It is clear from this tabulation that there is good evidence for the thesis that the ratio between hereditary potential and realized ability was generally lower for Negroes than Whites" (p. 283).

Osborne: "The h^2 differences are not remarkable, but on seven of the eight spatial tests h^2 was higher for Negroes than for whites suggesting more rather than less genetic or biological contributions for Negro children than for white children" (Osborne and Gregor, p. 738f). "The findings cannot support the hypothesis of differential heritability ratios for white and Negro children on tests of numerical ability" (Osborne and Miele, p. 538).

These opposite conclusions were reached from the same data, indeed apparently from copies of the same computer printout (kindly

TABLE 5.1. *Comparison of Holzinger heritability coefficients and identical-twin intra-class correlations in black and white samples from the Osborne-Vandenberg studies.*

Test	H (Osborne)		Same, for Vandenberg Scoring[a]		H' [b]		Identical-twin Correlations	
	B	W	B	W	B	W	B	W
Arithmetic test	.49	.60	—	—	.52	.63	.78	.85
Cube Comparisons	.49	.29	—	—	−.72	.38	.49	.51
Surface Development	.70	.60	—	—	.45	.56	.62	.75
Paper Folding	.46	.18	.60	.16	.03	.18	.46	.49
Object Aperture	.01	.41	.40	.34	.04	.10	.28	.57
Newcastle Spatial	.65	.46	—	—	−.92	.55	.86	.80
Mazes	.78	.33	.45	.38	.31	.27	.82	.39
Identical Pictures	.41	.51	.40	.51	.62	.34	.61	.75

Sources: Osborne and Greger, 1968; Osborne and Miele, 1968; Vandenberg, 1970; and unpublished data supplied by Osborne.
[a] From original computer output. Reported only for measures for which scoring differs between studies.
[b] Calculated from Fs reported by Vandenberg. See Appendix G for details.

supplied to us by R. T. Osborne), which was produced by a program of R. C. Nichols and S. Carson that calculates various heritability co-efficients and other statistics from twin data. Most of the tests were scored in more than one way and in some instances one author used one alternative while the other author used another alternative, but this does not appear to be an important source of the discrepancy in conclusions. Osborne's two papers treat only about half the measures covered by Vandenberg, but this is not the source of the discrepancy either. The key difference appears to lie in the choice of method of computing heritability, as Table 5.1 shows for the eight measures common to both reports.

The first pair of columns in Table 5.1 gives Holzinger heritability coefficients taken from Osborne's papers (see Appendix G for a discussion of this not-too-satisfactory coefficient). The coefficients are consistent with his general conclusion that there are no marked differences between the groups—or if anything, heritabilities are higher in the black subsample on the spatial tests. The second pair of columns shows that choice of scoring formulas was not decisive— indeed, Osborne might have drawn his conclusion even more strongly had he employed the scoring formulas that Vandenberg chose. The third pair of columns shows Holzinger heritability coefficients computed in a different way, from within-pair variances (actually, these were calculated from Vandenberg's reported F ratios—see Appendix G for details). The coefficients for the white groups in these columns are larger than those for the blacks for three-fourths of the tests, consistent with Vandenberg's conclusions. Note the particularly dramatic reversals on some of the spatial measures, such as Cube Comparisons or the Newcastle Spatial Test. The two large negative H' estimates for blacks suggest, however, that there is trouble somewhere.

The equivalence of the two methods of computing heritabilities depends on the equivalence of the total variance in the identical- and fraternal-twin groups, and as one might guess from these discrepancies, such equivalence does not obtain. The apparent source of difficulty is the very small black fraternal-twin sample (11 pairs), which in addition to being small seems to have been aberrant—particularly on the spatial tests the subjects in this sample had considerably lower average scores and strikingly reduced variability compared with the black identical-twin pairs. Indeed on some measures their scores were no higher than what could be obtained by random guessing of the answers. Thus heritability estimates depending on this group can hardly be very meaningful.

Since the black identical-twin sample is somewhat larger (32 pairs), and has variances more comparable with those in the white samples, the possibility suggests itself of a direct comparison of identical-twin correlations. These will in general provide inflated heritability estimates, since they reflect shared environments as well as identical genes, but if the overlap in twin environments is similar in the black and white groups, a difference in heritability should be reflected in a difference in identical-twin correlations. These correlations are shown in the righthand pair of columns in Table 5.1. It appears that they are fairly comparable in magnitude for blacks and whites. So far as this line of evidence goes, therefore, it suggests no important difference in black and white heritability of cognitive abilities.

The Nichols Study

In a recent doctoral dissertation done at the University of Minnesota Paul L. Nichols has presented data from somewhat larger black twin samples, plus a large sample of sibling pairs (Nichols, 1970). These data derive from the Collaborative Study of Cerebral Palsy, Mental Retardation, and Other Neurological and Sensory Disorders of Infancy and Childhood, which was coordinated by the National Institutes of Health. In this large-scale study a systematic sample (every nth pregnancy) was selected at each of the participating institutions (mostly public clinics) and any offspring followed up with various physical, psychological, and neurological examinations until the children were 8 years old.

The population from which Nichols drew his sample consisted of the offspring of approximately 18,000 white and 20,000 black mothers enrolled in the study at 12 hospitals distributed across the United States. His main sample consisted of 1251 white and 1264 black pairs of siblings (including twins and half-sibs) both of whom were included in the Collaborative Study and were tested with a short form of the Stanford-Binet at the age of 4 years. He also reports data for a somewhat larger number of sibling pairs (2030 black and 1767 white pairs) tested at age 8 months with the Bayley Mental and Motor Scales, and a smaller group of 543 sibling pairs who were tested with the Wechsler Intelligence Scale for Children and several other ability and achievement tests at age 7 years. (Only part of the total sample had reached this age at the time of Nichols's study.)

Nichols concluded that there was a lower heritability of intelligence among blacks than among whites in his sample. He based this conclusion primarily on the sibling correlations for the 4-year-olds' scores on the Stanford-Binet. For the 1100 ordinary sibling pairs in the white group the intraclass correlation was .52; for the 970 pairs in the black group it was .37. There is no question that this is a statistically dependable difference with samples of this size. It will be noted that the value of .52 in the white sample is quite typical of the values found in other studies with Caucasian populations (median of .49 in Table 4.1, p. 82). The value of .37 is definitely lower. The difference is probably not an artifact of something like different variability in time of testing (there was a month or so leeway in the age at which children were tested) or different illegitimacy rates in the two populations, since both weight and height correlated equally for black and white siblings at age 4 years.

The data from the 8-month Bayley tests and the 7-year WISC tell a rather different story. At 8 months 1830 white and 1390 black sibling pairs correlated .20 and .19, respectively, on the Bayley Mental Scale. These low correlations may in part reflect differences in the time or circumstances of testing. However, Nichols and Broman (1974) report that statistical adjustment for age at testing did not much affect sibling correlations in a sample largely overlapping the one we have been discussing. These infant tests, of course, measure a somewhat different set of variables than do later IQ tests.

With the 7-year-olds, however, there again appeared to be no consistent difference in sibling resemblance. The tests given included: seven subtests of the WISC, the Bender-Gestalt, the Illinois Test of Psycholinguistic Abilities, the Draw-a-Man test, and Wide-Range Achievement Tests of spelling, reading, and arithmetic. The sibling correlation was higher in the white sample for six of the thirteen tests, and in the black sample for seven. Few of the differences were large, and they do not appear to be systematic for such subgroupings as verbal versus perceptual tests, or aptitude versus achievement measures.

Only about a quarter of the total sample had been tested at age 7 years when Nichols made his study, and one cannot tell, of course, what trends might develop as more of the sample is tested. However, the available scores on 543 sibling pairs (presumably more-or-less equally divided between blacks and whites, though this is not clearly stated) should be sufficient to reveal a difference of the magnitude found at age 4 years if it still existed at age 7 years.

Twin data are not reported by Nichols for the 7-year-olds (not enough twins had yet been tested to make it worthwhile) but the twin correlations at 8 months and at 4 years do not suggest consistent heritability differences between blacks and whites. These correlations and heritability coefficients calculated from them, are shown in Table 5.2. Opposite-sex as well as like-sex fraternal pairs have been included, contrary to usual practice, because the like-sex fraternal samples are rather small (25 and 29 pairs on the Stanford-Binet). Inclusion of opposite-sex pairs often tends to inflate heritability coefficients somewhat, but the coefficients should remain comparable

TABLE 5.2. *Black and white twin correlations and heritabilities.*

				No. of Pairs	
Sample and Test	r_i	r_f	h^2 [a]	I	F
Whites, 8-month Bayley Mental Scale	.83	.53	.64	60	97
Blacks, 8-month Bayley Mental Scale	.83	.51	.68	85	117
Whites, 4-year Stanford-Binet IQ	.62	.51	.23	36	65
Blacks, 4-year Stanford-Binet IQ	.77	.52	.53	60	84

Source: Based on data from the Collaborative Study—Nichols, 1970.
[a] Jensen's formula—see Appendix G. Fraternal pairs are same- and opposite-sex combined.

across racial groups and the larger sample sizes should make them appreciably more stable. Note that the only out-of-line correlation (4-year-old white identicals) is based on the smallest sample (36 pairs) The heritability coefficients are on the low side, and erratic, but neither they nor the identical-twin correlations offer any support for a lower heritability in the black than the white sample.

Nichols presents several additional kinds of evidence suggestive of the effects of environmental variables on intelligence as measured in this study—for instance, on the 4-year Stanford-Binet the second-born of the two siblings tended to score slightly higher than the first-born, and twins averaged about 10 IQ points below singly born siblings. These phenomena were observed in both the black and white samples, although the first was slightly more marked among blacks (average of 3 versus 1 IQ points). Both suggest, at any rate, that the same sorts of mechanisms operate to affect IQ scores in both populations. Nichols also presents data showing similar subtest intercorrelation patterns in both samples. More recently he has reported that IQ correlations between nonadjacent siblings in these data are appreciably lower than between adjacent siblings—strong evidence that there are environmental factors that influence these IQ scores, since the siblings are all measured at the same age (Nichols and Broman, 1973).

The Scarr-Salapatek Study

By far the largest set of data on black and white twins so far reported is that of Scarr-Salapatek (1971a), who obtained scores for 506 pairs of black twins and 282 pairs of white twins from aptitude tests

routinely administered to children from grades 2 to 12 in the Philadelphia public school system. She also obtained achievement-test
scores for a smaller sample of 320 black and 163 white pairs, about
60 percent of these overlapping with the aptitude-test sample. While
each of the tests was given in the same number of grades in 1968
(2, 4, 6, 8, 10, and 12 for the aptitude tests, 3 through 8 for the achievement tests), the aptitude-test sample was larger because (1) some twins
in grade 5, 7, and 9 were used for whom aptitude tests were available
from the preceding year; (2) achievement-test scores were sometimes
not available for twins performing substantially below normal grade
level; and (3) the school district made more effort to retest absentees
in the case of aptitude tests (Scarr-Salapatek, personal communication). It will be noted that the sample for aptitude measures covers a
wider age range than that for achievement measures. Different aptitude tests were used at the different grade levels; Scarr-Salapatek
selected from each a verbal subtest and a nonverbal subtest (usually
numerical), and reports results for these plus a total score based on
all subtests administered. For the achievement tests, four subtest
scores and a total score were obtained.

A subgroup of twins relatively disadvantaged in socioeconomic
status (SES) was identified by selecting twins whose homes were in
low-SES census tracts. These were identified as tracts that in the 1960
census were below-median on both income and education in the set
of census tracts from which the twin sample came. This low-SES
group contained 63 percent of the black pairs and 21 percent of the
white pairs from the total sample.

Data are presented in Table 5.3 for both the low-SES twins and
the entire sample for the selected aptitude subtests and total score,
and the achievement total score. Correlations between twins are presented for black and white same-sex and opposite-sex twins, as well
as a heritability estimate derived from the difference between these
(see Appendix G).

For the aptitude tests, the twin correlations in the white sample
appear to run slightly higher than those in the black sample, and
those for the low-SES group run a bit lower than those for the total
sample (this tendency is less clear within the black sample).

However, the division of twin pairs into same- and opposite-sex
groups could as well have been done by a table of random numbers:
there seems to be no systematic tendency for either to be more similar.
This is an astonishing outcome, since the same-sex group, in addition

TABLE 5.3. *Intraclass correlations and estimated heritabilities for black and white Philadelphia twins.*

Test and Sample	Black			White		
	Same-sex	Opp.-sex	h^2 [b]	Same-sex	Opp.-sex	h^2 [b]
No. pairs in sample						
Low SES	(211)	(107)		(41)	(16)	
Total group	(333)	(169)		(192)	(82)	
Verbal aptitude						
Low SES	.49	.42	.34	.48	.55	—
Total group	.54	.44	.52	.67	.59	.30
Nonverbal aptitude						
Low SES	.51	.52	—	.52	.62	—
Total group	.54	.49	.25	.63	.66	—
Combined aptitude						
Low SES	.53	.60	—	.60	.63	—
Total group	.57	.58	—	.75	.69	.23
No. pairs in sample						
Low SES	(139)	(69)		(27)	(16)	
Total group	(203)	(117)		(116)	(47)	
Achievement[a]						
Low SES	.54	.33	.99	.54	.29	.98
Total group	.60	.47	.59	.68	.49	.74

Source: Based on Scarr-Salapatek, 1971a.

[a] Total score. Data from Scarr, 1971.

[b] Negative values omitted (shown by dashes).

to probably receiving more similar treatment, presumably contains a large proportion of twins who are genetically identical, while the opposite-sex twins are necessarily fraternal.

Given this lack of a systematically greater similarity of same-sex twins, heritability estimates are virtually meaningless—indeed they come out negative in Table 5.3 as often as not. The near-zero heritabilities in the white sample in Scarr-Salapatek's aptitude data are strikingly at variance with the results of previous studies in the United States and abroad summarized in the preceding chapter.

When we come to the achievement data in Table 5.3, we find results somewhat more consistent with previous studies, in that the same-sex twins are now more similar than the opposite-sex twins, and the calculated heritability coefficients are appreciable in magnitude. Indeed, in the low-SES groups the heritabilities are higher than is credible, given the moderate correlation of the same-sex twins. The questionable assumption of equal environmental similarity for the two types of twins is a plausible candidate for the source of the difficulty, although sampling error could well be a factor also, particularly in the low-SES white sample, which contains only 27 and 16 pairs.

The difference in outcome between the aptitude and achievement data is especially puzzling, since many of the same twins are included in both, and the correlation between aptitude and achievement measures is fairly high: the two total scores correlate around .70 in both black and white samples. Scarr-Salapatek also reports rather similar patterns of subtest intercorrelations in both groups, suggesting that the tests are measuring something consistently, and that this is the same thing in both samples.

Scarr-Salapatek's paper has evoked some vigorous criticism on technical grounds (Eaves and Jinks, 1972; Dawes, 1972; Allen and Pettigrew, 1973; Erlenmeyer-Kimling and Stern, 1973) to which she has replied, essentially, that imperfect data are better than none, and that further studies currently in progress should resolve some of the existing discrepancies (Scarr-Salapatek, 1972, 1973). Indeed, a preliminary report from one such study suggests substantial and approximately equal heritabilities for blacks and whites on aptitude tests in another Philadelphia twin sample (Barker, Scarr-Salapatek, and Katz, 1974).

Jensen's Data on Siblings

Correlations for a substantial number of black and white sibling pairs in a California school district were obtained by Jensen in a study in which some 8000 children, virtually all of the pupils in the district, were given a battery of ability and achievement tests (Jensen, 1973a). A number of representative correlations are given in Table 5.4. Aside from some variation among the achievement tests—which were given

TABLE 5.4. *Age-corrected correlations for black and white siblings on various tests.*

	Correlation		No. Families in Sample	
Measure	**White**	**Black**	**White**	**Black**
Ability tests				
Digit memory	.26	.22	429	260
Figure copying	.26	.36	435	277
Verbal IQ	.38	.36	707	346
Nonverbal IQ	.39	.34	709	359
Achievement tests				
Word meaning	.33	.35	206	278
Spelling	.37	.21	84	64
Arithmetic computation	.31	.45	88	76
Physical measures				
Height	.42	.45	744	414
Weight	.38	.37	743	414

Source: Data from Jensen, 1973a, p. 111.

to much smaller samples—it appears that the black and white siblings show rather similar levels of correlation in this population. Thus this study tends to agree with Nichols's finding of similar black-white correlations in siblings at 7 years, rather than his finding of a substantially lower black sibling correlation at 4 years. On the whole, the roughly equal correlations would tend to suggest, though not to prove, equal heritabilities among black and whites, at least at school ages.

An Earlier Study

In addition to the four recent studies described above, we have found one earlier study reporting IQ correlations among relatives in a U.S. black population, a study by Tomlinson (1944) using the Stanford-Binet, which yielded a correlation of .26 in IQ for 75 black sibling pairs aged 4 to 9 years in Austin, Texas. Tomlinson attributes the low correlation to a restriction of range in her sample, rather than to a racial difference—the standard deviation was about 11, compared with the 15 typical for this age range in the white population. We will return to this point.

Discussion

In brief, the studies we have reviewed have reported some evidence suggesting lower heritability of intelligence for blacks than for whites and a rather larger body of evidence suggesting approximately equal heritabilities in the two groups. Let us consider the discrepancies more closely.

If we ignore the one set of highly questionable heritability estimates depending on the Vandenberg-Osborne black fraternal-twin sample, the evidence in favor of lower black heritabilities consists of the following three items: (1) the lower black sibling correlation on the 4-year Stanford-Binet in Nichols's study; (2) the somewhat lower twin correlations for the black groups in Scarr-Salapatek's study; and the low sibling correlation in Tomlinson's study. We have seen that in one case (Tomlinson's) this low correlation was associated with a reduced total variability of IQ in the black sample. What about the other two?

The black variability is lower in both. In Scarr-Salapatek's sample, for the two aptitude subtests and total score, the standard deviations are: blacks, 18.2, 19.1, 18.5; whites, 21.2, 21.8, 20.8. In Nichols's sample, for the 4-year Stanford-Binet the standard deviations are: blacks, 13.6; whites, 15.4.

What about the variability in cases where there were *not* consistent differences in sibling or twin correlations between blacks and whites? These include: equal black and white sibling correlations on the 8-month and 7-year tests in Nichols's study; equal black and white twin correlations on the 8-month and 4-year tests in Nichols's study; equal black and white identical-twin correlations in the Osborne-Vandenberg study; and equal sibling correlations in the Jensen study. In two of these cases—Jensen's sibling sample and Nichols's 4-year-old twins—variabilities are not reported. In the other cases, the standard deviations either do not differ systematically between blacks and whites or are larger for blacks. On six of Nichols's 7-year measures the blacks were slightly more variable, on seven the whites were. In a sample that largely overlapped Nichols's, standard deviations on the 8-month Bayley Mental Scale were higher for black twins, 11.3 against 8.4 for whites, and for black siblings, 6.2 versus 5.2 for whites

(Nichols and Broman, 1974). Finally, in the Osborne-Vandenberg sample, the white identical twins were more variable on five of the eight measures summarized in Table 5.3, the blacks on three—and most of the differences were small.

Thus the evidence for lower heritabilities in the black population is lowered sibling and twin correlations in some samples from this population; furthermore, these lowered correlations tend to be found in samples when the total variance is lower for the blacks than for the whites, and tend not be found when it is not. Lowered correlations in association with reduced variance suggest that in the group in question between-family variance has been reduced, while within-family variance has not.

To summarize the empirical findings, then: (1) Methods of estimating heritability that rely primarily on within-family variation (such as comparison of identical- and fraternal-twin differences) tend not to show consistent differences in the heritability of IQ between U.S. blacks and whites in the populations so far studied. (2) Methods of estimating heritability that rely primarily on between-family variation (such as twin and sibling correlations) sometimes suggest lower IQ heritabilities for blacks, although more often they do not. When they do, it tends to be in conjunction with reduced total variance among blacks.

To what extent do these results shed light on the various mechanisms discussed in Chapter 4 (pp. 88–89)?

First, the data do not provide much evidence for black-white differences in gene-environment correlations that derive from the response of the environment to the individual, since the effects of this should be observable in heritability estimates derived from within-family variation. This offers little support for views that place heavy emphasis on a gene-environment covariance component in IQ variation, although it remains possible that such a component exists but does not differ between the blacks and whites in these studies.

Second, we see little evidence for higher black heritabilities based on a simple reduction of environmental variance in the black population. A decrease in the between-family portion of the environmental variance—for example, via cultural, social, or economic mechanisms that act primarily on the family as a unit—could explain those instances in which lowered black variances and sibling correlations occur together; however, one must be very cautious here, for in at least one set of data (the Nichols study) lower black sibling correlations did and did not occur at different times in the same families.

Third, the data offer no evidence for the existence of different amounts of genetic variability within the populations compared (unless, of course, such differences are being masked by one of the other effects discussed above). This lack of difference cannot be considered a very powerful finding, however, since these studies used samples that are restricted in various ways, relative to the total U.S. black and white populations.

Finally, we may ask how these results bear on the extent to which the average IQ differences between U.S. blacks and whites are genetic or environmental in origin. In the light of our earlier discussion of the theoretical issues involved, clearly the answer is that these within-population heritabilities cannot provide decisive evidence on this question. However, to the extent that the IQ-influencing environmental variables on which the black and white subpopulations in our society differ are also variables on which individuals and families differ within both groups, the within-group heritabilities are relevant. Environmental variables that don't account for much IQ variance within groups are not promising candidates for explaining between-group IQ differences, unless the between-group differences on these variables are very large in proportion to the within-group variation.

To put it in concrete terms, if within-group heritability is high, someone who wants to attribute a between-group difference to environmental factors would do well to focus on something like the direct effects of racial prejudice, which sharply contrasts the groups, rather than something like income or education, which, while showing average differences between the groups, varies tremendously within each group as well.

INTERRACIAL ADOPTION STUDIES

A potentially powerful design for separating genetic and environmental influences on a trait is to compare adopted children with their adoptive and biological parents. Unlike the twin study, this design can be applied directly to assessing between-race differences by examining children of one race adopted at birth by parents of another. Such a design is not altogether free from problems of interpretation, since parents who adopt across racial lines are far from a random sample of the general population, and since possible prenatal influences are not controlled; nevertheless, such data would be of great interest. Unfortunately, while we have been able to locate a few studies of interracial adoptions, their focus has largely been on the adopting parents, and they provide little information concerning the intellectual development of the children—many of whom were still in infancy at the time of the study (e.g., Falk, 1970; Fanshel, 1972; Priddy and Kirgan, 1971; see also Billingsley and Giovannoni, 1969, and Open Door Society, 1970). Fanshel's study of 97 American Indian children adopted into white homes provides a partial exception. He concludes, based on interview data, that "most of the parents appear to have very little question about the intellectual and cognitive competence of the youngsters and are anticipating normal school experience for them" (p. 323). This was when the children were 5 years old. It would, of course, be desirable to have test scores to confirm this impression, as well as IQs for the biological and adoptive parents.

Also, nearly all interracial adoptions in the United States occur in one direction; i.e., white parents adopt children of other races. Even so, follow-up investigations of samples of mixed-race adoptions could contribute materially to answering the questions with which we are concerned.

Another possibility is to look at children in institutions. A recent study from Great Britain reports intelligence-test data on white, black, and mixed-race children who had spent an appreciable part of their early lives in residential nurseries (Tizard, 1974). If anything, average IQ scores tended to favor the nonwhite children, although for the most part the differences were not statistically dependable. The children were tested at ages ranging from 2 to 5 years. While they had spent varying periods in the institutions, the majority had been admitted during the first year of life. A subgroup admitted prior to 4 months of age and tested at $4\frac{1}{2}$ years showed results similar to those for the group as a whole.

These results are of course consistent with the hypothesis that black-white IQ-test differences have their origin in the early childhood environment rather than in genetic or prenatal differences between blacks and whites. Two reservations must be noted, however. First, the black parents were West Indians or Africans, and thus the results cannot be generalized with confidence to U.S. blacks. And second, intelligence-test scores were not available for the parents, leaving open the possibility that the black parents of these children might have been a nonrepresentative group. Indeed there is some evidence to suggest that they were. It is reported of the biological fathers whose occupation was known that "there was no significant difference between the proportions of manual and nonmanual workers in the different racial groups." Given that there is some occupational discrimination along racial lines in Britain, plus the fact that many of the black parents were presumably fairly recent immigrants, such equality suggests the presence of differential selection in the parental groups. Obviously, additional information on the biological parents of these children would be most valuable.

HALF-SIBLINGS

An interesting group for disentangling heredity and environment is half-siblings, that is, persons who share one biological parent but not the other. The special interest of half-siblings chiefly derives from cases in which shared environmental factors are more closely associated with one parent than the other. An obvious instance is prenatal effects of the mother's anatomy and physiology, which half-siblings related through the mother share but half-siblings related though the father do not. Genetically the two kinds of half-siblings are about equally similar: only "about" because of some complexities introduced by genes on the X-chromosome and because of the possibility of differential assortative mating—the possibility, say, that there is a greater tendency among women than among men to select a new marriage partner who is similar to a former partner. But in most cases, if maternally related half-siblings are decidedly more alike on some trait than are paternally related half-siblings, it is presumptive evidence that environmental factors in the form of the mother's influence on the child, before birth or after, are having a substantial effect on the trait.

Another informative comparison uses half- and full-siblings. Genetically, half-siblings should resemble one another about half as much as full siblings (slightly less if genetic dominance is involved, slightly more if persons tend to select two spouses who resemble each other on the trait in question). On the environmental side, things are apt to be somewhat untidy, for there tends to be considerable variation in half-sibling families in the length of time a child lives with his original parent and his step-parent. In addition, on either the genetic or the environmental side, half-sibling and full-sibling families may often differ from each other in significant ways.

TABLE 5.5. *Black and white sibling and half-sibling resemblance.*

	Blacks		Whites	
Measure	**Intraclass Correlation**	**No. of Pairs**	**Intraclass Correlation**	**No. of Pairs**
Bayley Mental (8 mo)				
Full-siblings	.19	1390	.20	1830
Half-siblings	.11	175	.06	43
Stanford-Binet (4 yr)				
Full-siblings	.37	970	.52	1100
Half-siblings	.26	150	.44	50
Height (4 yr)				
Full-siblings	.27	970	.25	1100
Half-siblings	.27	150	.43	50

Source: Data from Nichols, 1970.

So the comparison of half- and full-siblings is likely to provide less clear-cut inferences than the comparison of maternally and paternally related half-siblings. Nevertheless, in particular cases one may often be willing to set limits on the plausible range of genetic hypotheses, and if the obtained results fall outside the predicted extremes this provides evidence of the importance—and direction—of environmental effects.

We are not aware of any studies comparing maternally and paternally related white or black half-siblings on IQ tests. Such data would be of great interest. There is, however, some information on half-siblings in the Collaborative Study data reported by Nichols, described in an earlier section of this chapter. Because these are all maternally related half-siblings, relatively high correlations would tend to suggest the importance of pre- or postnatal maternal environmental influences. The correlations for black and white half-siblings and full-siblings on three measures are shown in Table 5.5. The measures are the Bayley Mental Scale, administered at 8 months of age, the Stanford-Binet, given to each child at age 4 years, and a measure of height, also made at age 4. The correlations for the full-siblings should be fairly dependable, since they are based on large samples;

the correlations for the half-siblings would be more subject to chance sampling functuation, especially for the whites. Approximately three times as many half-sibling pairs were available in the black as in the white sample.

The relationships between half-sibling and sibling correlations for the Bayley measure at 8 months are more-or-less consistent with a genetic hypothesis, but the lowness of all the correlations suggests that environment (or at least gene-environment interaction) must be playing the dominant role here. On the Stanford-Binet at 4 years the half-sibling correlations are rather more than half the full-sibling correlations, suggesting the possible presence of some maternal environmental effects, although given the sample sizes these trends are not dependable statistically. The tendency toward a relatively higher white than black half-sibling correlation, if it were to be confirmed with larger samples, might suggest either stronger maternal environmental effects in whites—which runs counter to some arguments giving great emphasis to black maternal influences—or stronger assortative mating in whites than blacks. We know of no specific data on black assortative mating for IQ, but the degree of assortative mating for education is very similar for the U.S. white and nonwhite populations as a whole (Garrison et al., 1968).

Correlations for height at age 4 years suggest that either these are atypical samples regarding the variables which influence height, or that something is wrong with the data. The correlations of full-siblings, both blacks and whites, are decidedly lower than those usually found, and a half-sibling correlation in excess of a full-sibling correlation is just not plausible for this trait on either a genetic or an environmental hypothesis. Chance error in sampling could be responsible, but the possibility of a more systematic source of bias must decrease our confidence in conclusions drawn from the IQ data, so long as the source of bias remains unknown.

Thus on the whole these half-sibling data must be considered as illustrative, rather than as greatly advancing our substantive knowledge in this area. More data would be most welcome.

INTELLIGENCE AND RACIAL MIXTURE

Scholars concerned with disentangling the relative influence of heredity and environment upon racial differences in intelligence have long recognized that in the absence of controlled experimentation one method of securing relevant information is to compare individuals who vary in the proportions of ancestry deriving from the racial-ethnic groups of interest. Such studies in principle could be done using estimates of racial admixture based on biological or genetic markers, such as the blood antigens. Some limited recent data of this sort will be discussed later in this chapter. However, there have been a few earlier studies of persons of known, or partially known, mixed racial descent and a much larger number of studies relating intelligence to morphological characters, such as skin color, which are very differently distributed in different subpopulations.

Early studies of groups of subjects of mixed racial backgrounds are illustrated by a series of investigations by Garth (1931) of Indian and part-Indian subjects, and an investigation of black subjects in Canada by Tanser (1939, 1941). Garth reports "As to the IQ's of mixed blood Indians, they are found to be higher than those of full bloods, tending to increase with the degree of white blood . . . we . . . found a positive correlation of .42 for degree of white blood and IQ as obtained by the National Intelligence Test with 765 subjects. . . . The IQ of one-quarter bloods was 77, of half bloods 75, and of three-quarter bloods 74" (Garth, 1931, p. 76). Many subsequent critics have pointed out the confounding of racial and cultural factors in studies like Garth's, since the groups of mixed ancestry tend also to be more exposed to Western ways. In the study by Tanser, 162 subjects were classified as Negro or Mixed on the basis of genealogical information collected from teachers and other informants and were compared in their performance on several tests of intelligence. In all comparisons the Mixed group was superior to the Negro but when a more refined breakdown (full, $\frac{3}{4}$, $\frac{1}{2}$, $\frac{1}{4}$) was employed, on two of three tests the group judged to be $\frac{1}{2}$ Negro averaged lower than the $\frac{3}{4}$ Negro group. The Tanser study has attracted a good deal of attention because the investigator reported that in the area where his investigation was conducted (Kent county, Ontario), black and white residents were treated in a completely comparable manner. This assertion has been challenged by Klineberg (1963) and Smart (1963). It seems clear that in these and all studies of this variety the role of genetic variation is very much entangled with different kinds of environmental inputs.

A number of studies relating intelligence-test scores to anthropometric measures in U.S. black populations are summarized by Shuey (1966). They are generally of limited value because of the relatively weak control of genetic variation and, in many cases, the possibility or probability of experimenter bias. In most cases racial similarity has been defined in terms of some one or more physical attributes such as color of skin, width of nostril, or thickness of lips. The majority of the studies with persons of mixed African-European ancestry found that groups of subjects judged to be of more African ancestry were on the average slightly inferior on the tests of intellectual functioning employed. Results from several such studies are briefly summarized in Table 5.6.

Because of the probability of complex and differential environmental response to physical differences and the likelihood of assortative mating complicating the genetic picture, in addition to the questionable reliability of the racial measures themselves, it is easy to decide that these findings lend themselves to no firm conclusions. One might go beyond this generalization and suggest that the observed findings provide little solace for extremes of either environmentalism or genetical determinism. The fact that there are significant associations between physical indices of racial mixture and measured intelligence cannot be particularly encouraging to those who prefer to view the development of intelligence as totally under environmental control. On the other hand, the magnitude of these correlations is so slight and variable as to provide little encouragement for the ardent genetic determinist. In fact, these data are quite consistent with a reasonably sophisticated position, whether emphasizing genetic or environmental variation, since a moderate correlation between physical attributes and intelligence can readily be accommodated within either frame of reference.

Blood Groups and Abilities

As a byproduct of the study of black and white twins reported in an earlier section of this chapter (p. 104), Osborne and Suddick (1971) examined the association between blood groups and mental abilities in their sample. Since blood-type and psychological-test data had been collected for the twin study, they were able to calculate for 42 black and 54 white adolescents correlations between the presence or absence of certain blood-group genes and performance on the ability tests. They report correlations for three ability factors (verbal, perceptual speed, and spatial), as well as a combined score;

TABLE 5.6 *Skin color and intelligence.*

Evidence of Racial Mixture	No. of Subjects	Results[a]		Test	Investigator
		M(IQ)	S		
Strong evidence of white	94	91.9	11.6	Otis	Codwell (1947)[b]
Intermediate	210	90.0	13.7		
Dominantly Negroid	176	87	13.2		
		Mdn(IQ)	M(IQ)		
Light skin	23	76	78	Various	Bruce (1940)
Dark skin	49	73	74		
Correlation of test score with light skin	83	.18		Stanford-Binet	Peterson & Lanier (1929)
	75	.30		Myers Mental Measure	
Correlation of test score with dark skin (with age constant)	139	−.12		Pintner-Patterson	Klineberg (1928)
Correlation of test score with skin-color ratings	115	blackness −.14 whiteness +.17		Thorndike College Entrance	Herskovits (1926)

Source: Adapted from Shuey, 1966.

[a] Abbreviations: M = mean, S = standard deviation, Mdn = median.

[b] Unpublished dissertation.

however, the three ability measures proved to be highly intercorrelated and to show similar relationships with the blood groups, so we will only discuss the combined measure.

The question of primary interest in the present context (although it is not emphasized by the original authors) relates to the black subsample. To what extent, in this racially mixed group, do characteristically European genes go with good intellectual-test performance?

This is a question that Shockley (1972), among others, has raised.

Any answer to this question based on so small a sample would necessarily be highly tentative. Fortunately, comparable data had been gathered by Vandenberg in his parallel study, which included a black sample of similar size. The data from both the Georgia and Kentucky samples were analyzed by Loehlin, Vandenberg, and Osborne (1973), with respect to the present question. These authors obtained, for each of 16 blood-group genes, two items of information. First, the extent to which it was more common in the white than in the black sample, and second, its association with ability in the black sample. It was thus possible to ascertain whether those genes predictive of good intellectual performance among blacks were also those genes relatively more frequent among whites, i.e., these genes most likely to have been derived from European ancestors.

In both samples the result was negative. The rank-order correlations over the set of 16 genes were −.38 in the Georgia data and +.01 in the Kentucky data. Neither of these correlations differs significantly from zero. Thus there was no evidence in these data to suggest that European genes in U.S. blacks are associated with good performance on intellectual tests. Indeed in the Georgia data alone the relationship was in the opposite direction, although not reliably so. In the light of the Kentucky data, this should probably be interpreted merely as a chance fluctuation from zero.

If such results were to be substantiated on larger and more representative samples of the U.S. black population, would this be evidence that there was no difference in the genes relevant to intelligence in the African and European populations from which U.S. blacks are derived? Such an inference would depend on the extent to which the presence in U.S. blacks of blood-group genes derived from European ancestors is predictive of the presence of genes affecting intelligence derived from the same ancestors. Among other things, this relationship should decrease with an increasing number of generations after the original introduction of European genes into the black population. Loehlin and his co-workers offer some empirical evidence that the degree of predictive power may now in fact be extremely slight. They argue that if European intelligence genes are predictable from European blood-group genes in black populations, then European blood-group genes should be predictable from one another in these populations. In their data they were not, as indicated by average correlations of −.04 and −.02 in the two black samples.

In short, while these data on the association of blood-group genes and ability in U.S. blacks fail to support Shockley's hypothesis that European blood-group genes are associated with higher ability in this group, this failure may not be very informative concerning black-white differences in genes affecting intelligence.

U.S. Interracial Matings

Two recent papers by Willerman, Naylor, and Myrianthopoulos (1970, 1974) provide evidence concerning the measured intelligence of children of cross-racial (black-white) matings. These data stem from the Collaborative Study mentioned earlier in this chapter. A total of 129 children were tested at 8 months of age and again at 4 years. When the children were classified according to the race of their mother it was found that at age 4 there was a significant interaction between the race of the mother and the IQ of the child, with the children of white mothers averaging approximately 9 IQ points higher than the children of black mothers. At 8 months the children of black mothers were approximately 2 points superior to the children of white mothers on the Bayley Scale of Mental Development, also a statistically reliable result. Results are reported also concerning differences between children of married and unmarried parents, and male and female children, but it is clearly the finding concerning IQ at 4 years among children of black and white mothers that is most interesting and upon which the authors focus their attention.

The investigators imply strongly that the determinant of this marked difference appears to lie in maternal effects: "it appears that the explanation for the superiority of the interracial children of white mothers most likely rests on postnatal environmental influences. A good place to look for these positive influences might be in the child-rearing practices of the high social classes" (1974, p. 89). One may speculate about the possibility that such nongenetic environmental factors as the uterine environment or nutrition might provide the causative basis for the observed difference, rather than socialization techniques. Moreover, without data on the IQ scores of parents it is impossible to rule out the possible role of various kinds of assortative mating. Indeed, Goldhamer (1971) has suggested on the basis of earlier occupational data (Wirth and Goldhamer, 1944) that on the average the white female and black male mating may be intellectually superior to its converse. Willerman et al. (1971) concede that in the absence of the missing parental IQs it is impossible to rule out this assortative-mating possibility but they suggest it is implausible in view of the large IQ differences between the two mating types that would be required to produce this effect genetically, and the near-equivalence of the two types of cross-racial matings in educational and socioeconomic terms in their own data.

However, in the final sample of these investigators the mixed-race pairs with white mothers averaged almost a year more schooling for both fathers and mothers than the pairs where the mother was black. Since this is in the direction of the observed difference in children's IQs, it seems plausible that there might be some parental IQ difference between the two reciprocal matings in their sample, and that this may have contributed something to their offsprings' IQ differences.

It is clear that comparable sets of data including information on parental IQs would be very desirable.

Offspring of U.S. Black Soldiers in Germany

One consequence of the U.S. occupation of Germany following World War II was the birth of many illegitimate children whose fathers were U.S. servicemen and whose mothers were German women. As many of the fathers were black it becomes possible to compare children of mixed African and European descent with children of predominantly European descent under conditions of considerable, although doubtless not complete, environmental similarity; i.e., born of and reared by German mothers under comparable conditons of social status, illegitimacy, and the like.

Eyferth (1961) and his colleagues gave IQ tests to 264 illegitimate children born in Germany between 1945 and 1953, whose fathers were members of the occupation forces. About two-thirds of these, 181 children, were selected as a representative sample of the approximately 4000 illegitimate children of mixed racial origin born in these years in occupied Germany (Eyferth, 1959; Eyferth, Brandt, and Hawel, 1960). The great majority of the fathers of these children, about 75–80 percent, were U.S. black servicemen. The remainder were mostly from the French North African forces. A comparison group of 83 illegitimate offspring of white occupation troops was also tested, matched to the mixed-race offspring for age and mother's circumstances. In many instances it was possible to select a control child from among the school classmates of a mixed-race child, thus controlling for locality and educational factors as well. About one-third of the children were between 5 and 10 years of age when tested, and about two-thirds between 10 and 13; boys and girls were about equally represented in each group. The children were all tested with a German version of the Wechsler Intelligence Scale for Children.

The results showed no overall difference in average IQ between the children whose fathers were black and children whose fathers were white. However, this simple finding concealed some underlying complexity: for each sex there was a difference between the offspring of black and white fathers, but in opposite directions. For boys, the average IQ was significantly higher for the sons of white fathers (mean IQ 101 versus 97); for girls, the daughters of black fathers had the advantage (mean IQ 96 versus 93). In addition, age made a difference: the differences in IQ between the Caucasian and mixed-race children were greatest among the younger girls and the older boys.

An analysis of the Wechsler subtests revealed sex differences—the Digit Span and Digit Symbol subtests ranked relatively high for girls, and Picture Arrangement for boys—but within the sexes the race of the father seemed to make little difference in the pattern of performance.

The overall finding is perhaps the most interesting for our purposes: in brief, there was no general tendency for the children who had approximately 40 percent of their genes of African origin to score lower (or higher) than children reared under similar conditions whose genes were largely or exclusively European in origin.

Since actual ability scores are not available for the parents, the possibility of selective factors cannot be ruled out, and thus the results cannot be completely conclusive on the question of a genetic black-white difference in the U.S. population, even disregarding the non-U.S. fathers. The two sets of mothers were selected to be reasonably comparable in socioeconomic terms. The U.S. black fathers would have been somewhat positively selected for IQ relative to the total U.S. black population—the rejection rate for blacks on the pre-induction mental tests during World War II was in the neighborhood of 30 percent compared with about 3 percent for whites, but the difference remaining between the average black and white inductee on the Army General Classification Test was at least one standard deviation (Davenport, 1946, Tables I and III). The apparent absence of an average IQ difference among their offspring would seem to imply either a remarkably strong degree of selection on IQ in one or both races in determining which soldiers fathered illegitimate offspring in Germany, or that the average difference in test performance in the populations from which the fathers were drawn was predominantly environmental in origin.

The opposite IQ differences between the male and female offspring of black and white fathers rather complicates the issue, however, especially since a somewhat similar pattern of relationships among race, sex, and ability has often been reported in the United States. Jensen has surveyed a considerable amount of evidence suggesting that "relative to females of the same race, white males do better than black males" (1971, p. 136). This has often been attributed to cultural factors, such as the greater prevalence of matriarchal families in the black community, but the presence of such differences in the present study suggests that a broader range of hypotheses, including genetic ones, may need to be considered. The differences between different age groups could implicate either maturational or sociological factors. Further research with populations like this one, of which several now exist, would seem to be of considerable scientific interest.

Racial Mixture and High IQ

As Francis Galton (1869) and many successors have pointed out, a moderate difference in means between two groups on a more-or-less normally distributed trait can make a striking difference in the relative proportions of persons making scores beyond a point some distance away from the mean.

By way of concrete illustration, let us assume that we have two normally distributed populations with means of 100.0 and 85.4 and standard deviations of 15.55 and 14.02, respectively. These particular numbers are, of course, not chosen at random* but for the moment let us pursue the discussion of purely hypothetical populations with these parameters.

If we arbitrarily select some score, say 90, we can ask what proportions of our two distributions lie above it. Tables of the normal curve inform us that about 74 percent of the members of our first hypothetical population and about 37 percent of our second will receive scores of 90 or better, a ratio of 2 to 1. If we ask, what proportions of our two populations will receive scores of 120 or better, the answers will be about 10 percent and about 0.7 percent, or a ratio of about

*They happen to be unweighted means for these statistics from the U.S. studies of ordinary schoolchildren reviewed by Shuey which: used verbal group intelligence tests, tested both whites and blacks, tested complete school or grade populations or random samples thereof, and reported both IQ means and standards deviations.

14 to 1. If we ask what proportions will receive scores of 140 or better, the answers will be about 0.5 percent and about 0.005 percent, a ratio of 100 to 1.

If we were to take these last figures at face value as applying to U.S. blacks and whites, taking into account that in the U.S. whites outnumber blacks nearly 10 to 1, we would conclude that of each 1000 children in this country at the high level of intellectual talent represented by an IQ of 140 or above, only one would be black. In fact, the disproportion is less. The distribution of IQs is not strictly normal (cf. Burt, 1963), having a greater proportion of scores at the extremes than would be expected in an exactly normal distribution, and the black distribution may be skewed upwards somewhat as well (cf. Kennedy et al., 1963). This leads to less of a discrepancy. In U.S. studies reviewed by Shuey approximately 1 percent of white schoolchildren had IQs of 140 or better, and 0.12 percent of black schoolchildren. This is about twice as many whites as would be predicted from the normal curve, and nearly 25 times as many blacks. Thus the ratio is more like 8 to 1 than 100 to 1. But this translates to a considerable disproportion in the U.S. population—i.e., about 1 black in each 75 children who test at this high IQ level.

All this is descriptive, depending on the actual properties of the IQ distributions, and not on whether these properties are a consequence of genetic or environmental factors.

But a hypothetical genetic model along these lines, applied *within* the U.S. black population, leads to interesting and testable predictions. It is known that there is a considerable proportion of Caucasian ancestry among U.S. blacks—one recent estimate is 22 percent, for a California sample (Reed, 1969). In a study by Herskovits (1930) almost 15 percent of the persons in several U.S. black samples reported genealogies that contained more white than black ancestry. If we assume a reasonably high heritability of IQ, and an average difference between the distribution of IQ-relevant genes in the two ancestral populations in favor of the Caucasians, then we would predict that among children of extremely high IQ in the black population there would be a disproportionately large number from that subgroup that has predominantly Caucasian ancestry. On the other hand, if we were to hypothesize an average genetic difference in favor of the Africans, we would predict that more very-high-IQ black children would come from groups with high proportions of African genes. And if we assume no average genetic difference in the ancestral populations, we would expect to find high-IQ black children showing a distribution of racial mixtures more-or-less similar to that of the total black population.

Table 5.7 reports genealogical information for 28 black children with IQs above 140, uncovered in a systematic search for high-IQ black children in Chicago (Witty and Jenkins, 1936; see also Shuey 1966, pp. 386ff). Clearly, these data fit the predictions of the third hypothesis much better than either of the first two.

Similar data (not shown) were reported by Witty and Jenkins for a more inclusive group having IQs above 125; the proportions of ancestry in this larger group of 63 children were very similar to the Herskovits samples, and to the subsample with IQs above 140.

The figures in both the Jenkins and Herskovits samples in Table 5.7 suggest a somewhat higher proportion of Caucasian ancestry (approximately 30 percent) than one might expect from Reed's data based on blood-group genes (Reed, 1969). But it is quite possible that this discrepancy is due in part to a bias in the method of classification used—for example, a person reporting all four grandparents as "mixed" would be classified as "about equally Negro and white" (Herskovits, 1930, p. 14), even though the odds are that such a person would in fact have more black than white ancestry, since more "mixed" blacks in the current generation were "more Negro than white" than were "more white than Negro." However, there is no obvious reason why such a bias should operate in a grossly discrepant fashion in the two studies. It is also probable that there is some upward socioeconomic bias in both the Jenkins and the Herskovits samples, but again there is no obvious reason why this should prevent the effect of different degrees of racial mixture from appearing.

If IQ is indeed substantially heritable within the U.S. black population, as data reported earlier in this chapter (see pp. 103–114) suggest, these results would seem to lead fairly strongly to the conclusion that the Caucasian and African ancestors of the present U.S. black population were not markedly different in the frequencies of genotypes favoring general intellectual ability. Such moderate correlation as has been found typically between indices of racial admixture and IQ (see pp. 120–122) could be attributed to environmental advantages of light-skinned Negroes. If so, one might predict that skin-color–IQ correlations might soon start reversing in sign, for black males at least, since blackness now appears to be socioeconomically favored (cf. Udry et al., 1971).

TABLE 5.7. *White admixture of black children with IQs above 140, compared to that of the general black population.*

Ancestry	Gifted Children[a]		Black Population[b]
	No.	%	%
All Negro	6	21.4	28.3
More Negro than white	12	42.8	31.7
About equal	6	21.4	25.2
More white than Negro	4	14.3	14.8

Source: Data from Witty and Jenkins, 1936.

[a] Ancestry as reported by parents.

[b] Based on 1551 black adults from Harlem, Howard University, and rural West Virginia studied by Herskovits (1930).

If the African and European ancestors of present-day blacks were indeed similar in average intellectual ability, this can be given either of two interpretations. Either (1) the U.S. slave and white populations did not differ appreciably in their average genetic intellectual potential, or else (2) the populations did differ as a whole, but there was selection of whites who mated with blacks such that the white partners were of about the black population average in genetic intellectual potential. (Note that selection of the black partners, or selection on both sides, will *not* give the same result, since the white genes introduced into the black population would then differ from the general black average.) Existing demographic evidence suggests that selection on both sides has characterized black-white marriages in this century; that is, the white and black partners tend on the average to be below the white and above the black population mean on educational and occupational criteria (cf. Glick, 1970; Henderson, 1971; Wirth and Goldhamer, 1944). Projection of this tendency back to black-white matings in the period of U.S. slavery would probably be unjustified, however.

A third logically possible alternative to the above would be that there is selection in the survival of interracial offspring that acts adversely against IQ. There is some recent evidence of elevated prenatal mortality among the offspring of parents of genetically diverse origins within the white U.S. population (Bresler, 1970); this excess mortality seemed to be independent of socioeconomic status. In the Willerman et al. (1974) study of black-white matings, males were in relatively short supply among the offspring (43 out of 101 for matings in which the mother was white, 11 out of 28 when the mother was black) and the ones that were born were relatively low in IQ (average male disadvantage of about 4 IQ points among white mothers' offspring, 19 IQ points among black mothers' offspring). These sample sizes are small, of course, so these figures can at best be regarded as only suggestive. But a low male sex ratio has historically been characteristic of that part of the U.S. Negro population identified as mulatto. The 1910 census, for example, reported a sex ratio of 97.2 among Negroes younger than 5 years classified as mulatto, compared with a sex ratio of 99.9 among Negroes of these ages classified as black (Wirth and Goldhamer, 1944, p. 313). U.S. census reporting of this period was far from dependable with respect to blacks, but it is not obvious why this should distort the sex ratio of children under age 5. All of this suggests that there *might* be some sort of special reproductive stress on the offspring of racially mixed matings, and (much more tenuously) that this could conceivably affect IQ.

Summary: Racial Mixture

Studies of the correlation of measures of intelligence with variables, such as skin color, which may be presumed to reflect the proportion of European ancestry in U.S. blacks, have generally found higher IQ to be correlated with lighter skin color, etc. These correlations have tended to be quite low, and thus compatible with either genetic or environmental explanations. Recent studies of U.S. interracial matings and ability–blood-group correlations suffer from methodological limitations and small samples, but on the whole fail to offer positive support to hereditarian positions concerning between-group differences.

A study of illegitimate children in Germany fathered by black and white occupation soldiers found no overall difference in IQ in the two groups. This result is clearly concordant with an environmentalist hypothesis concerning U.S. black-white IQ differences, although a lack of information on the fathers precludes a firm interpretation in these terms.

Studies of racial admixture in phenotypically extreme populations offer a potentially powerful tool for testing hypotheses about differences between the ancestral populations. One such study suggests that black children with IQs above 140 show no larger proportion of white ancestry than do U.S. blacks in general. If confirmed, this would strongly suggest that the African and European ancestors of present-day U.S. blacks had, on the average, approximately equivalent genes for IQ. This could be interpreted as meaning that the average genetic intellectual potential of the U.S. slave and white populations did not differ. Alternatively, however, it might conceivably reflect either a special selection of the white partners entering into mixed racial matings, or an adverse effect of interracial matings on the survival of infants of high potential ability.

Genetic Designs: Conclusions

In summary, the studies we have reviewed in this chapter provide no unequivocal answer to the question of whether the differences in ability-test performance among U.S. racial-ethnic subpopulations do or do not have a substantial component reflecting genetic differences among the subpopulations. We have reviewed evidence from studies of twins and siblings that for the most part suggests appreciable and similar heritability of IQ within the U.S. black and white subpopulations, but this speaks only indirectly to the issue of differences between populations. Only very limited data exist from such potentially informative groups as adopted children and half-siblings. A variety of studies of individuals of mixed racial ancestry are available; most are impaired by limited samples, probable biases, incomplete information, or combinations of these factors. On balance, such studies can probably be assessed as offering fewer explanatory difficulties to environmentalists than to hereditarians, although they admit interpretation from a range of viewpoints.

CHAPTER 6

Temporal Changes in IQ

ONE OF THE DIMENSIONS on which genetic and environmental effects are sometimes distinguishable is the dimension of time. In this chapter we will examine several kinds of temporal change that may have implications regarding the effects of the genes and environment on cognitive abilities. First we will consider trends over time in measured IQ within populations, with special attention to the relative status of different racial-ethnic groups. Next we will examine age trends in individuals of different groups in the development of mental abilities. Finally we will give brief consideration to the effects of exceptional environmental treatments intended to produce major changes in intellectual capacity—the controversial topic of "compensatory education."

POPULATION IQ TRENDS

Under ordinary circumstances, the gene pool of a human population may be expected to show only very small changes over the course of a few generations. Rather substantial environmental changes may, however, occur within a few years or decades. Thus if a human population shows substantial change in a particular trait on a time scale of a few decades, it is reasonable to suspect that the trait is responding to environmental changes rather than to genetic ones. Conversely, if a trait is stable in the face of marked environmental changes, one has grounds for supposing that the trait is relatively insensitive to at least the particular aspects of the environment that are changing.

Since our present methods (such as they are) of measuring individual cognitive differences have been with us for less than a century, really long-term temporal comparisons using such techniques are clearly out of the question. Over a longer time span one must fall back on the methods of the historian (e.g., Calhoun, 1973). But in recent decades, the issue of whether the average IQ of a population is rising or declining is one that has interested both educational theorists and eugenicists, and has led to a number of attempts to measure comparable population samples at two separated points in time. Most such studies have been made on Caucasian populations, and thus are only indirectly relevant to racial comparisons, but they have some features of interest for our purposes.

Has IQ changed markedly in the U.S. and other western populations in the period since the beginning of IQ testing? The answer to such a question may have some bearing on our judgments regarding the likelihood of future changes in particular subpopulations. The relevant studies may be sorted into two categories: those that suggest essentially no change over time, and those that suggest an upward shift in measured IQ. We know of no large-scale empirical studies that suggest a downward trend in overall IQ. (Many problems of comparability of samples and comparability of tests are involved in studies of populations over time. For a discussion of some of these, see Appendix J.)

Studies Showing Little IQ Change

Of the studies that obtained either no temporal IQ change or a rise of a point or two, which might easily be attributed to a population increase in test-taking skills or the like, perhaps the most impressive is the Scottish Survey (Scottish Council for Research in Education, 1949). In this study, in 1932 and again in 1947 most of the 11-year-old children in Scotland were tested with a group intelligence test. In addition, a sample of the 11-year-old population was given an individual Stanford-Binet intelligence test in each of the two years. The results suggested that little change had taken place over the 15-year period. There was an increase equivalent to about 2 IQ points on the group test, and essentially no change on the individual test. In another study, 11-year-olds in ten education districts in England were tested in 1947 with group tests that had been used 8–12 years earlier in these same districts. The girls' scores averaged about 1 IQ point higher in 1947 than those from a decade earlier, the boys' about 1 IQ point lower (Emmett, 1950). In a similar study in which 10-year-olds were tested with a group test in the city of Leicester, England, in 1936 and 1949, there was a net average increase of just over 1 IQ point (Cattell, 1950). None of these studies suggests much change in IQ for the populations studied.

A similar inference may be drawn from the data of the 1937 Stanford-Binet restandardization, in the U.S. (Terman and Merrill, 1937). In connection with the restandardization, a subgroup of 178 children from ages 5 to 18 years were tested with both the 1916 and 1937 versions of the test. At most of the ages these children, who were selected to have IQs averaging near 100 based on the 1937 standardization, proved also to have IQs averaging near 100 according to the 1916 norms. There was some disagreement at ages older than 14, but at these ages the 1916 standardization was grossly inadequate. The good agreement at ages 5 through 13 implies that the performance of an average child in this age range in the 1937 testing was approximately the same as that of an average child of the corresponding age in the 1916 testing, suggesting little change over a 20-year interval.

Another comparison, over a more recent 16-year time span from 1947–1948 to 1963–1965, can be made between the standardization sample of the Wechsler Intelligence Scale for Children (Seashore et al., 1950) and a U.S. national sample tested with two WISC subtests, Vocabulary and Block Design as part of a nationwide health survey (Roberts, 1971). At most ages, the 1964 sample averaged slightly lower on Vocabulary and slightly higher on Block Design than the original sample. If we place the individual subtest scores on an IQ scale, the changes would be equivalent to an average drop of about

$1\frac{1}{2}$ IQ points for Vocabulary and an average rise of about 2 IQ points for Block Design, or little net change.

In both the WISC and the Stanford-Binet studies, questions can be raised concerning the adequacy and the comparability of the samples. For instance, the WISC standardization sample was based only on the white population, but included a subsample of institutionalized feebleminded children, while the Health Survey excluded the latter, but included nonwhites. The 1916 Stanford-Binet standardization was based on California children, while the 1937 standardization used a national sample. However, while not conclusive, the two studies appear to be consistent with the British studies, in suggesting little net IQ change in the age groups studied over time spans of a decade or two.

Studies Showing Substantial IQ Changes over Time

In contrast with the preceding studies, several investigators have reported fairly large increases in IQ-test performance over comparable time spans. Wheeler (1942) reported tests of East Tennessee mountain children in 1930 and again in 1940 that suggested an 11-point average increase in IQ during the decade, from a median IQ of 82 to one of 93 on a group IQ test. Stevenson Smith (1942), in a multiracial Hawaiian study that we will discuss in detail later, found an overall improvement of about .85 σ on a nonverbal group test during the 14-year period between 1924 and 1938—in IQ terms, an average rise of about 13 IQ points. A similar but less dramatic change was obtained in a recent study from New Zealand, in which a group IQ test originally standardized on 9- to 14-year-olds in 1936 was restandardized 32 years later in 1968. The results suggested there had been an average upward shift in performance equivalent to about 7 IQ points during this period (Elley, 1969). An appreciable sex difference in favor of the girls had also emerged during this time.

A comparison of test performance of U.S. enlisted men in World War II with that in World War I led Tuddenham (1948) to conclude that there had been a considerable improvement in average performance over the 25-year interval. A comparison of percentile scores on the two distributions suggests an average difference in performance of .8 to .9 σ favoring the World War II sample, or about 12–14 IQ points. A similar comparison between World War II Army General Classification Test norms and the nationwide Project TALENT sample of 1960 suggested that a further rise in performance had taken place since the 1940s (Tupes and Shaycoft, 1964).

Finally, in a recent study Schaie and Strother (1968) drew samples of adults in five-year age intervals from the population of subscribers to a health plan, testing one set of samples in 1956 and another set, matched for age at testing, seven years later in 1963. They found increases, averaging between .1 σ and .2 σ, on four of five Primary Mental Abilities—Verbal Meaning, Space, Reasoning, and Number. The increases were fairly consistent over age groups, holding at 7 of the 10 ages tested for Reasoning and Verbal Meaning, and at 9 of 10 for the other two. In IQ terms, these are average increases on the order of 2 or 3 IQ points; less than those reported in some of the earlier studies, although appreciable, considering the short time interval (7 years). Interestingly, performance on the fifth of the PMA tests, Word Fluency, showed a marked and consistent decline during the same time span—on the average, about .35 σ, equivalent to about 5 IQ points. While this kind of differential change may offer potential clues to understanding the processes taking place, this result does not in itself contradict an overall upward shift in measured IQ, since Word Fluency is not very strongly implicated in usual IQ measures. Preliminary reports from the testing of a third matched sample in 1970 (Schaie, 1971) suggest a continuing trend toward improved performance on most of the PMA measures. The decline on Word Fluency has not continued—indeed the 1970 sample may have performed slightly better than the 1963 sample on this measure, although it remains below the 1956 level.

Thus we seem to have two rather distinct categories of study: one reporting very little change in average IQ over a period of 10–20 years, and the other suggesting rather substantial rises in average IQ over comparable periods.

Can we make any generalizations concerning the conditions under which these different outcomes are obtained? Probably the most obvious is that those investigations finding small or no changes are ones in which the educational system was relatively stable during the period spanned by the measurements (e.g., elementary schools in the United States and Great Britain), whereas those finding larger shifts were studies of populations undergoing major educational changes—either in expansion at the secondary school level, or in the improvement of school conditions in relatively backward communities. (Hawaiian public schools seem to have been somewhat backward in

1924, since Hawaiian whites averaged about .65 σ, or 10 IQ points, lower than a Seattle public school sample on the nonverbal test used in Smith's study.)

Educational changes may not, of course, be the whole story. A great many cultural and other environmental changes have been taking place during this century, so formal education is only one of many logically possible candidates as explanatory variables.

If temporal changes of the sort we have been discussing are indeed due to environmental changes, educational or other, is this inconsistent with the evidence we have reviewed earlier (pp. 82–86) suggesting that abilities measured by IQ-test scores have a fairly high degree of heritability? Logically, not at all. A major environmentally determined temporal trend is theoretically compatible with *complete* genetic determination of individual differences within the population at any given time. All that is required is uniformity of change. In practice, of course, one would be astounded to find a heritability of 1.00 for IQ in a population changing in response to environmental improvement, since it is unlikely in real life that this improvement would reach all members of the population simultaneously and to an equal extent. However a heritability of .75 is consistent with substantial within-population environmental effects, whether in the form of temporal trends characterized by different timing in different subgroups within the population, or random events affecting individuals.

From the point of view of social consequences, the possibility that a general change of level might occur in a population without greatly disturbing the range of individual and subgroup differences within it is important to keep in mind. A shift from nearly everyone in a population being illiterate to nearly everyone being literate may constitute a highly significant social advance, regardless of whether this happens to increase, decrease, or leave unchanged the disparity of intellectual performance levels within the population.

Temporal Changes in Different Racial Groups

The Hawaiian study (Smith, 1942) mentioned earlier is of particular interest because it identified within the racially very diverse population of Honolulu a dozen different ethnic subgroups for which separate trends were reported. These groups included: Chinese, Japanese, Portuguese, Hawaiian, "white," Korean, Puerto Rican, Filipino, and four mixed groups—Chinese-Hawaiian, Portuguese-Hawaiian, White-Hawaiian, and White-Portuguese. Some of the groups were fairly small, having less than 100 children in the 1924 sample (Puerto Rican, Filipino, and White-Portuguese); the largest group was the Japanese, with 2799 children tested in 1924. The subjects were all the children in the Honolulu public schools between the ages of 10 and 15 years (presumably, all those in attendance on the test day), except that in 1938 only a systematic subsample was taken of the two biggest groups (children of Chinese and Japanese origin).

A three-part nonverbal intelligence test was administered, involving tracing mazes, selecting the unlike figure from a set, and copying patterns. In addition, two English vocabulary tests were given, one spoken and one printed. Exactly the same tests and procedures were used in the two years, in part administered by the same tester. We will confine our discussion mostly to the results from the nonverbal test. (The results from the vocabulary tests were similar on the whole, except for an obvious advantage for the native English-speaking groups, and some psychometric problems caused by the fact that the verbal tests proved a bit too easy for the older subjects in the 1938 testing.)

The results were quite striking. Despite the large upward shift in average performance, the relative standing of the 12 ethnic groups in the two testings was virtually identical: the correlation between rankings on the two occasions was .98. The oriental groups (Korean, Japanese, Chinese) and the whites were close together at the top in average performance, and the Filipinos, Hawaiians, Portuguese, and Puerto Ricans followed below in that order. There may have been a tendency for the higher-scoring groups to gain more over the 14-year interval than did the lower-scoring groups. Certainly no decrease of difference was evident. The mixed groups pretty consistently fell about midway between the two groups from which they were derived, except that the mixed Portuguese-Hawaiians did somewhat better than might have been predicted from the two separate groups. Interestingly, the mixed groups were not much more variable than the original groups, suggesting (on either genetic or environmental grounds) that intermarriage was probably occurring assortatively with respect to ability.

On the U.S. mainland, black-white differences in IQ test performance have been under investigation for many years. Therefore gross changes over time should be detectable, even in the absence of single studies making well controlled comparisons over substantial time

TABLE 6.1.   *Average black and white IQs reported in studies before and after 1945.*

Group	Before 1945		1945-1965		Black-White Differences	
	Black	White	Black	White	Pre-1945	1945-1965
Preschool children	96	105	91	107	9	16
School children (individual test)	85	99	82	96	14	14
School children (nonverbal group test)	83	99	88	101	16	13
School children (verbal group test)	85	98	83	99	13	16
Highschool students	86	97	83	102	11	19

Source: Based on Shuey, 1966.

Total numbers of studies: preschool, 17; school children, 43, 41, 103; high school, 55. Not all studies tested whites.

spans. A rough look at the situation is afforded in the studies reviewed by Shuey (1966), as summarized in Table 6.1.

On the whole, the IQs in Table 6.1 fail to suggest much change over time in black-white differences in the groups for which there is the most data—and probably the most representative data—the elementary school children. The other groups, the preschool children and the highschool students, suggest if anything an increase in average black-white differences in recent decades. However, the magnitudes of the IQs suggest that these latter data may not be altogether representative—the group of young children is a rather select one (it consists mostly of nursery school and kindergarten children), and the highschool samples average somewhat on the low side (they happen to be rather heavily weighted with subjects from the South).

By far the largest-scale mental testing of adult blacks and whites in this country has been in connection with military service. Since scores are available as far back as World War I, this provides an opportunity for asking whether the difference in average intellectual-test performance seems to have widened, narrowed, or remained about the same for the adult population over nearly a fifty-year span. Any such interpretation is of course complicated by differences in the size of the military forces and variations in draft policies and procedures during the different wars, but at least rough comparisons are possible. Table 6.2 shows such a comparison.

Essentially, Table 6.2 gives the percentages of black and white military recruits falling in each of several score categories on the general aptitude test used. Since the tests are different, and since the score categories differ in width, comparisons have been made by assuming an approximately normal underlying distribution of ability in each population, and converting the percentiles to standard score equivalents. Differences in standard score units between the two distributions at the four category boundaries are shown in the far right column. Each of these numbers reflects the difference between the distributions; their mean may be taken as an estimate of the difference between blacks and whites in standard score units. IQ equivalents (based on a conventional IQ σ of 15) are also shown for these average values.

The lowest score category for the Vietnam draft represents those men failing to qualify for service by virtue of a low test score. The World War II figures are based on tests taken after induction, but the lowest score category has been expanded to include a proportionate share of those screened out on preinduction tests (for details, see Appendix L). The World War I figures were also derived from men already in service. Since in World War I mental tests were not used in prescreening inductees we have not attempted to adjust these figures. Presumably only the grossly mentally incompetent were screened out of military service in World War I. Their inclusion should not markedly change the overall proportions given in the table.

Loss from the top part of the distribution, through direct enlistment as officers or deferment in essential civilian roles, remains as a possible bias in the figures for World War I and II. If such loss is proportionately greater from the white than from the black distribution, as is probable, the difference between these subpopulations may be underestimated in Table 6.2.

Two points stand out fairly sharply in the table. First, the average black-white differences are relatively large. Second, they appear to have increased since World War I.

TABLE 6.2. *Test scores of U.S. black and white military recruits during three wars; see text and Appendix L for explanation.*

Score Category	%		σ Equiv.		σ Difference
	White	Black	White	Black	
		World War I[a] *(Yerkes, 1921)*			
18+	6.7	0.4	1.50	2.64	1.14
14–17.9	33.8	6.5	0.24	1.48	1.24
10–13.9	48.0	41.5	−1.20	0.04	1.24
6–9.9	10.9	45.8	−2.58	−1.57	1.01
0–5.9	0.5	5.8			mean 1.16 ≈ 17 IQ points
		World War II[b] *(Davenport, 1946)*			
130+	4.3	0.1	1.72	2.98	1.26
110–129	25.5	1.6	0.53	2.11	1.58
90–109	33.1	7.1	−0.33	1.35	1.68
60–89	31.8	43.1	−1.62	−0.05	1.57
0–59	5.3	48.1			mean 1.52 ≈ 23 IQ points
		Vietnam War[c] *(Karpinos, 1966)*			
89–100	6.6	0.1	1.51	3.03	1.52
74–88	29.5	2.3	0.36	1.98	1.62
53–73	34.3	13.2	−0.54	1.01	1.55
25–52	9.0	12.5	−0.82	0.58	1.40
0–24	20.7	71.9			mean 1.52 ≈ 23 IQ points

[a] Black sample selected proportionately to black male population of states. White sample includes groups selected in other ways, but distribution conforms closely to proportionately selected subsample. Scores on combined scale.

[b] Based on inductions between June 1944 and May 1945. Lowest score category adjusted upward to reflect preinduction screening on mental tests (see Appendix L). Scores on AGCT.

[c] Based on preinduction examinations of 1964–1965, excluding cases disqualified on medical or administrative grounds. Scores on AFQT.

Actually, the World War I difference of 17 IQ points is not much out of line with the typical differences between school-age blacks and whites reported in Table 6.1 (p. 141), considering that the latter exclude regional differences that tend to inflate apparent racial differences in a nationally representative sample. A disproportionate share of the black population is Southern and rural, both factors that tend to be associated with lower IQ scores independently of race. However, any such effect should lessen, not increase, by the time of World War II and the Vietnam War, with the increasing migration of blacks to Northern cities.

Because there are a number of ways in which these samples are unrepresentative of the total U.S. male population, we are not willing to draw strongly the conclusion that the black-white gap in average measured ability has actually widened since the time of World War I. Certainly we would not conclude on the basis of these data that blacks were becoming less intelligent—if there has been an overall rise in adult intelligence-test performance in the United States during this period the blacks may simply have lagged behind the whites in the rate of improvement.

It would be theoretically convenient if during this period whites had increased their exposure to education more rapidly than had blacks. But the converse seems to have been the case. In 1910, 45 percent of black children between the ages of 5 and 20 years were in school and 61 percent of white children. The gap between these percentages shrank in every subsequent decade until in 1960 the figures were 79 percent and 82 percent, respectively (Broom and Glenn, 1965, p. 82). If we are to argue that it was the expansion of education that led to an overall improvement in test performance for the U.S. adult population as a whole, we ought to predict on the same grounds that U.S. black-white differences in average test performance should simultaneously have diminished. This does not appear to have occurred.

Equalizing school attendance for blacks and whites does not necessarily equalize the quality or appropriateness of schooling, of course. But so long as education is having a net positive effect on test scores, extending it to more members of a group should tend to improve the group's average performance. Thus unless one wished to argue that the schooling of blacks, relative to contemporary white schooling, was steadily worsening in quality as it improved in quantity during the present century, it is hard to see why one would not predict on educational grounds some diminution of the black-white IQ difference.

One alternative factor worth considering is the possible influence of occupation on IQ-test performance among adults. If intellectual skills become rusty with disuse, adults in lower-status occupations which place less demand on such skills might be expected to suffer in their performance on traditional intelligence tests. Has the black-white "occupational gap" shown the same decrease as the "educational gap" during the present century?

There is some evidence to suggest that it has not, and in fact that up until World War II the gap in average occupational status between U.S. blacks and whites may actually have been widening (Broom and Glenn, 1965, p. 107). Since World War II, and especially in the last decade or so, the relative proportion of U.S. blacks in white collar jobs has been increasing, but the difference in average occupational status between blacks and whites is still large. In short, a widened gap in adult IQ-test performance between World Wars I and II—if real— might primarily have been reflecting occupational rather than educational changes.

Another possible interpretation that deserves consideration is the possibility that in the black population, individuals of low intelligence are having more children than individuals of higher intelligence, to an extent enough greater than in the white population to widen the average difference between the races. This may be hypothesized on genetic grounds (e.g., Shockley, 1972), or through the environmental mechanism of poor learning opportunities provided by low-IQ mothers (e.g., Heber et al., 1972). Of course, both mechanisms might be operating. This process, however, seems somewhat implausible as a primary explanation in the present instance, on quantitative grounds. Even if blacks with IQs below the black mean were producing on the average, say, twice as many children as blacks with above-mean IQs this should only lead to a drop of around 2 or 3 IQ points in a generation (see Appendix K for details). Continued over ten or twenty generations this could have drastic effects, of course, but it would not by itself easily account for a 6-point widening of the IQ gap in the 25 years between the two World Wars.

Thus uncertainties remain. And since in the absence of adequate diagnosis, one cannot be optimistic about prescriptions for cure, this is grounds for some concern.

Summary: Population Trends

Our review of temporal trends in IQ within populations suggests that when education is reasonably stable little change takes place, but that when there is rapid educational improvement or expansion an average rise of as much as 10–15 measured IQ points may occur within a relatively brief span of years—though other environmental factors than education might also be involved. Relative differences in average measured IQ between racial-ethnic groups in the United States have tended to remain fairly constant or to increase somewhat during the period over which such measurements have been made, although differences in the amount of schooling appear to have been decreasing.

What implications does this evidence have for the general question of the relative importance of heredity and environment in accounting for racial-ethnic differences in IQ?

The evidence that suggests there have been substantial changes over time in average IQ-test performance in certain U.S. subpopulations, apparently as a result of educational or other environmental changes, would seem clearly to establish that some subgroup differences in IQ are environmental in origin. However, the stability of racial-ethnic group differences in the face of environmentally induced changes must at least suggest the possibility that racial-ethnic differences are fundamentally different in character. One possibility of course is that the differences are genetic, but other alternatives exist, such as differences in some relatively stable features of the subculture —for instance, characteristic mother-infant interaction patterns, nutritional conditions, attitudes toward achievement, or the like.

AGE AND RACIAL-ETHNIC IQ DIFFERENCES

In discussing the possible genetic and environmental origins of IQ differences between U.S. racial-ethnic subpopulations, one of the kinds of evidence we wish to consider is the course of development of such differences during the life-span of individuals in these populations. An individual's environment undergoes many changes during his lifetime, but his genetic composition is fixed at the moment of his conception and, barring rare biological accidents, remains the same in all the cells of his body until his death. For this reason, it has sometimes been supposed that if a trait is mainly influenced by the

genes it should remain constant during the life of the individual—
and thus, that individual change is synonymous with environmental
influence. Unfortunately for a simple view, this is not the case. The
fact that all the genes are present in a cell does not mean that all the
genes are continuously affecting the phenotype; indeed, the recent evidence from cell biology and biochemical genetics suggests rather that
the activity of genes gets switched on and off in complex regulatory systems in the course of development, and thus that profound changes
during the organism's lifetime may and regularly do take place under
genetic control. Uniformity of change among members of a species has
sometimes been suggested as a criterion for inferring a genetic basis
for a trait. But even this is not entirely satisfactory, because not all
uniformity is genetic—environmental universals do exist, ranging
from gravity to mothering—and because there is much genetic variability within species. Indeed since the effects of genes on the adult
phenotype are mediated by the effects of genes on the course and
timing of developmental processes, one might argue that within-species
genetic variability should be at least as evident in variation in developmental events as in variation in adult phenotype.

Stability or change within an individual's developmental history
are thus not in themselves evidence that influences are genetic or
environmental. Taken in appropriate context, however, such factors
may provide relevant, even decisive, information. If a trait regularly
changes in response to the experimental manipulation of something
that also varies naturally in the organism's environment, one can
ordinarily be confident in attributing part of the natural variation of
the trait to this environmental source.

Thus we wish to examine the evidence concerning racial-ethnic
differences in changes in IQ during life. While developmental change
can be assessed in various ways, most of the studies we will discuss
use measurement of the same persons at two or more times. In particular, we will focus on studies in which persons measured in this
way come from two or more racially or ethnically different groups.

The Emergence of Racial-ethnic IQ Differences

Some evidence on emergence of IQ differences is provided by two
large studies, both of which examined children from different ethnic
groups in the first year or two of life, and then retested them during
their early school years. One of these studies was carried out on 635

TABLE 6.3.   *Average IQs of children from five ethnic groups in Hawaii
at 2 and 10 years.*

Group	Cattell IQ at 20 mo	PMA IQ at 10½ yrs	No. of Children
Anglo-Saxon Caucasian	98	112	18
Japanese	103	108	253
Filipino	95	101	138
Full- and part-Hawaiian	96	99	180
Portuguese	99	96	46

Source: Data from Werner et al., 1968.

children from five Hawaiian ethnic groups. The other investigation
followed 626 black and white children in Portland, Oregon, as part
of the NIH Collaborative Study.

Such studies present a problem in comparability of measurement.
The dimensions of intellectual performance that can be evaluated in
an infant are different in many ways from those emphasized in school-
age IQ tests (cf. discussion in Chapter 3). Nevertheless, it is still
interesting to ask just when differences between racial-ethnic and
socioeconomic groups first emerge in those behaviors that seem best
to reflect intellectual competence at the ages in question.

The Hawaii study (Werner et al., 1968, 1971) began with all pregnancies on the island of Kauai in 1955, and the investigators were
able to follow up some 90 percent of the live births when the children
were 20 months and $10\frac{1}{2}$ years old. They report results separately for
five ethnic groups that constituted some 83 percent of the island's
population. The groups, from largest to smallest, are: Japanese,
part- and full-Hawaiian, Filipino, Portuguese, and Anglo-Saxon
Caucasian (there were only 18 children in the last-named group).
At 20 months the children were tested with the Cattell Infant Intelligence Scale, and at $10\frac{1}{2}$ years with the Primary Mental Abilities tests.
The results are summarized in Table 6.3. There is not much ethnic
differentiation in IQ at age 2, although the relatively strong showing
of the Japanese children is perhaps worth noting, particularly since
they constitute a fairly large sample. At age $10\frac{1}{2}$, however, the Caucasian and Japanese children are obtaining decidedly higher average IQ
scores than the children of Portuguese ancestry, with the Filipino and

TABLE 6.4.   *Average IQs of white and black children from the Oregon sample of the Collaborative Study at 8 months and at 7 years.*

Group	Bayley IQ[a] at 8 mo	WISC IQ at 7 yr	No. of Children
White males	95	98	208
White females	94	98	189
Black males	93	90	116
Black females	95	91	113

Source: Data from Goffeney et al., 1971.

[a] Raw scores from Bayley Mental Scale converted to IQ equivalents using mean of 80.74 and σ of 6.35, from Bayley (1965), Table 4.

Hawaiian groups being intermediate. The rank ordering of the ethnic groups at the later age agrees with that of Smith's earlier Honolulu study (described on p. 139), except that in it the Japanese children ranked slightly ahead of the Caucasians. But much of the Caucasian advantage in the Kauai study stems from the PMA Verbal subtest; with that omitted the two groups are virtually identical. And of course the Caucasian sample is very small; it is also quite select in terms of social status, coming largely from families at professional and managerial levels.

The results from the Oregon study (Goffeney et al., 1971), shown in Table 6.4, are quite similar. At 8 months, children of the two racial-ethnic groups were essentially indistinguishable in terms of their average performance on the "mental" activities (mostly attention and perceptual discrimination) that can be evaluated at this age. At 7 years they show a clear average IQ difference (as usual, there is much overlap among *individuals* in the two groups). Both groups average somewhat below norms at both ages. The sample in this study was drawn from a county hospital serving Portland families of below-average economic and educational status, which could account for low IQ-test performances; however, scores on the Bayley Mental Scale do not differ by socioeconomic status in other samples from the Collaborative Study (Bayley, 1965; Willerman, Broman, and Fiedler, 1970), so low economic status is probably not the whole story.

Both the Hawaii and Oregon studies suggest that average racial-ethnic differences in mental abilities are slight or nonexistent as these abilities are measured in the first year or two of life, but have become substantial when the same children are measured by traditional intelligence tests at elementary-school age. These two studies do not locate very precisely the point at which ethnic differences in mental abilities are first observable. Other studies, which have tested groups of children of various ages, suggest that for U.S. blacks and whites, at least, average differences on measures intended to tap mental abilities are minor or nonexistent during the first year or two of life (e.g., Bayley, 1965), but fairly regularly detectable by around age 3 (e.g., Rhoads et al., 1945; Horton and Crump, 1962).

Now there is considerable evidence to suggest that, in general, infant intelligence tests either do not measure the same intellectual functions as tests for children of school age, or that these functions are quite labile during the first year or so of life. There tends to be low predictability from infant measures of intelligence to intelligence tests taken at later ages (McCall, Hogarty, and Hurlburt, 1972). Nor would we wish to suggest that racial-ethnic behavioral differences are completely absent during infancy—in fact there is some evidence (e.g., Freedman, 1971) that such differences may be detectable in newborns. But it does seem that the ethnic group differences in intelligence-test performance that emerge during the preschool years are not easily explained as a consequence of differential capability in the infant, at least as far as the more obvious precursors of later mental development are concerned.

This fact is in itself neutral as regards a genetic or an environmental interpretation. An environmentalist could attribute a racial-ethnic difference emerging at around three years of age to the increasing impact of relevant cultural factors as the infant's capacity for complex cognitive learning expands rapidly at this period. A hereditarian could attribute it to racial differences in the frequencies of one or more genes affecting this same cognitive capacity. A study of interracial adoptions would probably provide the most straightforward way of discriminating between these two alternative views.

The emergence of differences in mental abilities between social-class groups appears to follow much the same temporal pattern as the emergence of racial differences—and this seems to hold within different U.S. racial groups. In a Boston sample of white children from the Collaborative Study, about 3000 infants, Willerman, Broman, and Fiedler (1970) failed to find significant differences in Bayley Mental

Scale scores between low, middle, and high SES infants at 8 months, but found an average difference of about 10 IQ points between the two extreme groups when the same children were measured at age 4 years on the Stanford-Binet. In two small New York black samples, Golden and co-workers (1971) found 18- and 20-point Stanford-Binet IQ differences at age 3 years between children of middle-class and welfare mothers. One group of children had been measured at 18 months with the Cattell Infant Intelligence Scale, at which time there was no difference in IQ between the middle-class and welfare groups; the other sample had been measured at 2 years on the Cattell test, at which time there was a small average difference between these groups (about 6 IQ points). However, in another larger New York black sample, Palmer (1970) found rather modest differences related to SES on the Stanford-Binet at around 3 years of age, and they were not obviously increasing within the age range tested (2 years 8 months to 3 years 8 months); thus the time of emergence of SES-related IQ differences in black groups remains in some doubt. Finally, in a Honolulu sample, presumably of mixed racial composition, Pearson (1969) found a substantial association between parents' education and child's IQ at ages from 24 to 48 months (r of about .40 between midparent education and Cattell and Stanford-Binet IQs). This might, of course, represent in part an expression of ethnic as well as social class differences, if parents from different racial-ethnic groups in the sample had different levels of education, which seems quite likely.

There would be obvious theoretical economy in postulating that whatever accounts for the emergence of substantial social-class differences in IQ by about age 3 years is also responsible for the emergence of racial-ethnic differences at about the same time, whether this factor is genetic or environmental, biological or social, or simply an artifact of changing measuring instruments. Some caution in this regard may, however, be indicated by studies of ability patterns in different ethnic groups and social classes (Lesser et al., 1965; Stodolsky and Lesser, 1967), to be discussed in the next chapter. In these studies, social-class differences are quite similar for different abilities, while ethnic-group differences are not. This could be evidence that different mechanisms are operating in the two cases.

Racial-ethnic Differences During the School Years

Do the ethnic differences in IQ established in the preschool years change during the years children spend in the U.S. educational system? The answer, subject to a few qualifications, seems to be "not much," provided we speak in terms of relative differences, i.e., that we express differences in terms of units such as standard scores or IQs that are defined relative to the spread of scores in the population at a given age, rather than in units that are independent of such spread, such as mental ages or grade levels (see the discussion of scaling mental measurements in Chapter 3).

We are not aware of studies repeatedly measuring the intelligence of the same children during the school years for U.S. racial groups other than blacks and whites. However, the data of the Coleman Report (Coleman et al., 1966) permit racial-ethnic comparisons at five different school-grade levels, and if we are prepared to assume that general populational trends were negligible at these ages during the period in question, this should provide a fair approximation to what we would expect to find if we repeatedly measured the same children over an equivalent time span.

Figure 6.1 shows results for the nonverbal and verbal ability scales used in that study. The graphs show the average performances in the six racial-ethnic groups at each of the five grade levels tested, expressed as standard scores. For the blacks and whites two contrasting subgroups are shown: the Northeastern metropolitan sample, which tended to score relatively high, and the Southern nonmetropolitan sample, which tended to score relatively low. On both tests, the four other ethnic groups rank fairly consistently in the order Oriental American, American Indian, Mexican American, and Puerto Rican. On the nonverbal test, the white averages overlap with the Oriental average at the top, and the black with the Mexican American and Puerto Rican averages at the bottom. The general standings of the different groups appear to remain fairly stable across the graph, with minor group-to-group variations in ups and downs, some of which may reflect sampling errors, testing artifacts, and the like. Scores on the verbal test are similar, except that the Oriental American and American Indian averages are a little lower relative to the other groups— which might reflect linguistic factors, since the tests were all in English. Again, the trend lines appear to run fairly level across the graph, except for a rather marked downward drift for the rural Southern black group after the third grade.

Thus in standard-score terms, the different racial-ethnic subgroups seem to retain a reasonably stable relative standing through the school years, with the exception of blacks in the rural South. One should,

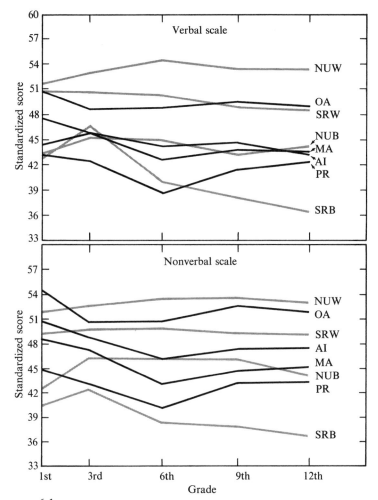

FIGURE 6.1

Average scores of various racial-ethnic groups in the United States at five grade levels on nonverbal and verbal tests. Black lines: Oriental American, American Indian, Mexican American, Puerto Rican. Gray lines: Northeast urban and Southern rural whites and blacks. (Data from graphs of Coleman et al., 1966.)

however, be cautious in making much of the apparent exception, since it is perfectly possible for a trend inferred from comparing different age-groups of children to disappear when a given group of children is followed longitudinally (see Kennedy et al., 1963, and Kennedy, 1969, for a case in point). Actually, an improvement in

Southern rural black education between 1956 and 1965 is a logically possible interpretation of the apparent "decline" on the graph— since successively younger grade groups performed better and better.

There have been a number of studies in which U.S. black children have been given intelligence tests on two or more occasions and compared in performance to white normative groups or to a white sample similarly tested. A classic Philadelphia study (Lee, 1951) traced IQ-test scores through school records for several groups of black children (see Table 6.5). Philadelphia born children showed little change in IQ from the first to the ninth grade. Those who had attended kindergarten averaged 3 or 4 IQ points higher than a group that had not—this is as likely to reflect selection as it is to represent an effect of the kindergarten experience. Finally, black children born in the South and migrating to Philadelphia scored below the Philadelphia-born children upon entering the Philadelphia school system, but tended to improve over time. Only the group that entered the Philadelphia schools in the first grade really fully caught up, however. Pretty clearly, the improvement in the southern-born children is in some way due to their change in environment, since it is directly associated with length of time spent in the North. The average change amounted to 7 IQ points for those entering in the first grade.

Several other studies have retested black children on one or more occasions after an initial testing. Baughman and Dahlstrom (1968) tested a small sample of rural North Carolina black children at ages 6 and 9 years. The girls' scores went up an average of about 1 IQ point, and the boys' went down about 2. Neither change was statistically significant. Kennedy (1969) retested 312 Florida black elementary-school children after 5 years. Their average IQ was 79.2 on the first occasion and 79.4 on the second—obviously no significant change. In connection with a compensatory-education study in Tennessee, Gray and Klaus (1970) tested two small black control samples at ages 3, 6, 7, and 9 years on the Stanford-Binet and the Peabody Picture Vocabulary Test. Both groups showed a marked jump in performance on both tests between ages 6 and 7, apparently associated with their initial school experience in the first grade. The average Stanford-Binet IQs dropped back down again by age 9, while the PPVT IQs remained roughly constant after the jump. Since the latter had started from a lower initial level, this meant that IQs on the two tests wound up fairly close to each other and to the typical average Southern black IQ values of the Kennedy sample. Osborne (1966) also reported data

TABLE 6.5.   *Average IQs of black children tested in the Philadelphia school system.*

| | IQ[a] in Grade | | | | | No. of |
Sample	1A	2B	4B	6B	9A	Children
Philadelphia-born, KG[b]	97	96	97	98	97	212
Philadelphia-born, no KG	92	93	95	94	94	424
Southern-born, entered 1A	86	89	92	93	93	182
Southern-born, entered 1B-2B		87	89	91	90	109
Southern-born, entered 3A-4B			86	87	89	199
Southern-born, entered 5A-6B				88	90	221
Southern-born, entered 7A-9A					87	219

Source: Data from Lee, 1951.

[a] From Philadelphia Tests of Mental and Verbal Ability (norm group—all Philadelphia children).

[b] KG means that the children in the sample attended kindergarten.

suggesting a rise in test performance following school entry: 111 black preschoolers scored an average of 84 IQ on the Wechsler Intelligence Scale for Children; one year later at the end of first grade 103 of them were retested, and obtained an average IQ of 93. It should be noted that sample loss or practice effects could be responsible for some part of the change in this instance.

A couple of studies have followed black and white children through later school years. Osborne (1960) found that a group of 815 white children in a county in the Southeast showed essentially no IQ change in three tests over a four-year time span (average IQs of 101, 101, and 102 in 6th, 8th, and 10th grades). In the same years, a group of 446 black students obtained average IQs of 79, 84, and 79. Thus on the whole, the relative standing of the two groups remained about the same with respect to the test standardization group. (The variability of both groups decreased during the 3 years, which may reflect some feature of the local school system or the sampling procedure. Attrition was reasonably comparable for blacks and whites—49 percent and 44 percent respectively.)

Another study, by Rosenfeld and Hilton (1971), followed a group of 316 black and 501 white students in a midwestern and a western city, testing them in the 5th, 7th, 9th, and 11th grades with the School and College Ability Tests (SCAT). The average performance of blacks and whites tended to diverge on both the SCAT verbal and quantitative scales, in absolute terms. Although the form in which the data are reported makes it somewhat difficult to judge, it appears probable that there was some divergence in relative terms as well over the six-year span of the study.

Finally, a New York City study (Harris and Lovinger, 1967) reported IQs at various grades from 1st to 9th for a group of 80 black students. They found no overall upward or downward trend, although there was some year-to-year fluctuation, probably attributable in part to differences in the norm groups for the various tests used.

Summary and Discussion: Age Changes

In our survey of evidence concerning changes in racial-ethnic IQ differences with age, we found little evidence of differentiation by race or social class in the intellectual functions measurable during the first year or two of life, but emergence of clear average differences between groups by age 3 or 4 years. Average racial-ethnic differences in measured ability tend to remain fairly stable during the school years, although positive change may sometimes occur with a shift from a deprived to a normal school environment.

Concerning adulthood and later life, we have less information. The military data (see pp. 141–144) suggest that average racial-ethnic IQ differences may be greater among adults than among school children. But more adequate sampling will be necessary before strong conclusions to this effect can be drawn.

The lack of differences in the test performance of infants from groups that later show substantially lower average IQs serves to place some restrictions on plausible hypotheses for explaining the latter. Thus it renders less attractive a hypothesis of generalized neural deficit due to (say) prenatal malnutrition or lack of peripheral stimulation in infancy, although subtle hypotheses along these lines are not altogether excluded. Similarly, if there is a genetic factor, it would seem appropriate to look first for a rather specialized one affecting only certain aspects of central nervous system functioning that are implicated in relatively complex intellectual tasks. If the difference is environmental, factors operating during the second and third years of life would seem to demand special scrutiny.

On the whole, the age trend evidence makes it appear that the schools can mostly be exonerated from the charges of creating the black-white difference in average IQ-test performance or of increasing it during the period of school attendance. Whether they should be— or could be—decreasing the difference is another question, best deferred until our more general discussion of social policy.

In summary, then, although studies of IQ changes during the life span do not provide decisive answers to our questions about the relative weight of heredity and environment in accounting for racial-ethnic differences in IQ, they do serve to place some constraints on plausible hypotheses in this domain, and thus should be of value in pointing towards better answers.

COMPENSATORY EDUCATION

From the time that the intelligence test began to be accepted as a relatively stable and significant predictor of important aspects of human performance, investigators have spent a good deal of energy and passion in attempts to demonstrate that marked shifts in intelligence could be produced through environmental manipulations. It was not sufficient that it be shown that the teaching of material closely related to the test content would produce changes in test scores. Rather, it was necessary to show that certain kinds of experience or instruction could produce enduring changes in test performance or other behavior that was not manifestly related to individual test items.

Initially, studies in this area were heavily motivated by theoretical concern over the relative stability of the IQ and its significance for understanding human development and intellectual functioning. More recently the goal of such studies has been quite specifically directed at dealing with the problems posed by groups that have on the average not done well within our school systems and occupational hierarchies. These studies, which have generally been grouped under the broad label of "compensatory education," have occupied a great amount of the time and effort of hundreds of social scientists and educators. The resulting literature is so vast that it is impossible to even begin to summarize it here. There are, however, several relatively recent surveys (e.g., Gottfried, 1973; Hellmuth, 1970; Stanley, 1972) that provide descriptions of many of the major studies that have been done or are currently being done in this area.

Later in this section, some examples of compensatory-education studies will be described. First, however, it should be emphasized that particular successes and failures in compensatory education bear only

tangentially on the central question at issue in this book: the extent
to which existing differences in intelligence-test performance between
U.S. racial-ethnic groups are genetic or environmental in origin.
Such successes and failures may, however, be of great interest in connection with an important subsidiary question, namely, *which* environmental variables should be manipulated to change IQ scores to reduce
between-group differences.

The general theoretical argument is straightforward. So long as
there is an appreciable environmental component in the variation of
IQ among individuals, there must be environmental changes lying
within the range of existing environments that will change IQs. One
still can't say what magnitudes of IQ changes should be expected
from environmental manipulations that are *educational*, as opposed,
for instance, to those that are nutritional or social. But it is also true
that estimates derived from variation within the existing range of
environments may underestimate the effects of novel educational
techniques, or of pushing existing treatments beyond their customary
ranges. In particular, it is often hypothesized that educational intervention at a much earlier age than the customary 5 or 6 years may
prove critical in the success of compensatory-education efforts.

In brief, a failure to find enduring effects on IQ from particular
compensatory-education programs does not mean that no such efforts
can succeed; at most it suggests that the effective environmental
variables are not being manipulated in the experiments in question.
Likewise, spectacular success of a compensatory program does not
mean that the heritability of IQ in the general population is low,
although it may suggest that something is being manipulated in the
experiment that ordinarily doesn't vary much in the natural environment.

This last point may be a nontrivial one, because it is our impression
that many authors of compensatory-education programs *think* they
are manipulating variables that *do* vary widely in the natural environment. Success might conceivably mean that they are mistaken about
what the effective variables in their experiment really are, and that
some unusual condition that they have incidentally introduced is in
fact what is important. This might in turn have some bearing on the
failures of replication that seem unusually prevalent in this area. If
you don't known what is important in your method, the chance of
losing it in a transfer to a new setting is greatly enhanced.

The Endurance of Gains

One of the commonest patterns in compensatory-education studies is the immediate gain that fades away on follow-up. A representative study is the Early Training Project in Tennessee (Klaus and Gray, 1968; Gray and Klaus, 1970). Two groups of black preschoolers who were provided with special enrichment training during two or three summers, plus weekly home visits during the rest of the year, showed modest gains on the Stanford-Binet IQ test. At the start of the experiment the IQs in the two groups averaged 88 and 92. At entry into first grade at the end of the training their IQs averaged 96 and 97, respectively, up 8 and 5 points. At a follow-up testing after third grade, however, the average IQs were 87 and 90, i.e., back at about the level from which they had started. There were two control groups in the study, one local and one in another city, which were given only the tests. They averaged 85 and 87 IQ at the beginning, and 85 and 78 at third grade. Only relative to the second control group could any lasting advantage be claimed for the experimental treatment, and the discrepancy between the two control groups makes the interpretation of this difference problematical to say the least.

Several early compensatory-education projects have reported substantially larger IQ gains than the preceding study. A widely cited example is the project of Heber and his associates in Milwaukee (Heber, Dever, and Conry, 1968; Heber and Garber, 1970; Heber et al., 1972; for a critical view see Page, 1972).

Heber's Study

Heber and his colleagues have worked with the children of black low-IQ mothers from a slum area in Milwaukee marked by high levels of mental retardation. Twenty of these children have been subjected since early infancy to an intensive program of educational intervention; another 20 infants assigned to a control group have been followed for purposes of comparison. Heber has summarized the experimental program as follows (Heber and Garber, 1970):

> At the Infant Education Center, the infants receive a customized, precisely structured program of stimulation. The infants are picked up in their homes early each morning by their infant teachers and are transported to the Center where they remain until late afternoon. Infant stimulation teachers follow an intensive pro-

gram which has been prescribed in detail. Essentially, it includes every aspect of sensory and language stimulation which we believe may have relevance for the development of intellectual abilities. Its major emphases are efforts designed to facilitate achievement motivation, problem-solving skills and language development.

The reported results are dramatic. The control group, given IQ tests at 3–6-month intervals between 2 and $5\frac{1}{2}$ years of age, averaged around 95 in IQ over this period; the experimental group, during the same time, was scoring at an average of about 125, roughly 30 IQ points higher (Heber et al., 1972).

Many qualifications need to be expressed before taking data of this kind at face value, and we can hardly do better than quote the researchers themselves (Heber and Garber, 1970):

> Our awareness of the numerous pitfalls and hazards of infant measurement leads us to extreme caution in interpretation of our present data. Our experimental infants have obviously been trained in skills sampled by the tests and the repeated measurements have made them test-wise. They have been provided with intensive training to which no comparable group of infants has ever been exposed, to the best of our knowlededge. Have we, thereby, simply given them an opportunity to learn and practice certain intellectual skills at an earlier age than is generally true? And if so, will their apparent acceleration in development diminish as they grow older?

Nonetheless, the further results of this study, as well as attempts at its replication, will be awaited with great interest. And if stable and consistent effects of this magnitude are obtainable, perhaps even more interesting will be studies that attempt to pinpoint which of the vast host of environmental variables being manipulated in such massive intervention procedures are indeed the critical ones.

Comparative Studies of Differing Treatments

In a commendable effort to isolate the variables that may contribute to the relative effectiveness or ineffectiveness of particular compensatory-educational techniques, a number of studies have been carried out that compare two or more such programs. To illustrate the problems of interpreting the results of such studies, we will briefly describe three investigations. In an Illinois study (Karnes, Hodgins and Teska, 1968), a highly structured experimental preschool program, which was specifically directed toward the improvement of language development and general cognitive skills, was administered to one group of 27 children, while a traditional nursery-school experience was provided for another group of 28 children. The mean Stanford-Binet IQ measured prior to the educational intervention (at about 4 years of age) was 96.0 for the group that received the experimental program, and 94.5 for the traditional nursery-school group. At the end of the year both groups obtained higher average IQ scores, 110.3 for the experimental group and 102.6 for the nursery-school group; the gain for the experimental group was nearly twice that for the nursery-school group. The authors interpreted the results as supporting their hypothesis concerning the superiority of structured over traditional preschool programs.

A Florida study gave even simpler results (Dwyer, Elligett, and Brost, 1972). One group of 32 5-year-old disadvantaged children attending a conventional Head Start program received $1-1\frac{1}{2}$ hours per day of a special structured treatment designed to improve word and number facility in a game-like context. Another group of 32 children simply received the ongoing Head Start program. Before the experiment, average Stanford-Binet IQs of the two groups were 89.6 and 88.3, respectively. Six months later, at the close of the experiment, the average IQs were 95.8 and 88.7, a statistically significant increase of some 6 points for the experimental group, and essentially no change for the Head Start group receiving a traditional unstructured program.

A third, Michigan study (Weikart, 1972), however, casts the whole matter again in doubt. This study compared three preschool groups. Two received structured programs: one Weikart's own cognitively oriented educational program designed for use with disadvantaged children, and the other the strongly academic language- and number-training curriculum of Bereiter and Engelmann. The third group received a traditional nursery-school program emphasizing social and emotional goals. The results fulfilled the expectations of the researchers for the structured programs: both groups of children showed substantial IQ gains. But quite contrary to the researcher's predictions, the group that received the traditional unstructured nursery-school treatment also showed IQ gains, and they were nearly as large as those of the structured groups. In short, it is not yet at all clear just what it is that makes successful compensatory-education programs go.

It does seem clear that the immediate effects of existing programs tend to diminish with time. Carl Bereiter, a veteran researcher in this field, has recently remarked (1972, p. 12): "However impressive the immediate results of preschool compensatory instruction may be, and however much encouragement may be drawn from followup achievement data, the fact remains that no preschool program shows any promise of making, by itself, any *permanent* difference in the scholastic success of poor children."

Bereiter goes on to argue that a continuation of compensatory effort through the school years may be the answer. This hypothesis has yet to receive an adequate test.

Compensatory Education
and Racial-ethnic Differences

As indicated earlier, the relevance of compensatory education to theoretical questions concerning racial-ethnic differences is somewhat oblique. All the more so, in that a majority of such projects have included only black children, a few others have included only whites, and the very small minority that were genuinely integrated tend not to report results separately by race (Gottfried, 1973). Thus differences in methods between studies tend to be confounded with population differences, both genetic and environmental.

To be sure, if it had turned out that compensatory education was easy—that a year of a Head Start nursery school left black children virtually indistinguishable from whites in their school performance thereafter—the case for an environmental source of the previous between-group difference would have been very strong. However, compensatory education turned out not to be so easy. Which did not prove that the between-group difference was genetic, since many early environmental conditions might be expected to have pervasive and persistent effects, but made it not unreasonable for Jensen (1969) and others to reopen the question of a possible genetic component.

Successful-but-difficult compensatory education has an ambiguous status. A sufficiently massive environmental intervention could well offset a moderate genetic disadvantage, even if the heritability of the trait in the population were quite high. Alternatively, the intervention might be reversing the effects of some earlier environmental condition. The mere fact of its success (or failure) doesn't tell which is happening. Only a direct research attack on the underlying variables can get at that question.

Finally, we should make it clear that we do not wish to prejudge the question of whether or not one *ought* to try to eliminate between-group differences, and if so, who should decide which ones. This raises important value questions that are best deferred to our concluding chapter.

Summary: Temporal Changes in IQ

In this chapter we have considered changes in IQ over time at the level of the population and at the level of the individual. In the former case, we concluded that at least some such IQ changes have occurred in the United States in recent decades, presumably in response to educational or other environmental changes, but that the environmental variables responsible appear to be reasonably independent of the genetic or environmental factors responsible for racial-ethnic group differences.

For individual development over time, we concluded that racial-ethnic differences in mental abilities are not very evident in those intellectual capacities that are presently measurable in the first year or two of life, but are substantial in IQ measurements made at three or four years of age. Racial-ethnic differences appear to remain fairly stable during the course of the school years, but may (possibly) increase somewhat in adulthood. At least for young children, specially designed stimulating environments, such as are provided in some compensatory-education programs, seem able to induce appreciable improvements in tested IQs. Often these improvements appear to be transient, but the data are by no means all in. Also, it is not at all clear what features of such special environments are in fact responsible for such changes as do occur.

On the whole, then, existing studies of temporal change suggest that environmental factors can and do have appreciable impact on measured IQs. However, such studies certainly do not rule out the possibility of a substantial genetic contribution to individual or to group differences in performance on mental tests.

CHAPTER 7

Cross-group Comparisons of Intellectual Abilities

IN THIS CHAPTER WE WILL FOCUS ON studies that compare different U.S. subpopulations on measures of one or more intellectual abilities. Such subpopulations may be presumed to differ environmentally as well as in gene frequencies and hence any observed behavioral differences are potentially ambiguous. Nevertheless, the magnitude and patterning of the ability differences between groups may shed some light on the causal influences that are operating, and the absence of differences, in the face of environmental or genetic variation, can also be instructive.

We will begin the chapter with an examination of racial-ethnic and social-class differences in general intelligence, and then proceed to a discussion of different patterns or profiles of ability in different U.S. groups.

RACE, SOCIAL STATUS, AND
GENERAL INTELLIGENCE

Social-class differences in the United States tend to be associated with average differences in level of performance on intelligence tests. So do racial- or ethnic group differences. Furthermore, ethnic-group membership and social status tend to vary together. Inherent in this pattern of facts is the opportunity for disagreement in interpretation.

Let us illustrate with some data derived from the Coleman Report, as reanalyzed by Mayeske et al. (1972). These authors examine the predictability of a composite achievement variable from several other composite variables scored in such a way as to maximize the prediction of achievement. We will be concerned with two of these composites: Socioeconomic Status (SES) and Racial-Ethnic Differences. The first combines data on father's and mother's education, father's occupational level, number of siblings, reading materials in the home, and appliances in the home, to give a single overall index of SES. The second variable scores ethnic-group membership so as best to predict average achievement: white and Oriental American highest in achievement, Mexican American and American Indian intermediate, black and Puerto Rican lowest. The achievement measure includes verbal and nonverbal ability scores, plus reading and mathematics tests. One would expect it to correlate highly, although not perfectly, with a traditional measure of intelligence. The variables and scoring in the various composites differ slightly from grade to grade; we may take the middle level studied, grade 6, as representative.

In grade 6, SES correlated .50 with achievement, Racial-Ethnic differences correlated .49 with achievement, and SES and Racial-Ethnic differences correlated .37 with each other. Table 7.1 shows what this means in terms of the proportions of the total variance in achievement predictable from these variables. Thus in these data we find roughly 25 percent of the total variance in achievement predictable from SES, and nearly the same amount from racial-ethnic group membership. However, slightly more than half of this in either case is overlapping. The joint racial-SES component is inherently ambiguous. As far as these data go, it is correct to say that 25 percent of the variance in achievement is predictable from SES, with an additional 11 percent predictable from racial-group membership. It is equally correct to say that 24 percent of the variance is predictable from

TABLE 7.1.   *Proportions of the variance in chil-*
dren's intellectual achievement predictable
from racial-ethnic group membership and
their families' socioeconomic status.

Source of Prediction	% of Variance
SES, independent of ethnic group	12
Ethnic group, independent of SES	11
Both SES and ethnic group	13
Total predicted variance	36
Variance within groups	64
Total	100

Source: Based on Mayeske et al., 1972.

racial-group membership, and an additional 12 percent from SES. The neutral way of describing the situation, shown in the table, seems preferable since it begs fewer questions.

This is not a purely academic issue. Writers in this area have often drawn rather strong conclusions based on an a priori allocation of joint variance in one direction or the other. An example is provided by Mayeske et al. (1973, p. 126) in another analysis of the Coleman Report data. They show that most of the variance in student achievement that is predictable from racial-ethnic group membership could be predicted instead by a collection of other variables correlated with ethnic-group membership, including socioeconomic status, family structure, attitudes toward achievement, and the properties of the student body of the school the student attends. This amounts to saying there is a large joint component of variance that is causally ambiguous: the other variables could be predicting achievement because they predict racial-ethnic group membership; racial-ethnic group membership could be predicting achievement because it predicts the other variables; both could be predicting some third variable that in turn predicts achievement; or any combination of these in any degree could be involved. Mayeske and his associates, however, take only one of these possibilities into account in their interpretation and unhesitatingly allocate the joint variation to socioeconomic rather than racial-ethnic factors.

But such questions aside, perhaps the most important fact to be noted in Table 7.1 is that nearly two-thirds of the total variance lies within groups. A small proportion of this represents error of measurement, but most of it means simply that the children within any given social-class and racial-ethnic group differ tremendously in level of academic performance—a fact that is all too easily overlooked when differences between groups are at the center of attention.

The Genes and Social Class

It must be emphasized that the variables of racial-ethnic group membership and of socioeconomic status do *not* coincide with the genes and the environment, respectively. Both variables cut across the heredity-environment distinction. It has for a good while been obvious to social scientists that being born and reared in a particular subculture carries with it many distinctive environmental inputs, as well as a share in a distinctive gene pool. It has not always been so obvious to social scientists that belonging to a particular social status may have genetic as well as environmental implications. However, several recent presentations of this view are available (Burt, 1961; Young and Gibson, 1963; Gottesman, 1963, 1968; Eckland, 1967; Herrnstein, 1971, 1973). Briefly, the argument runs as follows: if status mobility exists within a society and is in part a function of individual differences in ability, and if individual differences in ability are in part genetic, then status differences in that society will tend to be associated, to some degree, with genetic differences. This is not an assertion of hereditary castes, as in an artistocracy—quite the contrary, since social mobility is the key to the genetic sorting-out process in each generation.

Indeed, one direct prediction of such a model concerns social-status *differences* between parent and child: those offspring with an advantageous selection from the family gene pool should tend to rise in social status, and those with an unlucky draw should tend to fall, leaving only the "average" child at the level of his parents when status stabilizes in the next generation. Recent evidence in support of such a model has been reported by Waller (1971). Studied were 131 Minnesota fathers and 170 of their sons, drawn from the extensive data of Reed and Reed (1965). Social status was indexed by questionnaire data on education and occupation, and intelligence by IQ scores from school records, for both generations. Of 27 sons higher by 23 or more IQ points than their fathers, 20 moved up in social status; of 11 sons lower by 23 or more IQ points, 9 moved down.

The same trends were present, although to a less marked degree, for fathers and sons differing by 8 to 22 IQ points. Similar data have also been reported from Great Britain (Young and Gibson, 1963; Gibson, 1970).

According to such a social-mobility model, children from families of different social status should differ less in average IQ than their parents do, although they would still be expected to differ appreciably. Then as the children mature and move to their own statuses through the educational and occupational sorting-out process, they should reestablish the higher IQ-status correlation of the parental generation.

A social-mobility model is not inherently a genetic model; one could presumably make parallel deductions from a model based on differential early experience. However, to the extent that the evidence (which we have reviewed in Chapter 4) for the association of genetic differences and individual ability differences is valid, a social-mobility model tends to predict some degree of association between SES and the genes.

Of course nothing in such a model implies that social status does not also have important *environmental* consequences for the developing child. We have every reason to believe that variables associated with SES have both genetic and environmental implications; indeed, that these are deeply intertwined, in that the genetic consequences are affected to a considerable extent by the environmental mechanism of social mobility, and that the different environmental inputs children of different social classes receive are in part due to genetic differences between their parents.

Do such processes operate to the same extent for minority-group members in our society? A priori, it is difficult to say. On the one hand, limitation of occupational and educational opportunities for members of minority groups might well restrict the operation of social-mobility mechanisms, and thus lower correlations between IQ and status. On the other hand, education might be an even more critical route to social advancement for a minority-group member than for a member of the majority, which could tend to elevate the correlation between status and IQ.

What is the evidence?

IQ and Social Status in Different U.S. Racial-ethnic Groups

Much of the available data on ability and social status in U.S. minority groups is based on children, and as we have noted, the social-mobility model predicts that correlations will be weaker among children than among their parents. We can, however, begin by citing a few correlations for black and white adults.

Duncan (1968) presents correlations between Armed Forces Qualifying Test scores and level of educational attainment for young adult black and white males, based on the extensive Selective Service data tabulated by Karpinos (1966). A correlation of .59 was obtained for whites, and .62 for blacks—very similar correlations between ability and education despite substantial average differences of the two groups on both. Level of educational attainment also shows a similar relation to income in both groups: for black and white males in 1969 the correlations were .42 and .41, respectively (Farley, 1971, Bureau of the Census data), again similar correlations within both groups, despite average between-group differences on both measures. (For women, the education-income correlation was actually somewhat higher for blacks: .50 versus .33). The correlation between education and occupational level, on the other hand, may be somewhat lower for blacks than for whites, at least for males. Duncan, Featherman, and Duncan (1972, Tables A.1 and A.3) report correlations of .41 for blacks and .61 for nonblacks, based on large samples of men 25–64 years old in the U.S. civilian labor force in 1962. Among the fathers of these men the correlations between education and occupational level were lower, but the difference was in the same direction: the correlations were .35 for the blacks and .49 for the nonblacks. The difference in correlations between blacks and whites appears to be mostly attributable to a relative restriction of range in occupational status among the blacks.

Taken together, these data suggest that the relation of mental ability to SES-related variables is similar for U.S. blacks and whites, although the education-occupation relationship may be slightly weaker for blacks.

Let us turn to the somewhat more numerous studies relating children's IQs and SES. Some recent correlations for U.S. black samples are given in Table 7.2. The average correlation between child's IQ and family SES in the table falls in the neighborhood of .30. This is close to the value found in some large-scale recent studies of white populations (Duncan, 1968; Sewell et al., 1970). At best, of course, comparisons such as these are indirect, since many details of sampling and measurement differ across researches. Let us turn to some studies in which direct comparisons between blacks and whites are possible.

TABLE 7.2.   *Some correlations between children's IQ and family socio-economic-status measures in recent U.S. black samples.*

Sample[a] and Test	Correlation	Study
New York City,		
Stanford-Binet & PPVT	.22[b]	Palmer (1970)
5 southeastern states,		
Stanford-Binet	.27	Kennedy et al. (1963)
New York City,		
Lorge-Thorndike	.37	Whiteman & Deutsch (1968)
Riverside, Calif.,		
WISC	.41[c]	Mercer (1971)

[a] First study preschool, others elementary grades.

[b] Mean of 6 correlations for three age groups.

[c] Multiple correlation based on 5 best of 16 SES indicators ($N = 339$). Some shrinkage would therefore be expected on cross-validation.

For example, Nichols's (1970) study of 4-year-old sibling pairs from the Collaborative Study sample yielded a correlation of .24 among blacks between IQ and an SES index. The corresponding correlation for whites in this sample was a bit higher, .33. Nichols also reports correlations for SES with 13 measures obtained at age 7 years from his sample, including 7 WISC subtests and miscellaneous ability and achievement measures. The median correlations of these measures with the SES index were .18 for blacks and .26 for whites; for 12 of the 13 individual measures the correlation was higher in the white sample (Nichols, 1970, Table 21).

A similar direct comparison, in this case among several racial-ethnic groups, can be made from the data of the Coleman Report (Coleman et al., 1966) as shown in Table 7.3. In this instance, the black and white ability-SES correlations are intermediate in size, and roughly comparable. The strongest association between SES indicators and the nonverbal ability measure is found for the Oriental American group, and the weakest for the American Indian group. However, somewhat less confidence can be placed in the correlations for the groups other than blacks and whites, because of smaller and probably less representative samples.

The Mayeske analysis of the Coleman data used a composite of

TABLE 7.3. *Correlation of sixth-grade nonverbal intelligence measure with four SES indicators, for various U.S. racial-ethnic groups.*

Variable	White	Black	Mexican American	Oriental American	American Indian	Puerto Rican
Reading material in home [a]	.21	.25	.24	.45	.16	.23
Items in home[b]	.26	.28	.31	.51	.22	.35
Parents' education	.21	.19	.10	.19	.00	.01
Small no. of siblings	.06	.07	.05	.32	.05	.11

Source: Data from Coleman et al., 1966, Suppl. Appendix.

[a] Dictionary, encyclopedia, daily newspaper.

[b] TV, telephone, record player, refrigerator, automobile, vacuum cleaner.

ability and achievement measures and a more broadly based SES score, and obtained a slightly higher correlation between the two for whites, .46, than for blacks, .39. The correlations in the other minority groups ranged from .30 to .38 (Mayeske et al., 1973, p. 16).

Other studies examining the relation of children's IQ, racial-ethnic group, and SES, present their data in terms of differences in group means, rather than in correlational form. Sometimes the question is asked, are average differences in IQ between racial-ethnic groups the same at different SES levels? Several relevant studies were summarized by Shuey (1966) as indicating a somewhat larger black-white difference for higher than lower SES groups. Her averaged figures are presented in Table 7.4, along with results from a number of more recent studies that offer comparisons on this point. The different studies differ in how the SES groups were defined, but in each instance there was a relatively higher and a relatively lower SES group, defined by the same criteria for blacks and whites, for which an average IQ was available or could be estimated. Use of the same classification criteria does not guarantee exact equality of the groups compared, if individuals are distributed differently within the categories, as is probably true for these data. It should, however, serve to attenuate considerably the SES differences in the racial comparisons. Since the definitions of the SES groups differ from study to study, and since some represent more extreme SES comparisons than others, simple conclusions cannot be drawn concerning the relative size of the ethnic-group and social-class differences. (Though on the whole they seem

TABLE 7.4.   *Comparison of average IQs for a higher and a lower social-class group defined in the same way for black and white samples in various studies.*

Study[a]	Average IQ				W-B IQ Difference, Within Class		H-L IQ Difference, Within Race	
	LB	LW	HB	HW	L	H	B	W
Six earlier studies[b]	82	94	92	112	12	20	10	18
Wilson (1967)	94	101	95	109	7	14	1	8
Tulkin (1968)	91	94	108	113	3	5	17	19
Sitkei & Meyers (1969)	77	93	96	106	16	10	19	13
Nichols (1970)	92	97	102	107	5	5	10	10
Scarr-Salapatek (1971a)[c]	82	88	87	101	6	14	5	13
Nichols & Anderson (1973)	101	102	103	111	1	8	2	9
Nichols & Anderson (1973)	91	94	96	104	3	8	5	10

[a] Tests and samples: (Wilson) Henmon-Nelson, 6th grade, professional and white-collar vs. skilled & unskilled labor; (Tulkin) Lorge-Thorndike, 5th & 6th grade, Hollingshead I & II vs. V; (Sitkei) PPVT, 4-year-old, middle vs. lower class; (Nichols) Stanford-Binet, 4-year-old sib pairs from Collaborative Study, upper-middle vs. lower-middle class hospitals; (Scarr-Salapatek) various aptitude tests, school-age twins, above- vs. below-median census tracts; (Nichols & Anderson) Stanford-Binet, 4-year-old children from Collaborative Study, Boston and Baltimore-Philadelphia samples, SES index above 60 vs. below 40. In some instances, two or more IQs from original sources averaged (unweighted means).

[b] Reported by various authors between 1948 and 1964, averaged by Shuey (1966).

[c] IQ equivalents calculated from standard scores, using IQ $\sigma = 15$.

comparable.) The racial-ethnic differences within social-class groups (5th and 6th columns) appear in general to run somewhat smaller in recent studies than in the earlier ones summarized in the first row.

On the whole the differences between blacks and whites in recent studies tend to confirm the trend observed by Shuey of being larger at higher SES levels. In five of the seven recent samples, there was a difference in that direction, in one there was no difference, and in one (Sitkei and Meyers) there was the opposite outcome, with a larger difference for the lower SES group.

It should also be noted that the basic data of Table 7.4 can be looked at from a different perspective (last two columns), as testing the hypothesis that IQs are more differentiated by social class among white children than among black children. This would be consistent with a social-mobility mechanism that worked more effectively within the white than within the black population (Duncan et al., 1972). Again, the tendency in this direction in the earlier studies receives some, but not uniform, support in the more recent studies.

This is perhaps a good time to reemphasize the point that the overwhelming proportion of total ability differences lies *within*, not between these groups. A child's race or his family's social status is a much poorer predictor of his intellectual competence than an IQ test given to the child himself.

Besides the Coleman Report data mentioned above, some limited information is available concerning the relation of IQ to SES indices in U.S. minority groups other than blacks. Mercer (1971) reports a multiple correlation of WISC IQ with five SES indicators that is about the same for Mexican American children as for black children: .37 versus .41. Christiansen and Livermore (1970) found about the same IQ difference between middle- and lower-class groups for Spanish American as for Anglo American children: 20 versus 17 IQ points, again on the WISC. The study of Lesser, Fifer, and Clark (1965) compared first-grade New York children from four ethnic groups on four ability measures. On the whole, social-class differences occurred consistently across verbal, reasoning, number, and spatial abilities in all of the groups, with middle-class children exceeding lower-class children in average performance; the social-class differences were largest for black children and smallest for Chinese Americans, with Jews and Puerto Ricans intermediate. A replication in Boston of the difference between black and Chinese American children has been reported (Stodolsky and Lesser, 1967), but there were some problems in matching SES groups in this study (Lesser, personal communication). Note that these results are somewhat at odds with the Coleman data, in which Oriental Americans showed a stronger association than blacks between ability and SES measures.

Finally, Backman (1972), studying twelfth-grade students of different ethnic groups in the large Project TALENT sample, found only a very slight tendency for the relation between ability and SES to differ among different ethnic groups. This tendency, although at a conventional level of statistical significance in this large sample, was judged too weak to be of any real practical importance. On the whole, the differences between ethnic groups (Jewish and non-Jewish white, black, and Oriental American) were larger than those between SES groups (upper- and lower-middle class) in Backman's data. Obviously, the SES comparisons were not very extreme.

On the whole, then, we may safely conclude that an association between SES and measured intelligence holds within different minority groups in the U.S. as well as within the white majority; however, the data do not yet permit us to draw strong conclusions about differences, if any, in the relative degree of correlation between ability and SES in different U.S. racial-ethnic groups. Some of the studies we have reviewed suggest a slightly weaker association between SES and intelligence among U.S. blacks than whites, but other studies suggest essentially no difference.

A Note on "Regression"

The social-mobility model predicts that the children of different SES groups will differ less in ability than their parents do. This is an instance of the phenomenon of "regression towards the mean," originally described by Galton in connection with the heights of fathers and sons. In a population whose height distribution is stable over generations, tall fathers will tend to have sons who are on the average shorter than they themselves are, and short fathers will tend to have sons who are on the average taller than they are. As Galton expressed it, the sons tend to "regress" toward the population mean on this trait.

Now regression is basically a statistical phenomenon, not a genetic one, although in this particular instance genetic factors play a central role. The regression results from the fact that a son's height is only imperfectly predictable from his father's height, because while some of the causal factors which lead to a father having the particular height that he has are shared by his son, others are not. The shared factors tend to make sons resemble their fathers. Those causal factors, on the other hand, that affect a son's height but are unrelated to his father's height tend on the average to make sons like the population at large. Both kinds of factors operate; hence the regression. It should be emphasized that these are phenomena of averages, and there is much individual uncertainty in the process, so that some tall fathers in fact may have sons who are taller than they, and some short fathers may have sons even shorter.

Some of the factors that are shared between fathers and sons may be genetic: in this example, the genes affecting height that are transmitted from father to son. Some of the factors *not* shared by father and son are also genetic: the son receives half his genes from his mother. Also, some of the genes transmitted by the father to his son may result in differences, not similarities between them, since the effect of genes often depends on the particular configurations in which they occur, and these can differ between father and son. On the environmental side as well, some height-influencing factors may be shared between father and son (e.g., dietary customs), while others are not (e.g., the uterus in which they develop). The regression depends on the proportion of factors that are shared, that is, on the correlation between father and son, and not on whether the shared factors are genetic or environmental. A father-son correlation of .50 predicts the same regression whether it is derived from shared diet or shared genes. The purely statistical character of the regression phenomenon may be appreciated by noting that it operates just as strongly in predicting the height of fathers from that of their sons as it does in the other direction. If one picks out exceptionally tall sons they will tend to have fathers who are relatively shorter than they—to the same extent and for the same reasons as in the opposite case.

Unfortunately this statistically descriptive use of the term "regression" frequently gets tangled up with an evolutionary sense of the word, as a relapse to an earlier, more primitive state. This confusion is particularly likely in the context of change between generations. Thus when Jensen wrote of high SES black children "regressing to a lower population mean than their white counterparts in SES" (1969, p. 83), it is likely that many of his readers interpreted this in a vaguely evolutionary and generally pejorative sense, as though the black population mean were somehow a malevolent dynamic force, pulling back those hapless children who were threatening to rise above its influence.

In genetic terms, this interpretation is meaningless (though one can imagine environmental mechanisms that might take on something of this character). Black children get their genes from their parents, not from "the population." The relevance of the black and white population means in this case is simply that black parents of a given above-average social status are a more highly selected group than are white parents meeting the same SES criteria; this selection will tend to capitalize on chance parental advantages in genetic configuration and environmental accident that are not transmitted across generations, as well as on genetic and environmental advantages which are; both of these kinds will be more strongly selected for in the black parents. In the offspring generation the first kind of advantage will be lost, although the second will not be. The loss will be quantitatively greater for the black group, since the selection for these advantages was stronger in the first place. (At the same time, however, the black offspring should be further above their population mean than the whites above theirs, because of the second kind of advantage that is not lost.) Quantitative prediction of the amount of regression depends on (1) the variability in both groups, (2) the degree of selection in both groups, and (3) the observed parent-offspring correlation in both groups. It does not depend in any direct way on the relative genetic or environmental determination of the trait. (Some formulas used by geneticists to predict regression do involve heritability coefficients. Such formulas usually *assume* an environmental correlation of zero, in which case the phenotypic correlation is a simple function of the genetic correlation and the heritability.)

Since regression depends on the observed correlation and not on the heritability, one might well ask why Jensen (1969, p. 84) and others (e.g., Scarr-Salapatek, 1971b, p. 1226; Eysenck, 1971, p. 64) express the view that evidences of parent-child IQ regression fit genetic hypotheses better than environmental ones. This would seem largely equivalent to a claim that genetic hypotheses better predict the size of observed parent-child IQ correlations than do environmental hypotheses. Thus if one assumes that a parent can transmit nearly all his environmental advantages to his child, but only about half his genetic advantages, then an observed parent-child correlation near .50 (or the corresponding regression) indeed strongly favors the hypothesis of genetic transmission of the trait. But if one assumes the child's relevant environment also to be only about half under parental influence, the same degree of regression would be entirely inconclusive concerning the genetic or environmental determination of the trait in question.

The evidence provided by parent-child regression is thus similar to (and interlinked with) evidence about variations, correlations, and other statistically deescriptive measures. Genetic theory can often make strong predictions about the relationships among such measures. Where environmental theories make strong (and different) predictions, empirical evidence concerning regressions, variances, and correlations can indeed be conclusive. In special situations (for example, involving adoptions) we may already be in a position to make such discriminations, but so long as environmental theories remain vague and qualitative in character, it would appear that IQ correlations and regressions among ordinary family members will remain equivocal on the heredity-environment issue. This cannot, of course, be counted to the scientific credit of environmental theories.

Summary: Race, Social Class, and IQ

In the preceding sections, we have examined the relation between racial-ethnic identity, social status, and IQ-test performance, as existent in the United States at the present time. We have discussed the problems raised by the fact that racial-ethnic status and socioeconomic status are partially confounded variables in the United States, and have pointed out that both of these also cross-cut the heredity-environment distinction.

We have reviewed the evidence concerning the relation of intelligence-test performance to SES indicators within U.S. racial-ethnic subpopulations, and concluded that while the data do not exclude some quantitative differences, on the whole the SES-IQ relations within U.S. minority groups resemble those in the white majority population.

Finally, we have pursued some of the implications of statistical regression toward the mean, especially for studies in which children are matched according to the SES of their parents, and concluded that such regression does not in itself offer decisive evidence of the influence of genetic or environmental factors, although it needs to be taken seriously in the interpretation of any study of this type.

ETHNIC DIFFERENCES
IN PROFILE OF ABILITIES

In light of the fact that different racial-ethnic subpopulations represent somewhat different gene pools that have evolved under somewhat different environmental circumstances, it has frequently been suggested that such groups should display differences from one another primarily in the *pattern* of abilities they display rather than in any generalized level of ability. Such a hypothesis has a measure of biological plausibility, and it also has the comforting feature of avoiding some of the more socially unacceptable aspects of hypotheses that imply a generalized intellectual inferiority or superiority of different groups. The argument proceeds essentially as follows: if there are genetically determined differences between groups that have been in relative breeding isolation, one would expect these variations to be influenced by differences in selection pressure determined by different environments. Thus, each group should be somewhat better adapted to the unique demands of its own average environment. The natural result of this would be that each group should display distinctive superiorities over other groups in certain settings but no group should display a generalized superiority in all settings. Such an argument does not avoid all hazards—for example, a thoroughgoing racist might happily concede that the talents of blacks are better suited to the African jungle than to Western society—but it has undoubtedly been a factor in focusing interest on the possibility of distinctive patterns or profiles of abilities in different racial-ethnic groups. In this light, it is understandable that several observers (e.g., Dreger and Miller, 1960, 1968) have called for more studies of specific components of mental ability, and that a number of studies have been carried out that attempt to identify such differences in intellectual performance.

Studies Comparing Several Racial-ethnic Groups

Two main questions can be asked of data from a battery of ability tests given to a number of ethnic groups. First, are the relationships among these measures similar in the different ethnic groups; that is, is it meaningful to speak of the same underlying dimensions of ability in each case? And second, if so, how do the groups compare along these dimensions, in the average performance of individuals, the range of variation, or the like?

A number of studies have examined the first of these two questions, and have found the interrelationships of different ability measures to be similar across ethnic groups. An early study by Michael (1949) found a generally similar factor structure among ability measures on black and white Air Force cadets. A study of 5–9-year-old children by Semler and Iscoe (1966) also obtained similar though not identical ability factor structures among blacks and whites. A recent study by Flaugher and Rock (1972) found similar factor structures in a battery of 9 ability measures administered to black, white, Mexican American, and Oriental American highschool males from low-income groups in Los Angeles. In a Hawaiian study, DeFries and others (1974) administered a battery of 15 cognitive tests to samples of persons of European and of Japanese ancestry. They obtained almost identical factor structures in the two samples. In each, four factors were identified: spatial visualization, verbal ability, perceptual speed and accuracy, and visual memory. A study by Humphreys and Taber (1973) investigated the factor structure of 21 ability measures from the Project TALENT test battery for large samples of ninth-grade boys in the top and bottom fourths on SES, and found the same six factors in each group. The relation of tests to factors showed virtually no differences by SES. (The boys in the study were not separately identified by race, but in this population the high and low SES groups would be expected to differ in ethnic composition as well.) Finally, as noted in an earlier chapter (pp. 109, 112) very similar subtest intercorrelation patterns were found by Scarr-Salapatek (1971a) and Nichols (1970) in U.S. black and white samples. Thus all these studies agree in suggesting that the underlying dimensions of ability vary little if at all across U.S. racial-ethnic groups.

The standings of different groups on these dimensions may differ, however. A number of studies have compared the average performance of members of different U.S. racial-ethnic groups on measures of cognitive abilities.

An ambitious and influential study by Lesser, Fifer, and Clark (1965) investigated the level and pattern of mental abilities in Chinese American, Jewish, black, and Puerto Rican children of middle- and lower-class background in New York City. A total of 320 first-grade children were studied, with an equal number (20) of subjects in each sex, class, and ethnic group. Mental abilities were assessed by means of a modified version of the Hunter College Aptitude Scales for Gifted Children, which included four scales, each intended to measure a different dimension or component of mental ability. The tests were revised to make them more fair to the past experience of all subjects, and tests were administered under conditions intended to minimize group difference in test-taking experience, rapport, and such. Testers were of ethnic groups corresponding to the children tested, and testing was done either in English or the native language, as appropriate to the individual child.

The major results of the study are summarized in Figure 7.1, which presents the average performance for each of the ethnic groups in each social class on the four subtests. It is clear that there are marked ethnic differences in overall level of ability, and there are also differences in the pattern of performance on the various tests among these groups. Social class had marked effects on the level of performance but did not appear to influence the pattern of abilities. Differences in

| | Verbal | | | Puerto | |
	Chinese	Jewish	Negro	Rican	
Middle	76.8	96.7	85.7	69.6	82.2
Lower	65.3	84.0	62.9	54.3	66.6
	71.1	90.4	74.3	61.9	74.4

| | Reasoning | | | Puerto | |
	Chinese	Jewish	Negro	Rican	
Middle	27.7	28.8	26.0	21.8	26.1
Lower	24.2	21.6	14.8	16.0	19.1
	25.9	25.2	20.4	18.9	22.6

| | Number | | | Puerto | |
	Chinese	Jewish	Negro	Rican	
Middle	30.0	33.4	24.7	22.6	27.7
Lower	26.2	23.5	12.1	15.7	19.4
	28.1	28.5	18.4	19.1	23.5

| | Space | | | Puerto | |
	Chinese	Jewish	Negro	Rican	
Middle	44.9	44.6	41.8	37.4	42.2
Lower	40.4	35.1	27.1	32.8	33.8
	42.7	39.8	34.4	35.1	38.0

FIGURE 7.1
Scores on ability scale. Mean scores are listed in the bottom rows and righthand columns. (From Lesser, Fifer, and Clark, 1965.)

the pattern of ability between ethnic groups are more easily visible in Figure 7.2 where the four tests are averaged across social classes and placed on a comparable scale.

A partial replication of the Lesser, Fifer, and Clark study was conducted by Stodolsky and Lesser (1967) in Boston. This study used

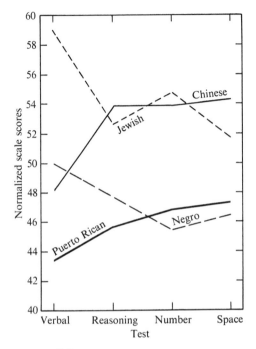

FIGURE 7.2

Patterns of Normalized Ability Scores for four ethnic groups. (From Lesser, Fifer, and Clark, 1965.)

the same tests but smaller groups of black and Chinese American children of middle-class and lower-class background. The main findings were quite similar to those obtained in New York. An additional group of Irish-Catholic children was included in this study but the results here failed to show either a distinctive ethnic-group pattern of abilities or distinctive social-class differences within this group.

In general the findings of the New York and Boston studies provide evidence suggesting that Chinese American subjects did least well in verbal tests and best on numerical, spatial, and reasoning tests. Black subjects performed best on verbal tasks and were poorest in numerical performance. Jewish subjects were best in verbal tasks and poorest in spatial tasks, and their performance in the numerical area was next to highest. The Puerto Rican children showed less variability between abilties than the other groups but their best ability was spatial and their poorest was verbal.

The Lesser study has been criticized by Feldman (1973) on the grounds that the shape of the ability profiles is dependent on the manner in which the tests are scaled. In a reply, Lesser (1973) agreed, but noted that the conclusions of the study do not depend in any critical way on the exact shape of the profiles. In any case, Lesser's scaling procedure—standard scores based on his total sample— would seem a reasonable one.

A study by Leifer (1972) compared 4-year-old disdavantaged New York children from Chinese, Italian, black, and Puerto Rican back-grounds on four tests requiring construction of mosaics, understand-ing of body parts, copying of geometric figures, and verbal ideational fluency. Relative to the other three groups, the Chinese American children were high on the first two tests and low on the verbal-fluency measure. There were no significant group differences on the figure-copying task.

The results for the Chinese Americans seem generally consistent with Lesser's findings, although one might have also predicted this group to perform well on figure copying. The relatively good verbal performance of the Puerto Rican children is somewhat at odds with Lesser's study; the fact that the verbal measure was one that em-phasized fluent verbal production may be relevant here.

A study by Backman (1971, 1972), utilizing data from Project TALENT, compared Jewish whites (1236), non-Jewish whites (1051), blacks (488) and Oriental Americans (150) in performance on six mental-ability factors. The factors studied were: verbal knowledge, English language, mathematics, visual (spatial) reasoning, perceptual speed and accuracy, and memory. The subjects were all in the 12th grade and they were classified as upper-middle class or lower-middle class, and included males and females.

The most marked differences in the profile of scores were attrib-utable to the sex of the subjects, with ethnicity and social class appear-ing to have much less influence upon the ability profile. "Considering differences in shape alone, sex accounted for 69 percent of the total variance, ethnicity 9 percent and SES 1 percent" (1971, p. 511). The average performance of each of the groups on the six factors is sum-marized in Table 7.5. Descriptively it appears that the Jewish sample was relatively superior in verbal knowledge and mathematics, the non-Jewish white subjects displayed on the average a relatively flat profile, the black subjects showed least disadvantage on perceptual speed and accuracy and memory, and the Oriental American subjects were distinctively high in mathematics.

TABLE 7.5. *Patterns of abilities for ethnic, SES, and sex groups.*

Group	Mean Standardized Score[a]					
	Verbal	**English**	**Math**	**Spatial**	**Perceptual**	**Memory**
Ethnic group						
Jewish white	57.1	50.8	58.6	46.0	51.0	47.8
Non-Jewish white	51.9	51.1	52.1	51.8	49.5	50.9
Black	46.0	47.5	47.3	45.1	50.9	50.4
Oriental American	49.0	52.5	59.1	49.4	50.3	51.6
SES						
Upper middle	53.0	50.6	56.2	48.9	50.5	50.0
Lower middle	49.0	50.3	52.4	47.2	50.3	50.3
Sex						
Male	53.7	40.9	63.9	54.5	49.1	44.3
Female	48.3	60.0	44.6	41.7	51.7	56.0

Source: Data from Backman, 1972.

[a] Standard errors of these means are between 0.3 and 0.6 for SES and sex, between 0.2 and 0.7 for the two white groups, between 0.4 and 0.8 for blacks, and between 0.6 and 1.2 for Oriental Americans.

It is clear that ethnic differences in profile are less dramatic than in the Lesser studies and it is also clear that direct comparisons between the studies are difficult both because of the different ability measures employed and because of considerable differences between the samples in age, ethnic background, and socioeconomic status. Nonetheless, several of the differences observed appear to be congruent with the findings reported by Lesser and his colleagues.

Another study involving several racial-ethnic groups used the Primary Mental Abilities Test, which measures verbal, reasoning, spatial, perceptual, and numerical factors. The study was conducted by Werner and her associates (1968, 1971), on a large sample ($N = 635$) of 10-year-old Hawaiian children classified according to ancestry as Japanese, part- and full-Hawaiian, Filipino, Portuguese, and Anglo-Saxon Caucasian. The general results are summarized in Figure 7.3, and indicate marked ethnic differences on the individual scales, except for scale P (Perceptual Acuity and Speed). The profile or pattern differences are less striking but generally consistent with the results reported by Lesser and co-workers where comparisons

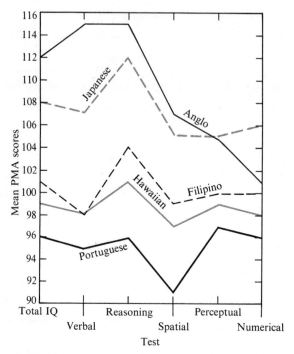

FIGURE 7.3

Patterns of Primary Mental Abilities for five ethnic groups. (From Werner et al., 1968.)

appear possible, e.g., Caucasian subjects performed best on verbal comprehension, and Oriental American subjects in both studies were relatively high-scoring on spatial, numerical, and reasoning factors.

While our chief interest is in U.S. racial-ethnic comparisons, we may note in passing a Canadian study by Marjoribanks (1972), which tested 11-year-old boys from five ethnic groups, and found differences both in level and pattern of abilities. In general, the Jewish group averaged highest on the tests, and the French Canadians and the Canadian Indians lowest. The profile for the Jewish group, with Verbal and Numerical abilities exceeding Reasoning and Spatial abilities, was similar to that found in Lesser's and Backman's U.S. studies. Marjoribanks also assessed cultural and family environmental factors in these groups, and found more cultural emphasis on intellectual achievement in the higher-performing groups. As is usually the case in studies of intact groups in natural settings, there is inherent ambiguity between cultural and genetic factors here: the

TABLE 7.6. *Wechsler verbal and performance IQs in U.S. black samples*[a].

Study	Ages	Number	Verbal IQ	Performance IQ
Osborne (1965)[b]	5–6	50	90	85
Semler & Iscoe (1963)	5–9	60	95	92
Nichols & Anderson (1973)	7	490	99	101
Nichols & Anderson (1973)	7	4091	91	93
Sartin (1950)[b]	8–9	45	86	97
Caldwell & Smith (1968)	6–12	420	91	83
Young & Pitts (1951)	6–16	40	79	67
Tuttle (1964)[b]	9–11	25	89	87
Young & Bright (1954)	10–13	81	74	67
Grandison (1951)[b]	11–12	21	109	95
Bonner & Belden (1970)	16–17	31	101	95
Wysocki & Wysocki (1969)	21–26	110	94	91
Fortson (1956)[b]	Grads.	50	106	101
Young & Collins (1954)	av. 26	52	82	83
Scarborough (1956)	av. 29	59	80	80

[a] Samples of neurotics, delinquents, venereal disease patients, retarded, etc., are excluded, although some normal control groups matched to such subjects are included.
[b] Unpublished, cited in Shuey (1966).

development of different traditions could in part be a function of differences in gene frequencies in the groups—which could in turn have been influenced by earlier cultural conditions.

Studies Comparing Ability Profiles in U.S. Blacks and Whites

As usual, the majority of U.S. studies involving racial-ethnic groups have confined their comparisons to blacks and whites. Easily the largest number of studies conducted with a single instrument are those employing various forms of the Wechsler tests of intelligence. Most of these studies have focused upon comparisons of blacks and whites, or else have compared the verbal and nonverbal performance of black subjects. The findings from a number of studies of the latter variety are summarized in Table 7.6. Although the results are by no means invariant, in about two-thirds of the samples black subjects have relatively higher scores on the verbal scale than on the performance scale, which is consistent with Lesser's results.

Data for black subjects on various subtests of the Weschler children's and adult scales are summarized in Table 7.7. Again it appears that black subjects perform relatively better on the first five subtests (Verbal) than on the remaining four (Performance). Also worthy of note is the inconsistency of the results for the Digit Span subtest, which in different studies ranks at the top and the bottom of black subjects' performance. This subtest is some special interest because Jensen (1972b) has identified it as a measure of Level I ability (which we discuss in the next section).

An extensive study of black and white children in the rural south by Baughman and Dahlstrom (1968), employing Thurstone's Primary Mental Abilities Test, produced findings that diverge from the Wechsler studies. Black subjects appeared to perform more poorly on a verbal scale (Verbal Meaning) than on two nonverbal scales (Perceptual Speed, Number Facility).

In an analysis of Stanford-Binet items, Nichols (1970) found blacks to score relatively higher on items requiring concentration and memory, and whites relatively higher on items requiring judgment and reasoning at age 4 years.

Still another measure, the Lorge-Thorndike Intelligence Test, was employed by Tulkin (1968) in a study of 389 fifth- and sixth-grade black and white subjects. In both upper- and lower-socioeconomic-status group black subjects had very similar verbal and nonverbal IQs. White subjects were significantly higher than black subjects in nonverbal IQ for both social classes and for verbal IQ in the upper social class.

A somewhat different approach to the study of differences in the patterning or structure of intelligence in ethnic groups was made by Sitkei and Meyers (1969). They studied 100 black and white subjects of middle- and lower-class backgrounds, each of whom was within 6 months of his or her fourth birthday. The study employed 22 specific tests that for the most part were intended to assess six general factors: verbal comprehension, ideational fluency, perceptual speed, figural reasoning, memory span, and picture memory.

The results indicated significant ethnic and social-class differences on verbal comprehension and a general lack of such differences on other factors when measured independently of verbal comprehen-

TABLE 7.7. *Wechsler subtest scores and ranks in U.S. black samples.*

Subtest	Scores					Ranks[b]					Combined Rank
	Osb[a]	C&S	Y&P	W&W	For	Osb	C&S	Y&P	W&W	For	
Information	7.4	8.4	7.0	7.0	11.0	5½	5	2	9	3	5
Comprehension	10.2	8.9	5.9	8.8	12.8	1	3	6½	3½	1	2
Digit Span	6.9	9.0	7.3	10.5	5.1	7	2	1	1	9	3
Arithmetic	7.7	9.3	6.0	7.4	9.4	3	1	4½	8	4	4
Similarities	9.7	8.8	6.5	8.8	11.8	2	4	3	3½	2	1
Picture Arrang.	6.8	7.6	5.1	8.6	9.2	8	6	8½	5½	6	8
Picture Compl.	7.5	6.9	5.9	8.2	9.2	4	9	6½	7	6	7
Block Design	6.6	7.3	5.1	8.6	8.2	9	8	8½	5½	8	9
Object Assembly	7.4	7.5	6.0	9.6	9.2	5½	7	4½	2	6	6

[a] Studies more fully identified in Table 7.6. "Osb" = Osborne, "C&S" = Caldwell & Smith, etc.
[b] Kendall's W over all ranks = 0.393, $p < 0.05$.

sion. While these results appear somewhat discrepant from others that have been cited, it is not clear whether it is the difference in age level of the subjects, the test battery, the method of analysis, or some other variable that is responsible.

Jensen's Theory of SES and
Level I and II Abilities

Although most of the studies reviewed in the preceding sections have been primarily descriptive in character, note should be taken of an explicit theory of the nature of the ability differences between different U.S. groups, namely Jensen's (1969, 1970a, 1972b, 1973c, 1974b) theory of Level I and Level II abilities. Jensen has proposed that relationships with socioeconomic variables that hold for IQ (which he classifies as a "Level II" ability) may not hold for other, simpler learning abilities ("Level I" abilities).

According to Jensen's theory of human abilities, there are two general categories of human ability: Level I—associative learning ability, the capacity to register and store incoming information (typical test—memory for digits); and Level II—conceptual learning and problem-solving ability, the capacity to transform and manipulate input (typical test—IQ test). The two kinds of abilities have largely independent genetic bases, although a moderate correlation has arisen between them. In part, this may be due to assortative mating— able people tending to marry able people, regardless of the particular mix of abilities involved—and in part to a slight functional dependence of Level II on Level I—some basic learning ability is necessary in order for higher intellectual abilities to develop and to be expressed, but above this minimal level the two may be fairly independent. In earlier writings (e.g., 1969) Jensen placed much more stress on the functional relationship between Level I and Level II, but he has since relaxed this position in the light of data from his own and others' studies.

The empirical relationships of Level I and Level II abilities that have, in Jensen's view, been best substantiated are: (1) Level II ability tends to differ more by social class and race than does Level I ability. (2) Level I and Level II abilities are more closely related in middle-class than in lower-class populations.

The connection between the empirical propositions and the rest of the theory is not always entirely clear. Thus the greater differentiation of Level II than Level I abilities reflects the fact that social stratification is more highly dependent on Level II than on Level I abilities (Jensen, 1972b, p. 269f). But insofar as this occurs by virtue of social-mobility mechanisms of the type discussed earlier in the present chapter, one would expect to find such differences occurring much more strongly across social-class lines, where there is much mobility, than across racial lines, where there is little or none. Yet, if anything, the opposite is the case (Jensen, 1973c).

One implication of the theory may clarify some puzzling results with the Wechsler Digit Span subtest noted earlier. It will be recalled that Digit Span (a Level I measure) gave quite inconsistent results in different black samples. It follows, however, from Jensen's model that at lower levels of IQ blacks should do better than whites of comparable IQ on Level I tests, but at higher levels of IQ they should do worse (Jensen, 1974b). And in fact, the study cited in Table 7.7 (p. 187) in which blacks performed worse on Digit Span than on all the other subtests used a sample of black graduate students. (However, the model does not predict that they should have done as poorly as they did in absolute terms.)

Much of Jensen's research on Level I and Level II abilities has relied on comparisons between rote memory for digits and IQ tests, which are measures that obviously differ in many other respects besides their employment of Level I and Level II abilities. Jensen has, however, reported some studies using an elegant procedure, the comparison of the recall of categorized and uncategorized lists. Twenty common objects are presented one at a time in random order to subjects with instructions to remember the names of as many as possible; at the end the subject is asked to recall the objects. In one condition the objects are easily classifiable into familiar categories (clothing, furniture, animals, etc.), in the other they are not. Nothing is said about this to the subjects; the instructions are identical in the two conditions—simply to try to remember the objects. Presumably, if a subject relies on Level I abilities, such as rote memory, both conditions will yield comparable results. If a subject makes use of Level II abilities, such as abstraction and classification, his performance should be facilitated on the categorized list. A recent study comparing second- and fourth-grade blacks and whites (Jensen and Frederickson, 1973) successfully replicated earlier studies in showing: no significant differences between blacks and whites in either grade on the uncategorized list; no significant difference between the groups at the earlier grade on the categorized list; a substantial difference in favor

of the whites in grade 4 on the categorized list. Racial-ethnic identification and socioeconomic status were confounded in this and earlier
studies using this technique, since the whites were largely from
middle-class families and the blacks from lower-class families, by
occupational and educational criteria. Thus it is not clear whether
the differential use of Level II abilities in these studies is due to
factors primarily associated with the racial-ethnic difference between
the groups, the social-status difference, or both.

A study by Scrofani (1972) addressed itself to the question of
whether the differences observed in the recall of categorized lists are
fairly basic differences in capacity or fairly superficial differences in
the readiness to use one or another learning strategy. He reasoned that
if the latter were true, appropriate pretraining on a classification task
might reduce or eliminate the group difference in performance. His
results suggested that one group of low-SES, low-IQ subjects gained
materially from the pretraining, relative to a middle-class, high-IQ
group, but another group of low-SES, low IQ-subjects did not. The
gainers were subjects who had low tested IQs, but performed well on
two Piagetian tasks. Since these two tasks (multiple-classification
and multiple-seriation) would appear to call upon Level II abilities,
it is difficult to find these results quite as contradictory to Jensen's
position as did the original author. Nevertheless, it is clear that a
distinction between an *ability* to perform in an abstract fashion and a
spontaneous *preference* for performing in this way is an important
one to make in connection with the categorized recall task. The study
by Jensen and Fredricksen provides an item of evidence relevant to
this point. Additional samples in their experiment were tested with
a categorized list that had the items grouped by categories rather than
in the usual random ordering. This had a negligible effect at grade 2.
At grade 4 it slightly reduced but did not eliminate the difference
between the black and white groups, mostly by improving the performance of the blacks on later trials in the experiment. Thus differences in readiness to employ categorization, rather than simply in
the ability to do so, could indeed be a factor making some contribution to observed group differences in performance on this task.

A Specific Perceptual Deficit Among U.S. Blacks

Tyler (1956), in reviewing the literature on U.S. black-white differences in performance on intellectual tests, pointed to a number of
findings suggesting that blacks often tended to show their most

severe handicaps on tests requiring complex perceptual discriminations, and conjectured that perceptual difficulties might play a key
role in retarding the development of skills important in IQ tests and
school performance. She was inclined on the whole to interpret such
a hypothetical difference environmentally, and to be optimistic concerning the possibility of modifying it by appropriate early environmental enrichment. In an assessment of recent data bearing on this
hypothesis Tyler found mixed results, some supporting, some not,
and concluded that the matter still remains open (1972, p. 191).

We have already surveyed a number of the kinds of evidence on
which Tyler based her hypothesis, such as the relatively poorer
performance of blacks on the performance subtests than on the
verbal subtests of the Wechsler scales. The Block Design subtest, in
which a pattern is to be copied with colored blocks, ranked at the
bottom in the scores of blacks in the studies surveyed in Table 7.7,
whereas the highly verbal Similarities and Comprehension subtests
ranked at the top. As we have seen, some of the data on patterns of
abilities tend to be consistent with a hypothesis of more perceptual
difficulties among blacks (e.g., Lesser et al., 1965), others do not (e.g.,
Sitkei and Meyers, 1969).

We wish at this point to cite a couple of additional items of evidence that may have some relevance to this issue, though we should
make it clear that we, like Tyler, consider it still very much a moot
question whether a specific perceptual deficit exists in black groups
generally.

The first type of evidence comes from studies using the Bender-
Gestalt test, in which the subject is asked to copy ten abstract geometric figures of lines and dots. The test is used with adults primarily
in the clinical detection of suspected brain damage, but with young
children performance on the test shows a correlation with other
indices of perceptual-motor and general intellectual development
(Koppitz, 1964). A couple of authors have recently reported data
with this test offering some clues to the *kinds* of errors made exceptionally frequently by black children. Albott and Gunn (1971) report
results for a study in which a small group of 35 rural Illinois black
first-graders was compared to white norms, and Snyder and co-
workers (1971) compared a larger sample of 185 inner-city black
third-graders to samples of 654 first-grade and 109 third-grade white
suburban children.

Both authors used the Koppitz scoring system, which scores the reproductions for errors of integration, perseveration, rotation, and distortion of shape and angles. Albott and Gunn report details of the errors made on the three most difficult figures for their group, number 4, which consists of three sides of a square with a curved line touching one corner, number 7, which consists of two partially over-lapping narrow six-sided figures, and number 8, which is a long flat six-sided figure with an inscribed diamond. Snyder and co-workers give a tabulation for their three groups on most of the 30 errors scorable in the Koppitz system.

Many of the errors occurred too infrequently in any group to be very discriminating, and at the first-grade level a few were made by nearly all of the children. Eight errors showed an absolute difference of 15 percent or more between the black and white third-graders in the Snyder et al. study: four of these were errors in reproducing shapes and angles, two involved integration of parts of a figure, and two involved rotation of figures. The two errors involving rotation were particularly interesting. They were the only two errors that occurred more frequently among the black third-graders than among the white *first*-graders: 31 percent versus 22 percent for a rotational error on Figure 4, and 45 percent versus 18 percent for a rotational error on Figure 7. Both errors were also much more frequent among Albott and Gunn's rural black first-graders than in the suburban white first-grade sample: 74 percent versus 22 percent and 51 percent versus 18 percent, respectively. According to Koppitz (1964, p. 66), rotational errors on the Bender-Gestalt test are often diagnostic of reading difficulties.

Another possibly related finding has been reported in a study by Barabasz and colleagues (1970), which compared a small group of 21 black 3- and 4-year-old urban preschool children with two groups of white preschoolers, one consisting of 41 deprived rural children in a Head Start program, and one a group of 23 children in a University Nursery School. The children were individually shown ten pairs of abstract figures and asked to indicate for each which member of the pair was upside down. (A preliminary screening eliminated any chil-dren who could not do this task accurately with a toy doll and pic-tured objects.) The two figures in each pair of abstract drawings differed only in whether the primary visual focal point was toward the top or toward the bottom of the figure—the latter were judged to be "upside down" about 85 percent of the time by the white children; the nondeprived and deprived groups did not differ. The black group made the judgment in this direction about 68 percent of the time, or only moderately above the 50 percent that would be expected if answers were based on guessing. The authors suggest that such a group difference might be either genetic or cultural in origin, but probably not socioeconomic, since the deprived and nondeprived white groups did not differ in how they interpreted the figures.

There is some suggestive cross-cultural evidence as well. Berry (1966) reported a striking difference between two primitive groups, the Eskimos of Baffin Island and the Temne of Sierra Leone, in their performance on four tests of spatial abilities, with the Eskimos performing at European levels, and the West Africans much more poorly. Vernon (1965) has noted similar differences between Canadian Indians and Eskimos, and Jamaican blacks. These findings have most often been given a cultural or ecological interpretation by their authors, and obviously there are many striking differences of these kinds among the groups. However, in view of recent evidence (Bock and Kolakowski, 1973) suggesting that the ability for spatial visualization may be substantially influenced by a single gene, the possibility that this gene might have a low frequency in populations of West African origin cannot altogether be discounted.

A fairly direct test of this hypothesis is possible from the data of Eyferth (1961). It will be recalled that he gave a German version of the Wechsler to illegitimate offspring of matings between German women and black and white servicemen of the occupation forces in Germany after World War II. If the gene for spatial ability is X-linked, and if the gene was more frequent among the white fathers of these children than among the black fathers, but equally frequent among the two sets of German mothers, there is a clear genetic prediction. The Caucasian and mixed-race girls should show a difference in spatial ability in favor of the Caucasians, since each girl received an X-chromosome from her father, and there should be no such difference among the boys, whose X-chromosomes all came from their German mothers.

In fact, the limited data in this case offer no support for the hypothesis. The Block Design subtest of the Wechsler is probably the best single measure of spatial ability used in the study, and the mean scaled scores on this measure were: girls with white fathers, 8.67; girls with black fathers, 9.34; boys with white fathers, 10.65; boys with black fathers, 9.41. The results for other Wechsler subtests with a spatial-ability component, such as Object Assembly, Picture Completion, and Picture Arrangement, were similar. In none of the three did the girls with white fathers do better than the girls with black fathers.

Since we have no information on the actual test performance of the fathers or mothers, and since the samples of offspring are somewhat limited (they range from 33 to 89 in the various groups), these results cannot be taken as entirely conclusive. As they stand, however, they offer no support for the notion that an X-linked "spatial-ability" gene is lower in frequency in African than in European populations. In fact, since there was no marked overall difference between the white and racially-mixed offspring in performance on these tests, there is little support for a *gene*-based black perceptual deficit of any kind in these data.

Summary and Conclusions: Profiles of Abilities

What conclusions, then, can be drawn from studies comparing U.S. racial-ethnic groups in terms of different patterns or profiles of abilities?

First, the interrelationships among ability measures have repeatedly been found to be similar across racial-ethnic groups, suggesting a similar underlying structure of abilities. However, the average levels of performance of different groups on such dimensions often differ. These results are far from entirely consistent. While most studies have obtained some significant subpopulation differences, there are inconsistencies in the particular traits involved. It is difficult to evaluate these discrepancies in view of the differences in measuring instruments and populations studied. Only in the black-white comparisons on the Wechsler scales is there a substantial number of studies using the same instruments, and here, although there is some variation in the findings, there appears to be a tendency for black subjects to do relatively better on the verbal scales than on the nonverbal scales. Other findings that show up in more than one study are the relatively good performance of groups of Oriental ancestry on quantitative tasks and the strong verbal and numerical performance of Jewish groups.

Second, the majority of studies find differences in level of performance as well as in pattern of abilities, among the ethnic groups studied. While such differences in level can be made to look larger or smaller by altering the relative weight given to different elements of the profile, it most cases it would not be easy to make them disappear by this means.

Third, while there is some evidence in support of Jensen's hypothesis that certain mental abilities ("Level I" abilities) may show relatively less difference across U.S. ethnic or social-class groups than do the other abilities that he classifies as "Level II," such support is not univocal, and there are difficulties of interpretation arising out of a correlation between race and social class in many of the pertinent studies.

Finally, Tyler's conjecture that U.S. blacks suffer from a perceptual deficit was examined. One specific genetic hypothesis concerning such a deficit was found testable by existing evidence, which did not support it.

In short, most of the studies we have reviewed are not at all decisive on the question of the possible genetic or environmental basis of observed differences in ability patterns among U.S. racial-ethnic groups. This is not to argue that studies of this type are inherently powerless to shed light on the issue of genetic versus environmental influences. On the contrary, a multidimensional pattern of ability differences places much more severe constraints on the particular genetic or environmental hypotheses that may be adduced to explain it than does a difference in average performance on a single dimension. It is merely that so far the empirical results are not sufficiently strong or consistent to provide much help in differentiating among competing theories about their origin.

Conclusion: Cross-group Comparisons

In this chapter a number of studies comparing levels or patterns of ability in different U.S. racial-ethnic or socioeconomic groups have been examined. It was concluded that ethnic group and socioeconomic status are separate but correlated variables, that both crosscut the heredity-environment distinction, and that ability differences among existing groups can rarely be unambiguously attributed to genetic or environmental differences between them.

Certain cross-group consistencies have emerged. Ability tends to show similar relationships to socioeconomic variables within different U.S. racial-ethnic groups. Different ability variables tend to be similarly interrelated in different groups. The question of characteristic differences in ability profiles among U.S. racial-ethnic groups has been considerably investigated, and some limited degree of consistency seems to be present in the data, but for patterns of special abilities as for general ability the variation within groups is much more impressive than the differences between them.

CHAPTER 8

Nutrition and Intellectual Performance

THE FACT THAT MORE AMERICAN BLACKS AND MEXICAN AMERICANS are seriously undernourished than American whites (U.S. Department of Health, Education, and Welfare, *Ten-State Nutrition Survey 1968–1970*, 1972) may contribute—directly or in interaction with other environmental factors associated with malnutrition and poverty—to the observed differences in group performance on intelligence tests. It is well established for both experimental mammals and man that severe protein undernourishment during critical periods of brain development in prenatal or early postnatal life can lead to irreversible brain damage or impairment, and in turn to reduced intellectual performance throughout the lifetime of the critically malnourished person, even if he receives good nutrition after infancy.

Cravioto and his colleagues stress that malnutrition, poverty, poor performance on standard intelligence tests, and correlated poor performance in school result in a vicious circle:

A low level of adaptive functioning, lack of modern knowledge, social custom, infection, or environmental insufficiency of foodstuffs produces malnutrition which gives a large pool of survivors who come to function in suboptimal ways. Such survivors are themselves more at a risk of being victims of their poor socioeconomic environment, being less effective than otherwise would be the case in their social adaptations. In turn, they will choose mates of similar characteristics and may rear their children under conditions and in a fashion fatally programmed to produce a new generation of malnourished individuals. (Cravioto and De-Licardie, 1973, 92–93)

A flow diagram illustrating this "spiral" is shown in Figure 8.1.

Qualitative Nutritional Requirements

A diagnostic feature of living organisms is that they take in food from the environment and remake it into the organic molecules characteristic of their species. Autotrophic ("self-feeding") organisms can use carbon dioxide as the sole source of carbon in building organic molecules. Thus organisms capable of photosynthesis, the manufacture of the sugar glucose ($C_6H_{12}O_6$) from CO_2 and water in the presence of sunlight and chlorophyll, are autotrophic. Heterotrophic ("feeding on others") organisms must obtain carbon in a complex form, such as glucose, which they obtain by ingesting cells from other organisms, ultimately derived from autotrophs. Man and other higher animals must use such organic compounds rather than inorganic CO_2 as a carbon source, and use oxidation-reduction reactions of organic molecules rather than sunlight as an energy source.

All the known, *major*, qualitative evolutionary trends in animal nutrition were established long before the origin of the human species some 300,000 years ago. The major qualitative nutritional requirements are mostly homologous for all higher animals, remarkably similar for most primates, and nearly but not entirely identical for all living varieties of man. For example, the essential amino acid requirements are nearly identical in the protozoan *Tetrahymena* the house fly *Musca*, salmon, rat, and man (Prosser, 1973, p. 118).

The nutritional requirements of human beings are inferred from the results of experimental studies on animals, especially the albino

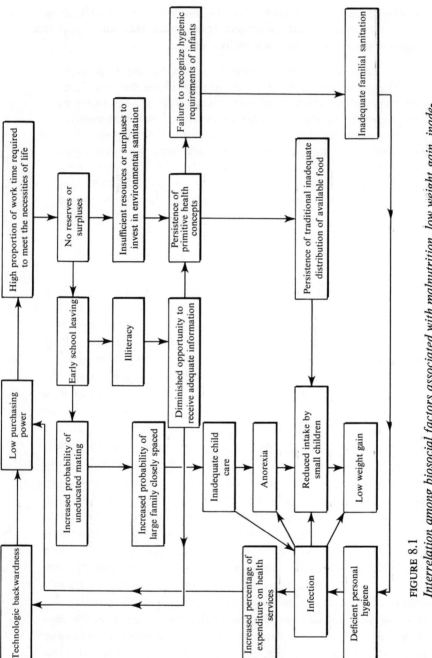

FIGURE 8.1

Interrelation among biosocial factors associated with malnutrition, low weight gain, inadequate child care and poor personal hygiene, increased morbidity, inadequate expenditure on health services, and low purchasing power. (From Cravioto, 1971.)

rat, correlated and corrected from such observations as can be made on human subjects. In animal experiments, the usual method of study is to omit specific chemically known substances from a controlled diet, in order to find which substances can be synthesized by the organism, and which are indispensable in the food intake.

Some examples of nutritional knowledge based on observations on man include the facts that if food intake during infancy is deficient in total calories marasmus results and that if it is sufficient in total calories but deficient in protein calories kwashiorkor results, both of which if uncorrected lead to death, or if not corrected soon enough, to mental defect; that vitamin C prevents scurvy, vitamin D rickets, and iodine (given other essential factors) cretinism; that persons suffering from phenylketonuria (PKU) because of an inherited lack of the enzyme phenylalanine hydroxylase will usually (but not always) be severely mentally retarded unless they receive, starting soon after birth, a diet low in phenylalanine (ideally, just sufficient to meet the changing requirements for that amino acid in protein synthesis); and that tyrosine is an essential amino acid in persons having PKU but not in other people.

The nutritional requirements of man must be specified in both qualitative and quantitative terms, not only what kinds of food are required but also how much and when. Although much progress has been made since the founding of the science of nutrition in 1790 by Lavoisier and Laplace (who measured metabolic heat production, oxygen intake, and carbon dioxide output in guinea pig and man), and although the assertion was confidently made in the 1930's that the science was perhaps nearing completion (e.g., McCollum, 1931), current knowledge must be regarded as approximate with varying degrees of incompleteness regarding individual and group variations in kinds, amounts, and critical periods.

Given the difficulty of their discovery, it is quite possible that some vitamins are still unknown. Moreover, it is probable that several trace elements remain to be established as essential nutrients in man and other mammals (Underwood, 1971). Of the nine trace elements well established as required plus three tentatively established, only two (iodine and iron) were demonstrated as essential before the turn of this century, copper only in 1928, manganese in 1931, zinc in 1934, cobalt in 1935, molybdenum in 1956, selenium in 1957, chromium in 1959, tin in 1970, and vanadium and nickel in 1971.

The question of whether tin is essential in the diet of man illustrates one of the technical problems in investigation of trace elements. In 1964 Schroeder, Balassa and Tipton concluded that "the evidence is convincing that measurable tin is not necessary for life or health" in human beings. The conclusion was based on the fact that no tin was found in *some* human cadavers. Schwarz (1971) points out that the prevailing methods of analysis were inappropriate for the detection of trace amounts of tin because they included drying the tissue specimens at 110°C and subsequently reducing them to ashes at 450°C and because some tin compounds boil at temperatures as low as 240°C, and the great majority of organotin derivative compounds evaporate at temperatures lower than 200°C. Schwarz, Milne, and Vinyard (1970) demonstrated that trace amounts of tin are essential for normal growth in rats. They used analytical techniques accurate to less than one part per million, an ultra-clean room, an air supply free of trace elements, modern isolator techniques, plastic apparatus free of metal, glass, and rubber, and highly purified, chemically defined diets containing amino acids in lieu of protein. The tin-deficient animals grow poorly, lose hair, develop seborrhea, are lethargic, and lack muscle tonicity. Near optimal growth is restored by supplying one part per million of tin in the form of stannic sulfate in the diet.

Schwarz (1971) concluded that 9 trace elements are established as essential nutrients in mammals; of the remaining 72 elements that could be potential candidates for trace-element function, 24 are under special consideration for that status, 32 are possible, and 16 are considered unlikely contenders.

Not all humans are identical in their qualitative nutritional requirements. It is commonly assumed that man cannot synthesize ascorbic acid. Rajalakshmi and co-workers (1965, 1967) concluded that some Asian Indian women do synthesize ascorbic acid, the evidence being that ascorbic acid lost in their milk and urine over long periods far exceeds the dietary intake, and the investigators' discovery that synthesis of ascorbic acid takes place in the Indian placenta when incubated after delivery. The fact that most primates do not have the capacity to synthesize ascorbic acid (Prosser, 1973) need not imply that the capacity is absent from all persons in all human populations (Davidson and Passmore, 1969, p. 213).

Deficiency of the enzyme lactase in the adult human is associated with intolerance of milk sugar (lactose) resulting in abdominal pain and diarrhea. Such adult lactose intolerance is characteristic of most world populations except those of Northern European origin—including African, Middle Eastern, Oriental, and Australian Aboriginal peoples. It is much more common in American blacks (70–75 percent) and American Indians than in whites (8–15 percent) (Bayless, 1973). In blacks the age of onset of the intolerance is variable, sometimes as early as the first six months, often in the first four years, and sometimes later (Cook, 1967). Rosensweig and his colleagues (1967) found evidence for three lactase levels, and suggest they might be determined by three genotypes at a single autosomal locus with the homozygous recessive lowest and the heterozygote intermediate in enzyme activity. Milk is an important part of most school lunches, and black children obtain a significant portion of their daily dietary intake from school lunches (*Ten-State Nutrition Survey 1968–1970*, 1972); if many black children avoid drinking all or part of the milk supplied with their lunches because of the discomfort it causes, this could make an appreciable difference in their total protein intake. Lactose intolerance levels are even higher in orientals, but Chinese and Japanese children in America are on the average probably less dependent than blacks on the contribution of school lunches to total dietary intake.

A growing number of genetic diseases are recognized that alter nutritional requirements in man (Dancis, 1970; Holtzman, 1970). We have already mentioned phenylketonuria, perhaps the best known example of such diseases. For a number of these genetic diseases, frequencies of the responsible genes show significant differences among American ethnic groups.

Of the better known inherited diseases, fifteen (of which PKU, galactosemia, fructosemia, histidinemia, and tyrosinemia are examples) are recognized that involve an accumulation of noxious metabolites proximal to a metabolic block, three involve a deficiency of an essential nutrient distal to the metabolic block, five involve an inability to conserve essential nutrients, and ten genetic diseases are known in which the biochemical defect is reversible by large doses of a vitamin (Dancis, 1970). Although the homozygous recessives for these inherited diseases are rare, the combined total of heterozygotes may reach 10 percent or more in local populations. Also, similar enzymatic disturbances may be associated with more common diseases: for example, transient dissacharide (e.g., sucrose, isomaltose, lactose) intolerance commonly complicates a variety of intestinal diseases. Also, partial reductions in enzyme activities of nutritional importance may be considerably more frequent than the metabolic diseases now recognized.

The qualitative nutrients established as normally essential for growth or maintenance in man, together with those that are probably essential, are shown in Table 8.1. They include 10 amino acids, 6 minerals, 12 trace elements, 13 vitamins, and 3 other organic compounds, a total of 44 nutrients. Authorities disagree on whether arginine is essential to human growth (Holt and Snyderman, 1961; Prosser, 1973). All but 7 of the 44 nutrients are believed to be essential for normal development and function of the brain and central nervous system (Lehninger, 1970; Rajalakshmi and Ramakrishnan, 1972).

Quantitative Nutritional Requirements

It is easier to show that a particular nutrient is essential to life, than to arrive at an accurate estimate of the quantity required for normal growth or maintenance. Nonetheless estimates of this kind are necessary for various purposes, and many have been made. The standards employed by the *Ten-State Nutrition Survey 1968–1970* (TSNS) are listed in Table 8.2 This is the most extensive nutritional survey ever carried out in the United States and the most reliable source on the comparative nutritional status of low-income blacks, Spanish Americans, and whites in the nation. The TSNS is described in some detail in a later section.

In general the intake values employed as standards in the TSNS are similar to those recommended by the U.S. National Research Council (1968) and the United Kingdom, Department of Health and Social Security (1969). Compared with the NRC recommendations the TSNS advocates a few more calories after age one year up to adulthood, more protein after age six months, more calcium to age six months but thereafter up to 46 percent less, and less vitamin A. Compared with the United Kingdom standards the TSNS has slightly more calories, less protein, less calcium, more iron, and more ascorbic acid.

Not all experts are in agreement concerning such specifications of nutritional requirements. As recently as 1973 four British physiologists proclaimed in *Nature* that the food-energy requirements of man and his balance of intake and expenditure are not known (Durnin, Edholm, Miller, and Waterlow, 1973). They reached this conclusion

TABLE 8.1. *Nutrients required by man. Deficiencies for nutrients marked with an asterisk are associated with impaired structure and function of the central nervous system (see Rajalakshmi and Ramakrishnan, 1972).*

Established as Essential		Probably Essential
Amino Acids		
*Arginine[a]	*Methionine	
*Histidine[a]	*Phenylalanine	
*Isoleucine	*Threonine	
*Leucine	*Tryptophan	
*Lysine	*Valine	
Minerals		
*Calcium	*Phosphorus	
*Chlorine	*Potassium	
*Magnesium	*Sodium	
Trace Elements		
Cobalt	*Manganese	Nickel
*Copper	Molybdenum	Tin
Chromium	Selenium	Vanadium
*Iodine	*Zinc	
*Iron		
Vitamins		
*Ascorbic acid (C)	*Thiamine (B_1)	*Biotin
*Folic acid	*Vitamin A	*Pantothenic acid
*Nicotinic acid[b]	*Vitamin B_{12}	*Vitamin E
*Pyridoxine	*Vitamin D	
*Riboflavin	Vitamin K	
Other Organic Compounds		
*Polyunsaturated fatty acids		
*Choline		
*Inositol		

[a] Required for normal growth (some disagreement on arginine), not essential for nitrogen balance in adults.

[b] Requirement may be met by synthesis from dietary tryptophan.

TABLE 8.2. *Standards for evaluation of daily dietary intake.*

Age	Sex	Calories, kcal/kg Body Weight	Protein, g/kg Body Weight	Calcium, mg	Iron, mg	Vitamin A, I.U.	Thiamine, mg/1000 kcal	Riboflavin, mg/1000 kcal	Nicotinic Acid, mg/1000 kcal	Ascorbic Acid, mg
0– 1 mo	FM	120	2.2	550	10	1500	0.4	0.55	6.6	30
2– 5 mo	FM	110	2.2	550	10	1500	0.4	0.55	6.6	30
6–11 mo	FM	100	2.2	550	10	1500	0.4	0.55	6.6	30
12–23 mo	FM	90	1.9	450	15	2000	0.4	0.55	6.6	30
24–47 mo	FM	86	1.7	450	15	2000	0.4	0.55	6.6	30
48–71 mo	FM	82	1.5	450	10	2000	0.4	0.55	6.6	30
6– 7 yr	FM	82	1.3	450	10	2500	0.4	0.55	6.6	30
8– 9 yr	FM	82	1.3	450	10	2500	0.4	0.55	6.6	30
10–12 yr	M	68	1.2	650	10	2500	0.4	0.55	6.6	30
10–12 yr	F	64	1.2	650	18	2500	0.4	0.55	6.6	30
13–16 yr	M	60	1.2	650	18	3500	0.4	0.55	6.6	30
13–16 yr	F	48	1.2	650	18	3500	0.4	0.55	6.6	30
17–19 yr	M	44	1.1	550	18	3500	0.4	0.55	6.6	30
17–19 yr	F	35	1.1	550	18	3500	0.4	0.55	6.6	30
Adults	M	40[a]	1.0	400	10	3500	0.4	0.55	6.6	30
Adults	F	35[b,c]	1.0[d]	400[e]	18[f]	3500[g]	0.4	0.55	6.6	30

Source: U.S. Department of Health, Education, and Welfare, *Ten-State Nutrition Survey, 1968–1970,* 1972, V. 2–4.
[a] Decrease for each decade up to 70 years, to 38, 37, 36, 34, and 34.
[b] Decrease for each decade up to 70 years, to 33, 31, 30, 29, and 29.
[c] For 2nd and 3rd trimesters of pregnancy, increase basic standard 200 kcal. For lactating, increase basic standard 1000 kcal.
[d] For 2nd and 3rd trimester of pregnancy, increase basic standard 20 g. For lactating, increase basic standard 25 g.
[e] For 2nd and 3rd trimester of pregnancy, increase basic standard 400 mg. For lactating, increase basic standard 500 mg.
[f] Reduce, from age 55 years on to 10 mg.
[g] For lactating, increase basic standard 1000 I.U.

because increasingly accurate and comprehensive studies of food intake and energy output show that in groups of 20 or more healthy subjects with similar attributes and activities, the food intake of individuals may vary as much as two-fold. Within such local groups there may also be large discrepancies between individual food intake and energy expenditure. Cross-cultural studies suggest that some populations keep healthy and active on food intakes that are grossly inadequate (for example, by a factor of 300 for sodium and potassium) by current British and United States standards (Davidson and Passmore, 1969). It is generally assumed that such population differences are due to unknown mechanisms of differential physiological adaptation rather than to unknown genetic differences, but certainly the details are quite unclear at this point.

Undernutrition and Brain Development

The first described and best known human nutritional disorders are adult deficiency diseases such as scurvy, beriberi, and pellagra in which a critically ill person can be restored to health rapidly by ingesting a missing essential nutrient. By extension, some investigators have assumed that all the consequences of serious prenatal and early postnatal undernutrition can be reversed completely by subsequent adequate nutrition.

Today there is substantial evidence, although not yet completely conclusive proof, that short periods of undernutrition in early life may permanently, irreversibly impair the structure and function of the central nervous system and thus permanently and irreversibly reduce the intellectual capacity of adults who were undernourished at a critical period early in life (Dobbing, 1970a, 1973, 1974).

Full proof of the permanent effect of critical-period undernutrition may not become available until the molecular bases of learning and memory are extensively known. Until then we must gain information on the problem from lower-animal experimentation (Balázs, 1972; Bass, Netsky, and Young, 1970a,b; Chase, 1973; Coursin, 1965; Davison and Dobbing, 1968; Dobbing, 1968a, 1970a,b; Levitsky and Barnes, 1972; Platt and Stewart, 1971; Scrimshaw, 1969; Winick, 1968b; Zamanhof, Van Marthens, and Margolis, 1968), well controlled psychological and nutritional retrospective and prospective studies on undernourished children (see references in Appendix M), postmortem examination of the brains of children who were undernourished (Fishman, Prensky, and Dodge, 1969; Winick and Rosso,

1969), and observational studies on the structure and chemical composition of adult brains from persons who were undernourished during critical periods of development, a field of study hardly yet begun (Dobbing, 1970b).

Platt and Stewart (1971) showed that most of the signs produced in growing experimental animals under protein-calorie malnutrition can be found in children who either are obviously malnourished or are members of very low socioeconomic groups; in a survey of the literature they found all of the following had been reported both in man and in studies on one or more of four experimental animals (rat, dog, pig, and rhesus monkey): low body weight for age, retarded growth of long bones, low concentration of serum albumin, presence of edema, presence of anemia, excess of fat in liver, excess of glycogen in liver, atrophy of thymus gland, changes in the structure or function of endocrine and exocrine pancreas and of the alimentary canal, abnormal gait or tremors of head and limbs, altered electroencephalograms, low brain weight for age, high brain weight/body weight ratio, low total amount of DNA or reduced number of brain cells, low proportion and amount of brain gangliosides for age, low amount of brain cholesterol for age, increase in glial fibers, and low amount of Nissl substance and cytoplasm in nerve cells.

The great expansion of the cerebral cortex, especially over the parietal and temporal lobes, is a distinctive feature of the evolution of the human brain (von Bonin, 1963; Jerison, 1973). Important parts of the neurological basis of human language are localized in the cerebral cortex (Lenneberg, 1967; Dingwall and Whitaker, 1974). Clark, Zamenhof, Van Marthens, Grauel, and Kruger (1973) not only confirmed, as had been previously reported, that when pregnant albino rats are maintained on calorie-deficient diets the brain measurements of their offspring (weight, DNA and protein content) are significantly reduced in comparison with those of rats that received adequate prenatal nourishment, but also showed that their cerebral cortical dimensions (thickness at several positions, width, area) are significantly smaller. The decreases are more pronounced at birth than at 10 days or later in development. Cortical thickness was reduced by almost double what would be expected from the reduction in the weight of the cerebrum as a whole, suggesting that the cerebral cortex is more affected by calorie undernutrition than the whole brain.

Extreme care must be used in attempts to transfer information from nonhuman animal experiments to man, especially when the

TABLE 8.3. *Brain weight in grams from birth to adult years.*

Age	Males	Females	% of Weight at Age 20 yr (Males + Females)
Birth	353	347	25.6
0–3 mo	435	411	30.7
3–6 mo	600	534	41.3
6–12 mo	877	726	54.5
1–2 yr	971	894	67.9
2–3 yr	1076	1012	76.0
3–4 yr	1179	1076	82.5
4–5 yr	1290	1156	89.7
5–6 yr	1275	1206	91.0
9–10 yr	1360	1226	95.0
14–15 yr	1356	1318	97.7
19–20 yr	1430	1294	100.0
20–60 yr	1355	1220	95.0

Source: Data from Krogman, 1941.

experimental animals are not primates. The timing of brain growth relative to birth differs markedly in rat, dog, pig, guinea pig, and man (Davison and Dobbing, 1968). Payne and Wheeler (1967) have shown that the rate of fetal growth in man and other higher primates is much slower in relation to the mother's body size in than nonprimate mammals. The slower growing primate fetus makes less exacting nutritional demands on the mother during pregnancy than the faster growing fetus of experimental or farm animals such as rats, dogs, pigs, and sheep. Payne and Wheeler suggest that this may explain why, for example, previously well nourished Dutch mothers subjected during pregnancy to some six months of serious undernutrition during World War II had babies with birth weights reduced by only 5–10 percent (Smith, 1947), whereas the offspring of farm animals of comparable body size and maternal undernutrition may be reduced as much as 20–25 percent.

The human brain weighs about 350 grams at birth, more than one-quarter of its adult weight (Table 8.3). The brain grows rapidly during the early postnatal period, increasing nearly 200 percent in weight during the first two years after birth; during the next 10 years, the additional weight gain is only about 35 percent. The brain reaches about 96 percent of adult size by age 10 years, may undergo a slight adolescent spurt associated with puberty (Tanner, 1962), and usually attains its maximum weight by around age 20 years. Brain weight in adults tends to decrease slightly with advancing age.

Dobbing (1974) and his associates examined a series of 139 human brains ranging in age from 10 weeks of gestation to 7 years after birth and 9 adult brains, all being from persons within one standard deviation of the expected body weight for age and without gross central nervous system pathology. Observations were made within two days after death on DNA in the forebrain, cerebellum, and brain stem; it is known that DNA remains stable under ordinary circumstances within this period. DNA levels reach 98 percent of adult volume by the fourth month after birth in the cerebellum, 75 percent in the forebrain, and 73 percent in the brain stem.

The incremental rates of DNA production show two velocity peaks, the first growth spurt occurring from 10 to 18 weeks of gestation, and the second from about 20 weeks of gestation to 4 months after birth (Figure 8.2). The early phase almost certainly represents the cell division of neurons and the late phase that of glial cells.

Although most of the cell divisions producing neurons occur before birth, the major brain-growth spurt is predominantly postnatal (Figure 8.2) and results from the production by cell division of glial cells, which are required to produce the great bulk of myelin characteristic of brain growth during the first four postnatal years.

Growth of the brain by cell division is mostly completed by 18 months of age. Subsequent increase in total brain weight results from increase in cell size, further differentiation of cells, or increase in extracellular substances. Schadé and van Groenigen (1961) found that pyramidal cells of the middle frontal gyrus increase rapidly in volume during the first two postnatal years, and less rapidly up to puberty, with little change thereafter.

The major growth change in the human brain after 18 months up to the age of sexual maturity reflects the interconnection of neurons by way of axons and dendrites. Conel (1939–1967), using camera lucida tracings made from microscopic sections, demonstrates a dramatic increase in neuronal interconnections in the cerebral cortex from birth to age 24 months. De Crinis (1934) and later workers report that in various areas of the cerebral cortex there are no den-

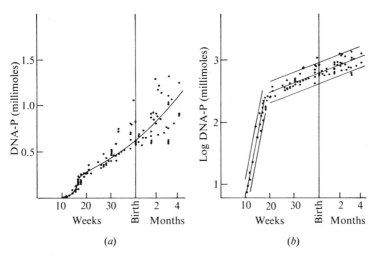

FIGURE 8-2

Total DNA-P (equivalent to total cell number) in the human forebrain from 10 weeks of gestation to 4 months after birth, showing two phases of prenatal cell multiplication, the earlier phase characteristic of neurons, and the later of glial cells. Figure 8.2(b) is a semi-log plot of the data in Figure 8.2(a) to show the sharp separation of the two phases at 18 gestational weeks. Regression lines with 95% confidence limits are added. (From Dobbing, 1974.)

drites, or only a few, in newborns but that many are well established by the fourth year.

All of these brain developmental processes, of course, presuppose a normal supply of essential nutrients, although the brain is favored and protected in its development relative to other parts of the body.

As more and more dendritic branches develop, which permits great numbers of interconnections between neurons to form, the cell bodies of the neurons move apart, and the neuron density decreases. This proceeds at a rapid rate during the first two years, and at a rate slowing to steady at or near puberty. The ratio of the volume of cerebral cortical gray matter made of neuronal interconnections to the volume of the neuron cell bodies contained in it, goes up from birth to age 20 years (Schadé and van Groenigen, 1961). And this ratio is higher in adult human than in adult chimpanzee brains (Haug, 1958).

Data based on the work of Brante (1949) and Folch-Pi (1955) summarized graphically by Lenneberg (1967) shows that the percentages of brain lipids, phosphatides, cholesterol, and cerebrosides—all required for normal brain function and all dependent on dietary intake of essential nutrients—increase from birth to puberty; cholesterol and cerebrosides increase roughly proportonally to the increase by age in fresh brain weight; the concentration of brain lipids and phosphatides may continue to increase during adult years.

There are two contesting, partially overlapping hypotheses about the biological basis of the period in which nutrition is critical to brain development in man and other mammals; they are known as the "cell-division" and "growth-spurt" hypotheses. The differences between the two hypotheses are of crucial importance in interpreting the consequences for intellectual development in children exposed to severe early undernutrition at different periods in the life cycle.

The cell-division hypothesis, proposed by Winick and Noble (1966), holds that undernutrition during periods of growth by cell division will lead to permanent reduction in total number of cells in the brain and other tissues. Undernutrition after cell division has stopped in a given tissue, when growth is by increase in cell size or extracellular substances, will result in a reduction of tissue or organ size that is reversible by nutritional rehabilitation.

The growth-spurt hypothesis, formulated by Dobbing (1968), states that the developing brain is most vulnerable to irreversible impairment from undernutrition during the transient period when it is passing through the rapid velocity phase of its $\int$-shaped growth curve.

The timing of the nutritionally critical period for brain development is significantly different under the two hypotheses. The adult number of neurons, usually considered the chief functional units of the brain, is established by about 42 days of gestation in the guinea pig, 2 days after birth in the rat, and 18–20 weeks of gestation (or 4–5 months before birth) in man (Dobbing, 1974, p. 573). Thus, according to the cell-division hypothesis, if neural cell division is critical, the effects of malnutrition on brain development should be reversible if the malnutrition occurs postnatally. To the extent that glial cells are important, the effects of malnutrition on the brain should mostly be reversible if the malnutrition occurs after the first year of life.

According to the growth-spurt hypothesis, permanent effects can result from malnutrition occurring at any stage of brain growth, but they will be greatest if the malnutrition occurs when growth is most rapid. Thus even mild undernutrition during or near the time of maximum velocity of the growth spurt may produce permanent restriction of brain development, and undernutrition timed farther away from the maximum will have a lesser effect, so that in adults even starvation leading to death may have no great effect on brain composition. Moreover, malnutrition at any one stage of development will produce different effects in different parts of the brain, and in different measures of brain development (neuronal cell number, glial cell number, protein and lipid content, total weight) according to the regional growth velocity prevalent at the time for each kind of cell or cell product.

According to Dobbing (1973, p. 48): "Much confusion of thought has unhappily resulted from a previous, erroneous report [he refers to Winick, 1968a] implying that the human brain spurt is over by about five postnatal months." Although the peak velocity of neuronal cell division is prenatal, and that of glial cell division is about three months postnatal, some glial cell division may continue past 18 months. After cell division is complete in the brain there is a marked increase in the growth of dendrites and neuronal interconnections, especially up to 24 postnatal months. The myelination in the brain is not well established until four years after birth. Some developmental changes continue in the brain, especially in the temporal and parietal lobes that have important roles in human symbolic and linguistic behavior, up to the adolescent growth spurt and puberty when the brain approaches adult volume. All of these changes require synthesis of new biomolecules, especially proteins and lipids, and thus an adequate supply of essential nutrients.

Because important aspects of brain growth continue through at least the first several years of life, it may not be easy to detect different degrees of developmental deficit in children severely undernourished at different times within the first two years after birth, say before and after 9 postnatal months (for example, Hansen et al., 1971, and Hertzig et al., 1972). Failure to find an age effect of severe malnutrition during the first two postnatal years does not demonstrate that early malnutrition is not associated with lasting adult mental deficit, but it does present some difficulties for both competing theories.

In the last decade a large number of studies on the cognitive effects of severe early malnutrition have been conducted in acutely and chronically undernourished populations in underdeveloped countries around the world. A number of these investigations are reviewed in Appendix M. These studies clearly show that severely malnourished children, whether in rural villages or in urban slums, often perform more poorly on tests of cognitive performance than do their better fed compatriots. Equally clearly, in many of these studies, poor nutrition is correlated with a host of other sociocultural and biological variables prognostic of less than optimal intellectual development (Cravioto, 1968; Warren, 1973). But some of the better studies (for example, those using sibling controls) strongly suggest a causal role of malnutrition in the later intellectual deficiencies, perhaps via brain-growth mechanisms of the kind discussed earlier in this section. Other mechanisms, such as the adverse effects of listlessness and apathy on critical early learning, have also been discussed. Further results of major long-term studies now underway in various countries are awaited with great interest.

Effects of Prenatal Nutrition
on Birth Weight and Later Intelligence

Intrauterine effects of malnutrition have been extensively studied in experimental animals and human populations. In a recent review of the literature, Platt and Stewart (1971) concluded nutrition is probably the most important among many interacting factors that may modify birth weight. Kaplan (1972) summarizes a number of reports suggesting that food shortages associated with wars, depressions, and poverty tend to lead to lowered birth weights, although she notes that other concurrent stresses could also be playing a role.

Hendricks (1967) reported that socioeconomic differences, including nutritional differences, had a greater effect on fetal growth than did racial differences in a Cleveland hospital sample. Gruenwald and co-workers (1967) note that the substantial increase in birth weight in Japan during the 20-year period following World War II was caused by better fetal growth and not by an increase in the duration of pregnancy. Burke and co-workers (1943) reported that mothers with poor or very poor dietary histories were likely to produce underweight, weak infants with poor prognoses for survival and normalcy.

A systematic quantitative estimation of the effect of various genetic and environmental factors on birth weight in a sample of mothers and their infants in the British Isles was made by Penrose (1954), using observed data on one- and two-egg twins, full sibs, and various kinds of first cousins. His estimates were:

Maternal genotype	0.20
Maternal environment: General	0.18
Maternal environment: Immediate	0.06
Age of mother	0.01

Parity of fetus	0.07
Fetal genotype: Without dominance	0.15
Fetal genotype: Effect of dominance	0.01
Sex of fetus	0.02
Unknown intrauterine environment	0.30
	1.00

General maternal environment refers to environment common to full sibships and immediate maternal environment to that of a given pregnancy, which, of course, would be common for twin pairs. If we label as "known" those sources of variation that can be attributed to observed maternal age, parity, sex and weight of infant, and type of biological relationship, then maternal genotype is the most important known single factor in the determination of birth weight, with general maternal environment and fetal genotype close behind in importance. Age of mother, parity, and immediate maternal environment are relatively unimportant, at least in these samples. Unknown intrauterine environment accounts for more variation than any single known factor. The state of maternal nutrition could be a factor in maternal environment and unknown intrauterine environment that account for a total of 54 percent of the variation in birth weight in this (presumably relatively well nourished) British population.

Several studies carried out in the United States correlate birth weight and later measured intelligence (among others, Wiener, 1962, Harper and Wiener, 1965, and Caputo and Mandell, 1970, review the literature). One of the most important of these studies is the extensive follow-up from birth to ages 12–13 years of a large sample of premature and normal births occurring in 1952 in Baltimore. The initial sample contained 500 single-born premature infants, which included all available survivors whose birth weight was less than 1501 grams and a sample of those weighing 1501 to 2500 grams, and 492 controls with birth weight more than 2501 grams (Knobloch et al., 1956). Premature and control children were matched for race, season of birth, parity, hospital of birth, and socioeconomic status. The 992 infants tested at 40 weeks were 85 percent of those initially selected, and 878 of the originally tested sample of 992 infants ($87\frac{1}{2}$ percent) were successfully followed up at ages 12–13 years (Wiener, 1968).

The children were examined at age 40 weeks, and at 3–5, 6–7, and 8–10 years, and school achievement records were obtained at 12–13 years of age.

Separate analysis by race was not reported for the Gesell Development scores, physical examinations, interviews with mothers, and behavioral observations obtained for the test and control children at 40 weeks (Knobloch et al., 1956). There were significantly more black infants with low birth weights (between 1000 and 2000 grams), and more neurological defects in this group. However, no substantial differences in mental or neurological status between races were observed when birth weight was controlled.

At ages 3–5 years, the low-birth-weight babies had a mean IQ of 94.4 compared with 100.6 for the controls based on Stanford-Binet Form L tests (Wiener et al., 1965). On the combined basis of Gesell and IQ tests, 16 percent of the undersized and 6 percent of the full-sized children were rated below the low average level among whites, and 32 and 21 percent among blacks. The racial difference varied with examiner, however, so it is difficult to interpret (Harper et al., 1959).

The examination at ages 6–7 years using Stanford-Binet Form L tests showed that intellectual deficit continued on the average for the low-birth-weight children after associated factors of race, sex, social class, and maternal attitudes were controlled (Wiener et al., 1965). The results of the findings at 6–7 years, combined with the index of neurological damage obtained on the same individuals at 40 weeks of age, strongly suggest that low birth weight leads to mental deficit by way of intervening neurological factors. The following partial correlations (r_p) were obtained for IQ, birth weight, and three other variables. Each represents the relationship of the given variable to IQ with the other three variables held statistically constant:

	r_p	p
Birth weight	0.10	<0.01
Maternal attitudes	0.18	<0.001
Socioeconomic class	0.32	<0.001
Race	0.18	<0.001

The multiple correlation between IQ and the above four variables was 0.57 in this sample.

Wiener (1968) reports a Pearsonian r of 0.14 between IQ and birth weight based on Primary Mental Ability and Kuhlman-Anderson tests administered in the first and second grades by the Baltimore City Public School System on 582 children being followed in the long-term study.

WISC tests were given to the Baltimore children at ages 8–10 years (Wiener et al., 1968). The scores of 157 white and 260 black prematures and 167 white and 238 black controls differed in favor of the full-sized group by about 5 points on Full Scale WISC scores after controlling for sex and social class.

The final round of evaluation, carried out using measures of academic achievement when the children were 12–13 years old, suggests a lasting average intellectual deficit in children with low birth weight (Wiener, 1968).

Discussion: Low Birth Weight

Thus we have some grounds for believing that a mother's nutrition during pregnancy may affect her child's birth weight, as well as evidence for a modest association between birth weight and later measured intelligence. It should, however, be noted that the latter is from a sample heavily weighted with premature births, and hence may exaggerate the relationship to be expected in the total population.

Against this positive evidence of an association between maternal undernutrition and child's intelligence, we must set the negative evidence from the Dutch World War II famine study. In this study, described in more detail in Appendix N, no relationship was found between severe nutritional deprivation during pregnancy and the intelligence of the offspring measured at age 19 years, although there was an effect on birth weight. It may be that the years of previous good nutrition of these Dutch women provided a nutritional reserve on which the developing fetal brain could draw, or it may be that any effect of prenatal nutrition on intelligence is transient, or it may be that some qualitative, rather than quantitative, feature of the diet is what is critical for normal fetal brain development. Only further research can answer such questions. In any case it is clear that there are many important differences between the Dutch famine and populations in which undernutrition may have been chronic for generations.

NUTRITIONAL STATUS OF AMERICAN RACIAL-ETHNIC GROUPS

Despite the lack of adequate cross-racial nutritional surveys on a nationwide basis, and especially data on nutrition during periods critical for brain development in the child, that is, during gestation, nursing, and preschool years, it is widely accepted by nutritional authorities that on the average American blacks from conception on suffer significantly more undernutrition than American whites.

Mayer (1965) reports that various recent surveys indicate the following percentages of families in both urban and rural areas of the South have diets of the indicated nutritional quality:

	Black	White
Obviously inadequate	60	25
Probably inadequate	15	45
Obviously adequate	10	20
Unspecified adequacy	15	10

According to Mayer (1965, p. A112):

> The Negro diets are characterized by monotony, a restricted choice of foods, and a low intake of protective elements. While the caloric requirements are generally covered for all members of the family, the protein intake in children tends to be only borderline. At least 25 percent and perhaps as many as 35 percent of Southern Negroes have a low calcium intake. Likewise the iron intake of perhaps one-third or more is low. The intakes of thiamine, riboflavin and nicotinic acid are low in 12 to 15 percent of the population, vitamin A requirements are not adequately covered by the diets of perhaps as many as 50 percent, and vitamin C intake is inadequate for much of the population, particularly in urban areas, for several months each year.

Further, the relatively poor nutrition of American blacks has prevailed for decades. Myrdal used survey data of the late 1930s and early 40s (see Table 8.4) to conclude: *"The majority of the Negro population suffers from severe malnutrition. This is true at least about the South. Conditions may be somewhat better in the North, for which we do not have any adequate information"* (Myrdal, 1944, p. 375). Myrdal's table suggests that the deficiency was mainly economic: within a given expenditure level and community type, black and white nutrition was generally comparable.

There is evidence that the nutrition of blacks can sometimes be improved greatly even without other wide-scale social or economic change simply by providing supplementary food. Zee and co-workers (1970) and Zee and Kafatos (1973) found that a USDA supplementary food program after a three-year period significantly elevated

TABLE 8.4. *Percentage of black and white families in the Southeast whose diets provide less than optimum requirements of specified nutrients: 1936–1937.*

Families by Weekly Food Value per Food-expenditure-unit	No. of Families in Sample	Percentage of Families Deficient in								
		Cal-ories	Pro-tein	Phos-phorus	Cal-cium	Iron	Vitamin A	Thiamin	Ascorbic Acid	Ribo-flavin
$0.69–$1.37										
Village families, Negro	84	48	70	66	93	58	67	68	96	94
Farm families, Negro[a]	109	50	57	24	60	22	52	47	96	79
$1.38–$2.07										
City families, Negro[b]	54	16	41	45	33	21	24	44	67	91
Village families, Negro	53	17	26	25	15	24	63	43	73	79
Village families, White	69	22	49	30	73	39	68	61	69	74
Farm families, Negro[a]	89	7	14	9	34	9	23	30	81	48
Farm families, White[c]	133	16	4	2	23	4	44	17	79	38

Source: From Myrdal, 1944, p. 1290; after U.S. Department of Agriculture, Bureau of Home Economics, *Consumer Purchases Study, Farm Series, Family Food Consumption and Dietary Levels, Five Regions,* Miscellaneous Publication No. 405 (1941), pp. 52–61 and 103; and *Urban and Village Series, Family Food Consumption and Dietary Levels, Five Regions,* Miscellaneous Publication No. 452 (1941), pp. 209–229.

Note: The following requirements were used for this tabulation: energy value, 3000 cal; protein, 67 g; phosphorus, 1.32 g; calcium, 0.68 g; iron, 12 mg; vitamin A, 6000 I.U.; thiamin, 1.5 mg; ascorbic acid, 75 mg; riboflavin, 1.8 mg. These requirements refer to the daily needs of a moderately active full-grown man. Needs of women and younger persons may be different from these—many are lower, but some higher. This complication is taken care of by computing the consumption per nutrition unit, whereby the needs of a full-grown man are used as a unit. The number of food expediture units are computed in a similar way (U.S. Department of Agriculture, Miscellaneous Publication No. 452, op. cit., pp. 251–252). Groups having less than 50 representatives in the sample are excluded from the table.

[a] Owners, tenants, and croppers.

[b] Atlanta, Georgia; Mobile, Alabama; Columbia, South Carolina.

[c] Owners and tenants, except croppers.

the nutritional status of 250 impoverished preschool blacks from a South Memphis, Tennessee, community in a number of variables that are associated with normal function of the central nervous system. For example, the incidence of anemia decreased from 25 to 11 percent ($p < 0.01$), and the percentage of low plasma vitamin A levels fell from 44 to 26 percent ($p < 0.01$).

The Ten-State Nutrition Survey

The Ten-State Nutrition Survey 1968–1970 (U.S. Department of Health, Education, and Welfare, 1972) is the largest nutrition survey ever conducted in the United States. The survey was carried out in Washington, California, Texas, Louisiana, South Carolina, Kentucky, West Virginia, Michigan, Massachusetts, and New York, including a separate survey of New York City. Within each state families were selected into the primary survey sample from the enumeration districts with the lowest quartile average income according to the 1960 Census. Because the income characteristics of some of the districts had changed since 1960, some middle- and high-income families were included in the primary sample.

Almost 30,000 families were identified in the initial survey; of these 79.6 percent were interviewed and a total of 40,847 persons (47.3 percent of those interviewed) attended the survey clinic for a nutritional examination.

There was a heavy representation of children in the group that received the detailed clinical evaluation, more than 50 percent of the series were 16 years of age or less, 30 percent were from 17 to 44, and 17 percent were 45 years of age or older.

Forty-six percent of those attending the clinic were white, 32.2 percent black, 12.2 percent Spanish American, 1.3 percent Oriental, 1.1 percent American Indian, and 1.3 percent of unknown ethnic group. The Spanish American group included two rather different populations: Puerto Ricans, mostly from New York City, and Mexican Americans from Texas and California. Because in urban areas adequate income is essential to purchase adequate food, the income level of each family was expressed by the Poverty Income Ratio (PIR) of Orshansky (1968) according to the criteria listed in Table 8.5. A family with a PIR less than 1.0 are living "below poverty," one with a PIR of 1.0 at the poverty line, and those with a PIR greater than 1.0 are living above the poverty level. For example, a nonfarm

TABLE 8.5.   *Weighted average of poverty criteria for families of different communities, by household size, sex of head, and farm or nonfarm residence, March 1967.*

| | Weighted Average of Incomes at Poverty Level | | | |
| | Nonfarm | | Farm | |
Number of Family Members	Male Head	Female Head	Male Head	Female Head
1 Member	$1710	$1595	$1180	$1110
Head under age 65	1760	1625	1230	1140
Head age 65+	1580	1560	1105	1090
2 Members	2130	2055	1480	1400
Head under age 65	2200	2105	1540	1465
Head age 65+	1975	1955	1380	1370
3 Members	2610	2515	1820	1725
4 Members	3335	3320	2345	2320
5 Members	3930	3895	2755	2775
6 Members	4410	4395	3090	3075
7+ Members	5440	5310	3795	3760

Source: Orshansky M.: The Shape of Poverty in 1966. Social Security Bulletin, March 1968.

four member family with a male head of household having an income of $3335 would have a PIR of 1.0 and a family with the same characteristics but an income of $2000 would have a PIR value of $2000/$3335 = 0.60.

Since farm families made up only 7.2 percent of the total clinic population, separate urban-rural analyses were generally not reported; however, farm families were assigned appropriate PIRs.

The mean PIR for all families for whom income data were available was 1.89 and the median was 1.39. Five states with a median PIR below 1.39 were designated as "low-income-ratio states": South Caroline, Louisiana, Texas, Kentucky, and West Virginia. The remaining five states with a median PIR equal to or greater than 1.39 were called "high-income-ratio states": Michigan, California, Washington, Massachusetts, and New York State including New York City. The

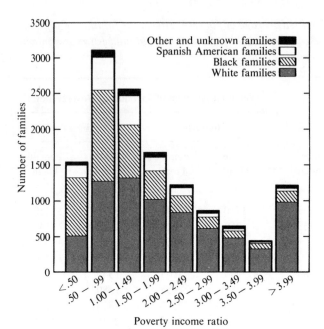

FIGURE 8.3
*Distribution of families by ethnic group and poverty income ratio group
for low and high income ratio states. See text for explanation. (From
Ten-State Nutrition Survey 1968–1970, 1972.)*

distribution of families by ethnic group and poverty income ratio is
shown in Figure 8.3.

The clinical evaluation included a medical history, physical examination, anthropometric measurements, X-ray examination of the
wrist, dental examination, and collection of blood for hemoglobin
and hematocrit determinations. Selected subgroups received more
detailed biochemical and dietary evaluations. Among these subgroups
were high-risk ones such as infants and young children, adolescents,
pregnant or lactating women, and persons over 60 years of age.

The sampling procedure is believed to have yielded a representative
sample of low-income families, but the population studied was not
representative of the entire population within the nation or within
any of the states sampled, and the survey findings cannot be extrap-
olated to the overall population of states from which the samples
were drawn. Table 8.6 illustrates the bias of the survey. In the low-
income-ratio states blacks constituted 61.7 percent of those receiving

TABLE 8.6. *Percentage distribution by ethnic group of persons attending TSNS clinics and of state populations in 1970.*

Population	Low-income-ratio States		High-income-ratio States	
	White	Black	White	Black
TSNS Clinic	38.3	61.7	74.5	25.5
1970 Census	84.0	15.9	91.3	8.6

Source: *Ten-State Nutrition Survey 1968-1970*, 1972, Tables 2A, 2B, Appendix, pp. II–27–28.

full clinical evaluation, but blacks constituted only 15.9 percent of the 1970 Census population in the five low-income-ratio states. Blacks were also overrepresented and whites underrepresented in the high-income-ratio states. Since only whites from lower-income areas were sampled, it is likely that the results of the survey underestimate the differences in nutritional level between blacks and whites on a national scale. It should also be emphasized that the Ten-State Nutrition Survey studied only a dozen or so of the nearly 40 nutrients known to be essential for good health, and presumably for optimal behavioral performance.

The dietary intake information in the TSNS was based on subjects' recall of all foods and beverages they had consumed during the preceding 24 hours. Discrepancies with the biochemical findings suggest that there was considerable overreporting of nutritional intake, especially of milk. The mean dietary intakes reported in the TSNS for infants and children from birth to 36 months were sufficient to meet the survey standards for all of the nutrients studied except iron. Yet the biochemical and anthropometric findings suggest that in black children of this age intake of a number of essential nutrients was less than adequate.

The complex problems of nutritional surveys in general are reviewed by Marr (1971) and the inadequacies of available information on childhood malnutrition in the United States is documented by Davis, Gershoff, and Gamble (1969) and by Gershoff (1971).

In order to provide a compact numerical summary of the TSNS findings, we have assigned arbitrary scores to reflect the extent of nutritional deficiencies in three racial-ethnic groups for seven nu-

TABLE 8.7. *Extent of relative nutritional deficiency for seven nutrients.*

Nutrient	Black	Spanish	White
Iron	24	16	16
Protein	21	5	0
Vitamin A	5	24	4
Vitamin C	5	2	4
Riboflavin	16	4	4
Thiamine	2	0	2
Iodine	0	0	0
Totals	73	51	30

Source: Based on data from *Ten-State Nutrition Survey 1968-1970*, 1972.

Note: The seriousness of nutritional problems is scored and summed for eight age and sex categories (0–5 years M and F, 6–9 M and F, 10–16 M, 10–16 F, 17–59 M, 17–59 F, 60 + M, and 60 + F): Relatively marked problem = 3, medium = 2, low = 1, minimal = 0. Maximum possible score for a given nutrient is 24, maximum total is 168.

trients known to be essential for normal development and function of the brain and nervous system. The results are given in Table 8.7. Although there is some variation for different nutrients, on the average blacks are significantly more malnourished than whites, and Spanish Americans are intermediate between the other two ethnic groups.

Protein supply is critical to the development of the brain of the fetus, especially during the middle and last trimesters of pregnancy. Serum albumin levels in the mother provide one index of protein consumption. The TSNS found the percentage of deficient or low serum albumin values (i.e., values less than 3.50 g/100 ml) to be 51.3 in Spanish American, 56.2 in white, and 73.9 in black pregnant women (Table 8.8). Interestingly, the percentages of deficiency were slightly higher in the high-income-ratio states, suggesting that income is not the only factor in good nutrition.

Protein supply is also critical to the later division of glial cells in the brain and to the differentiation and interconnection of axons and dendrites during the first two or more postnatal years. Table 8.9 shows young black and Spanish American children have a higher frequency than whites of low serum protein values during the first six

TABLE 8.8.   *Serum-albumin deficiency (< 3.50 g/ml) in pregnant women of various racial-ethnic and income groups.*

Income Ratio	White		Black		Spanish	
	No.	% of Sample	No.	% of Sample	No.	% of Sample
Low	20	50.0	66	63.6	28	46.4
High	190	56.8	95	81.8	48	54.2
Totals	210	56.2	161	73.9	76	51.3

Source: *Ten-State Nutrition Survey 1968-1970*, 1972.

TABLE 8.9.   *Percentage of children having low serum protein values, in five low-income-ratio states.*

Age and Sex	White	Black	Spanish
< 6 M	0.8	4.1	8.1
< 6 F	0.0	3.7	2.3
6–12 M	1.7	3.9	4.1
6–12 F	2.1	3.7	5.0
13–16 M	3.0	3.6	2.6
13–16 F	2.4	3.5	6.2

Source: *Ten-State Nutrition Survey 1968–1970*, 1972.

years of life, and continuing throughout the period when the brain is developing to adult size.

Later we will return to differential findings between racial-ethnic groups in blood levels of ascorbic acid, and in head circumference and obesity.

Local Studies of Malnutrition

A number of local studies also report significantly higher malnutrition rates for blacks. In an intensive study of the health of 5170 black school children from 6 to 14 years of age in Atlanta, Georgia, Sterling

(1928) found that 21.4 percent of boys and 19.0 percent of girls had poor or very poor nutritional status. Poor nutrition was evenly distributed through the age groups. At least two bony evidences of rickets were observed in 13 percent of the children.

Browning and Northcutt (1961) report the results of a nutritional survey made by the Florida State Board of Health during the period July 1956 to July 1961 on 439 members of migrant and 423 members of nonmigrant black families doing farm work in the vicinity of Belle Glade, Florida. Belle Glade is a city of 11,000 located on the southeastern shore of Lake Okeechobee in Palm Beach County. Some 7,500–10,000 migrant workers do seasonal agricultural work in this vicinity each year. They are a part of the estimated 50,000 black workers in the migratory farm force known as the "Atlantic Coast Migrant Stream." Some 6,000–8,000 blacks are permanent residents in the area, most of whom do farm labor.

Although detailed medical examinations for evaluation of nutritional status were not performed, general physical examinations showed that 97 of the 439 migrant (21.1 percent) and 57 of the 423 nonmigrant (13.5 percent) black patients examined in the Migrant Project Family Clinic had a nutritional abnormality. Several children showed evidence of scurvy, rickets, nutritional anemias, or marasmus, and one case of kwashiorkor was found.

There is local variation. Some local surveys have found black children to be better nourished than whites in the same community. In a survey in which some 900 "suburban" school children in Georgia were examined medically more carefully than in the usual school examination, Bivings (1927) found only 6 percent of 266 blacks were malnourished, as defined by clinical appearance and being at least 10 pounds underweight, while 27 percent of 111 white children from families of similar economic level, and 25 percent of the total white sample of 648 children were malnourished. This finding for one group of semirural black school children in Georgia was in marked contrast to Bivings's experience over several years in the black clinics of Atlanta where signs of malnutrition and rickets were common.

Despite some local variation, over all the evidence is substantial that U.S. blacks and Spanish Americans are, on the average, considerably less well nourished than U.S. whites. American Indians may be even worse off nutritionally (e.g., Moore et al., 1972).

In a five-year study conducted during 1963–1967 at the Public Health Service Indian Hospital in Tuba City, Arizona, 4355 Navajo children under 5 years of age were admitted to the pediatric service. Of these 616 (14.14 percent) received diagnoses of malnutrition, including 15 (0.34 percent) with kwashiorkor and 29 (0.66 percent) with marasmus, a total of 44 cases (1.01 percent) of severe malnutrition. Fourteen of the children with marasmus and two of those with kwashiorkor died from the diseases (Van Duzen, Carter, Secondi, and Federspiel, 1969).

NUTRITION AND
BLACK-WHITE IQ DIFFERENCES

What is the evidence that better nutrition might increase IQ? Would the black-white racial difference in mean IQ scores disappear if blacks were as well nourished as whites?

The best evidence needed to answer these questions is lacking, and the relevant, usable information is scanty, and of unknown or dubious reliability. The best evidence would come from carefully designed prospective studies in which a broad spectrum of intelligence tests and tests of nutritional status were given to ample population samples of blacks and whites, with and without, and before and after nutritional supplementation (see Pollitt, 1969; Kaplan, 1972; and Warren, 1973, for suggestions on the design of such studies).

There are a few U.S. studies that report substantial increases in measured IQ following nutritional improvement. In a retrospective study Poull (1938) found an average increase of 10.0 IQ points in a group of 41 mentally retarded New York City children who were seriously malnourished at the time of a first intelligence test at ages 2 to 7 years and well nourished at the time of a second test after intervals from 8 months to 7 years. The rise in IQ scores was higher in the children treated for malnutrition at earlier ages, up 13.0 points in 11 two-year-olds and up 14.4 points in 15 three-year-olds. Kugelmass, Poull, and Samuel (1944) reported on an additional group of 50 malnourished New York children in the normal intelligence range. These children showed an even larger increase in tested IQ following nutritional remediation, averaging 18 IQ points. Few details are reported. Control groups for both samples, well nourished at both the first and second testings, showed essentially no average IQ gain between testings.

Harrell (1947), in a well designed and controlled study with an orphanage population, found small IQ improvements for an experimental group given a 2 mg/day thiamine supplement for a year, compared to a matched control group given a placebo. The children were of somewhat below-average intelligence (mean IQ at pretest 91.6) but probably not especially ill-nourished. The interpretation of Harrell's results is made problematical by the second year of the study, in which half the experimental group was switched to the placebo, and vice versa. The group switched from thiamine to placebo showed just as much improvement during the second year as the group switched from placebo to thiamine, on the two intelligence tests used. By contrast, a measure of visual acuity responded in a much more straightforward way to the supplementation, showing improvement in the experimental group during the first year and the expected crossover of results during the second.

A third study, by Kubala and Katz (1960), discussed in more detail in Appendix O, reported an increase of mean IQ scores of 3.5 points in a generally well nourished school population following 6 months during which the children were given supplemental orange juice.

Finally, Harrell, Woodyard, and Gates (1956) reported that IQs were relatively higher by 5–8 points among the children of 111 welfare mothers (mostly black) resident in Norfolk, Virginia, who received a daily dietary supplement of 2 mg thiamine, 4 mg riboflavin, 20 mg niacinamide, and 15 mg iron for an average of 134 days during pregnancy. The control group consisted of 133 mothers attending the same maternity clinic who received a nutritionally inert placebo during pregnancy. At 3 years of age the mean IQ of children from supplemented mothers was 103.4 and that of the controls 98.4. Neither set of children in this generally undernourished population received dietary supplements after birth. At age four the treated children had a mean IQ score of 101.7 and the untreated controls 93.6. A parallel study, carried out with poor white mothers in the Kentucky mountains, yielded no significant effect on the offsprings' IQs.

Thus there is some evidence from U.S. subpopulations to suggest that improved nutrition may sometimes be associated with rises in IQ scores. Can we predict, from knowledge of black-white differences on one or more variables associated with nutritional status, how much quantitative decrease in black-white IQ differences might be anticipated from improvement in nutrition? In Appendix O we attempt such predictions for four variables considered on the basis of one or more investigations to relate nutritional status to intelligence test scores. The four indicator variables are: obesity, blood level of ascorbic acid, birth weight, and head circumference for a given age. We place almost no confidence on the reliability of obesity as an indicator, little on that of ascorbic acid level, and suggest caution in interpretation of the evidence on birth weight and head circumference. In all four cases, evidence on the indicator variables comes from populations different from the one in which we wish to apply them. However, in Appendix O we consider all four, and the predictions range from just slightly in the wrong direction (for obesity in males) to about 3 or 4 IQ points decrease in black-white difference (for ascorbic acid in blacks from low income states), with 1 or 2 IQ points being typical. Because these variables are presumably correlated with one another and with other nonnutritional variables related to intelligence, it could not be confidently predicted that there would be *large* effects on black-white IQ differences in the U.S. population as a whole as a result of manipulating variables like these, singly or in combination. Effects of a few IQ points remain, however, a reasonable possibility.

Summary and Discussion:
Nutrition and Intelligence

To what extent can the observed lower average scores on intelligence tests made by blacks and Spanish Americans compared with those of whites be explained by the observed higher prevalence of malnutrition among blacks and Spanish Americans? This question raises many others examined in this chapter. First, what is the status of nutrition as a biological science in general?

We have emphasized that the most intensive current nutritional surveys, including the excellent Ten-State Nutrition Survey, are limited to the study of only a few of the nearly forty nutrients known to be essential for proper development. The quantitative requirements of several essential nutrients are unknown and those for many of the essential nutrients little known. An agreed-on standard is not available for the classification of "deficient" values of serum albumin nor serum protein from birth to age 16 years—yet available protein in this period is clearly critical to the development of intelligent behavior. Authorities differ by a factor of nine on the optimal daily intake of ascorbic acid—yet in one study mean IQ rose about 3.5 points as the ascorbic-acid concentration in the blood plasma was increased over a period of six months from about 1.00 to 1.50 mg/100 ml of

plasma. We simply do not know the possible behavioral correlates
of several poorly studied nutrients including zinc, magnesium, and
vitamin E, not to mention molybdenum or selenium. Because there
is considerable ethnic, economic, regional, and rural-urban variation
in the kinds and amounts of foods consumed, the average information
available from current surveys on the qualitative and quantitative
distribution of essential nutrients is inadequate—and we cannot
even know at present just how inadequate it is. Certainly, current
field methodology is not adequate to monitor the nutritional status
for all, or even most, essential nutrients in the major subdivisions of
any population including the United States.

Yet we do know for certain that total calories, protein calories, iron,
iodine, vitamin A, vitamin C, riboflavin, and thiamine (to keep the
list short) are essential for good health and normal intellectual performance and we do have some evidence concerning the distribution
of these essential nutrients in the diets of black, Spanish, and white
Americans.

Every broad indicator of nutritional status in the two large surveys
of 1936–1937 and 1968–1970, whether estimates of dietary intake,
biochemical values, weight-height ratio, or estimates of relative brain
size for stature, show blacks on the average are significantly more
malnourished than whites, and that Spanish Americans in this respect are intermediate between the other two ethnic groups.

Protein supply is critical to the development of the brain of the
fetus, especially during the last trimester of pregnancy. The TSNS
found that the percentages of deficient or low serum albumin values
in pregnant women were 51.3 among Spanish Americans, 56.2 among
whites, and 73.9 among blacks.

The percentages of deficient or low hemoglobin values were 15.6
among whites, 20.6 among Spanish Americans, and 37.4 among
blacks. The prevalence of low values for vitamins A, C, riboflavin,
and thiamine were consistently higher among blacks. The iodine
levels for blacks were slightly lower than for whites, who had values
a little lower than the Spanish Americans.

There were three times as many blacks and Spanish Americans
having two or more deficient or low biochemical values as whites.

Thus, the evidence is ample and consistent that on the average
American blacks from conception on are significantly more malnourished than American whites. However, the rate of *severe* mal-

nutrition (marasmus and kwashiorkor) is low in all ethnic groups in America.

What is the evidence that better nutrition will increase IQ? There is evidence from several U.S. studies that IQ test scores sometimes rise following nutritional improvement, although we know of no consistently replicated evidence of intellectual improvement following supplementation of moderately deficient levels of specific nutrients in any U.S. group. There is theoretical disagreement and empirical uncertainty about whether and when the effects upon intellectual performance of malnutrition early in life can be reversed by subsequent nutritional improvement. There is striking evidence from outside the United States (the Dutch wartime famine) that six months of nutritional deprivation during pregnancy, in a previously and subsequently well nourished population, may have no detectable effects on the IQs of offspring measured at maturity.

We considered four specific variables—head circumference, birth weight, ascorbic acid level, and obesity—that permit some sort of tentative prediction of black-white IQ differences under improved nutrition. None of the four variables offers much direct promise for modifying existing IQ differences between U.S. blacks and whites, although the possibility of some modest effects is not excluded, particularly with ascorbic acid in low-income blacks.

We conclude that the nutritional status of U.S. blacks and Spanish Americans is significantly poorer on the average than that of whites. There is at least some evidence that better nutrition may sometimes be associated with better scores on IQ tests. We think there are more compelling reasons for improving the nutritional status of U.S. minorities than the chance that this might boost their average IQs a few points. But it seems quite clear that further investigation of the effects of nutrition on intelligence-test performance remains very much in order.

PART III

CONCLUSIONS AND IMPLICATIONS

CHAPTER 9

Summary of the Empirical Findings

BEFORE PROCEEDING TO A DISCUSSION of broader social, political, and scientific implications, it may be useful to summarize briefly some of the empirical generalizations that appear to us to emerge from the studies we have reviewed in the preceding chapters.

The first two generalizations have to do with the quality of the evidence rather than with its substance.

1. The design, execution, and reporting of studies concerned with racial-ethnic differences in intelligence often leave much to be desired. The conclusions that we have attempted to draw from these data are necessarily limited by this fact.

2. We have been concerned privately by the number of instances in which the political and social preferences of the investigators apparently have grossly biased their interpretation of data. Such dis-

tortions appear to be at least as prevalent at environmentalist as at hereditarian extremes. While we have preferred in this book to report findings directly rather than their authors' interpretations of them, we must face the possibility that the influence of the investigators' preconceptions may in some instances have crept in earlier in the scientific process, and affected the gathering of the data as well. Consequently, any evidence deriving from a single unreplicated study must be viewed with more than the normal caution stemming from statistical considerations.

The next three generalizations have to do with the heritability of measured intelligence.

3. Within populations of European origin, both the genotype and the environment demonstrably influence IQ, the former tending under present conditions to account for more of the individual variation in IQ than does the latter. It is quite possible that part of the variation attributed to the genotype may in fact be the result of gene-environment correlation, and that part of the variation attributed to the environment may in fact be the result of gene-environment interaction, but there is little direct evidence that these factors play a large quantitative role.

4. Estimates of the heritability of intelligence that are based on within-family data (e.g., twin comparisons) tend to be of comparable size in U.S. black and white samples. Many of these estimates tend to be somewhat lower than the heritability estimates for IQ commonly reported in the literature; this is probably due in part to measurement limitations and restricted range in the samples in the studies we have discussed.

5. Estimates of the heritability of intelligence that are based on between-family data (e.g., sibling correlations) are less consistent, sometimes being approximately the same in both groups, but sometimes being appreciably lower in black than in white samples. When the heritabilities for blacks are lower, this tends to be in conjunction with a lesser overall variance of IQ among the blacks, suggesting that a decrease in between-family differences of some kind is involved in these cases.

The following five conclusions derive from studies of racial mixture. Except for the first, they are each based on very limited data, with all the hazards this implies.

6. The correlation in U.S. black populations between IQ and lightness of skin color or similar anthropometric indices of European

admixture has traditionally been found to be positive, but low (typical correlation coefficients are about .15). Such correlations may easily be reconciled with either genetic or environmental interpretations.

7. There was negligible association in two recent small U.S. black samples between intellectual ability and blood-group genes likely to be of European origin. This is compatible with an environmental interpretation of the between-group IQ difference, or with there having been a number of generations since the racial crosses, or both.

8. A study of black children with very high IQs did not find increased European admixture. If replicable, this would argue fairly strongly against an average difference in the genetic potential for intelligence of the African and European ancestors of present-day U.S. blacks. This could in turn either reflect an absence of average difference in IQ-relevant genes between the U.S. slave and white populations, or a special selection of whites who mated with blacks. An alternative possibility would be reproductive effects among hybrid offspring that acted adversely against intelligence.

9. Offspring of black-white pairs in which the mother was white had higher IQs than those from black-white pairs in which the mother was black. This suggests a maternal environmental effect (pre- or postnatal), rather than a genetic effect. The alternative possibility of a difference in average parental intelligence in the two types of matings was, however, not entirely excluded.

10. A study of the offspring of occupation forces in Germany after World War II found no overall IQ differences between mixed-race and white children; similar results were reported from a study of children in residential nurseries in Great Britain. Information on the parents' IQs was not available in either study.

The next seven generalizations have to with comparisons among socioeconomic and racial-ethnic groups, and changes over time involving these.

11. Racial-ethnic differences and socioeconomic differences, while correlated, are sufficiently distinct to demand separate treatment. This is supported empirically. It is also indicated on theoretical grounds, since the models underlying possible genetic effects are quite different in the two cases, in the one emphasizing natural selection and genetic drift, in the other, assortative mating and social mobility.

12. IQ scores have generally the same socioeconomic correlates in U.S. minority groups as in the majority group. The evidence does not justify a strong assertion that the correlations are of exactly equal

magnitude in the various groups, but at any rate large and consistent differences are not apparent (despite differences of this character among the group averages on both kinds of variables).

13. Social changes can affect (and have affected) average levels of IQ-test performance in various U.S. subpopulations, and perhaps among U.S. adults as a whole, but average racial-ethnic group differences seem not to have been particularly responsive to such environmentally induced changes.

14. Racial-ethnic group differences (and social-class differences) are minimal on tests purporting to measure intellectual capacities during the first year or two of life, but become substantial by age 3 or 4. (It is not clear to what extent this may simply be a function of the difference in what the tests measure at these ages.) Most studies suggest that relative to individual differences group differences remain fairly constant during the school years. (This implies that IQ differences, standard score differences, etc., will stay about the same, although absolute grade level differences will increase.)

15. Stimulating environments can sometimes have substantial effects on the measured IQs of young children. It is not yet clear what environmental changes are effective, nor how lasting the resulting IQ changes may be. It is clear that the gains have not endured in some studies, but the returns are by no means all in.

16. Differences in patterns or profiles of ability between different U.S. racial-ethnic groups have some support in the data, although study-to-study discrepancies are often considerable. The most often supported generalizations are: relatively stronger verbal than nonverbal performance among U.S. blacks, high verbal and numerical performance in Jewish groups, relatively stronger quantitative than verbal performance among groups of Oriental ancestry. There is some evidence that these differences are fairly independent of socioeconomic status, but it is not yet clear whether other cultural factors or genetic factors are responsible.

17. The majority of the variation in either patterns or levels of ability lies *within* U.S. racial-ethnic and socioeconomic groups, not between them. Race and social class are not very powerful predictors of an individual's performance on tests of intellectual abilities. Much of this evidence comes from studies of children. Predictions from social status to ability level should be somewhat stronger for adults, but individual differences, not group differences, would still account for the largest portion of the variation.

The final three generalizations are concerned with nutrition.

18. There is good evidence that malnutrition in prenatal and early life, if sufficiently severe, can have adverse effects on brain and cognitive development.

19. There is substantial and consistent evidence that, on the average, U.S. blacks are less well nourished than U.S. whites. Nutritional levels for Spanish Americans are usually found to be intermediate between those for blacks and whites. However, very severe malnutrition (marasmus or kwashiorkor) is uncommon in any U.S. ethnic group.

20. Some studies suggest that moderate nutritional deficiencies in the pregnant mother or in the young child can lead to lowered levels of performance on IQ tests. Other studies, however, fail to find much evidence supporting such a relationship. Thus it remains a possibility, although by no means a certainty, that improvement of the nutrition of U.S. minorities, which is presumably desirable on other grounds, might as a byproduct result in some decrease in existing group differences in IQ-test performance.

In the concluding chapter of this book we will examine what seem to us to be some of the more significant scientific and social implications of these findings, and some of the kinds of further research that might profitably be conducted.

CHAPTER 10

Implications
and Conclusions

IN THIS FINAL CHAPTER, WE WILL FIRST CONFRONT the central question: Considering the theory and empirical findings we have reviewed in the preceding chapters, what conclusions are justified concerning the sources of observed differences in average IQ score among U.S. racial-ethnic groups? Can we say anything about the importance of cultural bias in the tests, environmental influences on intellectual development, and genetic differences between the groups? Next we will consider the question: If genetic factors should contribute (in some measure) to group differences in intellectual performance, what practical implications, if any, would this have for society? We will wish to examine this question regardless of whether there seems to be at present any good evidence for such genetic differences. After all, a negative judgment on this point could be mistaken, or could be

refuted tomorrow by new and unexpected evidence, and it is important to examine what the consequences of such future findings might
be. Finally, we will look at the kinds of relevant research that we feel
might be pursued most profitably, taking into account potential
scientific contribution, social importance, and social acceptability.

WHAT CONCLUSIONS ARE JUSTIFIED?

In Part I of this book we discussed a variety of theoretical questions
relating to the origin and extent of biological racial differences, to
intelligence and its measurement, and to the estimation of heritability.
In Part II we reviewed a variety of evidence that bears on the interpretation of differences in intellectual performance among different
U.S. racial-ethnic groups. The major empirical findings were summarized in Chapter 9. While we will not recapitulate these findings in
detail here, we will remind the reader that they include: studies of
heritability, which suggest that there is a substantial genetic component to variation in IQ within both black and white populations;
studies of racial mixture, which are consistent with either moderate
hereditarian or environmentalist interpretations of the difference between U.S. blacks and whites, but perhaps are more easily accommodated in an environmentalist framework; and studies suggesting
that racial-ethnic differences in levels and patterns of abilities are distinct from socioeconomic differences, and seem fairly stable in the face
of general environmentally induced performance changes—an outcome consistent with a genetic interpretation but not necessarily excluding a subcultural one.

Given the empirical findings, and the theoretical arguments we have
discussed, what conclusions about racial-ethnic differences in performance on intellectual tests appear justified? It seems to us that
they include the following:

1. Observed average differences in the scores of members of different
U.S. racial-ethnic groups on intellectual-ability tests probably reflect
in part inadequacies and biases in the tests themselves, in part differences in environmental conditions among the groups, and in part
genetic differences among the groups. It should be emphasized that
these three factors are not necessarily independent, and may interact.

2. A rather wide range of positions concerning the relative weight
to be given these three factors can reasonably be taken on the basis of

current evidence, and a sensible person's position might well differ for different abilities, for different groups, and for different tests.

3. Regardless of the position taken on the relative importance of these three factors, it seems clear that the differences among individuals *within* racial-ethnic (and socioeconomic) groups greatly exceed in magnitude the average differences between such groups.

Let us emphasize that these conclusions are based on the conditions that have existed in the United States in the recent past. None of them precludes the possibility that changes in these conditions could alter these relationships for future populations. It should also be noted that the probable existence of relevant environmental differences, genetic differences, and psychometric biases does not imply that they must always be in the same direction as the observed between-group differences.

On the whole, these are rather limited conclusions. It does not appear to us, however, that the state of the scientific evidence at the present time justifies stronger ones.

SOCIAL AND PUBLIC-POLICY
IMPLICATIONS OF GENETIC DIFFERENCES

We will preface our discussion by asserting unequivocally that *no* public-policy implications follow from scientific conclusions alone, no matter how firm the empirical findings may be. Public policy flows from facts *and values*. A particular set of facts concerning genetic differences between racial groups might lead, given different sets of values, to policy recommendations as disparate as total racial segregation, maximum encouragement of intermarriage, and simply ignoring the differences.

This, of course, does not imply that scientific facts are irrelevant to social policy. Given certain values or social goals, scientific facts can bear on the feasibility of alternative means of achieving the goals, the relative costs that may be incurred, the probable consequences, and the like.

Let us begin by stating three social goals that relate to the status of different subgroups of the U.S. population, and for which the issues of fact with which we have been concerned in this book may have some relevance. We believe these social goals would command assent among most Americans, although we recognize that individuals may differ considerably in the priority they would assign to these relative to other goals, and in the specific interpretations they might place on such phrases as "equal access" or "full opportunity."

1. Members of different U.S. racial-ethnic groups should not feel their group membership to be the occasion for feelings of humiliation, shame, and inferiority, but rather for dignity, self-respect, and pride.

2. Members of all such groups should have full opportunity for economic productivity and rewards, and for social and political participation.

3. Members of these groups should have equal access to general social benefits and services, including education, health care, and all forms of governmental assistance.

All three of these goals may be seen as deriving from a deeper and more fundamental goal: namely, that all individual Americans should feel the satisfaction of being full participants in a democratic and productive society. If there are members of U.S. racial-ethnic groups for which any of the three goals stated above are unsatisfied, achievement of this more fundamental goal thereby falls short.

Let us examine what the implications would be, for each of these three goals, if it were indeed true that there were differences among U.S. racial-ethnic groups in the distributions of one or more genes affecting intellectual development, which led to differences in average performance on tests of intellectual abilities. As we have indicated, such genetically based differences have not been firmly established, and thus we are pursuing a hypothetical question. But it is not a trivial question. We consider it quite likely that *some* genes affecting *some* aspects of intellectual performance differ appreciably in frequency between U.S. racial-ethnic groups—leaving open the issue of which groups, which aspects, and which direction of difference. Thus we consider it most unwise to base public policy on the assumption that no such genetic differences exist. If someone defends racial discrimination on the grounds of genetic differences between races, it is far more prudent to attack the logic of his argument than to accept the argument and deny any differences. The latter stance can leave one in an extremely awkward position if such a difference is subsequently shown to exist.

What implications, then, might it have, for each of the three stated social goals, *if* genetically based average ability differences were shown to exist between U.S. racial-ethnic groups?

Self-respect

First, as to the goal of feelings of dignity and worth. Undoubtedly, to label members of one racial-ethnic group as generally intellectually inferior to members of another would, given our present value system, represent a serious step backward in the attainment of this goal. Thus it would seem extremely important to establish the clear understanding as widely as possible, that the detection of a difference between racial groups in the frequency of some gene affecting intellectual performance would not in any way imply that individual members of the one group were by this fact rendered generally intellectually inferior to individual members of the other. This simply does not follow. Quite clearly, the people who have the gene in both groups remain equal. The people who don't have the gene in both groups remain equal. The individual person is not affected. It is simply the case that the proportions of the two kinds of persons differ somewhat between the two groups. (With a polygenic trait, it is less simple, but the principle still holds: the person's genotype with respect to intelligence remains what it is—and equivalent to any similar genotype —regardless of how someone may elect to classify individuals into racial or other groups.)

Concomitantly, it would seem advisable to continue to broaden and diversify the dimensions along which intellectual abilities are assessed. If group A should turn to out have a greater frequency than group B of a gene that favorably influences intellectual dimension X, it is quite likely that there is some other intellectual dimension Y which is favorably influenced by a gene that has greater frequency in group B than group A. The more that is known about the genetic basis of intellectual abilities, and the distribution of the relevant genes in different groups, the more likely it is that one will be able to demonstrate differences in patterning of abilities, rather than overall inferiority-superiority, as characteristic of group differences.

Economic Opportunity

Let us consider the implications for the goal of equality of job opportunity, if two U.S. racial-ethnic groups were discovered to differ in the frequency of some gene or genes related to intellectual ability. To a rational employer, in the vast majority of instances, this should make no difference at all. He is interested in whether the particular person he hires does or does not have the ability in question, not in whether it is relatively more or less common in the person's racial-ethnic group. In any event the employer has no particular reason to care whether a prospective employee's ability or lack thereof stems from his *genes*—as opposed to his prenatal nutrition, or his early experience—what matters is how it affects the job he can do now or his trainability for another one.

These same considerations apply in assessing the presence or extent of discrimination in employment. If different patterns of ability show different frequencies in different racial groups, one would expect that hiring purely on the basis of ability would result in an unequal representation of members of different racial-ethnic groups in jobs requiring different patterns of skills and talents. One would have to assess hiring bias against the background of the existing distribution of talent, rather than by the simple rule that discrimination exists unless a given racial-ethnic group constitutes a proportionate share of the persons in every occupation. But whether the different ability patterns derive from differences in genes or from enduring differences produced by early experience is not relevant to assessing discrimination in hiring. Where it *could* be relevant is in deciding what, in the long run, might be done to change the situation. Even here, the issue is by no means clear-cut, for there might well be instances in which the same compensatory educational strategy would be appropriate to deal with a genetic disability as with, say, a prenatal nutritional one. However, there are likely to be important differences in the kinds of preventative actions that might be undertaken in these two cases.

Even if genetic influences on ability patterns should differ between racial groups, one should not overestimate the likely impact of this on occupational patterns. The fact that much more genetic diversity exists within major racial groups than between them suggests that no matter how strong the associations may prove to be between the genes and the intellectual abilities—and this, of course, is a matter still under debate—one will never find a strict alignment of occupational and racial groups, a caste system, arising on purely biological grounds. Gene configurations adequate to support every level and pattern of performance presumably exist in persons of every racial-ethnic background. At most, the relative frequencies of such configurations may differ.

Of course, societies may sometimes elect other grounds than ability for hiring and promotion, for example, ethnic quotas or seniority. To the extent that such other criteria predominate, group differences in ability will have less impact on employment patterns, although not necessarily any less effect on the operation of the industries or institutions involved.

Equality of Access to Other Social Benefits

Much that is relevant to this topic has already been discussed in connection with the previous two goals, but it may be appropriate to comment briefly on education. Historically, intelligence tests were developed in order to predict school performance. They subsequently proved able to predict trainability in other contexts (e.g., industrial and military), and to predict occupational level and income —to a quite modest degree—independently of family background and education (Duncan, 1968). Still, it is in the educational realm that the tests have been most successful and most influential. One of the points made by Jensen in his 1969 *Harvard Educational Review* article, a point that subsequently rather got lost in the furor over racial differences, was that success in U.S. and other western schools tends to be based on a rather narrow portion of the total spectrum of intellectual abilities, and that it is largely by means of this narrow set of abilities that the traditional IQ test predicts so well.

There are risks, however, in proposing as a solution a pluralistic educational strategy. (This in fact was Jensen's proposal, although he probably invited trouble by the fact that in much of his discussion his plural was only two, and hence became mistakenly identified in many minds with black versus white education, or rich versus poor; Jensen's intent, presumably, was that persons from all social and racial groups whose Level I abilities functioned more effectively than their Level II abilities would receive an education designed to capitalize on this fact.) One risk in a pluralistic educational system is that certain educational paths will come to be regarded as "better" than others, in terms of some actual or imagined tendency to lead to higher-status positions within the society. Another risk is that the common educational experience that many have felt to be so crucial an element in a democracy, the core of shared knowledge, values, and experiences that permits easy intercommunication and effective cooperation among citizens in the pursuit of common goals, may be seriously attenuated or lost in an overly individualized educational system.

The risk in a uniform scheme of education, on the other hand, is that by forcing individuals of diverse capacities, interests, and talents into a common educational pattern, failure and frustration will accrue to many persons ill-suited to that mold, and there will be a consequent loss to society of their unique and idiosyncratic talents.

These are genuine dilemmas, but they would be just as acute if there were no racial-ethnic differences at all, since the issues arise primarily at the level of individual differences, and only secondarily at the level of subgroups within society. From a genetic viewpoint, and, we are persuaded, from an environmental one as well, most of the relevant variation in our society must be presumed to lie within racial-ethnic groups, not between them.

Past, Present, and Future

In considering the relationships between heredity, environment, and society, there is probably no dimension more crucial than the temporal one. Racial-ethnic group differences are no exception. Suppose that incontestable evidence were to be uncovered suddenly showing that existing U.S. racial-ethnic differences in performance on intellectual tests were almost wholly genetic in origin. Such a finding would mean only that under the environmental conditions prevailing at present and in the recent past this was the case. What would prevail in the future would depend, in part, on society's response to this finding. Nor in this instance need one be especially pessimistic concerning the possibility of change. A clear understanding of the developmental basis of a trait, regardless of whether the genes or the environment are now acting as primary determinants, is surely the most promising basis for effective intervention in that process. Indeed one could well argue that discovery of a genetic basis for a trait, if this were to lead to intervention possibilities at a nutritional or pharmacological level, might be much more strongly predictive of relevant environmental change than would the discovery that variation in the trait in the existing environment was largely a function of cultural or interpersonal variables.

Suppose, for example, that it were discovered that U.S. blacks have an elevated frequency of some gene that makes brains vulnerable to deficiencies in some trace dietary element. The remedy could conceivably be as simple and painless as commercially adding the trace element to table salt. Contrast this with the social effort that would be required to modify a purely environmental condition, if it were to be discovered that, say, the lack of a father in the home during child-rearing was the critical variable responsible for low IQ.

Again, we do not wish to give the impression there is a simple one-to-one connection between genetic causes of variation and biochemical treatments or between environmental causes of variation and sociological or educational therapies. It is perfectly conceivable that educational methods might be the most appropriate way of dealing with a genetic deficit, or that pharmacological treatment might be the method of choice for a problem of environmental origin. The point is simply that if one is motivated to change the incidence of some human characteristic, the more clearly he understands the effective factors in its development, the more likely he is to be able to devise an effective way of producing this change.

There is, however, another quite different strategy for dealing with human differences, of groups or individuals, and this is, not to change them, but to cherish them. Given this alternative strategy, there are perhaps fewer *policy* reasons for wanting to understand the underlying basis of human differences, although such differences may retain or even enhance their interest from scientific, esthetic, or personal viewpoints.

We do not have any simple answers to offer on the question of whether—or when—it is better to change or to cherish human differences. We think it likely that human societies will continue in the future, as they have in the past, to do some of each. There is fairly broad consensus in our own society that some behavioral traits— such as impulsive violence or extremely low intelligence—should if possible be changed rather than cherished. Further, we suspect that it will be well to maintain some social constraints on the notable human preference for changing someone else's individuality while cherishing one's own. But we do not think most of us would like a world in which no human changes were possible, and we are sure that few would like one in which no human diversity existed. Indeed the lesson of biology suggests that diversity is the key to survival.

How Important is IQ?

One issue on which experts have been in less than perfect agreement is on how much difference intelligence makes to an individual in our society. If U.S. blacks and whites differ (as they do) both in average income and in average IQ, it becomes of some social importance to know if these two differences are closely associated. If income, not IQ, is the primary determinant of access to social benefits, and if the wish is to equalize such access for different individuals or groups, will decreasing the inequalities in IQ, even if feasible, be expected to have any appreciable effect? In his recent book on *Inequality*, Jencks (1972) has argued that, in fact, income in the U.S. is predominantly determined by nonintellectual factors, and hence that to reduce inequalities in income by attempts to change IQ differences would be a very inefficient process indeed, even if such attempts were much more successful than they have been heretofore. With specific regard to black-white income disparities, Jencks concludes that for the present "it seems wiser to concentrate on eliminating racial discrimination, which is both practical and effective, than to concentrate on equalizing black and white test scores, which is much harder and far less effective" (1972, p. 219).

By contrast, other writers seem to argue for a fairly strong association between IQ-test scores and success in life; Jensen, for example, cites correlations in the .80s and .90s between measures of the prestige of different occupations, the level of education and income of persons in those occupations, and psychologists' ratings of the intellectual demands the occupations make (1969, p. 14).

Part of this disagreement is more apparent than real. Jensen's argument places primary weight on the averages for different occupations, Jencks's on the individual variation within them. As we have emphasized in other contexts in this book, between- and within-group relationships are not necessarily the same. Duncan (1968) estimated the correlation between income and IQ-test scores for young adult U.S. white males in 1964 to be about .30. This implies that less than 10 percent of the individual variation in income was predictable from IQ-test scores. Nonetheless, IQ predicted relatively well compared to other variables in Duncan's study—IQ-test scores predicted a man's earnings better than did measures of his father's education or income, for example. Sewell and co-workers (1970) obtained similar results in a study based on Wisconsin high school seniors. These are, of course, average relationships. For some persons—or at some levels of intelligence—20 points of IQ may represent the difference between an independent and productive life and dependency or social failure. Yet the modest overall correlations suggest that most Americans are not close to such critical thresholds with respect to IQ.

On the whole then, we conclude that while IQ is of some genuine importance it is very far from all-important in determining what life will be like for most persons in the United States at the present time. In the future? Herrnstein (1971) argues that in an increasingly technological society IQ may play an increasingly more decisive role in social prestige and economic success. This is indeed a possibility. But one might conjecture alternatively that in a leisure-oriented society, with expenditures increasingly influenced by fashion, popularity, and whim rather than the basic necessities of life, Jencks's "personality factors and luck" might continue to come out ahead after all. Or one could speculate that abilities may be crucial, but abilities spanning a far broader range than the traditional IQ. Or even that ethics may once again assume priority (e.g., Cattell, 1972). Obviously, the future holds many possibilities, only some of which auger an increasing role for IQ.

DIRECTIONS FOR FUTURE RESEARCH

The Social Context of
Research with Racial-ethnic Groups

The object of research in a behavioral science, as in any other science, is to answer questions. Social or political input into this process may take several forms: social pressures may influence what questions are asked, what methods are used to attempt to answer them, and what answers are obtained. We believe that the first two of these kinds of influence are, in appropriate circumstances, perfectly proper, but that the third is totally inappropriate and self-defeating. It makes no sense for society to organize and support an investigative process if it has decided in advance what the answer is to be. This may on occasion be good politics or propaganda, but it is corrupt and emasculated science. If society is to spend valuable resources on the question-answering apparatus of science, it should insist on getting its full money's worth in return: honest answers.

Society may, however, quite properly exert some influence on which questions are asked, and put some constraints on the methods used to answer them. Since society is to some greater or lesser degree paying for the research, it may legitimately express its relative concerns with social problem areas by the distribution of its support. Not all behavioral research is directed toward social problems, of course. We are strongly convinced that both by virtue of the sheer adventure of exploring the unknown, and the potential—though unpredictable—payoffs from this enterprise, a society is well advised to invest a good proportion of its research resources in basic research: that is, research that is *not* directed primarily at achieving immediate practical goals.

For basic research, society pretty much needs to trust the scientist's own sense of direction. But applied research is needed, too, and for research that *is* aimed toward specific social problems, surely society should have some voice in choosing the problems to attack.

Society has a right as well to place constraints on the means used by scientists to answer research questions. Social science research, in particular, typically involves the observation or manipulation of people or social processes, and society has every interest in insuring that the potential benefits of the research outweigh any social costs that are incurred. Ideally, social scientists should be sufficiently sensitive to social and ethical issues that problems do not arise—and indeed, mutual respect and trust between the scientist and his subjects has undoubtedly been characteristic of the overwhelming majority of actual empirical investigations in the social sciences. But when conflicts of interest do occur, clearly it is the public or its representatives, not the social scientist, who should be the ultimate judge of the acceptability of the side effects of the scientist's research methods. Social scientists, biomedical investigators, universities, governmental agencies, and indeed society at large have become increasingly aware of and concerned about these problems. Ethical standards for research are widely disseminated. "Informed consent" is now a standard term and a powerful constraint in all research involving humans.

These general issues bear concretely on some of the recent controversies about research involving members of U.S. minority groups. Suppose a particular research project, let us say a study of childrearing practices among lower-income black mothers, comes under fire from members of the black community. What are the issues? First, is it legitimate research; i.e., could it contribute significantly towards answering some meaningful questions in this area? If not, obviously there is no reason to defend it. Many existing studies, for example, are so insensitive to the fact that racial-ethnic groups differ on multiple genetic and environmental dimensions as to be practically uninterpretable. Second, is the research question being asked of sufficient social or theoretical importance to justify the cost that carrying out the study may impose on the black community? This is a difficult question, of course, since the indirect costs and benefits of research are not easily assessed. But members of minority groups have at least a *prima facie* case when they argue that a great deal of the research done in their communities in the past has been primarily for the academic benefit of the majority-group investigators, and has had, if anything, adverse consequences for the members of the communities in which the studies were carried out. Thus it would seem incumbent upon an investigator or his sponsors to communicate sufficient information to the potential participants in a study to enable them to make a reasonably informed judgment on its costs and benefits to them. If this judgment lies against the research, it would appear that the study should be modified or dropped. Finally, is the objection to the study solely that it might yield an unpalatable answer? If so, in our view, the objection is *not* justified, although it may sometimes be necessary to carry out appropriate education to convince people that firm knowledge, even unpleasant knowledge, is more constructive and ameliorative in the long run than refusing to confront facts.

One objection that is particularly likely to be raised in connection with studies of racial-ethnic group differences, is the objection that the results of such studies are likely to be used by bigots to justify repressive social policies. While we agree that bigots may well make this attempt, there is no need to permit them to succeed. As we have tried to make clear in the preceding section of this chapter, the discovery of differences between U.S. racial-ethnic groups in the distribution of one or more genes influencing intellectual abilities would not provide a rational basis for treating individuals other than on their merits as individuals—whether in employment, education, or social or political life. Ignorance, misinformation, and superstitious beliefs about genetic differences would seem to provide richer opportunities for bigotry and prejudice than any set of facts that research is ever likely to bring to light. To refuse to investigate racial-ethnic differences out of sheer fear of what might be found is surely to concede game, set, and match to the bigot.

Two Kinds of Study
Involving Racial-ethnic Groups

There are at least two major classes of problems that might lead an investigator to wish to do studies of U.S. racial-ethnic groups. The first focuses on general issues of human evolution, and includes studies of genetic differences among persons of different racial ancestry, the consequences of racial intermixture, and the like. For example, the one-sided historical definition of a "Negro" as anyone with any African ancestry has resulted in individuals with widely varying mixtures of African and European ancestry living in the United States under a relatively restricted set of social conditions.

If there are genes that affect behavior which differ sharply in frequency between the ancestral populations, there should be opportunities for detecting their effects in such a mixed population. As another example, the increasing number of interracial marriages in the United States raises the possibility of investigations into the biology of characteristics for which the original populations differ, such as sex ratio or twinning rate; it may also permit comparisons of the advantages of hybrid vigor to the possible disadvantages of the breaking up of coadapted gene configurations in crosses between long-separated populations. Not all such questions are biological in character. Issues of cultural and linguistic evolution may also be illuminated by a study of U.S. racial-ethnic subpopulations, and the microculture of the family of mixed origins may also provide interesting research possibilities.

The second category of problems leading to studies involving U.S. ethnic-group members centers on matters of immediate social concern rather than on broader scientific issues. Examples of problems of this kind might include such questions as the modifiability of group differences in ability and temperamental traits, the developmental consequences of group differences in diet patterns, the mechanisms of racial discrimination and prejudice, the effects of sickle-cell anemia, the psychological implications of minority-group membership, the effectiveness of particular educational practices, such as special preschool programs or racially integrated schools, and many others. Studies in this second category almost necessarily involve minority-group members because that is what the investigators are primarily interested in; investigations in the first category involve particular racial-ethnic groups because they happen to be populations in which the phenomena of interest can conveniently be studied.

Of course in practice the separation between studies concerned with scientific issues and those concerned with social problems is far less sharp than this description would suggest. A particular investigation of discrimination against New York City black policemen may have the direct practical goal of eliminating such discrimination, and at the same time be addressed to general psychological issues concerning how men perceive their fellows. Nevertheless, the conceptual distinction between the two kinds of study seems to remain worth making. And the practical consequences of a refusal of U.S. minority-group participation are quite different in the two cases. In the one case, the scientific questions are simply studied in other somewhat less powerful or efficient ways. In the other case, one doesn't find out the answers to the questions. Both kinds of losses are regrettable, but in terms of an intelligent social policy the second is much more serious.

Thus in summary we would urge that (1) scientists should consider research involving members of different U.S. racial-ethnic groups when (a) this is the method of choice on scientific grounds, or when (b) practical questions related to the groups in question are at issue; that (2) when such research is done it be done honestly, with great care that the possible political implications of various answers not affect what answers are obtained; and that (3) considerable education be undertaken with minority-group members and the public in general concerning the social benefits of research of both kinds, along with continued scrutiny of the research undertaken to insure that it does indeed offer such benefits.

Some Promising Areas of Research

In indicating some of the kinds of research on racial-ethnic group ability differences that we feel to be interesting in themselves or to have special promise for illuminating socially important questions, we do not intend to be in any way prescriptive, but only to suggest some likely possibilities. We are sure that many other promising avenues of research are missing from this list, either because they didn't occur to us, or because we failed fully to appreciate their potential merits.

Studies causally linking abilities to specific genes or specific antecedent environmental conditions. This would permit much more powerful statements about racial-ethnic group differences in abilities than can be made at present, as both of these kinds of knowledge tend now either to be nonspecific or merely qualitative. A heritability coefficient says only that *some* unspecified genes and environmental factors contribute in such-and-such proportions to the variability of the trait in this population under these conditions. If one were able to identify *particular* genes and environmental factors and their respective contributions to the variation of the trait, one could ask directly whether those genes or environmental factors differed between the groups in question.

Studies that simultaneously compare several racial-ethnic groups on a number of ability measures. A comparison of two groups on a single ability measure, for example, blacks and whites on an IQ test, while it may sometimes provide data of practical interest, is virtually power-less to provide explanatory leads. Any of the multitude of differences between the two groups might conceivably be responsible. In con-trast, a varying pattern of ability differences between several racial-ethnic groups is much more constraining upon possible explanatory hypotheses, since very few environmental conditions, for example, are likely to vary in just the particular fashion among the groups that would fit the pattern of observed differences.

Developmental studies, especially on children in the first three years of life. As the evidence reviewed in Chapter 6 suggests that this is the period in which the primary racial-ethnic differentiation of abilities takes place, it would seem highly relevant to concentrate on environ-mental and biological factors known to be operating during this period. Furthermore, the pattern of changes of abilities over time, like the pattern of change across different groups, can place constraints on explanatory hypotheses that are much stronger, and hence more scientifically useful, than a difference noted at a single point in time.

Cross-racial adoptions.   As increasing numbers of adoptions are made across racial lines in the U.S., a powerful means of partially disentangling genetic from family environmental factors becomes available. Such studies will be somewhat handicapped by the fact that families adopting children of a different race are a highly selected subset of U.S. families, as well as the fact that such adoptions are made almost entirely in one direction, i.e., minority-group children are adopted into majority-group homes. Clearly such studies must in-corporate an assessment of selective factors in the adoption process. A particularly attractive type of family for research purposes is one in which several children of different racial origins are adopted into the same home.

Racial mixture studies in the United States.   Such studies should ideally employ either good genealogical evaluation of racial mixture, or sophisticated empirical evaluation using blood-group and protein markers. The former method should work well where the racial mix-ture dates back only a few generations, as among some of the mixed racial-ethnic groups in Hawaii, for example. The latter approach has received recent theoretical development (e.g., MacLean and Workman, 1973; Shockley, 1973; Reed, 1973) but it is still not entirely clear how accurately such estimates can be made in practice. The pursuit of studies of this kind in extreme groups, such as U.S. blacks of very high IQ, should magnify their potential resolving power. A multivariate study, in which changes in the ability profile are examined across varying degrees of racial admixture, should also provide relatively powerful inferential possibilities.

Mixed-race offspring of U.S. soldiers overseas. The studies of the offspring of matings between German women and black and white U.S. servicemen (Eyferth, 1961) are prototypic here. Studies of this kind should be possible in Japan, Korea, and Southeast Asia as well. If the studies could be expanded by military-test data from the fathers' service records, this would render them considerably more powerful, although the problem of accurately identifying parentage would doubtless be a formidable one. Presumably the mothers could be identified and tested, however. Again, a multiple-trait approach is clearly desirable.

Studies comparing genetic and social criteria of race. It would be useful to have studies in which blood groups or other genetic marker variables, physical cues to race such as skin color or facial features, and social and self-identification were studied concurrently in a mixed-racial population, in relation to abilities or other suitable dependent variables.

A large twin study of U.S. blacks and whites at difference socioeconomic levels. It would be even better if this were expanded to include parent-offspring and ordinary sibling correlations in each group. Comparison of family correlations and heritabilities of different ability traits among the various groups should be most instructive; however, the study would need to be carried out on a considerably larger scale than existing investigations of this kind if differences of a size likely to be found are to be statistically dependable. Extension to other racial-ethnic groups would be attractive, but the required sample sizes might make this impractical.

Half-sibling studies. Comparison of the resemblance of maternally and paternally related half-siblings is a powerful test of maternal environmental effects. The fact that there are many half-siblings in some U.S. black groups should make such a study a promising way to evaluate the hypothesis that maternal influence plays a critical role in shaping observed ability patterns in blacks.

Educational, nutritional, and other environmental manipulations.   There is a tremendous research potential inherent in the introduction of environmental changes that are undertaken primarily for reasons other than research (Campbell, 1969). With a little advance planning, the effects of a change in educational or nutritional practices, say, can be evaluated both within and across racial-ethnic groups. Such research may be highly instructive even though the change is made for reasons quite unrelated to racial-ethnic differences. If the change is intended to affect such group differences, rational social policy would appear to dictate that an appropriate means of evaluating the effectiveness of the change be included as part of the process—and opportunities for informative and effective supplemental research become multiplied. Such an emphasis on the evaluation of social programs has been increasingly evident in recent U.S. government policy.

The kinds of research studies listed above seem to us particularly likely to shed light on the relative influence of genetic and environmental factors in producing differences between U.S. racial-ethnic groups in average levels and patterns of abilities. A host of other kinds of investigations—paleontological, anthropological, sociological, psychological, psychometric, linguistic, genetic, and many others—are essential to provide the matrix of knowledge within which studies like these may be most powerfully conceived, effectively implemented, and sensibly interpreted.

Above all, we would urge a diversity of research approaches. What falls through one net may be caught by another. A lingering doubt about a bias in one method may be dispelled when another approach, starting from different assumptions, yields confirming results. Investigators from different disciplines, through their differently distorting spectacles, can help keep one another honest. In the evolution of knowledge, as in the evolution of life, diversity plays a key and central role.

How Urgent Is Research on Racial-ethnic Differences?

This is obviously a question to which no simple answer can be given. By almost any criterion, some kinds of such research are more urgent than others. If an educational or other ameliorative treatment is introduced with the avowed intention of decreasing average racial-ethnic differences in performance on IQ tests, it would appear to be fairly obvious and urgent that concomitant research should be carried out to determine whether in fact it does so, particularly if the treatment is costly, or may have unwanted side effects. By contrast, studying the genetics of intelligence by means of racial comparisons is likely to be grossly inefficient compared to studying it by twin and family studies within a race. One would seldom wish to incur considerable social cost in order to make the cross-racial study, if his main interest were in the development of intelligence in individuals.

For studies of human evolution, including the evolution of human behavior, the comparison of existing racial groups would seem to provide one of the more powerful methods available, and hence should deserve a reasonably high scientific priority. For studies of educational methods and policies, research into individual differences is almost certainly more critical than research into group differences, since more of the variation is associated with the former than with the latter. Still, group differences may be large enough to justify some degree of research attention.

The urgency of studying possible eugenic or dysgenic trends within U.S. racial-ethnic subpopulations is a controversial issue, with which the name of William Shockley has been particularly associated in recent years. Such trends are in our view a perfectly legitimate object of study, although the interpretation of data of this kind is far from simple, as our earlier discussions should have made clear. However, the urgency of such research is very much a matter of point of view. From the standpoint of effects on the gene pool, given the long time scale of human genetic change, the remarkable lability of reproductive patterns in the U.S. in recent decades, and the uncertainty of the prediction of genotype from phenotype, such research seems to us not very urgent. At least so far as intelligence is concerned, any changes in gene frequency that are likely to take place in the next fifty years could presumably be reversed in the following twenty-five, if in the light of our later knowledge this seems desirable. However, from the standpoint of the social consequences to a minority community (such as U.S. blacks) of a slight shift upward or downward in the average level of intellectual performance, one might wish to consider research into eugenics-dysgenics as rather more urgent. For a slight average shift can markedly change the proportions of phenotypes at the extremes of a distribution, and in terms of the effects on social stereotypes, changes at the extremes may make much more difference than changes near the mean. Obviously, genetic change should not be the only kind considered. These same arguments apply with at least equal force to phenotypic changes produced by shifts in the environment; in addition, the possibility of altering gene-environment covariance should not be neglected—it can have very pronounced effects at the extremes of the distribution.

One kind of research that deserves priority is the replication of certain key studies that are of relatively powerful design and have obtained striking results tending to support one or another position in the race-IQ controversy. It is in many ways appalling that after thirty or forty years of reference to such findings, in some cases, we still do not know if what was reported in the original research is true, in the sense of being replicable by other investigators on other occasions. Examples of such studies include Witty and Jenkins's 1936 research on the distribution of ancestry of high-IQ black children (see Chapter 5, p. 130), Stevenson Smith's 1942 investigation of the stability of racial-ethnic differences in Hawaii (see Chapter 6, p. 138), Harrell, Woodyard, and Gates's 1956 study of vitamin supplements for pregnant black women (see Chapter 8, p. 226), Lee's 1951 longitudinal study of black migrants from the South in Philadelphia schools (see Chapter 6, p. 154), and, somewhat more recently, but still more than a decade ago, Eyferth's 1961 study of the illegitimate offspring of black and white soldiers in Germany (see Chapter 5, p. 126). When one considers the hundreds of inconclusive comparisons of black and white IQs that have appeared in published studies in the scientific literature in the last several decades, the thousands of pages of print devoted to discussion of race and IQ, and the massive commitments of human and financial resources based on *assumptions* about matters to which these studies are directed, one can hardly help but feel some serious misgivings about the responsiveness and responsibility of the system of rewards and support that determines which research gets done in the social sciences.

In short, some research on ability differences between U.S. racial-ethnic groups seems to us to be of fairly high scientific and social priority. Other perfectly legitimate research may well be of less pressing concern. Given the social and political sensitivities that exist in this area, however, it may be wise to precede and accompany any such research with extensive public education concerning what is being done and why.

A FINAL WORD

When we have mentioned our general conclusion to colleagues—that the solid evidence to date is compatible with a relatively broad range of intellectual positions on the "race-IQ" question—a typical response is "yes, but what do you *really* think?" Well, what we really think is just that. Based upon our reading of the available evidence, we would offer the following propositions for the consideration of fellow social scientists, public-policy makers, and concerned citizens in general.

1. Further evidence should be sought in order to narrow the range of positions that an intellectually honest person might take on this question—we have identified some reasonable research possibilities and we are confident that others exist.

2. Humane and enlightened public-policy measures need not be, and should not be, bound by either hereditarian or environmentalist dogmas. Improving the educational opportunities of U.S. blacks, for example, seems to us such a good idea that it should not be made to depend on the risky assumption that this will make the distribution of performance of U.S. blacks on IQ tests indistinguishable from that of U.S. whites (or American Indians, Asian Americans, or any other group). The same applies to improving the nutritional status of U.S. minorities.

3. Any public policy should be responsive to the fact that individual variation within U.S. racial-ethnic groups greatly exceeds average differences between groups. The empirical fact that many members of any U.S. racial-ethnic group exceed in intellectual performance the typical member of any other group is in itself a compelling case against racism. Ironically, some of the more intemperate critics of Jensen, Eysenck, and Herrnstein, by focusing attention on group averages as opposed to individual differences, have probably tended to detract from, rather than to strengthen, public understanding and acceptance of this truth.

4. Finally, although IQ is an empirically significant variable, it is not everything—not nearly everything. First, IQ-test performance is clearly not identical with intelligence as socially defined, although in an unselected sample of the U.S. population the correlation between these variables is likely to be quite high. Second, real-life intellectual achievements are not solely a matter of ability, but reflect motivational, temperamental, and opportunity factors as well. And third, the cor-

relation between intellectual achievement, however broadly defined, and the social rewards of money, leisure, power, affection, and esteem is surely only moderate at best.

While de-emphasizing IQ may have the soothing effect of somewhat down-playing the race-IQ controversy, it does raise a sobering possibility: Are we in for a re-enactment of the whole IQ affair in some other domain, such as personality traits? We sincerely hope not. There are, of course, some important differences. The personality domain is much more complex, contingent, and multidimensional in character, with no massive central axis like "general intelligence." Thus simple orders of merit between groups are much harder to come by, although not impossible to suggest. In addition, the technology of testing is much less advanced in the personality domain, and theory is very divergent, so that it would be much more difficult to claim scientific consensus in support of any particular public policy. Finally, we may at least hope that the lessons of the race-IQ controversy will not have been altogether lost on social scientists, policy makers, and the public. Thus the next time around, if there must be a next time, a higher proportion of the efforts and emotions of all concerned might be focused on decidable questions and the evidence that bears upon them, rather than on polemics and politics.

We do *not* believe that the lack of a definitive answer to the questions with which we began is either disastrous or disappointing. Moral and political questions never have had scientific answers. The factual questions involved, if phrased in limited and specific form, should indeed be answerable, and it is probably worth society's time and money to try to answer a good number of them. It is part of our own fundamental conviction as social scientists that on the whole better and wiser decisions are made with knowledge than without.

APPENDICES

APPENDIX A

Glossary of Some Genetic Terms Used in This Book

In general, technical terms used in the text in only one place and explained there have not been included in this glossary. Also, these are not necessarily comprehensive definitions, but are restricted to the senses of these terms used in this book.

Additive effect: A combined effect of two or more genes on a trait that is equal to the sum of their separate effects.

Allele: A variant form of a gene. All of the alleles of a given gene occur at the same locus.

Assortative mating: Mating between individuals in a population who tend to resemble one another in a specified trait (positive assortative mating) or who tend to be opposites for the trait (negative assortative mating).

Autosome: Any chromosome except the sex chromosomes.

Chromosomes: Structures in the cell nucleus that carry the genes.

Cline: A continuous monotonic change in a species' gene frequencies across a geographic region.

Clone: A line of individuals descended by equational division from a single cell, hence having the same geneotype.

Dizygotic twins: "Fraternal" twins; i.e., formed from separate fertilizations of two ova, and hence genetically no more similar than siblings born at different times.

DNA: Deoxyribonucleic acid, the long molecular chain that carries genetic information.

Dominance: Interaction between the two alleles at a locus. If the effect of possessing a given allele on either chromosome is the same as having it on both, that allele is described as *dominant*, and the allele with which it is paired in the heterozygote is described as *recessive*. The *dominance component* of the population variance of a trait reflects the existence of dominance at one or more genetic loci influencing the trait.

Drift: Changes in gene frequency resulting from random fluctuations in transmission of genes across generations. Genetic drift has an appreciable effect only in small populations.

Dysgenic: Tending to lead to the deterioration of a population's gene pool (contrasted with *eugenic*).

Electrophoresis: A method of identifying proteins by their differential movement in an electric field.

Endogamy: The custom of mating within the tribe, village, or other population subunit.

Epistasis: The interactive effect on a trait of genes at different chromosomal loci. Also, a component of the population variance of a trait deriving from this source.

Eugenic: Tending to lead to the improvement of a population's gene pool.

Exogamy: The custom of mating with an individual from outside the tribe, village, or other subpopulation unit.

Gamete: The sex cell (sperm or ovum).

Gene: The unit of inheritance. A section of the DNA molecule that codes for a single polypetide.

Gene frequencies: The relative proportions of the different alleles of a gene in a given population.

Gene pool: The genes of a population.

Genotype: The genetic constitution of an individual (sometimes, with reference to a given trait).

Heritability: (In the broad sense, h_B^2) the proportion of the variation of a given trait in a population that is genetic; (in the narrow sense, h_N^2) the proportion of the variation due to the additive effects of genes, transmissable across generations. Variation due to genetic dominance and epistasis is included in h_B^2, but excluded from h_N^2.

Heterosis: Increase in size, vigor, etc., with outbreeding.

Heterozygote: An individual who has different alleles on his two chromosomes at the locus in question.

Homozygote: An individual who has the same allele on both of his chromosomes at the locus in question.

Hybrid: An offspring of a mating between members of two populations that have been relatively isolated genetically.

Hybrid vigor: Same as *heterosis*.

Inbreeding: Mating between individuals who are more closely related than members of the population in general (or some reference population).

Linkage: Patterns of association between traits resulting from the location of genes on the same chromosome.

Locus (plural, *loci*): A position on a chromosome occupied by a particular gene or its alleles.

Monozygotic twins: "Identical" twins; i.e., formed from the splitting of a single fertilized ovum, and hence having the same geneotype.

Mutation: A change in a gene that is preserved in its replication.

Natural selection: The increase in relative frequency of certain alleles of a gene in a population due to increased survival of individuals carrying the alleles, their more effective reproduction, or both.

Outbreeding: Mating between genetically remote individuals (contrasted with *inbreeding*).

Overdominance: A gene's having a greater effect on a trait in the heterozygous than in the homozygous condition.

Penetrance (of a gene): The probability that a given gene will be expressed in the phenotype.

Phenotype: The actual observed traits of an individual (as contrasted with his *genotype*).

PKU: Phenylketonuria, a metabolic disease caused by homozygosity for a particular recessive gene. It results in a severe mental defect unless the affected infant is protected by a special diet.

Pleiotropy: A given gene's having an effect on more than one trait.

Polygenic (of a trait): Being influenced by more than one pair of genes (often many).

Polymorphic: Having more than one form in a population.

Random mating: Mating in which the trait is not systematically associated with mate choice.

Recessive: See *Dominance*. Many rare recessive alleles are deleterious to the organism when they are homozygous, but are harmless when paired with normal dominant alleles.

Secular trend: A change in some population characteristic over time.

Sex-linkage: Occurrence of a gene on a sex chromosome (usually X, in man).

X chromosome: The sex chromosome that is homozygous in normal human females (XX).

Y chromosome: The sex chromosome that is present in heterozygous form in normal human males (XY).

A Brief Explanation of Some Statistical Terms Used in This Book

This is intended to give a reader who is unfamiliar with these statistical concepts a sufficient sense of their meaning to enable him to understand their use in the text. For more complete discussions and explanations, and computational details, any introductory textbook in statistics may be consulted.

Mean (M): An ordinary arithmetical average, obtained by adding a set of numbers and dividing by the number of items added. The mean of 5, 7, and 6 is 18 ÷ 3 or 6. The mean is used as a representative or typical value to characterize a set of scores: thus one can convey the information that a certain student group is of high ability by reporting that the students' mean IQ is 122.4.

Median (Mdn): The value of the middle item or items in a set of numbers arranged in order of magnitude. This is another way of arriving at a typical value for a set of scores. The median of 5, 7, and 6 is 6 (as is the mean), and so is the median of 5, 6, and 10 (whose mean is 7). The fact that the median is relatively insensitive to the numerical values of scores at the extremes makes it useful where the meaningfulness of extreme scores may be in doubt.

Standard deviation (σ): A measure of the scatter, or dispersion, of a set of scores around their mean value. It is the square root of the average of the squared distances of individual scores from the mean. For the set of scores 5, 6, and 7,

$$\sigma = \sqrt{(1^2 + 0^2 + 1^2)/3} = \sqrt{2/3} \approx 0.8.$$

For the set of scores 4, 6, and 8,

$$\sigma = \sqrt{(2^2 + 0^2 + 2^2)/3} = \sqrt{8/3} \approx 1.6.$$

In a normal distribution about two-thirds of scores lie within the distance from one σ above to one σ below the mean.

Variance (*V*): Another index of scatter, or variation, of scores. It is the average of the squared distances of individual scores from the mean; thus it is equal to the square of σ. In the examples in the paragraph above the variances are 2/3 and 8/3 respectively. The standard deviation is ordinarily used when one simply wishes to describe the variation of a set of scores, but the variance is more useful when one wishes to analyze the variation of scores into components deriving from different causal influences. When independent influences combine in a simple (additive) fashion, the variance of their combined effect is equal to the sum of the variances of their separate effects, i.e., $V_{A+B} = V_A + V_B$. For example, if the variance due to genetic effects on some trait is 15, and that due to independent environmental effects is 10, the total variance of the scores on the trait will be 25 (such a simple additive relation will not hold for the corresponding σs).

Covariance: The variance that is common to two variables (when expressed on equivalent scales). A measure of their tendency to vary together in the population.

Raw score: A score expressed in its original units, such as number of items correct on a test.

Standard score: A score expressed as a distance from the mean in standard deviation units. Thus an individual whose score happens to be two standard deviations above the mean of some population has a standard score of $+2.0\ \sigma$; one whose score is one-half σ below the mean has a standard score of $-0.5\ \sigma$. A standard score always has reference to some particular population, and is a description of an individual or subgroup in terms of the average level and scatter of scores in that population.

Normal distribution: A set of scores in which most individuals are concentrated around the average, with smaller numbers tailing off symmetrically toward both extremes, in the manner of the so-called "normal curve"—a bell-shaped theoretical distribution that is produced when many independent influences act on scores. Many sets of behavioral measures (for example, IQs) tend to take the form—more or less—of a normal distribution.

Skewed distribution: A set of scores in which scores tend to be spread out to a greater extent in one direction from the mean than in the other. When scores are more spread out above the mean, the skew is called *positive*, when they stretch out below the mean, the skew is called *negative*.

Correlation coefficient (*r*): A measure of the relationship or association between two sets of scores. The relationship is expressed on a scale from .00 (no relationship) to 1.00 (perfect relationship). If the relationship is positive (i.e., a high score in one set tends to go with a high score in the other, and a low score with a low score) the correlation coefficient has a plus sign; if it is negative (high tends to go with low and low with high) the coefficient has a minus sign. Correlation coefficients may be used to indicate the resemblance of two related sets of individuals on a single trait (e.g., the extent to which husbands of high IQ tend to have wives of high IQ), or they may be used to indicate the relationship between two traits measured on a single set of individuals (e.g., the extent to which persons high in IQ tend also to be high in social status). When the two sets of scores have the same variance, the correlation coefficient can be interpreted as the proportion of that variance that is common to the two, and its complement $(1 - r)$ as the proportion of the variance of each that is independent of the other.

Multiple correlation (R): The highest obtainable r between one measure and a weighted sum of several other measures. It indicates how closely the single measure (e.g., IQ) is related to an ideal composite variable based on the other measures (e.g., several SES indicators).

Factor analysis: An analytical procedure that interprets the correlations among a set of measures in terms of a few hypothetical underlying variables, the *factors*. Thus a factor analysis of several ability tests might yield (among others) a "verbal factor," identified by its high correlations with, say, two vocabulary tests and a synonyms test. The relationships among tests and factors define the *factor structure* of the domain under consideration.

Path analysis: A procedure that assumes certain causal sequences among variables, and then estimates the extent to which each variable influences those subsequent to it along such causal paths. The indices of relative influence are called *path coefficients*.

Statistical significance: A *significance test* asks if a given outcome could plausibly have resulted from the operation of chance in the selection of cases to be observed from some larger population. If, on the basis of the variability of the observations and the number of cases observed, there is any reasonable likelihood that the outcome may have been due merely to a fortuitous selection of cases, the result is said not to be statistically significant. A "reasonable likelihood" is usually defined as one chance in twenty or better. Thus only when an outcome appears to have less than one chance in twenty of having resulted from the operation of chance factors is it taken seriously in a scientific sense. Statistical significance does not guarantee that the observed result is interesting or important or means what the researcher thinks it does, it merely provides reasonable assurance that a relationship not due to chance alone is present in the data.

The calculation of the probability that the obtained result could have been expected to occur by chance is basic to the significance test. Such calculations are usually made with the aid of tables, and involve special quantities known as F, t, χ^2, etc.; thus they may be referred to as "F-tests," "t-tests," "chi-square tests," and the like.

APPENDIX C

Brief Descriptions of Intelligence Tests Referred to in This Book

These descriptions are intended to provide brief characterizations of these tests for the general reader. For further technical details and references to published literature on most of these tests, the reader may consult Buros's *Mental Measurements Yearbooks* (1972 and earlier editions).

Armed Forces Qualifying Test (AFQT): A modification of the Army General Classification Test used after 1950, and like it intended to predict potential success in general military training and performance. Contains items to test verbal, numerical, spatial relations, and mechanical abilities.

Army Alpha: A verbal group-administered intelligence test used by the U.S. Army during World War I. Consists of 8 subtests intended to measure ability to follow directions, numerical ability, reasoning, verbal ability, and information. Served as a prototype for many subsequent group IQ tests.

Army Beta: A nonverbal group-administered intelligence test used by the U.S. Army during World War I to test recruits not literate in English. Consists of 7 subtests in the spatial, reasoning, and perceptual areas. Items similar to those used in this test appear in many present-day IQ tests.

Army General Classification Test (AGCT): A 40-minute group test used by the U.S. Army during World War II to estimate the capacity of men entering military service to absorb different kinds and levels of training. Consists of typical intelligence-test items in the verbal, numerical, and spatial relations categories.

Bayley Mental Scale: For infants age 1–30 months. For the first year, mostly attention and responsiveness items ("looks at moving spoon," "smiles at image in mirror"). For the later periods, more varied items reflecting verbal, sensorimotor, and social development ("says two words," "scribbles with crayon," "follows direction"). Originally published in 1933, restandardized on the nationwide Collaborative Study sample in 1955.

Bender-Gestalt Test: Used primarily as a clinical test (to assess brain damage, etc.), but can also be used as an ability test for children younger than 12 years. Ten geometric figures are copied by the testee, and the errors made are scored and interpreted. Originally published in 1938.

Cattell Infant Intelligence Scale: Intended as a downward extension of the Stanford-Binet scale to test infants 3–30 months old. Items for earlier ages emphasize attention to stimuli ("follows moving object with eyes") and simple coordination ("hits cup with spoon"). At later ages some Stanford-Binet items are used. Standardized in 1937 on a sample of Boston infants, mostly of lower-middle SES.

Draw-a-Man Test: Child draws pictures of a man and a woman, and these are scored for basic structure and details. Originally developed in 1926; restandardized in 1963 under the title of the Goodenough-Harris Drawing Test.

Henmon-Nelson Tests of Mental Ability: A group intelligence test designed primarily for school use. Includes verbal, perceptual, numerical and reasoning items, with most emphasis on verbal. Standardized on a representative sample of the U.S. school population. Originally published in 1931.

Illinois Test of Psycholinguistic Abilities: An experimental individual test published in 1961 intended to measure different aspects of language ability in children (ages $2\frac{1}{2}$ to 9 years). Uses picture booklet, cards, and familiar objects, and yields 10 subscores with labels such as "visual decoding," "auditory-vocal association."

Lorge-Thorndike Intelligence Tests: A group intelligence test designed primarily for school use. Verbal and nonverbal subtests of such familiar types as vocabulary, arithmetic reasoning, number series, figure classification, and analogies. Standardized on a nationwide sample representing the U.S. school population. Originally published in 1954.

Myers Mental Measure: An early (1921) group nonlanguage test. Includes following oral directions, completing pictures, and detecting similarities.

Otis Self-administering Tests of Mental Ability: An early group intelligence test, originally published in 1922 by one of the developers of the Army Alpha. Mostly verbal, with some numerical and perceptual reasoning items.

Peabody Picture Vocabulary Test (*PPVT*): An individual test in which the examiner reads a word and the testee points to the one of four pictures on a card that illustrates it. Standardized in 1959 on white children and adolescents in and around Nashville, Tennessee. (For ages $2\frac{1}{2}$ up.)

Pintner-Paterson Scale: An early (1917) scale consisting of 15 performance tests not requiring the use of language by either examiner or testee (most of the tests use formboards into which geometric or pictorial pieces are to be fitted).

Porteus Maze Test: Pencil-and-paper mazes of graded difficulty, with performance scored both quantitatively and qualitatively. Originally published in 1914, and widely used in cross-cultural studies and with juvenile delinquents and other special groups.

Primary Mental Abilities: A group-administered test battery designed to assess five of L. L. Thurstone's ability factors: Verbal Meaning (e.g., vocabulary test); Space (e.g., recognizing rotated figure as same or different); Reasoning (e.g., detecting the rule underlying a series of letters or numbers); Number (e.g., simple arithmetic); and Word Fluency (e.g., listing words beginning with a given letter). Additional Perceptual Speed and Motor factors are measured at younger ages. Originally published in 1941.

Raven's Progressive Matrices: Various versions developed since 1938 in Great Britain and elsewhere; intended as a test of general ability relatively independent of specific schooling. Perceptual reasoning items, in which testee selects the alternative that best completes a two-dimensional sequence.

School and College Ability Tests (SCAT): A group test intended to measure general academic aptitude. Yields a verbal and a quantitative subscore. Standardized on a representative sample of the U.S. school population. Originally published in 1955.

Stanford-Binet: The classic individually administered IQ test, for ages $2\frac{1}{2}$ years up. A variety of verbal and performance items, with verbal predominating, especially at later ages. The current standardization is based on a 1937 sampling of American-born U.S. white children and adolescents. The original publication was based on a 1911 translation of Binet's 1908 scale, and major revisions were made in 1916, 1937, and 1960.

Wechsler Scales (Wechsler-Bellevue, WAIS, WISC): Individually administered IQ tests, with items grouped into 10–12 separately scored subtests, classified into a *verbal* group (e.g., Information, Vocabulary) and a *performance* group (e.g., Picture Completion, Block Design). The WAIS (Wechsler Adult Intelligence Scale), a 1955 revision of the earlier Wechsler-Bellevue scale, was standardized on a sample of the U.S. population aged 16–64. The WISC (Wechsler Intelligence Scale for Children, 1949) was standardized on sample of U.S. white children aged 5 to 15 years.

Details of Some of the Calculations in Chapter 2

Selection required to produce a given genetic difference (p. 44)

$$g = ah^2 \qquad \text{(see C-S \& B, eq. 9.70, p. 604)*}$$

where g = mean genotypic value to be achieved (i.e., 1σ), a = mean phenotypic value of selected individuals, and h^2 = regression of additive genetic value on phenotype = h_N^2, which we take as .64. (The narrow-sense heritability is used, because we are concerned with the effect on generations subsequent to the immigrants.) It follows that $a = 1.56\,\sigma$.

$$a = z/q \qquad \text{(see C-S \& B, eq. 9.44, p. 556)}$$

where $a = 1.56\,\sigma$ = mean standard score of individuals above threshold of selection, q = proportion of population above threshold, and z = ordinate of normal curve at threshold; from which $q = 0.15$, via normal curve tables. Thus 15 percent of the population at one extreme must be selected to produce an average genotypic value of plus (or minus) $1\,\sigma$ in the selected population.

Effects of mild selective migration (p. 44)

Mean IQ of individuals above the mean in IQ:

$$a = z/q,$$

as in preceding section; $q = .5$ and $z = .3989$, so $a = .80\,\sigma$ (and the mean of individuals below the mean is correspondingly $-.80\,\sigma$).

Individuals below the mean are 25 percent more likely to be selected, therefore 55.5 percent of selected individuals are below and 44.4 percent of selected individuals are above the mean ($.555/.444 = 1.25$), and the average IQ of the selected group is $.444\,(.8) + .555\,(-.8) = -.079\,\sigma$.

*Throughout this appendix, the citations are to Cavalli-Sforza and Bodmer, 1971.

The average genetic difference is again obtained from $g = ah_N^2$, thus $g = -.051\,\sigma$. If we assume $\sigma = 15$ for IQ, this is equivalent to $-.76$ IQ points.

Change of gene frequency under weak selection (p. 45)

Number of generations to go from .01 to .50:

$$T = -\log_e(p_0/q_0)/s \qquad \text{(C-S \& B, p. 134),}$$

where T is a number of generations, p_0 is the initial frequency, q_0 is $(1 - p_0)$ and s is the coefficient of selection. For $p_0 = .01$ and $s = .01$, T is 460 generations. To go from .50 to .99 will take another 460 generations, for a total of 920; thus 1000 generations will take the frequency somewhat beyond .99.

Differential selection of a quantitative trait with a graded threshold (p. 47)

We wish to find the increase per generation with a threshold function following a cumulative normal distribution centered on $\mu = -3.33\,\sigma$ ($=50$ IQ), with a standard deviation $S = .33$ ($=5$ IQ points). Thus 2.3 percent reproduce at $\mu - 2S$ ($=40$ IQ), and 97.7 percent reproduce at $\mu + 2S$ ($=60$ IQ).

The mean of selected individuals, m, is given (in standard deviation units) by:

$$m = \frac{\exp[-\mu^2/2(1 + S^2)]}{A\sqrt{2}\,\mu(1 + S^2)} \qquad \text{(C-S \& B, eq. 9.73, p. 607)}$$

where A is the area under the normal curve above $\mu/\sqrt{1 + S^2}$, μ and S are as defined above, and the numerator is e raised to the power in the square brackets. A is .9987, and m is .00255 σ. With μ shifted upwards 5 points to 55 IQ ($= -.3\,\sigma$), A is .9965 and m is .00662 σ for Population B.

The mean effects for the offspring generation are given by $g = ah^2$, where h^2 is the narrow heritability, which we will take to be .64. These will be about .0016 σ and .0042 σ, or .024 and .064 IQ points for Population A and B, respectively, a difference of .04 IQ points.

Cross-cultural Studies of Sense Perception

If cultural factors can be shown to be of importance in the differential results of cross-cultural tests of sense perception, where the path from gene to sensory behavior is more direct, culture might be expected to be of even greater importance in accounting for transcultural differences in scores on intelligence tests, where the final, complex behavior is more remote from the multiple, primary gene action.

The Cambridge Anthropological Expedition to the Papuan natives of the Torres Straits Islands between New Guinea and Cape York Peninsula, Australia, in 1898 made a pioneer attempt to measure objectively the sensory capacities of primitive subjects and to compare their performance with that of European subjects. The expedition was organized by the physical anthropologist-ethnographer A. C. Haddon and included on its staff the psychologist-anthropologist W. H. R. Rivers and the psychologists C. S. Myers and William McDougall. Rivers (1901) found that the nonliterate Papuans of the Murray Islands were generally superior in visual acuity to Europeans but he was skeptical of the result because of differences in the test situation.

In a review of much more extensive data from the world literature, R. H. Post (1962) found that the frequency of defects in visual acuity among several different samples of hunters and farmer-hunters was strikingly lower than in populations with relatively long histories of agriculture and settled habitations. A variety of primitive peoples including African and Oceanic blacks, African and Asian pygmies, Ainus of Hokkaido, and American Indians surpass on the average European and North American whites in keenness of vision.

The most familiar tests of visual acuity measure the distance at which the subject can read the block letters or figures on a Snellen chart. Snellen defined

TABLE E.1. *Visual acuity tested by the* E *method.*

Subjects	Sample Size	Average Acuity
Murray Islanders, Torres Straits	115	10.3/5 = 2.06
Mabuiag, Torres Straits	36	11.6/5 = 2.32
Kiwai, Fly River, New Guinea	19	10.3/5 = 2.06
Pooled samples, Torres Straits and Fly River	170	10.6/5 = 2.12
Singalese and Hindus	23	14/6.5 = 2.15
Heligoland males	100	10.6/6 = 1.77
German sailors	100	12.6/6 = 2.10
Normal European subjects	Large	5/5 = 1.00

Source: Rivers, 1901, p. 25.

visual acuity by the minimum angle at which the subject can recognize the form of an object. The degree of visual acuity (V) may be expressed by the formula $V = d/D$, where D is the distance at which a given figure subtends an angle of 5 minutes, and d is the greatest distance at which this figure can be recognized. Thus $V = 5/5 = 1$ means that figures subtending the specified angle at 5 meters can be read at 5 meters, and $V = 10/5 = 2$ means that the same figures can be read at 10 meters. The so-called normal vision (for Europeans) is defined as $V = 1$.

Although such tests of visual acuity have high reliability, they may in fact be somewhat culturally biased against civilized peoples (Kroeber, 1948). Usually visual acuity is tested by the ability to distinguish objects or marks of a standard size and shape *at a distance*; the greater the distance at which one can see a letter or figure on the test charts, the higher one's score. Civilized Chinese, Japanese, and European subjects commonly read and work at a distance of about 14 inches. They read small characters (in Chinese with as many as 57 strokes), work with small tools, use fine, sharply pointed needles with fine thread, sharp knives, and thin paper and fabrics. Close accuracy is stressed, hazy distant observations are neglected.

The nonliterate hunter, fisher, or herdsman, on the other hand, is an out-of-doors person, who scans the horizon, looks for game at a distance, takes an interest in dim tracks, and uses large tools and blunt needles with cords as thread. In general the culture of primitive peoples gives them training and practice all their lives to see at medium and far distances, and thus, in effect, to make high scores on Snellen-type visual tests. There could also, of course,

TABLE E.2. *Percentages of refractive deviations (± 1 diopter) determined in ophthalmologic examinations in five populations.*

Group	Age	Sex	No. of Eyes	% Myopic	% Normal	% Hyperopic
Gabon Negroes	18–37	Male	1154	1	85	14
Greenland Eskimos	15–29	Male	227	1	86	13
Swedes (conscripts)	20	Male	5122	6	68	26
Germans (patients)	25+	Both	48000	11	43	45
British (recruits)	17–27	Male	2066	7	45	48

Source: Data from Post, 1962.

be genetic selection for this sort of visual capacity under primitive cultural conditions (Post, 1962).

The Kalmuks, herdsmen living on the steppes of western Mongolia and Dzungaria, are reputed to have unusually acute vision. Rivers (1901) cites an observation by Pallas in 1776 recording that on one occasion a group of Kalmuks distinguished the dust made by a herd of cattle at a distance of about 20 miles. Kotelmann (1884), using Snellen charts, reported that the visual acuity of 17 Kalmuks averaged 2.7, and that one male Kalmuk had a $V = 42/6.5$—that is, over six times the "normal" visual acuity for Europeans —and one Kalmuk woman, a $V = 5.4$.

Rivers used charts with the block letter **E** in different positions to test the natives at Torres Straits and the Fly River region of New Guinea. The person being tested reported which side of an **Ш** was open, or placed a model **Ⴀ** he was holding in the same position as one pointed out to him on the chart. The average acuity of two population samples from Torres Straits, one from Fly River, and several others are given in Table E.1. The 170 Papuans averaged 2.12, more than double the "normal" standard for Europeans, and as acute as the average for 100 German sailors whose induction into the navy required good vision.

Today it is possible to estimate objectively the refractive error in a person's vision by using retinoscopy and other methods that are too technical to be described here. The results of studies using such modern techniques tend to suggest, as did the earlier studies, that the frequency of visual defects is much lower among primitive than among European and other long-civilized peoples in the Near and Far East (Post, 1962). Table E.2 compares the proportion of near- and farsighted persons in two primitive and three European groups. It will be noted that the primitive peoples have lower incidences of both near- and farsightedness.

Eyes that permit normal or nearly normal visual work show important variation in their individual optical components including the refraction of the corneal center, depth of the anterior chamber, refraction of the lens, volume of the vitreous body, and transverse diameter of the eyeball. These variations are polygenic in inheritance.

In an excellent review of the massive literature on total refraction and the variability of its individual components, Waardenburg (1963, vol. 2, pp. 1201–1285) argues for a polygenic hereditary basis for the common varieties of normal, long, and short sightedness. He concludes that the excessive convergence and accommodation required to do the close, fine visual work of civilized and industrialized societies has not been proved as an environmental cause of myopia. In a number of European and Near-Eastern agricultural populations, the illiterate peasants show frequencies of myopia similar to those of the literate upper classes. Harem women of the Middle East, who do little visual work, have the same frequencies of myopia as the general population.

Nor is there clear evidence that overcrowding, poverty, poor health, bad eye hygiene, or either inferior or superior mental ability cause myopia, although correlations with these kinds of factors are occasionally reported, including such oddities as the finding of Ask (1904) in Sweden and E. Holm (1926) in Denmark that university students concentrating in languages have a higher proportion of myopia than those majoring in mathematics.

In addition to polygenic variation in total refraction, a number of mutant, major genes result in pathological myopia. The less severe degrees of pathological myopia are usually determined by autosomal dominant genes with high penetrance while the more severe conditions follow various modes of inheritance, e.g., autosomal dominant, partial dominant, or recessive, and X-linked recessive, some with reduced penetrance.

Additional evidence for the heritability of total refraction is presented by twin studies. Table E.3 shows the concordance of a total of 1063 monozygous (MZ) and dizygous (DZ) twin pairs, pooled from five studies summarized by Post (1962). In these data 62 percent of MZ and 44 percent of DZ twin pairs are concordant, suggesting an appreciable influence of the genes, but by no means total genetic determination.

The common types of myopia would seem significantly less of a handicap among agricultural and industrial peoples than among nonagricultural hunters. We may assume that natural selection operates against myopia under primitive conditions, and that there is relaxation of selection under civilized conditions (Post, 1962). The same explanation holds for the increased frequency of myopia and other refractive anomalies among domestic or captive mammals: 30 percent myopia in horses, up to 69 percent in cattle, and high incidences in dogs, rabbits, monkeys, and apes, varying from 6.5 to 24.1 percent (Waardenburg, 1963).

Vision of course requires the brain as well as the cornea, lens, eye chambers, and retinas. Retinal images are transmitted over the optic tracts to the visual cortex at the back lobe of the cerebral hemispheres. We do not understand just how the brain interprets retinal images, but it is clear that the interpre-

TABLE E.3. *Twin-pair differences in total refraction.*

	Concordant[a]	Discordant	Totals
Monozygous	371	225	596
Dizygous	207	260	467
Totals	578	485	1063

Source: Post, 1962; pooled data from five studies.
[a] Concordant $= < \frac{1}{2}$ diopter difference.

tation depends in part on individual experience, which in turn depends in part on the culture acquired by individuals. Sailors see a distant shore where landsmen see only a haze on the horizon. Pastoralists, including modern ranchers, can distinguish a horse from a cow a mile away where city dudes cannot.

Thus we may conclude that the results of tests of visual acuity may depend both on genotype and on individual and cultural experience and training. If sensory psychologists were to reverse their measurement techniques to test for ability to see fine differences at close range, it is possible that civilized Chinese, Japanese, and Europeans might improve in their tested "visual ability" and the primitive hunters get worse, although some of the evidence cited by Post and Waardenburg suggests that the outcome of such an experiment is far from certain.

The early quantitative tests on the acuity of hearing may also have been biased culturally, but in the opposite direction, for the test procedures probably tended to favor the civilized and to disfavor the primitives. During the Torres Straits Expedition Myers (1903) found the Papuan natives of Murray Island were generally inferior in auditory capacity to European subjects. Data are not available to decide whether, and to what extent, the Europeans did better because they were of European genotype, had less pathology of the ear, especially middle ear infections, or because they were of European culture and familiar with the experimental apparatus and setting. Manuals for auditory testing instruct that "the test must be made in a sufficiently quiet room," but, through lack of a suitable room on Murray Island, Myers was forced to test his subjects in the open amid the "constant rustle of the palm-leaves and the beating of the surf on the sea-shore." The test apparatus included tuning forks, ticking stop watches, pith balls falling through metal tubes on felt disks, or metal spheres dropping on metal plates.

Of 12 Murray Island boys, 7 were inferior in auditory acuity to Myers (whose hearing was slightly better than that of the average English adult), and 4 out of 5 adult Murray Islanders had remarkably low auditory acuity.

However, the upper limit of hearing high pitches tested by means of a

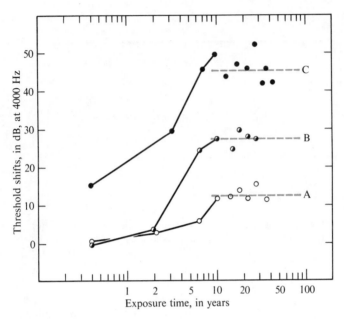

FIGURE E.1

Noise-induced permanent threshold shifts in hearing ability plotted against years of occupational exposure to noise. All cases are corrected for the average changes with age found in persons without occupational exposure to loud noise. The graphs are for a test tone of 4000 hertz and the data points are medians. The average sound levels were 83 decibels for group A, 92 decibels for group B, and 97 decibels for group C. (From Nixon and Glorig, 1961.)

Galton whistle was very nearly identical in the Papuans of Torres Straits and the people of Aberdeenshire.

Variable and fixed (256 vibrations per second) tuning forks were used by Myers to test the smallest perceptible tone differences in the Murray Island natives. The average difference in vibration frequency just distinguished by the adults of Murray Island was 15.4, and of Aberdeenshire 7.6 vibrations per second, and by the children, 12.5 and 4.7 vibrations per second, respectively.

As with variation in visual acuity, we know that major genes, polygenes, and environmental factors including cultural differences are all important in determining the observed variation in auditory performance within races, and probably between them. The first psychometric conclusions on the superiority of Caucasian hearing acuity were reached in the early 1900's. Today auditory acuity is measured with audiometers, not falling pith balls.

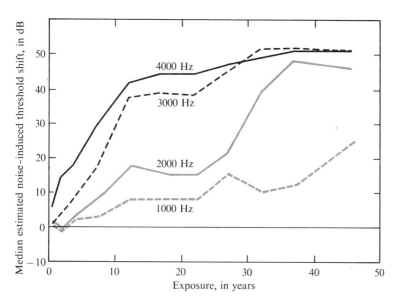

FIGURE E.2

Median noise-induced threshold shifts in hearing ability for jute weavers with occupational exposure to noise with sound level of about 98 decibels. These threshold shifts are corrected for the expected changes in threshold with age in persons who are not exposed to loud noise. (From Taylor et al., 1965.)

And today the difference in hearing acuity is often reversed due to hearing loss resulting from the continual, noisy insults to the ear suffered by urban, commercial, industrial Japanese, Europeans, Americans, and others.

Workers in some industrial environments may be exposed to noise levels of 80–100 decibels. As the exposures are repeated day after day, year after year, the ear becomes less and less able to recover from the temporary threshold shift (hearing loss) at the end of each day. After long exposure, the hearing loss becomes permanent or nearly so.

Age-corrected threshold shifts tested at 4000 hertz are shown in Figure E.1 for male workers in noisy industrial work spaces in the United States (Nixon and Glorig, 1961).

Similar data were collected by Taylor et al. (1965) on female jute weavers, many of whom received nearly constant exposures of above 98 decibels in the mills over periods ranging up to more than 50 years. The median threshold shifts, corrected for the expected change in thresholds with age in persons who are not exposed to high levels of noise are given in Figure E.2, and some idea of the range of individual variation is expressed in Figure E.3.

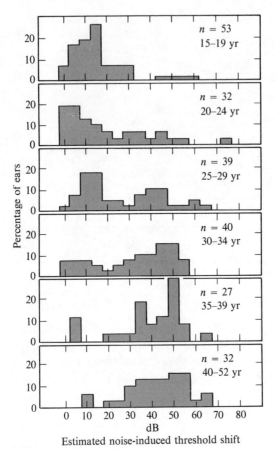

FIGURE E.3

The distribution of noise-induced threshold shifts in hearing ability of jute weavers exposed for 6 different periods of years. The test frequency was 2000 hertz. Note the great variation between people in the effects of noise on the magnitude of the threshold shift. (From Taylor et al., 1965.)

Even occasional, but repeated, exposure to high level noise may result in permanent hearing loss. Taylor and Williams (1966) found modern sports hunters had permanent hearing loss in contrast with an age-matched control group, especially for the test zone 2000–8000 hertz (Figure E.4).

In short, tests used to measure racial differences in the acuity of visual and auditory perception are tests not only of group differences in frequencies of

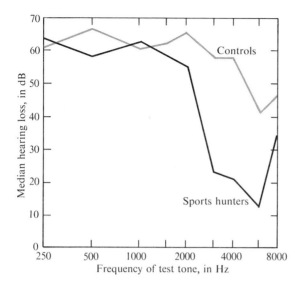

FIGURE E.4

Median left-ear hearing loss in habitual sports hunters and age-matched controls. The sample size in the hunters is 32 and in the control group 9. (From Taylor and Williams, 1966.)

genotypes but also of differences in the average experiences and habits of peoples of different cultures.

The untested *assumption* that observed differences between peoples are due exclusively to one or the other class of determinants—an assumption that has been made both ways, at one time or another, by writers of different prejudices—would seem to be both unnecessary and inappropriate.

APPENDIX F

Cross-cultural Studies by Piagetian Methods

The developmental or genetic psychology of Jean Piaget studies the stages of cognitive development from infancy to adolescence. Piagetian psychologists do not give standardized tests that have answers and quantitative scoring. Rather they look for the steps and the paths, the stages and substages, by which a growing child acquires the full cognitive abilities of the adult. The method is clinical and open-ended. The children are given tasks or questions designed to test specific cognitive powers; their answers or solutions are not scored as correct or incorrect, rather the investigator probes to find the child's own reasons for the responses given. This allows great flexibility. It can also make for difficulty in comparing different studies. The richness of Piaget's developmental psychology makes his main results difficult to summarize. See Piaget and Inhelder (1969) for a compact summary of Piagetian psychology. Other introductions to the field are given by Flavell (1963), Ginsburg and Opper (1969), and Furth (1969).

Piaget identifies four main stages in the development of human intellectual behavior:

1. The sensorimotor stage (0–2 years in Swiss children)
2. The preoperational stage (2–7 years)
3. The concrete operational stage (7–11+ years)
4. The formal operational stage (11–15+ years)

Although the open-ended, clinical methodology of Piaget is easily adapted to different cultural situations, the results of cross-cultural studies are not always strictly comparable because of variation in techniques, scoring methods, age ranges, and the extent to which verbalization is taken into account (Dasen 1972a). One might add to this list the prejudices and style of the individual experimenter. Goodnow (1969), in an excellent review of methodological issues, points out that there are major differences between various conceptualizations of Piaget's developmental psychology, and that the interpretations prevalent in English-speaking countries often differ from those found among Piaget's own students and associates.

Are stages universal?

A number of workers have questioned whether Piaget's stages are universal or whether they are a product of cultural factors. Dasen (1972a) provides a good summary of these cross-cultural studies. For western cultures the succession of stages has been verified by longitudinal studies. For nonwestern cultures it has not; however, many cross-sectional studies have been carried out.

A large number of cross-cultural studies show much variation between cultures in the proportion of subjects who complete the transition from the preoperational to the concrete operational stage and in the age at which the transition is completed. Some but not all adults of all cultures reach the concrete operational stage. Some Chinese and Japanese make the transition at an earlier age than is typical for Europeans (Tuddenham, cited in Dasen, 1972a). In a number of the nonwestern cultures sampled, all make the transition but the rate of reaching concrete operational thinking is slower than in Europeans. But, in a few societies, some persons 12–18 years of age have not reached the concrete operational stage.

There is also some evidence concerning the formal stage in different cultures. Goodnow (1962) found that middle-class Hong Kong Chinese children receiving English schooling performed as well as or better than Europeans on tasks of combinations and permutations, while lower-class children receiving Chinese schooling performed somewhat less well on the same tasks. Three investigators using a variety of tasks and population samples found no evidence of formal thinking in 14–16 year-old Papuans in New Guinea (Waddell, cited in Dasen, 1972a; Prince, 1968, 1969; Kelly, 1970).

On the whole, cross-cultural studies of Piaget's stages tend to suggest that there are more cultural differences in the rate of development than in the structure of thinking. The cognitive structures underlying the stages may thus be universal. We have not found any quantitative genetical studies (in the sense of biology rather than developmental psychology), using Piaget's methods. However, one widely quoted Piagetian study with some genetic implications, that of DeLemos (1966, 1969) on Australian Aborigines, will be discussed later in this appendix.

Dasen also reviews a number of cross-cultural studies on the sequential application of the same structures of thought to different contents. It is well established that among Europeans there is a succession of difficulty in manipulating concepts of quantity, weight, and volume. The concepts of substance, weight, and volume are acquired in this order in a variety of cultures but the sequence is not universal. The cross-cultural variation is a function of test familiarity, daily activities peculiar to a given culture, and general ecological demands and cultural characteristics, such as those described by Berry (1966) for perceptual and spatial skills.

Piaget found that the responses or reactions of Swiss children to individual tests had a constant, hierarchical organization into a succession of steps for each particular concept, the number of stages varying with each kind of problem. Some investigators of nonwestern cultures found it difficult to classify children's rractions into easily identifiable stages, but the majority of investigators found a similar hierarchy of steps in a variety of cultures. Dasen (1972a) concludes that the hierarchies described by Piaget, if, when, and where they develop, could be qualitatively the same in all cultures.

Animism

In his early work, Piaget (1929) distinguished the three attitudes that develop in succession in a child's conception of the world as (1) *realism*, (2) *animism*, and (3) *artificiality*. Child realism confuses symbols about human thoughts, feelings, and wishes with happenings in the external world. Child animism grows out of realism and tends to regard inorganic objects as living and endowed with will. Artificiality characterizes the attitude of modern science.

Jahoda (1958) made a critical review of cross-cultural research on the extent to which child animism is universal. Animism has been investigated among children of whites, Hopi, Navajo, and Zuni Indians in the United States, English, Swedish, and Chinese youngsters, and African children in Ghana and the former Belgian Congo. Most investigators found (a) some of the responses of younger children were animistic, and (b) the proportion of such responses declined with increasing age.

The only report of complete absence of child animism was by Mead (1932) on Manus children. Dennis (1943) considered that Mead's results were inconclusive because her data were not obtained using the methods employed by Piaget and others. Also her subjects were somewhat older than allowed by Piaget's theory. In fairness to Mead, Dennis points out that her field work was done in the winter of 1928–1929, before the publication of Piaget's *The Child's Conception of the World* (1929), which formed the basis for more recent cross-cultural research on child animism. Jahoda (1958) concluded that the quantitative data on the frequency and age distribution of child animism between cultures are unreliable because of wide differences in the methods used in the various studies.

Dennis (1943) proposed "that the earliest ideas of children are uniform in all societies and are the product of universal child experiences and of mental immaturity." Dennis found that low intelligence is not the explanation of the more extensive animism found in the Hopi than in white American children. Probably cultural factors account for the fact that the white children give up childish animism at a faster rate than the Hopi.

Factors in mental development

Piaget recognizes four general factors in mental development:

1. Organic growth, especially the development of the central nervous system. Here both genetic and environmental factors are clearly involved and important. Some 100 mutant genes are known to prevent normal mental

development. Many environmental effects, including protein malnutrition, social isolation, and lack of affection, also interfere with normal cognitive growth.

2. Acquisition of individual logico-experimental experience based on learning the results of actions performed on objects and the results of coordination of two or more actions. Here again both genetic factors and environmental factors (including cultural ones) are crucial to any explanation of the observed variability.

3. Social interaction of the child with the members of his society and the acquisition of culture by the child within a given generation.

4. A cybernetic interconnection of ontogenetic processes in the developing individual and the sociocultural processes that transmit the successive cultural content of each generation during the evolution of culture.

> Basically, the mental development of the child appears as a succession of three great periods. Each of these extends the preceding period, reconstructs it on a new level, and later surpasses it to an even greater degree. This is true even of the first period, for the evolution of the sensory-motor schemes extends and surpasses the evolution of organic structures which takes place during embryogenesis. Semiotic relations, thought, and interpersonal connections internalize these schemes of action by reconstructing them on the new level of representation, and surpass them until all the concrete operations and cooperative structures have been established. Finally, after the age of eleven or twelve, nascent formal thought restructures the concrete operations by subordinating them to new structures whose development will continue throughout adolescence and all of later life (along with many other transformations as well). (Piaget and Inhelder, 1969, pp. 152–153).

It is interesting that several of Piaget's sequences of stages have been observed in a wide spectrum of cultures. In fact Jolly (1972, pp. 295–319) found a number of interesting correspondences with Piagetian stages, in the object manipulation, motor development, and social interaction of monkeys and apes. Piaget set out in his early work to test Lévy-Bruhl's thesis that the minds of primitive and civilized man were different in kind. On the whole, Piaget and his followers did not find support for this, but rather found a high degree of similarity in the sequential development of cognition in all or nearly all cultures tested. They also found differences in rate of development and level achieved. We know that both genetic and nongenetic factors are important in the variation observed for Piagetian tasks within cultures. However, we do not have the data to partition the variation *between* races or cultures into innate and learned fractions.

A racial mixture study of conservation

A widely cited study by DeLemos (1966, 1969) with Australian Aborigines illustrates one possible approach to assessing the role of the genotype in cognitive development within a Piagetian framework. In this research, adaptations of Piaget's tests of the process of conservation were given to Australian Aboriginal children. Conservation refers to the capacity to perceive constancy in some attribute when the stimulus object is changed in an irrelevant manner; e.g., the volume of a given amount of fluid should be perceived as the same even though it is poured into a different shaped container. The most significant of the various comparisons used six tests of conservation (quantity, weight, volume, length, area, number) administered to 38 children whose ancestry was completely Aboriginal and 34 children whose ancestry was a mixture of Aboriginal and European. The latter children were several generations removed from their European ancestors and the majority were classified as "7/8th Aboriginal." It is also reported that "there were no apparent differences in the present environment of the part-Aboriginal and full-Aboriginal children." The children "formed a single integrated community, and the children were brought up under the same mission conditions and attended the same school." On all six tests of conservation the part-Aboriginal children were superior and in four of the six comparisons the difference attained conventional statistical significance.

In view of the absence of any evident environmental differences between the two groups DeLemos is inclined to interpret the differences in performance as heavily influenced by genetic factors:

> It would therefore seem reasonable to attribute the significant differences between the part- and the full-Aborigines in this study to genetic differences between Aborigines and Europeans, resulting in the part-Aboriginal children having a higher probability of inheriting a higher intellectual potential. Our results indicate that such differences are likely to be statistical differences in average potential rather than absolute differences, since some of the full-Aboriginal children showed performances equal to the best performances of the part-Aboriginal children. (1969, p. 268)

There are a number of difficulties in arriving at any unambiguous interpretation of these findings. First, the assertion that there are no environmental differences between the two groups compared may be questioned. Aside from the probability of physical differences between the two groups that might lead to differential treatment, it seems unlikely that in a society where there is a very substantial interest in kinship as a major determinant of social organization there would not be a general awareness of which individuals had European ancestry and it would be surprising if this did not produce some concomitant environmental differences. Second, it should be noted that comparisons between Aboriginal groups raised in different mission schools showed variations in performance on conservation tests that was comparable to the difference observed between the part-Aboriginal and full-Aboriginal children. Thus, it appears that test performance is not any simple function of the proportion of Aboriginal genes in a given population. Third, the reported differences tended to be much larger than one would expect on a simple genetic hypothesis, given the very small amount of European admixture (Willerman, 1972).

A recent study by Dasen (1972b) has attempted to replicate the findings of DeLemos comparing full- and part-Aboriginal children on measures of conservation. The 90 subjects were drawn from one of the mission schools used in the DeLemos investigation and were evenly divided in terms of being full Aboriginals or part Aboriginals (having not more than $\frac{1}{8}$ Caucasian genes) and included samples from each age from 6 through 16 years. The measures of conservation were similar to those used by DeLemos but not identical, and in addition there was a different interval of time between administration of the tests. Moreover, Dasen counterbalanced the order of administration of tests while DeLemos did not.

Contrary to the findings of DeLemos the results of this study revealed no difference in the conservation performance for the two Aboriginal groups. The existence of some procedural differences between the two studies in addition to the possibility of experimenter bias in either or both studies makes it impossible to interpret these contradictory results. Although neither experimenter was explicitly aware of the classification of particular subjects as being full or part Aboriginal it seems very likely, and indeed it is suggested by Dasen, that physical cues made it possible for the experimenter to classify more of the subjects correctly than would be expected on the basis of chance.

On the whole then, these studies can shed no clear light on the role of genotype in cognitive development in the Piagetian sense. Only as further research resolves the contradictions between studies, and clarifies the genetic and environmental factors involved, can studies such as these provide significant evidence on the primary issues confronting us in this volume.

Heritability Formulas and Related Matters

Intraclass correlations and variance proportions

The intraclass correlation is V_b/V_t, or $(V_t - V_w)/V_t$, where V_w and V_b are components of variance within and between classes, respectively, and they sum to V_t, the total variance. Thus the intraclass correlation is the proportion of the total variance that lies between rather than within classes, and reflects the extent to which class members are similar on the trait in question, relative to members of the population at large. The intraclass correlation may be obtained from an ordinary one-way analysis of variance as:

$$r_i = \frac{MS_b - MS_w}{MS_b + (n - 1)MS_w},$$

where MS refers to the mean square between or within groups, and n refers to the number of individuals per group (McNemar, 1969, p. 322). With twins or other paired data, $n - 1 = 1$, and the equation becomes simply $(MS_b - MS_w)/(MS_b + MS_w)$. An F test on MS_b/MS_w provides a simple way of testing the significance of the departure of r_i from zero. Confidence limits on a nonzero r_i may also be set (Hays, 1963, p. 424ff). An alternative way of obtaining r_i from paired data is by an ordinary Pearson r calculated from a double-entry table, a method often used in earlier studies. This will closely approximate the analysis of variance method if the number of pairs is not too small.

The interpretation of a correlation as a proportion of variance common to two sets of scores may be seen from the definition of the Pearson correlation coefficient as:

$$r = \frac{\Sigma xy}{N\sigma_x\sigma_y}.$$

If x and y refer to twin A and twin B (randomly so designated), we expect

σ_x to equal σ_y in a large sample and $\sigma_x\sigma_y$ will thus approximate σ^2. Since $\Sigma xy/N$ defines the covariance of twins' scores, we have the correlation approximately equal to the ratio of covariance to variance. Since the covariance also equals $(V_t - V_w)$, we have the equivalence to the proportion first described.

Readers familiar with the analysis of variance approach to test reliability will see analogies here.

Heritability coefficients

A simple, general heritability formula may be derived from the following expression:

$$r_i = r_g(h_B^2) + r_e(1 - h_B^2),$$

where r_i is the observed intraclass correlation on some trait in some group of relatives, h_B^2 is the broad heritability of the trait, and r_g and r_e are the genetic and environmental correlations for that trait in that group. If from some population of interest we have two kinds of relatives whose environmental correlations r_e may be assumed to be equal, we can readily derive from this the expression:

$$h_B^2 = \frac{r_{i1} - r_{i2}}{r_{g1} - r_{g2}},$$

where r_{i1} and r_{i2} are the observed intraclass correlations for the two kinds of relatives, and r_{g1} and r_{g2} are the theoretical genetic correlations. (This is essentially the derivation given by Jensen, 1967.)

Falconer (1960, p. 185) gives $2(r_I - r_F)$ as an upper-bound formula for heritability. This is equivalent to the expression just given if all variance is additive and mating is random, since under these conditions the genetic correlation between siblings is .50.

If the correlation between environments is zero, which may approximately obtain for children reared in separate families, then an even simpler heritability expression may be derived, namely:

$$h_B^2 = \frac{r_i}{r_g}.$$

Thus the correlation between identical twins reared in separate families may be taken directly as an estimate of h_B^2, since in this case $r_g = 1$.

Another heritability coefficient often encountered is Holzinger's (Newman, Freeman, and Holzinger, 1937). It is intended specifically for use with twins, and comes in two versions, one based on intraclass correlations, and one on within-pair variances. These are, respectively:

$$H = \frac{r_I - r_F}{1 - r_F}, \text{ and } H' = \frac{V_{WF} - V_{WI}}{V_{WF}}.$$

These two expressions are equivalent only if the total variances are equivalent for the identical and fraternal twins. They will yield the same values as the preceding formulas only if r_F is equal to the genetic correlation between siblings, which in general will be the case only if the environmental correlation between siblings is close to .5, or if heritability is very high.

There is a simple relationship between the H' version of Holzinger's coefficient and the F-test based on V_{WF}/V_{WI}, which is a test for significance of the genetic component in the within-family variance (Vandenberg, 1966); namely:

$$H' = 1 - \frac{1}{F}.$$

If only correlations based on same-sex and opposite-sex twin pairs are available, rather than correlations on same-sex twins identified as identical and fraternal, it is still possible to obtain a heritability estimate, if one is willing to assume that there is no differential selection or difference in environmental correlation between the same-sex and opposite-sex fraternal twins in the sample. These are often difficult assumptions to justify. Essentially, the procedure is based on the assumption that the same-sex sample consists of a group of fraternal twins of the same size and with the same correlation as the unlike-sex sample, plus a group of identical twins with an unknown correlation that can be deduced from knowledge of the sample sizes and correlations in the fraternal and total groups. An expression for the unknown identical twin correlation is:

$$r_I = \frac{N_{SS}r_{SS} - N_{OS}r_{OS}}{N_{SS} - N_{OS}},$$

Where SS and OS refer to same and opposite-sex twin pairs. This estimate of the indentical-twin correlation may then be entered into any appropriate heritability formula, using r_{OS} as the estimate for fraternal twins.

Finally, the correlation between identical twins reared together can be employed as an upper-bound estimate of h_B^2. It is often useful as a check on heritabilities calculated by the other methods described. If they yield higher estimates than the identical-twin correlation (as happens not infrequently in practice), there is strong reason to suspect a violation of underlying assumptions—most likely, that of equal r_es in the groups under consideration.

Precision of heritability estimates

In general, the accurate estimation of heritabilities requires fairly substantial samples. An expression for the approximate standard error of a broad heritability coefficient calculated according to the first general formula given is:

$$\sigma_{h_B^2} \approx \frac{1}{r_{g1} - r_{g2}} \sqrt{\frac{(1 - r_1^2)^2}{N_1} + \frac{(1 - r_2^2)^2}{N_2}},$$

where N_1 and N_2 are the numbers of pairs in the two groups; the other symbols are as in the expression for heritability. By way of illustration, for an estimate based on identical and fraternal twins with typical values of IQ correlations and 50 pairs in each group, the standard error of h_B^2 is approximately .23; for 500 pairs in each group it is about .07. The former value probably does not represent enough precision to justify a quantitative estimate of h_B^2, but the latter, with a 95 percent confidence interval of about $\pm.15$, would probably be a satisfactory approximation for most practical purposes.

Where the heritability estimate only involves one empirical correlation, as in the second general formula, the precision is substantially greater. An approximate expression for the standard error in this case is:

$$\sigma_{h_B^2} \approx \frac{1}{r_g} \sqrt{\frac{(1 - r^2)^2}{N}}$$

For example, if the correlation between identical twins reared apart is approximately .75, an estimate of heritability based on 50 pairs will have a standard error of about .06.

The studies summarized by Erlenmeyer-Kimling and Jarvik included a total of about 3000 twin pairs reared together, and about 100 identical twin pairs reared apart. These numbers should be discounted somewhat, because of the loss of accuracy in taking medians of rs based on different studies, but it is probably fair to assume they would yield as much precision as the .07 and .06 in the examples given.

Both of the formulas yield only approximations to the standard errors, especially when samples are small or correlations are high. For some more sophisticated methods of estimating the precision of heritability coefficients and variance components, the reader is referred to Jinks and Fulker (1970) and Eaves (1972) and further references cited in those articles. The simpler methods of this section should be useful, however, for obtaining a rough idea of the magnitude of errors likely to be present in particular estimates of heritability.

Agreement of heritability estimates made by different methods

Heritability estimates made on the same character in the same breeding population at the same time using different methods based on differing sets of biological relatives are often in satisfactory agreement provided the methods are appropriate, i.e., that methods assuming absence of a common environment or of maternal effects are not used when such factors are present. For example, Clayton, Morris, and Robertson (1957) estimated the heritability of abdominal bristle number in a population of *Drosophila melanogaster* as $0.51 \pm .07$ by offspring-parent regression, $0.48 \pm .11$ by half-sib correlation, and $0.53 \pm .07$ by full-sib correlation. However, when the environment is important in the development of a character, heritability estimates based on full-sub or parent-child resemblance made without taking the common environment into account may greatly overestimate the heritability as estimated by other methods, e.g., from half sibs. Roberts (1973) summarized heritability estimates for production of immunoglobins G, A, M, and D among the Mandinko of Gambia, West Africa, as follows:

Immunoglobin	Full-sibs	Father-child	Half-sibs
G	0.37	0.42	—
A	0.61	0.60	0.00
M	0.38	0.28	0.33
D	0.50	0.50	0.08

For immunoglobin M the three methods are in fairly good agreement, but for A and D the estimate from half-sibs suggests that the heritabilities based on full-sib and parent-child resemblance are greatly inflated by common environmental effects. (The methods used in the present book take common environments into account.)

Relationship of within- and between-group heritability

DeFries (1972) has pointed out that there are formal relationships between heritability within groups (h_w^2), heritability between groups (h_b^2), and total heritability in the combined population (h^2), which may be expressed in terms of two parameters, the genetic correlation (r), and the phenotypic intraclass correlation (t) describing group resemblance on the trait.

DeFries provides an algebraic derivation, but the relevant relationships may perhaps be more easily seen in the form of a diagram (see Figure G.1), in which the areas to the left and right of the vertical line represent the genetic and nongenetic portions of the variance, the upper unshaded area (A + B) represents within-group variance, and the lower shaded area (C + D) represents between-group variance. The proportion of the total variance that is between groups is equivalent to the phenotypic intraclass correlation (t). The proportion of the genetic variance that is between groups is equivalent to the genetic correlation (r). As shown below the diagram, h_b^2 and h_w^2 can be defined directly in terms of r, t, and h^2, and by minor rearrangement and substitution the other equations follow.

What implications can be drawn from these equations? Of most immediate interest is the implication that an estimate of h_w^2 obtained by twin, foster-sibling, or other suitable method can be used to estimate h_b^2 if either h^2 or r is known (t can readily be determined from the data).

Obtaining an estimate of h^2 or r is not easy, however (Jensen, 1972). Direct estimation of h^2 in, say, the combined U.S. black-white population would seem to present formidable problems, because the twins or other pairs of relatives on which such estimates might be based are ordinarily found only within races, not across them. Parent-child and sibling or half-sibling resemblances from racially mixed matings would offer possibilities in principle if the individuals entering such matings were randomly selected members of their respective populations, but of course they tend not to be.

DeFries has suggested an alternative strategy—to obtain an indirect estimate of r from other sources, and then apply this to the trait of interest.

An estimate for r for blacks and whites based on blood-group and protein genes can be obtained from the data of Nei and Roychoudhury (see p. 37). If two individuals, both black or both white, are matched at random, the average probability of finding a difference between them at a given genetic locus is .098 for protein loci and .180 for blood-group loci. If one individual is black and one white, the average probability of finding a difference is .108 for protein and .192 for blood-group loci. The probability of a difference between two individuals selected at random from a mixed group consisting

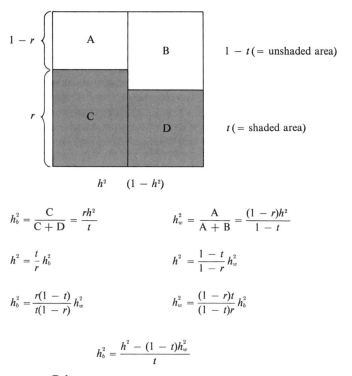

$$h_b^2 = \frac{C}{C+D} = \frac{rh^2}{t}$$

$$h_w^2 = \frac{A}{A+B} = \frac{(1-r)h^2}{1-t}$$

$$h^2 = \frac{t}{r} h_b^2$$

$$h^2 = \frac{1-t}{1-r} h_w^2$$

$$h_b^2 = \frac{r(1-t)}{t(1-r)} h_w^2$$

$$h_w^2 = \frac{(1-r)t}{(1-t)r} h_b^2$$

$$h_b^2 = \frac{h^2 - (1-t)h_w^2}{t}$$

FIGURE G.1

Equations interrelating within- and between-group heritabilities.

of equal numbers of blacks and whites lies approximately halfway between these values, if the groups are reasonably large—i.e., .013 for the protein loci and .186 for the blood-group loci. The genetic correlation r expresses the increased genetic resemblance produced by classifying individuals into groups. Two estimates of r may be obtained: from the protein loci r may be estimated as $(.103 - .098)/.103 = .049$, and from the blood-group loci as $(.186 - .180)/.186 = .032$; i.e., averaging about .04. If we calculate the between-group heritability using .04 for r, .75 for h_w^2, and DeFries's estimate of $t = .20$ for black-white IQ differences, we obtain an estimate of $h_b^2 = .125$. That is, about one-eight of the variation between groups would be genetic, as opposed to three-fourths of the variation within groups. This estimate assumes that the genes influencing IQ are average with respect to racial differentiation. However, it might be argued that this assumption is a rather awkward one to have to make, since it is an important part of the question at issue. If the genes influencing IQ have been subject to differential selection in different races they might well differ more than the average gene.

Kamin on Separated Identical Twins and Adopted Children

There is always difficulty in dealing with evidence gathered in field situations, especially in the social sciences. Such evidence invariably has shortcomings. A sufficiently determined critic can thus always discover some grounds for rejecting any item of it that he happens not to care for. It is not surprising, therefore, that writers who have drawn hereditarian or environmentalist conclusions from studies of adoptions—whether of single children, siblings, or identical twins—have found themselves the focus of critical attack. Yet to reject evidence out of hand because it is in some way flawed is a policy that if pursued to its logical extreme must lead to the rejection of all empirical evidence whatsoever. Clearly some judicious weighting of the evidence with regard to its probable validity is a more reasonable course.

The study of adopted children has long commended itself to scientists interested in the heredity-environment question. Conceptually, it is extremely elegant: if offspring are drawn randomly from the pool of biological parents in a population, and placed in a random sample of the homes in the population, then the eventual resemblance of these children to the parents who conceived them or the parents who reared them provides an index of the relative importance of genetic and environmental influences on the trait in question. Likewise, if identical twins are placed in separate homes randomly chosen from the population, their continued resemblance to each other gives testimony to the effects of the genes, their differences to the effects of the environment.

In real life, of course, it is never quite like this. The parents who conceive children that wind up in adoptions can rarely be assumed to be a random sample of the population. The homes into which the offspring are placed are selected by the adoption agencies on certain criteria of economic and emotional stability, and are self-selected by a desire for children. In real life there is always an awkward gap between conception and placement in the adoptive home, a gap that may permit pre- or early postnatal environmental factors to join genetic ones in producing resemblances (or differences) between biologically related individuals.

And yet the researcher in the field is not totally helpless in the face of these problems. He can compare adoptive families with ordinary families matched on socioeconomic and cultural variables. He can assess how restricted the traits of interest are in the population of biological or adoptive parents, or to what extent social agencies exercise selective placement with respect to economic, educational, or other criteria. He can make internal comparisons within his data to control for various possible sources of bias—for example, he can compare the degree of resemblance of children to their mothers and their fathers as a check on pre- or postnatal maternal environmental effects.

Most important of all, perhaps, is the mutual support provided by studies using different designs to attack the same problems. A shortcoming or bias that affects one study may be absent in another, or affect its results in a different way. Thus selective placement of children will tend to raise heritability estimates based on some adoptive comparisons, and to lower heritability estimates based on others. A lack of comparability of tests at different ages that creates serious problems for interpreting parent-child correlations may be trivial for a twin study based on a restricted age range. This balancing out of biases means that many doubts which may legitimately be raised cor•erning individual studies carry much less force when the literature is considered as a whole.

Over the years, most reviewers of the studies of separated twins and adopted children have come to the conclusion that these studies provide evidence of a substantial genetic component in performance on IQ tests. In a recent invited address before the Eastern Psychological Association, Leon Kamin launched a violent assault on this evidence.

Kamin's paper (Kamin, 1973) has two main parts. The first accuses the pioneers of the U.S. testing movement of more or less deliberately using the intelligence test as a weapon to keep down the underprivileged classes. Kamin finds—as one certainly can—in the psychological literature of the 1910's and 1920's a variety of statements that by today's standards are shockingly bigoted toward ethnic minorities and lower-income groups. However, he does not mention the statements that one can also find in that same literature, often by the same authors, suggesting that an important motivation of the testing movement has always been to circumvent traditional social class barriers by locating and encouraging talented youth from all sectors of society. The success of this effort is open to some debate—it has probably worked better with the lower middle class than with the really poor. But the intent certainly seems to have existed. And many children of impoverished immigrants, among others, have been its beneficiaries.

In short, it is not too difficult to find both good things and bad in the history of the intelligence-testing movement. Kamin, for whatever reasons, has elected to report only the bad.

However, our principal concern is not with Kamin's views on historical issues, it is with his critique of the evidence suggesting that intelligence-test scores have substantial heritability.

Kamin begins with the studies of the late Sir Cyril Burt, proceeds to the three other studies of identical twins reared apart, and finally considers studies of adopted children. He does not discuss the oldest and most widely used method of estimating IQ heritability, the comparison of the resemblance of identical and fraternal twins.

Kamin's scrutiny of Burt's published work amply demonstrates what is in fact clearly the case—that Burt's empirical studies in this area are inadequately and often carelessly reported, at least in sources readily available to the U.S. investigator (Jensen, 1974a). If one wishes to use Burt's data, one must take a lot on faith—which Kamin clearly is not inclined to do. Alternatively, one could presumably attempt to *find out* the explanations for some of the anomalies in the data: while Burt himself is dead, doubtless some of his former students and research associates could shed light on the details of some of the researches, and it might not be out of the question to track down some of the "unpublished theses" and "LCC reports" that Burt refers to as the primary documentation of the studies. Kamin prefers simply to dismiss Burt's data as "not worthy of serious scientific attention."

Next, Kamin turns his critical eye on the three studies of identical twins reared apart other than Burt's, those by Newman, Freeman, and Holzinger (1937), Shields (1962) and Juel-Nielsen (1965). He correctly notes that the degree of separation in such studies is often exaggerated in secondary accounts: in Shields's study, for example, the criterion for inclusion was merely having been reared in separate homes for at least five years during childhood, and in many cases the homes were those of relatives. Still, even these homes are presumably less alike than the *same* home, and so it is not at all clear, on Kamin's hypothesis, why the separated identical twins in all these studies should be more highly correlated in IQ than typical like-sex fraternal twins who are reared together.

Before we proceed to examine some of Kamin's particular criticisms, remarks on some shortcomings in his treatment of statistical significance may be in order—one relatively minor, one more serious. The first matter is the Ns he uses when evaluating the significance of correlations between age and IQ in various twin samples. He takes as N the number of individual twins, which gives an exaggerated level of significance, rather than the number of pairs, which gives a conservative test. The two members of a twin pair, whose IQs are correlated in the .70s, say, can hardly be regarded as drawn independently from the IQ distribution—let alone from the *age* distribution! When testing the significance of an age-IQ correlation based on as few as three twin pairs (as Kamin does on two occasions) the question of the proper number of degrees of freedom is not altogether academic.

The other more serious matter is in treating post hoc correlations on small subsets of the data as if they were a priori. In small samples, numerically large correlations can easily arise by chance, and to pick out and report a few such correlations after the fact as "statistically significant" makes the stated probability values virtually meaningless. For example, Kamin makes much of age-IQ correlations. From the two smallest studies of separated twins, Newman, Freeman, and Holzinger's 19 pairs and Juel-Nielsen's 12,

TABLE H.1. *Kamin's reporting of "pseudo-paired" correlations among identical twins reared apart.*

Sample	Intraclass	"Pseudo-paired"
Newman, Freeman, and Holzinger		
7 male pairs	.58	.67[a]
10 pairs, mixed (including the 7 above)	.65	.47[a]
12 female pairs	.69	−.02[b]
Shields		
14 male pairs	.71	.09[b]
24 female pairs	.81	−.40[b]
Juel-Nielsen		
9 female pairs	.59	.59[a]
3 male pairs	(.34)	(meaningless)

[a] Reported by Kamin.

[b] Not reported by Kamin, calculated by us.

Kamin calculates no less than 7 age-IQ correlations for various subsets of the data. Four of these correlations are above .60 in absolute value. But they are based on 7, 3, 9, and 3 twin pairs. And Kamin does not report age-IQ correlations for some larger available samples, such as Shields's 14 male and 24 female pairs. For the reader's benefit we provide them here. They are .15 for the male and −.05 for the female pairs. When reporting is this selective, clearly statements of statistical significance cannot be taken at face value.

Kamin invents a statistical device called the "pseudo-paired correlation," which estimates the correlation that would be produced by age matching alone. Kamin's general logical point is quite correct: that a poorly standardized test can result in some degree of inflation of identical-twin correlations, and hence of heritabilities estimated from them. (On the other hand, such improper standardization will often result in a *decrease* of heritabilities estimated from the adoption designs that he later discusses, but Kamin does not extend this reasoning to that context.) At any rate, if the "pseudo-paired" correlation were to approach the intraclass correlation in magnitude in a large sample, it would be strong grounds for mistrusting the latter. But a few large "pseudo-paired" correlations picked out from small samples mean just about as much as a few large correlations of any other kind under similar circumstances. Table H.1 may perhaps speak for itself on this matter.

One additional issue that Kamin raises regarding Shields's study should be mentioned. Kamin notes a considerably greater average difference in IQ for the 5 twin pairs who were not both tested by Shields, and offers this as evidence of "an unconscious experimenter bias introduced during the administration and/or scoring of the tests." First, the tests and conditions of administration were not such as to lend great a priori plausibility to such an interpretation. Both the tests used by Shields, the Dominoes and the Mill Hill Synonyms, are of the objective multiple-choice type, so there is not much scope for bias in the scoring. Nor does the administrator participate actively in the testing, other than in giving the initial instructions. We quote Shields on the typical conditions of administration (1962, p. 59): "It will be recalled that some were tested on quite separate occasions. Some did the test (supervised) in the same room. But in most cases they were tested separately on the same occasion. While one was being interviewed the other did the Dominoes in another room. The Mill Hill was generally done by the twins together, but supervised to avoid their comparing notes during the testing."

In short, while we agree wholeheartedly with Kamin's general argument—that it is methodologically superior in a twin study to have two separate testers, each testing one twin of each pair—and while we ourselves have worried about this matter in connection with Shields's personality ratings in this study, we simply do not find it credible that "unconscious experimenter bias" would have produced a large effect on ability scores under these conditions. Are there alternative hypotheses?

One is that colleagues are most likely to be called in to test a twin at a remote location, and hence a twin who may have been subjected to a greater-than-average degree of cultural and educational disparity from his partner. For example, in one of the five pairs in question (Pair S f 19) one sister spent her life in South America, mostly in prosperous circumstances, and was tested there, while the other lived in poverty in South America until age 9, in Scandinavia until 35, and subsequently in England, where Shields tested her. As Shields properly notes, since the native language of neither twin was English, their scores on the vocabulary test must be considered of doubtful validity as an intelligence measure, although he did retain the pair in the study.

Another possibility is that colleagues cannot always be counted on to do the job right. Shields says of another pair, both tested by others (Pair S m 1) "These boys of 14 appear to have worked too fast on the Dominoes. It is suspected that they did not grasp the instructions equally well . . ." (p. 63). A twin in another pair who scored only one point on the Dominoes was also tested by a colleague. Some of her replies (impossible answers) made it pretty clear that she did not understand the test instructions. Shields excluded the pair (S f 3) from his calculations, but Kamin does not, and the 27-point difference makes a major contribution to his evidence for "unconscious experimenter bias."

Thus in three of the five cases there are other plausible reasons for large obtained differences. And in one of the remaining two, the difference was in fact close to the average for the sample of separated twins. On the whole, then, the evidence for experimenter bias is hardly compelling.

Finally, let us consider Kamin's treatment of the adoption data. He begins with the Burks (1928) and Leahy (1935) studies, which compared correlations within adoptive families to those within biological families matched to the adoptive families on a number of variables. He concedes the major finding of both studies—that the parent-child correlations are much higher in the biological than in the adoptive families, but challenges the interpretation usually made, that this is because of the presence of a genetic resemblance between parent and child in the biological families that does not exist in the adoptive ones. Kamin's thesis is, essentially, that adoptive families are environmentally different from biological families in ways that fail to generate the large correlations among their members that are found in biological families.

Kamin notes that on some variables for which the families were not matched (age, income, family size) there were average differences between the biological and adoptive families, of a sort that one might expect—the adoptive parents tended to be somewhat older, with higher incomes and fewer children. He also notes that in Leahy's data the correlations between spouses were higher for intelligence and lower for education in the adoptive than in the control families. The actual correlations were .57 versus .41, and .59 versus .71, respectively—this might seem rather modest support for the claim that "The entire nexus of environmental IQ determinants appears to differ across the two types of families."

Kamin does, however, point to some limited but theoretically relevant data: the IQ correlation between parents and biological children *in adoptive families*. On the basis of 20 such cases in Leahy's sample and an additional 28 from the adoption study of Freeman, Holzinger, and Mitchell (1928), Kamin concludes that biological children in adoptive families show markedly lower correlations with their parents than do biological children in ordinary families, a result which fits his hypothesis that adoptive families are different in a way that leads to lower IQ correlations. Clearly, a larger body of data on this point would be welcome, as well as some information on how representative adoptive families with biological children are of all adoptive families —an essential link in Kamin's argument here.

Kamin then goes on to examine Skodak and Skeels's study (1949) in which adoptive childrens' IQs were shown to correlate .32 with the education of their biological mothers, but only .02 with the education of their adoptive mothers, another finding that has often been interpreted as evidence in favor of the influence of genes on IQ. Kamin fields this tricky datum approximately as follows: (1) the adoptive mother's education doesn't correlate with the adoptive child's IQ because at the levels of education from which adoptive parents come, parental education is not a relevant variable in influencing the child's IQ, and (2) the biological mother's education *does* correlate with the child's IQ, because social workers in placing children in adoptive homes put children of more educated biological mothers in homes that have more of the environmental characteristics that produce high IQs in children. Kamin then proceeds to demonstrate that children of more educated biological mothers were selectively placed in the homes of more highly educated adoptive mothers, apparently forgetting that the adoptive mother's education level is not supposed to affect the child's IQ, or indeed to be correlated with variables that do, otherwise the argument in step (1) comes tumbling down.

If it isn't education, what else might it be? Kamin vaguely hints at "cultural and environmental amenities." But two composite measures of such amenities in the Burks study correlated only .21 and .25 with child's IQ in the adoptive families, although the reliabilities of both measures were in the .90s, and several similar indexes in Leahy's study had correlations ranging from .13 to .26 with child's IQ in this group. In both studies these variables were much more highly correlated with child's IQ in the control group of biological families: .42 and .44 for Burks, and .37 to .53 for Leahy. This difference is not because the adoptive families were more highly selected on these variables than the control families. Burks states that the distributions of her indexes were quite similar in the two groups. Data that Leahy presents suggest that her composite "Environmental status" index also had a roughly equal variability in both groups (although there was a difference in mean in favor of the adoptive families). "Environmental status" is similarly related in both groups to occupational level, and occupational level to parental IQ. But all of these are much more highly related to child's IQ in the biological than in the adoptive families. Thus it cannot be restriction of range on variables like these that is accounting for lowered correlations in the adoptive families. In fact, it cannot very well be selection for *any* important environmental variables, for if the relevant causal variables—whatever they may be—are dramatically restricted in range in adoptive families relative to matched biological families, then the consequent products, the children's IQs, should also be dramatically restricted. A modest reduction of range was found in Leahy's study; little or none in Burks's or Skodak's.

In short, while an explanation of the data from adoption studies in purely environmental terms may be logically possible, on the whole Kamin's interpretation seems much less plausible than a view that allows a place for substantial genetic factors—unless, perhaps, one begins with a strong a priori commitment to a purely environmentalistic position.

Not all environmentalists, by the way, will thank Kamin for the emphasis he puts on selective placement. While it may be necessary to invoke selective placement in the Skodak and Skeels study to save the hypothesis of zero IQ heritability, the more general consequence of postulating selective placement in adoption studies is to *raise* heritability estimates. Some of the moderate observed correlations between adoptive parents and children, or adoptive siblings, which in the absence of selective placement must be attributed to environmental factors, may be genetic if selective placement is going on.

One final general issue deserves comment. In his critique, Kamin seems more than once to slip into the "either-or" fallacy regarding the heredity-environment question. Thus he appears to take significant evidence that the environment can influence IQ as somehow refuting the possibility that the genes can. All the authors of the separated twin and adoption studies believe that the environment influences scores on IQ tests, and cite evidence from their studies to demonstrate it. All behavior geneticists who divide the variance of IQ tests into genetic and environmental portions thereby signify their belief that one ought to be able to show the influence of environmental variables (of some sort) on IQ-test performance. (Burt would not have accepted this for the underlying trait of intelligence, which he *defined* as innate, but he clearly accepted it for the observed test scores.) Thus Kamin gives a somewhat misleading impression when he suggests that by ferreting in the appendix of Shields's book he has somehow brought to light damaging evidence of environmental effects—that twins brought up in related families turn out more alike than twins brought up in unrelated families. Shields not only reports this evidence in his main text (see his Table 21), he positively insists on it (p. 105).

On the whole, then, although Kamin's critique emphasizes some methodological points worthy of attention in conducting and evaluating studies in this area, it does not, in our view, constitute an unbiased survey of the data, and it suffers from enough logical and statistical difficulties that Kamin's "reasonably prudent man" will want to think twice before accepting its conclusions.

There is, obviously, room for some range of opinions concerning the exact quantitative implication of the studies of separated identical twins and adoptive families for the heritability of IQ. Slightly different assumptions in the analysis can easily push heritability estimates up or down 10 or 20 points, as examples we cite elsewhere in this book make clear. Correcting or not correcting raw figures for test unreliability, age, and restriction of range can make an appreciable difference, and these are matters on which experts do not always see eye to eye. Consequently we suspect that for some time to come the individual social scientist's preferences will have some bearing on the exact heritability figure he most favors for IQ in the U.S. population. But we believe that the data do place some real constraints on the plausible values of this index, and that for at least the last 30 years these values have not included either zero or one.

Postscript

While type was being set for this appendix, Kamin published in book form a considerably expanded version of his critique of IQ heritability studies (*The Science and Politics of I.Q.* Potomac, Md.: Lawrence Erlbaum Associates, 1974). In it he amplifies his earlier presentation, and adds additional material—for example, chapters on kinship correlations (including twins), and on prenatal effects. Kamin's chapters on separated identical twins and adopted children generally follow along the lines of the paper we have discussed, and the majority of the specific comments made in this appendix, and the general conclusion, would apply to the book as well, although they would fall short of doing it full justice.

APPENDIX I

Jencks's Heritability Estimation

In Appendix A of his book *Inequality* (1972) Jencks arrives at estimates of the heritability of IQ that are rather lower than those typically reported (Jensen, 1967, 1969; Jinks and Fulker, 1970; Vandenberg, 1971; Burt, 1972). In part this is a result of his making certain arbitrary but not indefensible decisions: for example, he excludes British studies, which tend on the whole to yield higher heritability estimates than U.S. studies, and he introduces a correction for restriction of the range of variability in single studies, a correction that tends generally to lower his heritabilities. Thus his estimates do not necessarily apply to exactly the same populations and conditions as those of others. But even making allowance for this, they are on the low side.

Jencks's approach is via path analysis. He first constructs a path diagram involving natural and adoptive parents and offspring. This is underdetermined, and so cannot be completely solved, but yields a table of sets of values of the genotype-phenotype correlation (h), the environment-phenotype correlation (e), and the genotype-environment correlation (s), for various assumed values of the parent-child genetic correlation (g). He then proceeds to a similar analysis of natural- and adoptive-sibling and twin data, attempting to find the best fits to these data from among the combinations of values generated in the parent-child analysis. Actually, he finds that different sets of data are fit more or less well by different combinations of values, and finally chooses as his "best guess" 45 percent for heredity (h^2), 35 percent for environment (e^2) and 20 percent for the covariance of genes and environment ($2hes$).

The estimate of gene-environment covariance from the parent-child analysis plays a key role in Jencks's subsequent analyses. Unfortunately, the path equations leading to the solution for this covariance present difficulties. Jencks's solution entails comparing the correlation between natural parent and child (Jencks's eq. 11) with that between adoptive parent and child (his eq. 12). But his paths for the latter case take an unnecessarily circuitous route

TABLE I.1.   *Comparison of the Jencks and revised solutions for parent-child equations.*

	Jencks			Revised		
g	h^2	e^2	$2hes$	h^2	e^2	$2hes$
.50	.29	.52	.19	.43	.41	.15
.45	.34	.47	.19	.49	.36	.15
.40	.40	.41	.19	.56	.29	.15
.35	.47	.34	.19	.65	.20	.15
.30	.59	.23	.19	.77	.07	.15
.25	.76	.06	.18	—	—	—

(see his eq. 5). They proceed from the child's genotype, via the natural parents' genotypes and phenotypes, to the adoptive parents' phenotypes. So far so good. But then the path detours via the adoptive parents' genotypes instead of proceeding directly via the child's environment to the child's IQ. Presumably it is the adoptive parents' *phenotypes* that are brought into correlation with the natural mother's phenotype via the selective placement process, and that constitute the relevant environment for the child. The adoptive parents' genotypes are beside the point. It would make no difference if the genotype-phenotype correlation for the adoptive parents were zero.

What happens if we use the more direct path? To minimize complications, we will make the oversimplified but not very critical assumption that the selective placement process acts purely by matching the adoptive to the natural mother, and we will accept Jencks's estimate of .16 for this IQ correlation, which becomes .20 when corrected for variance between samples (to be consistent with his practice elsewhere). We can now replace Jencks's equation 12 for the correlation of adoptive parent's and child's IQ with:

$$r_{\text{IQAP, IQC}} = 1.57\,ew + 1.57\,xgh(h + se)$$

where x is the selective placement correlation, i.e., .20, w represents the effect of parent's IQ on child's environment, and the 1.57 takes into account the IQ correlation between spouses. We will make one further change in Jencks's procedure, namely to exclude the Freeman study in deriving the empirical value for the correlation between adoptive parent and child. It seems doubtful that the selective placement process in the Freeman study (which included a more varied sample of adoptions, and involved many late placements) would be comparable to that in the studies from which the parental placement correlation was estimated. If not, an appreciable degree of distortion would be introduced. The weighted parent-child correlation from the remaining studies is .174; corrected in Jencks's usual way it becomes .23. Combining our modified equation with Jencks's equations 11 and 10 the solution for the covariance term $2hes = .153$ is straightforward.

This value of approximately .15 (Jencks originally obtained .19) makes an appreciable difference in the estimates of h^2 and e^2 for various values of g, as shown in Table I.1. The values of heritabilities for given values of g run about .15 higher in the revised solutions. The revised values also greatly decrease the discrepancy noted by Jencks between his predicted values (.30 to .32) for the correlation between natural mother and adopted child, and Skodak and Skeels's obtained value of .45. Use of the revised figures yields a predicted value of .40 for this correlation.

Extending the analysis to twins and siblings, substituting our Table I.1 values for Jencks's, but otherwise following Jencks's procedures and assumptions, we obtain a best fit to the data with $h^2 = .61$, $e^2 = .23$, and $g = .37$.

Neither our values nor Jencks's come close to fitting his estimates of the overall average IQ correlation between unrelated children reared in the same home. The values are reasonably consistent with the correlations in two studies, those by Burks and Leahy, but not with those of Freeman et al. and Skodak and Skeels. Skodak and Skeels's adopted pairs were not *all* unrelated—at least one appears to have been a pair of same-sex twins (their 47G and 48G). But it would take more than deleting this one pair to bring their figures into line with the others. As noted earlier, the Freeman sample was quite diverse, including for example both legitimate and illegitimate children, many late adoptions, and a substantial proportion of children with one or both parents recorded as mentally defective, so adoptive-sibling correlations might be somewhat unrepresentative in this sample.

Finally, Jencks's equations for identical twins reared apart yield an estimate of h^2 in the neighborhood of .55 (again, following his assumptions and empirical estimates, but using the revised values from Table I.1). This last result is based only on Newman, Freeman, and Holzinger's 19 pairs, the one U.S. study, and hence would be subject to a large sampling error.

Thus, the two plausible changes we have made in Jencks's analysis would appear to modify his "best guess" values from around 45 percent for heredity, 35 percent for environment, and 20 percent for gene-environment covariance, to around 60 percent, 25 percent, and 15 percent, respectively. Clearly, making still other assumptions could modify them further, up or down. The point simply is that Jencks's mode of analysis does not inherently yield results completely incommensurate with those obtained by others.

Some Issues in Studies of Population Change

Interpreting the difference in average IQs measured at two different times in a population can be a ticklish business, and it is quite safe to say that no single study cited in the text avoids all possible sources of difficulty in interpretation. However, since the difficulties vary from study to study the main trends observed are probably dependable.

One rather critical matter concerns the definition of a population as being "the same" at two different times. Obviously, different persons are tested on the two different occasions. If sample selection differs from one testing to the next in a systematic way, a spurious apparent rise or fall in average IQ may result. Studies that test entire populations, say, of school children, present the least difficulty from this standpoint. Some attrition through children's absence from school on the test day is always present, but it is most unlikely that this is an important biasing factor in the major studies cited, since (1) the fraction of pupils absent on a given test day was usually not large—e.g., it was about 6 percent in the Scottish study; (2) many of the absences that do occur are for reasons unrelated to intelligence, and in only some of the remaining cases would the association with intelligence be strong enough to have an appreciable statistical effect; and (3) most biasing factors are apt to be reasonably similar in their operation on the two test occasions, and thus to cancel out.

The studies testing samples from larger populations are open to more question on this score, especially since only a few have used modern sampling techniques. And even a well designed recent study such as Schaie and Strother's that uses stratified random samples drawn from a complete roster of the population comes into some question because of the exceptionally high loss rate (over 80 percent) from persons who were selected for the sample refusing or being unable to cooperate. This offers a good deal of scope for the operation of bias, even though the authors do present some assurance of the comparability of the samples on SES measures.

Other problems that arise in the interpretation of studies on population change have to do with the comparability of tests over time. Several studies are cited in the text in which a group was given at the same time two tests, one based on a recent normative group, and one on a earlier normative group, thus indirectly comparing the two normative populations. If some items in the earlier test have become obsolete because of cultural change, one is faced with the choice of using a revised version of the earlier test of uncertain equivalence (as Tuddenham did) or of having a test containing some items whose difficulty may be quite different from what they were at the time of the original normalization (as would probably be true for the Stanford-Binet restandardization).

Another potential source of distortion, which would particularly affect subgroup comparisons based on standard scores, would be systematic changes in trait variability within the population. An apparent divergence of subgroup means expressed in standard score units might in fact be produced by decreased variability within the groups rather than an increase in mean difference between them. This is not necessarily a spurious effect in terms of social consequences, which may depend as much on the discriminability of the two groups in performance as on the absolute size of the average difference between them; however, in seeking causal explanations one would surely want to distinguish change of means from change of variability. Fortunately, there is little reason to believe that this particular source of distortion is of much importance in most of the investigations cited in the text. The Scottish and English studies report little change over time in raw-score standard deviations (mostly, slight increases). The Honolulu data show some decrease in variability, but the observed widening of between-group differences cannot be attributed to this, since all standard score conversions were based on the 1924 population. Likewise, the Schaie and Strother study standardized all scores on the basis of the first test administration.

Finally, a perfectly genuine and appropriately measured difference may be subject to different interpretations. Particularly important as an alternative to hypotheses that attribute IQ trends to environment are hypotheses based on in- or out-migration that is differential by IQ. By no means all of our studies provide evidence adequate for rejecting the alternative of migration, although several discuss it in some detail. It is clear that in the total U.S. population the levels of immigration and emigration in recent decades have been nowhere near high enough to account for IQ shifts on the order of 10–15 IQ points in a generation, even if the immigrant and emigrant IQ means were to depart much more drastically from the total U.S. population mean than seems likely to be the case. However, the situation may be quite different for local populations. There pretty clearly was differential migration by racial subgroup into Honolulu during the period covered by the Smith study, as well as differential rates of intermarriage between groups. In this case, the striking uniformity of test-score improvement across racial groups makes it difficult to believe that differential migration is playing a central role in the results. However, the racial intermarriage could be a factor contributing to the observed slight increase in racial differences, if lower-IQ members of higher-scoring subgroups and higher-IQ members of lower-scoring subgroups are marrying one another and contributing their offspring to the mixed groups. Such assortative mating by ability is suggested by the fact that the variability of the mixed groups is not much higher than that of the component racial groups (as noted in the text).

APPENDIX K

Calculation of Effects of Higher Reproduction by Lower IQ Mothers

The average IQ of mothers below the mean in a normal distribution is, in σ units, y/q, where y is the ordinate of the normal curve at q, and q is .5. Thus it is .3989/.5, or approximately .8 σ. This is equivalent to 12 IQ points below the mean, for $\sigma = 15$. Similarly, the average IQ of mothers above the mean is $+12$ IQ points. If the mothers below the mean have twice as many offspring as those above, and there is no regression toward the mean, the offspring generation should differ on the average by $(12–24)/3 = -4$ IQ points. An appreciable degree of regression toward the mean would be expected, however, so a decline of 2 or 3 IQ points in a generation would be a more plausible prediction.

The actual reproductive differential between mothers below and above average IQ in the U.S. black population may well have been slightly less extreme than 2 to 1 in recent decades. For example, some U.S. census figures are available on differential reproduction by educational level for white and nonwhite—mostly black—women (Mitra, 1966). While education and IQ are not perfectly correlated, of course, it seems likely that education would be at least as strongly associated with reproductive behavior as IQ would be. In 1960, in a sample of married nonwhite women aged 45–49, who had presumably completed their families, mothers who had not gone beyond elementary school (about 60 percent of the sample) had, on the average, 3.83 children, and mothers who had more education than this had, on the average, 2.11 children, a ratio of approximately 1.8 to 1.

A more precise estimate of reproductive differentials among black women would need to take several additional factors into account. First, the data cited include some nonblacks. Second, they do not represent all black women —it is quite possible that including the substantial group of black women who have children but no husband present might tend to increase the fertility differential by IQ. Third, the generation interval needs to be considered as well: if low-IQ black mothers not only have more children but have them on the average earlier in life, the fertility differential would again be increased. And finally—and in the other direction—the data cited do not take into account the sharp drop-off of reproduction at very low IQ levels. For U.S. whites this last factor is sufficient to wipe out completely any association between low IQ and increased fertility in the population as a whole (Higgins et al., 1962; Bajema, 1963), even though in data such as Mitra's, white wives, like nonwhite wives, show a substantial reproductive differential by education.

APPENDIX L

Some Details
on Table 6.2 (p. 143)

The World War I figures are based on data from Yerkes (1921, Table 332). The combined score places the different tests used (Alpha, Beta, individual examinations) onto a common scale.

The World War II figures are based on Davenport's (1946) Tables I and III. The period from June 1944 to April 1945 was chosen from Table III to overlap maximally with the September 1944 to August 1945 period on which Table I was based. Overall rates of disqualification on mental ability grounds (last row of Table I), were calculated by weighting the various service commands in terms of the white and Negro populations of their component states in 1940 (Statistical Abstract of the U.S., 1953, Table 25). The proportions from Table III were then modified by expanding the lowest scoring group to reflect preinduction rejections on mental-ability grounds. This was done by expressing mental-test failures as a percentage of total men processed, and adding this to the percentage in the lowest scoring group of inductees after so readjusting percentages that the total would equal 100. This in effect assumes that if a proportionate number of those failing the preinduction tests had been inducted and allowed to take the AGCT, they would all have placed in the lowest scoring category. This would probably have been true in most cases, but there would no doubt have been exceptions. Any appreciable effect of this would very likely be confined to the estimate of the lowest interval boundary; moreover, there is no particular reason to assume the effect would be differential by racial group.

The Vietnam figures are based on Karpinos's (1966) Tables 1 and 3. Those disqualified for medical or administrative reasons are excluded, and the adminstrative acceptees are included with those scoring below 24.

The assumption of an underlying normal distribution of ability is reasonably well supported by the World War I data, for which complete distributions are available (Yerkes, 1921, Table 165, Fig. 7). While neither the

Table 6.2 Details 309

white nor the black distribution is strictly normal—the latter shows a slight positive skew and the former may be a bit leptokurtic—the departures from normality are fairly minor. Certainly neither the white nor the black curve is dramatically skewed or truncated. The displacement of the curves estimated on normal curve assumptions in Table 6.2 (1.16 σ) is reasonably close to the difference between means calculated directly (1.24 σ).

Severe Early Malnutrition and Intellectual Performance

The classical definition of malnutrition covers the well known deficiency diseases: that is, if a person does not take in the minimal required amounts of one or more nutrients over long periods, specific symptoms of the deficiency appear, in conditions such as anemia, beriberi, goiter, pellagra, scurvy, or growth retardation.

Gershoff (1971) distinguished two additional kinds of malnutrition. The second type results when a person experiences repeated periods of prolonged hunger even though his total intake during 24 hours or in a month is sufficient to prevent development of a deficiency disease. This type of undernutrition is widespread among American children from impoverished families who often go to school without breakfast, have no lunch, and eat only one substantial meal each 24 hours, usually late in the day (Citizens' Board of Inquiry into Hunger and Malnutrition in the United States, 1968), or whose families run out of food in the last week or few days of each month.

Gershoff's third type of malnutrition derives from members of a social or cultural subgroup being unable to acquire sufficient food meeting social and cultural approval, or unwilling to use nutritious food that is available but not culturally acceptable. For example, the vitamin-deprived poor of the rice-producing areas of the world prefer the polished rice eaten by members of the middle and upper classes to the nutritionally better, vitamin-rich, unpolished rice. Many American Indian and some black mothers refuse to feed their protein-malnourished babies the powdered milk provided by government agencies, probably on the nutritionally wrong grounds that since milk gives abdominal pains and diarrhea to many adults in their communities (those who lack adult lactase), it is not good for babies.

It is usual to divide the degrees of malnutrition into severe and moderate, also called chronic, categories. We now consider at some length the consequences for later intellectual performance of severe early undernutrition. An excellent summary of the medical aspects of protein-calorie malnutrition is presented by Viteri and Arroyave (1973).

Effects of severe malnutrition in young children

Protein-calorie malnutrition (PCM) refers to a group of diseases arising from inadequate diet especially in childhood. Marasmus and kwashiorkor are the two extremes of the PCM group of diseases.

Marasmus, from a Greek word meaning "to waste," is caused by a continued restriction of total food intake including protein. Marasmus, the childhood equivalent of starvation in adults, usually develops in infants younger than one year and is most frequent in the towns and cities of the underdeveloped areas.

Kwashiorkor, a word derived from the language of the Ga tribe living in and around Accra, Ghana, means "the sickness the older child gets when the next baby is born," that is, after the older child is weaned. Kwashiorkor results when food intake, even if adequate in calories, is deficient in protein. The protein deficiency may be quantitative (that is, all essential amino acids may be present in the diet but not in sufficient amount) or qualitative (that is, one or more essential amino acids may be absent from the diet). Kwashiorkor occurs mostly in the second year after birth and is most frequent in the rural areas in underdeveloped countries. However, the disease has long been known in Europe and the United States under various names including nutritional edema and *Mehlnährschaden* (Pesé, 1966).

In between these two extreme forms of PCM are diseases due to varying combinations of protein and calorie deficiencies together with deficiencies of minerals and vitamins and associations with infections. Two examples of the intermediate diseases are marasmic kwashiorkor and nutritional dwarfing.

The mental impairment in PCM may be associated with loss of potassium from the brain (Garrow, 1967). In severe PCM up to 40 percent of the total body potassium may be lost (Garrow, 1965). The low level of potassium is not due to a deficiency of dietary intake of potassium, but seems to be related to difficulties in regulation of extracellular body fluids in these patients.

Severely undernourished children exhibit characteristic changes in mental state starting with irritability and proceeding to apathy, stupor, coma, and death. The mental changes are more pronounced in kwashiorkor than in marasmus and the total body potassium is also more reduced in kwashiorkor than in marasmus.

Brown (1965), in an examination of 1094 autopsy records at Mulago Hospital, Kampala, on Ugandan children from newborn to 15 years old, presents evidence on the brain weight of 96 malnourished children contrasted with a control group of 104 children who were not recorded as malnourished. The average brain weight in malnourished children under one year of age was 73 grams less than the well nourished children, a difference that with his sample size fell short of statistical significance. Infants 1–2 years old who were malnourished had a brain weight of 105 grams less than the controls, and those

2–3 years old had a brain weight of 162 grams less than the controls, both results being significant at the 1 percent confidence level. The brain weight of children 3–4 years old was 107 grams less than the controls, and that of children 4–5 years old 142 grams less than the controls, these results being significant at the 5 percent confidence level. The weight of the malnourished brain was for all ages 87.6 percent of the weight of the controls and ranged from a low of 84.6 percent for the 2–3-year-old age group to a high of 90.0 percent in the 3–4-year-old group.

Studies on lower animals report similar findings. For example, Zamenhof, Van Marthens, and Margolis (1968) fed two groups of female rats, four in each group, on a high and low protein diet for one month before mating and through gestation. The four mothers fed on the 27 percent protein diet had 32 offspring and the four mothers fed on the 8 percent protein diet had 31 offspring. The body weight of the offspring from the mothers on low protein diet was 30 percent below that of offspring from the high-protein-diet mothers; brain weight (the cerebral hemispheres without the cerebellum and olfactory lobes) was 23 percent less; the amount of DNA (reflecting the number of cells) was 10 percent less, and the amount of protein in the cells of the brain 19.8 percent less. Thus the brain weight and body weight of offspring of mother rats malnourished before and during pregnancy is reduced, with fewer cells, and less protein content in the cells of the brain. If, at birth, brain cells of the rat are predominantly neurons, and the number of neurons becomes final at around the time of birth, then protein undernourishment before and during pregnancy may result in offspring with a permanent brain neuron deficiency.

A number of investigators have attempted to find direct evidence associating protein-calorie malnutrition with impaired mental development in humans. The earlier studies measured intelligence-test performance or mental development in groups of severely malnourished children after nutritional rehabilitation. Stein and Kassab (1970) reviewed a number of such studies, including: Géber and Dean (1956) in Uganda; Stoch and Smythe (1963) in Capetown, South Africa; Cabak and Najdanvic (1965) in Yugoslavia; Cravioto and co-workers (1967) in Mexico; Champakam and co-workers (1968) in the Telengana area of Andra Pradesh, India; and Mönckeberg (1968) on three samples of children in Chile. A variety of behavioral and developmental indicators were applied; in general the severely malnourished children after rehabilitation were inferior to controls on one or more indicators. A majority of the investigators concluded the damage was irreversible when the malnutrition was early, severe, and prolonged.

Methodological issues in studies of early malnutrition

The interpretation of the lower intelligence and developmental scores, as well as the anthropometric indicators of physical growth, is difficult, because the effects of malnutrition tend to be confounded with ecological, social, cultural, and economic factors. The differences in physical status and behavioral performances could be mediated by biochemical disorders resulting from nutritional shortages or imbalances, or by biosocial factors associated with malnutrition, or by some interaction of nutritional and nonnutritional variables (Pollitt, 1969; Kallen, 1973). Certainly single variables, for example, stature alone, are not dependable indicators of the nutritional background of children. Pollitt and Ricciuti (1969) showed that differences of stature in a sample of children from the slums of Lima, Peru, confounded differences in nutritional background with other important biosocial factors: more of the short children had short mothers, who had a greater number of marriages, more pregnancies, and fewer years in school.

Kaplan (1972) suggests that an adequate study of the effects of malnutrition on mental development should meet six criteria: (1) Known duration of malnutrition and extent of physio-psychological effects. (2) Exposure to malnutrition during approximately the same period of development for all subjects. (3) Control of other appropriate physiological variables—prematurity, chronic disease, congenital malformations. (4) Control of pertinent environmental variables—family income, socioeconomic class, diet, parental education. (5) Measurement of mental development with a variety of tests—IQ, cognitive, perceptual and motor skills, emotional and personality development. (6) Repeated mental-development measures taken at intervals over a period of 10 years or more.

None of the studies listed above meet all six of Kaplan's criteria, but she felt that several of the studies she reviewed—including Cabak and Najdanvic (1965), Chase and Martin (1970), Pollitt and Granoff (1967), and Stoch and Smythe (1967)—employed relatively thorough methodologies and presented very convincing results.

In a critical article Warren (1973) concluded that the four studies Kaplan found "relatively thorough and very convincing" were "inherently inadequate in design and thus incapable of testing their own hypotheses." He considers the ideal design of a study of early severe malnutrition and later intellectual performance would be *prospective* from the prenatal period, *experimental* with random assignment of subjects and nutritional supplementation to level of nutrition and age of malnutrition, and *longitudinal* at least up to physical and mental maturity. He points to a number of studies in progress in Columbia, Guatemala, and Mexico that closely approach the ideal design.

Some existing studies of infant malnutrition and intelligence

Rather than delay further review and comment until the results of the new prospective, experimental, and longitudinal studies are published, we assemble here available quantitative data on the problem in Table M.1 below, and outline some of the more interesting studies that support the data in that table.

Stoch and Smythe (1963, 1967, 1968) present evidence that severe undernutrition during the first two years of life, when brain growth is most active, results in a permanent reduction in head circumference (and, by inference, in brain volume) and a restricted intellectual development.

Twenty Cape Coloured infants, grossly undernourished in infancy, were followed for 11 years starting in 1955. They were matched for age and sex

TABLE M.1. *Studies of the relationship between undernutrition and intellectual development.*

Investigators	Age at Recovery from Malnutrition, in mo	No. of Test Children	Age at Time of Testing, in yr	Test Used	Mean IQ or Developmental Index	
					Control	Test
Cabak & Najdanvic, 1965	4–24	36	7–14	Binet	101, 109	88*
Stoch & Smythe, 1967	>10	20	8–13	New S. Afr. Ind. Scale	76.7 ± 9.4	61.2 ± 8.1*
Champakam et al, 1968	18–36	11	8–9	Specially developed	56.1	17.0*
		5	9–10	for study	69.8	37.9*
		3	10–11		78.5	40.4*
Mönckeberg, 1968	3–11	14	3–6	Binet	?(100)	62*?
Birch et al., 1971	6–30	37	5–13	WISC	81.5 ± 17.23	68.5 ± 13.35*
Chase & Martin, 1970	2–12	19	2–6	Yale Rev.	99 ± 7	82 ± 16*
Evans et al., 1971	10–48	40	9–14	New S. Afr. Ind. Scale	77.7 ± 14.8	77.4 ± 15.2
				Harris Draw-a-Man	79.6 ± 18.0	75.5 ± 17.8*
Brockman & Ricciuti, 1971	12.2	10	1.2	10 sorting tests	21.0	9.2*
	19.2	10	2.9	10 sorting tests	40.0	20.0*
Hertzig et al., 1972	<24	71	5.9–10	WISC Full Scale	65.99 ± 13.59	57.75 ± 10.75*
				WISC Verbal	73.70 ± 14.55	64.92 ± 11.80*
				WISC Performance	63.69 ± 13.30	56.30 ± 11.85*

Source: Enlarged and revised from Chase, 1973.

*Difference between control and test children significant at the 5 percent level or beyond.

with the control group of 11 boys and 9 girls who were not severely under-nourished. Although both groups were from the lowest socioeconomic level and lived in urban poverty, the control-group children lived in relatively stable home environments, whereas unemployment, alcoholism, illegitimacy, and broken homes were the rule in the undernourished group.

There were no significant differences between the parents of the two groups of children in measurements of head circumference or intelligence quotients. The children came to the attention of the investigators from various health agencies. Fourteen of the children were between 10 and 16 months old when first seen; the rest ranged up to 3 years of age. Height and weight of the ex-perimental children were markedly reduced, as was head circumference. Their EEGs showed a number of deviations from normal. In tests over the follow-up period, the undernourished children showed inferior performance on the Gesell and Merrill-Palmer scales and adaptations of the Stanford-Binet and Wechsler intelligence tests.

Champakam, Srikantia, and Gopalan (1968) studied the mental develop-ment of 19 children who were treated for kwashiorkor in the clinical unit of the Nutrition Research Laboratories in Hyderabad, India. The subjects, 8 boys and 11 girls, were between 18 and 36 months of age on admission for treatment, and were 8–11 years of age when tested.

Each undernourished child was matched with 3 children from his school class. Matching was attempted for age, sex, religion, caste, economic status, family size, birth order, and educational level of the parents. Matching was apparently only partially successful. The control group finally reported com-prised 25 males and 25 females.

Special tests of intelligence and sensory development in the Telugu and Urdu languages were developed and standardized in the area. Measurements of height, weight, and head circumference at the time of testing were obtained.

The average height of the males was 93.9 percent of that of the controls, while that of the females was 96.3 percent of the controls. The head circum-ference of males was 98.6 percent of the controls and that of the females 98.5 percent.

The children who had been treated for kwashiorkor made strikingly lower average scores than the control group on the ability battery and its subtests. The boys averaged only 41.3 percent of the score made by the controls on the test as a whole, and the girls 40.1 percent; on the subtests the average scores for both sexes combined were 51.5 percent for memory, 36.7 percent for perceptual ability, 36.8 percent for abstract ability, 47.5 percent for verbal ability.

The investigators emphasize that despite attempts at matching, differences are likely to exist between families in which a child is severly malnourished and control families, so that the large performance differences may not be exclusively attributable to malnutrition.

Hertzig, Birch, Richardson, and Tizard (1972) investigated the conse-quences of severe malnutrition during the first two years of life in 71 boys in Jamaica, West Indies, who were given intelligence tests 3–7 years after mal-nutrition recovery. All of the boys had been hospitalized for marasmus, kwashiorkor, or marasmic-kwashiorkor. Of an initial larger roster of severely malnourished cases, three were dropped because matched comparison children could not be studied, two were lost because the family had moved and could not be located, and one with Down's syndrome and one with infantile hemiplegia were excluded. On the average the malnourished boys received eight weeks of inpatient care, and follow-up visits in the homes of most were conducted for two years following discharge. Detailed clinical and metabolic records for all of the boys were available.

The subjects were compared with two groups of school-age boys, the first group of 38 consisting of the available brother or half brother closest in age to each subject, and the second group composed of 71 unrelated male classmates or neighbors close in age to the subjects. The subjects and unrelated controls were 5–10 years old and the sibling controls were from 6–12 years old at the time the WISC intelligence tests were given.

The results on the two subscales and full scale of the WISC for the three groups are given in Table M.2. The severely malnourished boys have the lowest mean scores, their sibs are intermediate, and the unrelated boys have the highest IQs. The greatest differences, all highly significant, were found between the severely malnourished boys and the unrelated controls, with the difference being greater for Verbal than for Performance IQ. The severely malnourished boys scored significantly lower than their siblings on Full Scale and Verbal but not on Performance IQ.

Although the sib group was a little older on the average than the other two groups, no age or birth-order trends in IQ scores were observed.

An analysis of variance found no significant differences in the IQs of children hospitalized for severe malnutrition early (0–7 months of age), medially (8–12 months), or late (13–24 months) during the first two years of life.

The method of selecting control cases in the Jamaican study narrowed, but did not fully equate social, economic, and familial characteristics between the three groups of children. It is not possible to conclude that the subjects differed from the control children solely in malnutrition; they may have been differentially subjected to stresses other than malnutrition that resulted in impaired mental development.

The sib-control method is, however, clearly an improvement in design over most of the earlier studies that did not use it. Sibs and half-sibs share, respectively, one-half and one-quarter of their genes, and share common familial and social circumstances, but differ, in the Jamaican study, in exposure to early, severe malnutrition requiring hospitalization.

The authors considered a number of nonnutritional factors that may contribute to intellectual differences in the Jamaican children and plan to report their findings in subsequent papers. It is hoped that they will also include the informative research design based on separate analyses of half- and full-sibs.

In a second report on the same Jamaican children, Richardson, Birch, and Hertzig (1973) compared the 62 of the severely malnourished children who were attending school with their matched classmates of the same age and sex from the unrelated comparison group. The 62 subjects did significantly less well on the Wide Range Achievement Test, class grades, and teacher's evalu-

TABLE M.2. *Means and standard deviations of WISC scores of Jamaican boys severely malnourished during first two years of life, a group of their siblings and half-siblings, and unrelated controls.*

Test	Malnourished $N = 71$	Sibs $N = 38$	Unrelated Controls $N = 71$
Full Scale IQ	57.72 ± 10.75	61.84 ± 10.82	65.99 ± 13.59
Verbal IQ	64.92 ± 11.80	71.03 ± 12.87	73.70 ± 14.55
Performance IQ	56.30 ± 11.85	58.03 ± 10.47	63.69 ± 13.30

Source: Data from Hertzig, Birch, Richardson, and Tizard, 1972, Table II.

ation. Male siblings of the severely malnourished boys received achievement-test scores like theirs, but had less trouble in school—their teachers' evaluations resembled those of the unrelated classmates. As in the initial study, no relation was found between behavioral performance and the age at which the subjects had been hospitalized for malnutrition.

An earlier study employing sibling controls was made in Mexico City by Birch, Piñeiro, Alcalde, Toca, and Cravioto (1971) on the relation between kwashiorkor in early childhood and intelligence at school age. The subjects probably were more homogeneous clinically than in most other studies of severe protein-calorie malnutrition. Strict diagnostic criteria of kwashiorkor were used, and no cases of marasmus or of undifferentiated protein-calorie malnutrition were included.

Intelligence was measured in 37 previously malnourished children (14 boys and 23 girls), and in 37 of their siblings who had not been hospitalized for malnutrition (21 boys and 16 girls), using the Spanish version of the WISC tests. The malnourished subjects had been hospitalized for kwashiorkor when they were between 6 and 30 months of age. The average time in hospital was 6 weeks, with a range from 1 to 2 months. During hospitalization the children were visited by their mothers for a 3–4-hour period every other day. All the children returned to their family after nutritional recovery.

At follow-up the children were 5–13 years of age and all were given intelligence tests at least 3 years after discharge from the hospital. Each control child was within 3 years of the age of the subject he or she had been paired with.

The mean WISC Full Scale, Verbal, and Performance IQs of the subjects were 68.5, 69.6, and 72.5, respectively, and those of the controls were 81.5, 80.8, and 80.2 The differences were 13.0, 11.2, and 7.7 IQ points, the Full Scale difference being significant at < 0.01 and the other two at < 0.05 levels. There were large differences in the distribution of high and low IQ scores in the two groups of children. Eighteen malnourished children had IQs below

70 while only 9 of their siblings were in this low category, and 10 of the subjects had IQs below 60 in contrast with only 2 controls. Ten of the control children had IQs of 90 or higher, but only 4 subjects did. No significant relation between IQ and age was found in either group. Among the mal-nourished children, the two sexes were not significantly different in IQ, but the 16 female controls had a mean IQ of only 72.8, or 9.5 IQ points below the average of the 21 male controls. Thus a significant effect of malnutrition was not shown for the females in this study.

The demographic and socioeconomic data for Mexico strongly suggest that families in which one child has been hospitalized for severe malnutrition are at high risk for chronic subnutrition in all children in the family. In conse-quence the comparison of Mexico City subjects and their sibs may under-estimate the overall effects of nutritional inadequacy on intellectual develop-ment. Nevertheless, these data strongly suggest that severe malnutrition (kwashiorkor) with hospitalization may have a long-term effect on intelli-gence measured three or more years later.

One apparently well designed and conducted study using sibling controls, that of Evans and his colleagues in South Africa (Evans et al., 1971; Hansen et al, 1971), failed to find an appreciable difference between 40 children who had been hospitalized early in life for kwashiorkor and 40 siblings within two years of their ages. All children were tested when they were 8–15 years old with the WISC-type New South African Individual Scale used by Stoch and Smythe, plus the Goodenough-Harris Draw-A-Man test. There was a sig-nificant, though small, difference on the latter test in favor of the sibling controls, but essentially no difference on the conventional intelligence test. Both groups achieved scores approximately equal to those of the controls in Stoch and Smythe's earlier study. This similarity of scores on the IQ test between subjects and their siblings was observed both for children hospital-ized early (at 10–15 months) and later (at 16–48 months), although the latter group scored lower on the whole and were worse off socioeconomically. There were no appreciable differences betwen subjects and their sibling controls in height, weight, or head circumference, which suggests that nutritional con-ditions may have been more nearly equivalent for the two groups than the presence of kwashiorkor in one sibling but not in the other might otherwise lead one to conclude. But at any rate, the study must count as negative evi-dence for the notion of a *specific* effect of kwashiorkor on intellectual devel-opment, due to potassium loss, or the like.

Discussion

The relevance of studies of severe malnutrition in underdeveloped coun-tries for interpreting racial-ethnic IQ differences in the United States is both debatable and debated. If one assumes that marasmus and kwashiorkor merely represent extremes on a nutritional continuum, and that lesser degrees of undernutrition may be expected to have similar but perhaps milder effects on intellectual development, then these studies have direct relevance to the United States, given the evidence reviewed in the text for poorer nutrition among U.S. minority groups than among the white majority. On the other hand, if one assumes the effects of severe undernutrition to represent a threshold phenomenon, involving the breakdown under extreme deprivational insult of the normal nutritional buffering of the brain, then one may, given the rarity of marasmus and kwashiorkor in the United States, largely discount the relevance of studies such as these for interpreting average U.S. racial-ethnic differences. (This, for example, is Jensen's conclusion—1973a, p. 337f.)

It is interesting that biases against according a majority role to nutrition in influencing IQ exist among both environmentalists and hereditarians.

On the one hand, some social scientists are suspicious of the possible importance of nutrition to intellectual performance simply because they view nutrition as "biological" and they oppose on general grounds making biological determinants important in explanations of variation in any social behavior, even when the biology is placed on the nongenetic side of the heredity-environment equation. At the other extreme strong hereditarians on the IQ issue may tend to minimize the role of nutrition in intellectual performance because it is, after all, an environmental factor.

It is clear that nutrition and nonnutritional factors are to some degree confounded in currently available data on humans, but the impressive evidence from animal studies (including those of Zimmermann, Strobel, Steere, and Geist, 1974, on rhesus monkeys), together with the results obtained from the better controlled human investigations, leads us to expect that the new prospective, experimental, longitudinal studies will support rather than contradict the thesis that severe undernutrition during the first 2–4 years of life can result in lasting brain and mental impairment varying in degree according to the timing and severity of the malnutrition. Studies bridging the gap between severe malnutrition and chronic or sporadic mild malnutrition are obviously needed.

Finally, most of the animal and human studies connecting nutrition and intellectual performance are concerned with the behavioral effects of undernutrition; very little is known about the behavioral consequences of "better-than-normal" diets (Brožek and Vaes, 1961). The scanty data do not allow us to make informed estimates of the contribution of better-than-minimum-standard diets to the differential IQ scores between U.S. blacks and whites. It seems quite possible that there is some contribution; and it is clear that significantly more whites than blacks belong to the better-than-standard-nutrition class.

APPENDIX N

Effects of the Dutch Wartime Famine on Later Intelligence of Offspring

For about six months during the winter and spring of 1944–1945 there was a very severe food shortage in the cities of the western Netherlands, caused by a transportation embargo imposed by the occupying German forces. Cities in the south, east, and north of the country, because of their proximity to sources of food supply, were relatively unaffected by the famine, but the western cities were hard hit. Up until the time of the embargo, apart from moderate wartime shortages, nutritional conditions in the western cities were generally satisfactory, and good nutritional conditions were rapidly established again after the embargo was ended by the Allied liberation forces.

In October, 1944, before the start of the famine, the official ration for a pregnant woman in the affected cities amounted to about 2100 calories per day, and while there was some variation in the actual availability of extra rations, postwar surveys estimated that the actual level of consumption by pregnant women in September, the closest month for which figures are given, averaged about 1925 calories per day (Smith, 1947). In January, the official ration was down by nearly one-half, to 1144 calories. Actual consumption was down even more—estimated at 731 calories in February. It seems that most women receiving extra rations shared them with their families. Protein consumption also dropped by about one-half: the official daily ration in the fall was 62 grams and the estimated actual consumption was 61 grams; corresponding values for January and February were 34 and 33 grams.

The famine affected all sectors of the population. The lowered nutrition had marked effects on women's menstrual cycles—approximately 50 percent became amenorrheic, and many of the remainder, irregular in their cycles. There was a corresponding sharp drop in the number of pregnancies. Infant birth weights declined somewhat in the western cities, by an average of 8 or 9 percent; the proportion of stillbirths did not show any rise, however, and may even have decreased (Smith, 1947).

Stein, Susser, Saenger, and Marolla (1972) reported analyses based on intelligence-test data for 19-year-old Dutch males who by virtue of date and place of birth were inferred to have been, or not to have been, exposed to the famine conditions either prenatally or early in postnatal life. The investigators compared the test scores of men born in seven cities in the western Netherlands that were in the severe famine area with those of men born in eleven relatively unaffected cities in the south, east, and north during the same period, for various cohorts ranging from those born before the period of the famine to those conceived after its termination. A total of some 125,000 males born in the famine and control cities during the years 1944–1946 were included in the study; about 20,000 of them were inferred to have been exposed to the famine via maternal food deprivation. The intelligence measure was a Dutch version of the Progressive Matrices test routinely given to youths at the time of registration for military service at age 19. Essentially all noninstitutionalized males born within the period and still resident in the Netherlands at age 19 were included in the testing.

No significant difference was found between the average intelligence-test scores of males born in the famine cities and those born in the control cities. This held for those exposed to the famine early in the prenatal period as well as for those exposed late. (Since the famine was of approximately six months' duration, there was no group exposed for the full nine months.) There was also no systematic difference in intelligence-test scores between cohorts who were exposed to the famine conditions and preceding or following cohorts in the famine or control cities.

The intelligence-test scores reflect other sorts of systematic influences known to relate to measured IQ, such as social class, family size, and birth rank (Belmont and Marolla, 1973). The apparent lack of a lasting effect of serious maternal nutritional deprivation on such scores must at a minimum suggest caution in interpreting intelligence-test data from underprivileged groups in the United States and elsewhere in terms of the immediate effects of maternal undernutrition. The situations are of course different in many respects. One important difference may well lie in the fact that women in underdeveloped countries and in minority groups in the United States often have been chronically malnourished all their lives, while the undernutrition of the Dutch women was abrupt and of relatively limited duration. Stewart (1968) has suggested that in chronically malnourished populations, in order to prevent the birth of weak, undersized children with a high neonatal death rate and a lowered intelligence among some of the survivors, it might be necessary to improve mothers' diets starting 15 to 20 years before the deliveries in question. Indeed some writers argue that one might even need to start a generation earlier, with the mothers' mothers.

Prediction of IQ Changes from Four Nutritional Variables

In this Appendix four variables are considered: obesity, head circumference, birth weight, and ascorbic acid levels. These four variables share the characteristics that they are indicators of nutritional status, that they show some association with IQ, and that they differ on the average between U.S. blacks and whites. The four variables will be used to predict how much change in average IQ difference might occur if black-white differences on the nutritional indicators were eliminated.

For a number of reasons, these predictions should be viewed with a great deal of skepticism. Much of the data on the association with IQ comes from populations quite different from the one in which we wish to predict. Some of the data comes from isolated small studies, whose findings may well be unrepresentative. Finally, quantitative statistical prediction is always hazardous when the relevant causal relationships are not well understood. Nevertheless, it seems worthwhile to pursue these four cases, if only to illustrate the kinds of predictions that might follow from more satisfactory data.

Obesity and intelligence

The term malnutrition has classically implied undernutrition of one or more essential nutrients in the diet. But, as Nitowsky (1968) points out, if we take malnutrition to imply a deviation from balanced nutrition, then a large segment of the American people who are obese are malnourished. Contrary to the situation in some African and Polynesian societies, in Western countries obesity is negatively correlated with socioeconomic status, the frequency of obesity tending to increase with decreased social position (e.g., Stunkard, d'Aquili, Fox and Filion, 1972; Whitelaw, 1971). Since socioeconomic status is correlated with measured intelligence in Western societies, it is plausible that average measured intelligence may be inversely related to the prevalence of obesity.

TABLE O.1.   *IQ and obesity in a Czechoslovakian working population.*

	% in IQ Category			
	Females		Males	
IQ	Obese	Normal	Obese	Normal
up to 90	47.1	20.1	14.8	13.9
91–110	37.3	40.2	61.1	41.1
111 or more	15.7	39.6	24.1	45.0
Total number	(51)	(169)	(54)	(280)

Source: Data from Kreze et al., 1974, Table 1.

Kreze, Zelina, Juhás, and Garbara (1974) studied the relationship between obesity and measured intelligence in 554 adult Czechoslovakian workers in occupations ranging from manual laborer to technician and clerk. The 334 men were between 18 and 58 years of age and the 220 women between 18 and 50 years. Subjects who were 20 percent overweight or more, according to standards for normal weight in the healthy Czech population, were classed as obese. The IQ scores were based on the Czech AR-B Intelligence Test. The proportions of obese and nonobese persons in various IQ categories are shown in Table O.1. In all, 23.2 percent of women and 16.2 percent of men were obese by the Czech criterion, and 40.0 percent of women and 29.6 percent of men obtained IQ scores equal to or less than 100. In both sexes obesity was significantly associated with lower IQ scores.

Using the data of Table O.1, and assuming that IQ is normally distributed in this population, one can estimate the average IQ of obese Czech women to be 92.0 and that of women whose weight is normal to be 105.8. The corresponding averages for men are 102.5 and 108.4, respectively.

The *Ten-State Nutrition Survey 1968-1970* (III–13–14. Tab. 20, Appendix) gives the distribution of obesity in blacks and whites by sex and income status. The TSNS defined obesity in adults as fatfold measurements greater than the 85th percentile of such measurements on young white adults recorded by Seltzer and Mayer (1965); the actual fatfold thickness defining obesity in the TSNS was 18.6 mm in males and 25.1 mm in females. (Fatfold is a way of measuring the thickness of subcutaneous fat.) The criterion for obesity in the Czech data would include a few more obese individuals out of the total distribution than the TSNS criterion. Since the argument we are about to present leads to a minor result, we have not made the small correction for this difference.

If the association between obesity and IQ were assumed to be the same in Czech and U.S. black and white females, what difference in mean IQ for U.S.

blacks and whites would be predicted? The U.S. survey gives for ages 18–50 the prevalence of obesity among black women as 0.338 and for whites 0.278. This difference in obesity, based on the Czech figures, would predict a difference of just under one IQ point in favor of white women. And since the prevalence of obesity is greater among white than black males in the age range 18–50 years, the same logic would predict a very slightly higher mean IQ for American black than for white males. In short, differential obesity rates are not a very promising explanation of observed differences in IQ-test performance between U.S. blacks and whites.

Head circumference and intelligence

The statistical fact that small head size for age and sex is associated with mental retardation has been known to clinicians at least since Kind's report on 500 mentally retarded persons in 1876. A majority of the earlier studies on head size and mental ability were based on persons in institutions for the mentally retarded. Results supporting a statistical association between mental retardation and reduced head size for age and sex are reported by Böök, Schut, and Reed, 1953; Mosier, Grossman, and Dingman, 1965; O'Connell, Feldt, and Stickler, 1965; and Pryor and Thelander, 1968.

The size of the head is mainly determined by the growth of the brain except in cases of hydrocephalus, craniosynostosis, or other cranial pathology. Head circumferences reach about 96 percent of the adult value at age 10. Some of the increase thereafter results from increased thickness of the skull bones and scalp tissues, some from further growth of the brain especially in the parieto-occipital lobes (Tanner, 1962).

The growth of the head is a result of a complex interaction of genetic and environmental factors. Trisomy 21, a chromosomal aberration, results in cessation of growth in head size after the age of approximately three years (Thelander and Pryor, 1966). Severe brain infections such as encephalitis, meningitis, and toxoplasmosis at early ages may prevent further growth of the brain and head (Thelander and Goebel, 1949). However, a variety of chronic illnesses, among them congenital heart disease, may result in growth deficits in height and weight without reduction in brain size; in a review of autopsy findings on 16 children who died of congenital heart disease, Robinow (1968) found brain weights were 2.2 percent above normal means for age; height, 6.3 percent below; weight, 35.9 percent below; and head circumference, 8.2 percent below. The evidence is conclusive from studies on experimental animals and man that severe malnutrition can result in reduced growth of the brain and head (Balázs, 1972; Coursin, 1965; Chase, 1973; Dobbing, 1970b; and Winick, 1970).

Nellhaus (1968) presents composite graphs of head circumference for boys and girls from birth to 18 years of age calculated from 15 reports in the world literature published between 1952 and 1965. He found no significant racial, national, or geographic differences in head circumferences among the representatives of the three major races included: Japanese, Negroes from the United States, and Caucasians from Europe and America. Table O.2 gives

TABLE O.2. *Average head circumference in American children.*

Age	Mean		Standard Deviation	
	In	**Cm**	**In**	**Cm**
Birth	13.8	35	0.5	1.2
3 months	15.9	40.4	0.5	1.2
6 months	17.0	43.4	0.4	1.1
12 months	18.3	46.5	0.5	1.2
18 months	19.0	48.4	0.5	1.2
2 years	19.2	49.0	0.5	1.2
3 years	19.6	50.0	0.5	1.2
4 years	19.8	50.5	0.5	1.2
5 years	20.0	50.8	0.6	1.4
6 years	20.2	51.2	0.6	1.4
7 years	20.5	51.6	0.6	1.4
8 years	20.6	52.0	0.8	1.8
10 years	20.9	53.0	0.6	1.4
12 years	21.0	53.2	0.8	1.8
14 years	21.5	54.0	0.8	1.8
16 years	21.9	55.0	0.8	1.8
18 years	22.1	55.4	0.8	1.8
20 years	22.2	55.6	0.8	1.8

Source: Watson and Lowrey, 1951, p. 49.

the standards adopted by Watson and Lowrey (1951, p. 49) for head circumference in American children, together with their standard deviations.

Several investigations in different areas of the world show that malnutrition, especially in the early years, will reduce the normal rate of growth in head circumference (see, for example, Stoch and Smythe, 1963). Further, Winick and Rosso (1969) demonstrate that reduced head circumference in children severely malnourished during the first months after birth accurately reflects the reduced number of cells and reduced protein content of their brains. These investigators studied the relation between head circumference and the cellular growth of the brain in children who had died of severe malnutrition and in control children who died of causes other than malnutrition during the first years of life. In marasmic children, brain weight and total brain protein were reduced proportionally to head circumference. Brain cell number as estimated by DNA content was reduced as much as, and in some cases more than, head circumference.

It is important to note than an abnormally small child does not necessarily have a proportionally small brain and head; O'Connell, Feldt and Stickler (1965) found the head circumferences of 31 children with normal intelligence *and* growth failure (due to such conditions as hypopituitary dwarfism, vitamin-D-resistant rickets, and congenital heart disease) were normal for age and sex.

Pearson seems to have been the first to investigate systematically the association of normal intelligence and normal head size in man (Pearson, 1902; Lee, Lewenz, and Pearson, 1903). Pearson and his co-workers correlated head length and breadth with intelligence levels estimated from performance in college work of Cambridge University undergraduates, and head length, breadth, and height with teachers' ratings of the intelligence of English school children. The mean of nine coefficients of correlation of absolute head dimensions with intelligence scores in these normal young people was .074, all nine *r*s being positive.

Pearl (1906, reprinted 1924) reanalyzed data collected by Eyerich and Loewenfeld (1905) on horizontal head circumference and estimated intellectual ability in 935 Bavarian soldiers in ordinary two-year service. The men were ranked by their officers in four levels of intellectual capacity: very well endowed, well endowed, normal, limited. The range in head circumferences was from 50.6 to 61 cm, with a mean of 56.5 cm, and a standard deviation of 1.41 cm. The correlation between head circumference and appraised intelligence obtained from a 2×2 table was $r = 0.14 \pm 0.04$.

Pearl (1924, p. 101) concluded that "there is a sensible, but *very slight*, positive correlation between intelligence and size of head." With regard to individual cases he agreed with Pearson's opinion that "For practical purposes it seems impossible, either in the case of exceptionally able men or in the bulk of the population, to pass any judgment from size of head to ability or *vice versa*." For the purposes of this discussion, Pearl's final conclusions (1924, p. 102) are worth repeating:

> If further statistics (of which there is great need) should show that generally there is a just sensible positive correlation between these characters, the correct interpretation of the fact would, it seems to me, probably by physiologic rather than psychologic. That is to say, the association between vigor in growth processes (leading to a well-developed body) and vigor in mental processes would most probably be the result of the action of good conditions of nurture. Other things being equal groups of men with well-nourished bodies are on the average likely to be more able intellectually than groups in which bad conditions of nutrition prevail. Such an interpretation of the facts seems at present to have much better justification than any which in effect implies that a big brain connotes *per se* an able mind.
>
> Rightly interpreted the facts regarding the correlation between size of head and intelligence seem to me simply to furnish, so far as they go, direct statistical evidence in favor of the adage: *Mens sana in corpore sano.*

Klein and co-workers (1972) obtained the following within-age correlations between head circumference and scores on ability tests taken by 3–6-year-old Guatemalan children:

Ability	Boys	Girls
Language	.23	.29
Memory for Digits	.18	.33
Perceptual analysis	.31	.32
Means	.24	.31

This village population suffers from some degree of malnutrition, but not as severe as that found in some urban Latin American populations.

The Ten-State Nutrition Survey provides data for both black and white children from high- and low-income-ratio states on average head circumference at ages from 1 to 6 years, as shown in Table O.3.

If we ignore the values for age 6, which are based on very small numbers of children, we find that the average differences between black and white children of a given age are, with one exception, less than 1 cm in absolute magnitude. They are also quite variable in direction. The black average is larger than the white average in eight instances, the white average is larger in nine instances, and there is no difference in three. There is a net overall mean difference of less than 0.1 cm in favor of the whites. In only two of the four groups is there any suggestion of a consistent trend in favor of a larger head circumference for either blacks or whites: these are the boys from the low-income-ratio states (whites larger) and the girls from the high-income-ratio states (blacks larger). In each the average difference is approximately 0.5 cm, i.e., somewhat under $\frac{1}{2}$ σ. Even if we assume correlations between IQ and head circumference as large as those found among Guatemalan children, these differences would only predict average differences of one or two IQ points in these two subgroups. For the total group, the predicted difference would be about one-fourth of an IQ point in favor of the whites.

Again, head circumference, while quite possibly a valid indicator of a link between nutrition and IQ, shows little promise of accounting for U.S. between-group IQ differences, even allowing for some underestimation of black-white nutritional differences in the Ten-State study.

Blood level of ascorbic acid and intelligence

Kubala and Katz (1960) carried out a study that tested for IQ and an essential nutrient using the same persons before and after supplementary feeding of that nutrient. They studied subjects from the fourth, fifth, and sixth grades of a private elementary school and from kindergarten through the sixth grade in a second elementary school. The subjects were divided into a higher-ascorbic-acid group (having more than 1.10 mg of ascorbic acid per 100 ml of blood plasma) and a lower-ascorbic-acid group (having less than 1.10 mg/100 ml). Forty-six subjects from the higher-ascorbic-acid group were matched with 46 from the lower on the basis of family income and education of the father and mother. The mean IQ was found to be greater in the higher-ascorbic-acid group than in the lower in each school. The mean IQ scores for the two groups were 112.8 and 109.9, respectively, a difference of 2.9 IQ points. Similar or slightly larger differences were also reported for small seventh to ninth grade and college samples.

TABLE O.3 *Mean head circumference by age, sex, and ethnic group for white and black persons one through six years of age for low-income-ratio states and high-income-ratio states.*

	Male					Female				
	High-income-ratio		Low-income-ratio			High-income-ratio		Low-income-ratio		
Age Midpoint, in yr	No. of Persons	Mean Head Circumference, in cm	No. of Persons	Mean Head Circumference, in cm	Difference,[a] in cm	No. of Persons	Mean Head Circumference, in cm	No. of Persons	Mean Head Circumference, in cm	Difference,[a] in cm
				White						
1	127	47.8	26	48.1	−0.3	128	46.2	23	46.6	−0.4
2	133	49.3	32	48.7	0.6	119	48.0	20	47.4	1.4
3	151	50.0	31	49.9	0.1	138	49.0	30	49.0	0.0
4	167	50.8	37	50.3	0.5	150	49.3	41	49.4	−0.1
5	188	51.2	41	51.6	−0.4	164	50.1	36	50.0	0.1
6	5	50.6	2	52.5	−1.9	16	49.7	4	49.8	−0.1
				Black						
1	45	47.8	59	47.2	0.6	52	47.1	39	46.0	1.1
2	40	48.6	78	48.9	−0.3	48	48.2	28	48.1	0.1
3	59	50.3	85	49.4	0.9	53	49.4	48	48.7	0.7
4	66	50.8	93	49.9	0.9	58	50.2	50	49.8	0.4
5	67	50.6	72	50.2	0.4	51	50.0	49	50.0	0.0
6	5	51.2	5	49.9	1.3	9	51.3	2	49.2	2.1

Source: *Ten-State Nutrition Survey 1968–1970*, 1972.

[a] Negative numbers indicate that the mean head circumference for the low-income-ratio states is greater than the mean head circumference for the high-income-ratio states.

After the initial test, the elementary school subjects were given supplementary orange juice during a period of six months. At the end of this period the average IQ of the higher-ascorbic-acid group remained unchanged at 112.8, while that of the low group moved up to 113.4, a rise of 3.5 IQ points.

Data presented by Kubala and Katz suggest that the mean rise of 3.5 IQ points accompanied a rise of about 0.50 mg/100 ml in ascorbic acid levels.

The Ten-State Nutrition Survey gives median ascorbic acid levels for blacks in the high-income-ratio states as 0.95 mg/100 ml and in the low-income-ratio states as 0.54 mg/100 ml. Whites in the high-income-ratio states had average ascorbic acid levels of 1.03 mg/100 ml. If we were to take Kubala and Katz's results at face value as applicable to the U.S. black population (a rather hazardous procedure), we would predict that bringing the ascorbic acid levels of U.S. blacks up to those of U.S. whites in the high-income-ratio states would make only a slight difference for the blacks in those states (about half an IQ point), but might mean a 3- or 4-point rise for blacks in the low-income-ratio states.

Birth weight and intelligence

It is well known that on the average twins have lower birth weights and are born after a shorter gestation than single births. Bulmer (1970) estimated that the mean birth weight of white twins standardized for duration of gestation was 1.3 pounds (590 grams) less than that of the singly born. Among all live births in the United States in 1960 white twins averaged 1.1 pounds less, and black twins 1.9 pounds less than the singly born (Bulmer, 1970).

Several investigators have shown that twins on the average score lower on intelligence tests by about 5 IQ points (Byrns and Healy, 1936; Mehrotra and Maxwell, 1949; Asher and Fraser Roberts, 1949; Barclay and Maxwell, 1950; Husén, 1959; Tabah and Sutter, 1954; Sandon, 1957; Record, McKeown, and Edwards, 1970). The difference in mean IQ is determined by a shifting downward of the entire distribution rather than by a concentration of twins at lower IQ levels (Barclay and Maxwell, 1950).

Identical twins provide the only direct evidence in human beings on the relation between birth weights and later intelligence in persons with identical genotypes and gestational ages. Scarr (1969) published individual birth weight and IQ data on 25 pairs of white identical twins given the Draw-a-Person test at ages 6–10 years, together with birth weights and performance IQs for 7 pairs of black and 20 pairs of white identical twins given the Wechsler Intelligence Scale for Children at ages 5–15 years by Willerman and Churchill (1967). She found an average difference of 320 grams and 9 IQ points between her series of heavy and light co-twins, and a difference of 270 grams and 5 IQ points for Willerman and Churchill's. On the average, then, a difference of about 7 points in IQ is associated with a difference just under 300 grams in birth weight within these identical twin pairs.

In a National Institutes of Health collaborative study based on some 20,000 pregnant women seen in 14 hospitals from all over the United States, Naylor and Myrianthopoulos (1967) reported the following mean birth weights in grams:

Group	Number	Mean birth weight	S.D.
White	8698	3286	557
Black	9374	3069	565
Puerto Rican	1848	3155	517
All	19920	3172	567

While the regression of birth weight on many socioeconomic variables, including family income, occupation, education, and housing density, is highly significant, little of the variation in birth weight is accounted for by these variables. The authors conclude that about 130 grams of the observed difference of 217 grams in mean birth weight between blacks and whites is genetically determined and that about 87 grams (40 percent) is environmentally determined.

In a larger sample from the National Institutes of Health collaborative study, the outcomes of some 38,000 pregnancies were followed in 15 university-affiliated medical centers in the United States. Niswander and Gordon (1972) report mean birth weights of 3272 grams for 18,481 white babies and of 3039 grams for 19,504 black babies, an average difference of 233 grams.

If we were to assume that the factors producing an association between birth weight and IQ within identical twin pairs held for births in general, we would estimate that the average birth weight difference of 233 grams between blacks and whites should be accompanied by an IQ difference of about 5 IQ points. However, if 60 percent of the weight difference is associated with racial factors that are independent of socioeconomic variables, as the analysis of Naylor and Myrianthopoulos suggests, and if these racial factors are not causally related to IQ differences, then a black-white difference of about 2 IQ points would be predictable from birth weight differences.

REFERENCES

References

Adams, J., and Ward, R. H. Admixture studies and the detection of selection. *Science*, 1973, *180*, 1137–1143.

Albott, W. L., and Gunn, H.E. Bender-Gestalt performance by culturally disadvantaged first graders. *Perceptual and Motor Skills*, 1971, *33*, 247–250.

Alland, A., Jr. *Human diversity*. New York: Columbia University Press, 1971.

Allen, G., and Pettigrew, K. D. Technical comment. *Science*, 1973, *182*, 1042–1044.

Anderson, V. E. Genetics and intelligence. *In* J. Wortis (Ed.), *Mental retardation (and developmental disabilities) an annual review*. Vol. 6. New York: Brunner/Mazel, 1974. Pp. 20–43.

Asher, C., and Roberts, J. A. F. Study on birth weight and intelligence. *British Journal of Social Medicine*, 1949, *3*, 56–58.

Ask, F. Studien über die Myopie in den vollständigen höheren Lehranstalten für Knaben. *Nordiskt Medicinskt Arkiv, Stockholm:* 1904, *10*, 1–70.

Backman, M. E. Patterns of mental abilities of adolescent males and females from different ethnic and socioeconomic backgrounds. *Proceedings of the 79th Annual Convention of the American Psychological Association*, 1971, *6*, 511–512.

Backman, M. E. Patterns of mental abilities: Ethnic, socioeconomic, and sex differences. *American Educational Research Journal*, 1972, *9*, 1–12.

Bain, R. A definition of culture. *Sociology and Social Research*, 1942, *27*, 87–94.

Bajema, C. Estimation of the direction and intensity of natural selection in relation to human intelligence by means of the intrinsic rate of natural increase. *Eugenics Quarterly*, 1963, *10*, 175–187.

Baker, J. R. Cro-Magnon man, 1868–1968. *Endeavour*, 1968, *27*, 87–90.

Balázs, R. Effects of hormones and nutrition on brain development. *Advances in Experimental Medicine and Biology*, 1972, *30*, 385–415.

Barabasz, A. F., Dodd, J. M., Smith, M., and Carter, D. E. Focal-point dependency in inversion perception among Negro, urban Caucasian and rural Causasian children. *Perceptual and Motor Skills*, 1970, *31*, 136–138.

Baratz, J. C. Language abilities of black Americans. *In* K. S. Miller and R. M. Dreger (Eds.), *Comparative studies of blacks and whites in the United States.* New York: Seminar Press, 1973. Pp. 125–183.

Baratz, S. B., and Baratz, J. C. Early childhood intervention: The social science base of institutional racism. *Harvard Educational Review*, 1970, *40*, 29–50.

Barclay, G., and Maxwell, J. The intelligence of twins. A comparative study of eleven-year-old twins. II. *Population Studies*, 1950, *4*, 333–344.

Barker, W., Scarr-Salapatek, S., and Katz, S. On sampling, factor-analysis, and heritability. Paper presented at Behavior Genetics Association annual meeting, Minneapolis, June, 1974.

Barnicot, N. A. Taxonomy and variation in modern man. *In* M. F. A. Montagu (Ed.), *The concept of race.* New York: Collier, 1969. Pp. 180–227.

Bass, N. H., Netsky, M. G., and Young, E. Effect of neonatal malnutrition on developing cerebrum. I. Microchemical and histologic study of cellular differentiation in the rat. *Archives of Neurology*, 1970, *23*, 289–302. (a)

Bass, N. H., Netsky, M. G., and Young, E. Effect of neonatal malnutrition on developing cerebrum. II. Microchemical and histogogic study of myelin formation in the rat. *Archives of Neurology*, 1970, *23*, 303–313. (b)

Baughman, E. E., and Dahlstrom, W. G. *Negro and white children: A psychological study in the rural South.* New York: Academic Press, 1968.

Bayless, T. M. Milk intolerance: Clinical, developmental and epidemiological aspects. *In* I. I. Gottesman and L. L. Heston (Eds.), *Summary of the Conference on Lactose and Milk Intolerance.* DHEW Publication No. (OCD) 73–19. Washington, D.C.: U.S. Department of Health, Education, and Welfare, 1973. Pp. 10–18.

Bayley, N. Comparisons of mental and motor test scores for ages 1–15 months by sex, birth order, race, geographical location, and education of parents. *Child Development*, 1965, *36*, 379–411.

Beckman, L. The relation between stature and parental birth place. *Acta Geneticae Medicae et Gemellologiae*, 1962, *11*, 39–42.

Belmont, L., and Marolla, F. A. Birth order, family size, and intelligence. *Science*, 1973, *182*, 1096–1101.

Bereiter, C. An academic preschool for disadvantaged children: Conclusions from evaluation studies. *In* J. C. Stanley (Ed.), *Preschool programs for the disadvantaged.* Baltimore: Johns Hopkins University Press, 1972. Pp. 1–21.

Berry, J. W. Temne and Eskimo perceptual skills. *International Journal of Psychology*, 1966, *1*, 207–229.

Bielicki, T. Typologists versus populationists and genetic theory. *International Social Science Journal*, 1965, *17*, 94–96.

Billingsly, A., and Giovannoni, J. Research perspective on interracial adoption. *In* R. R. Miller (Ed.), *Race, research and reason, social work perspectives*. New York: National Association of Social Workers, 1969. Pp. 57–77.

Binet, A., and Simon, Th. Le developpement de l'intelligence chez les enfants. *L'Année Psychologique*, 1908, *14*, 1–90.

Birch, H. G., Piñeiro, C., Alcalde, E., Toca, T., and Cravioto, J. Kwashiorkor in early childhood and intelligence at school age. *Pediatric Research*, 1971, *5*, 579–584.

Bivings, L. The Negro school child compared with the white school child. *Archives of Pediatrics*, 1927, *44*, 191–193.

Boas, F. The half-blood Indian. *Popular Science Monthly*, 1894, *45*, 761–770.

Boas, F. *The mind of primitive man*. (2nd ed.) New York: Macmillan, 1938.

Bock, R. D., and Kolakowski, D. Further evidence of sex-linked major-gene influence on human spatial visualizing ability. *American Journal of Human Genetics*, 1973, *25*, 1–14.

Bonin, G. von. *The evolution of the human brain*. Chicago: University of Chicago Press, 1963.

Bonner, M. W., and Belden, B. R. A comparative study of the performance of Negro seniors of Oklahoma City high schools on the Wechsler Adult Intelligence Scale and the Peabody Picture Vocabulary Test. *Journal of Negro Education*, 1970, *39*, 354–358.

Böök, J. A., Schut, J. W., and Reed, S. C. A clinical and genetical study of microcephaly. *American Journal of Mental Deficiency*, 1953, *57*, 637–660.

Brace, C. L. A nonracial approach towards the understanding of human diversity. *In* M. F. A. Montagu (Ed.), *The concept of race*. New York: Collier, 1969. Pp. 103–152.

Brante, G. Studies on lipids in the nervous system with special reference to quantitative chemical determination and topical distribution. *Acta Physiologica Scandinavica*, 1949, *18* (Supplement 63).

Bresler, J. B. Outcrossings in Caucasians and fetal loss. *Social Biology*, 1970, *17*, 17–25.

Broadhurst, P. L., Fulker, D. W., and Wilcock, J. Behavioral genetics. *Annual Review of Psychology*, 1974, *25*, 389–415.

Brockman, L. M., and Ricciuti, H. N. Severe protein-calorie malnutrition and cognitive development in infancy and early childhood. *Developmental Psychology*, 1971, *4*, 312–319.

Broman, B., Dahlberg, G., and Lichtenstein, A. Height and weight during growth. *Acta Paediatrica, Uppsala*, 1942, *30*, 1–66.

Brooks, H., and Bowers, R. The assessment of technology. *Scientific American*, 1970, *222*(2), 13–21.

Broom, L., and Glenn, N. D. *Transformation of the Negro American.* New York: Harper and Row, 1965.

Brown, R. E. Decreased brain weight in malnutrition and its implications. *East African Medical Journal,* 1965, *42,* 584–595.

Browning, R. H., and Northcutt, T. J., Jr. On the season. A report of a public health project conducted among Negro migrant agricultural workers in Palm Beach County, Florida. *Florida State Board of Health Monographs,* 1961, No. 2.

Brožek, J., and Vaes, G. Experimental investigation on the effects of dietary deficiencies on animal and human behavior. *Vitamins and Hormones,* 1961, *19,* 43–94.

Bruce, M. Factors affecting intelligence test performance of whites and Negroes in the rural South. *Archives of Psychology,* 1940, *36,* No. 252.

Bulmer, M. G. *The biology of twinning in man.* Oxford: Clarendon Press, 1970.

Burke, B. S., Beal, V. A., Kirkwood, S. B., and Stuart, H. C. Nutrition studies during pregnancy. *American Journal of Obstetrics and Gynecology,* 1943, *46,* 38–52.

Burks, B. S. The relative influence of nature and nurture upon mental development: A comparative study of foster parent-foster child resemblance and true parent-true child resemblance. *27th Yearbook of the National Society for the Study of Education,* 1928, Part I, 219–316.

Buros, O. K. (Ed.), *Seventh mental measurements yearbook.* Highland Park, N.J.: Gryphon Press, 1972.

Burt, C. Intelligence and social mobility. *British Journal of Statistical Psychology,* 1961, *14,* 3–24.

Burt, C. Is intelligence distributed normally? *British Journal of Statistical Psychology,* 1963, *16,* 175–190.

Burt, C. The genetic determination of differences in intelligence: A study of monozygotic twins reared together and apart. *British Journal of Psychology,* 1966, *57,* 137–153.

Burt, C. Inheritance of general intelligence. *American Psychologist,* 1972, *27,* 175–190.

Burt, C., and Howard, M. The multifactorial theory of inheritance and its application to intelligence. *British Journal of Statistical Psychology,* 1956, *9,* 95–131.

Byrns, R., and Healy, J. The intelligence of twins. *Journal of Genetic Psychology,* 1936, *49,* 474–478.

Cabak, V., and Najdanvic, R. Effect of undernutrition in early life on physical and mental development. *Archives of Disease in Childhood,* 1965, *40,* 532–534.

Caldwell, M. B., and Smith, T. A. Intellectual structure of Southern Negro children. *Psychological Reports,* 1968, *23,* 63–71.

Calhoun, D. H. *The intelligence of a people.* Princeton, N.J.: Princeton University Press, 1973.

Campbell, B. G. Conceptual progress in physical anthropology: Fossil man. *Annual Review of Anthropology*, 1972, *1*, 27–54.

Campbell, D. T. Reforms as experiments. *American Psychologist*, 1969, *24*, 409–429.

Caputo, D. V., and Mandell, W. Consequences of low birth weight. *Developmental Psychology*, 1970, *3*, 363–383.

Cattell, J. McK. Mental tests and measurements. *Mind*, 1890, *15*, 373–380.

Cattell, R. B. The measurement of adult intelligence. *Psychological Bulletin*, 1943, *40*, 153–193.

Cattell, R. B. The fate of national intelligence: Test of a thirteen-year prediction. *Eugenics Review*, 1950, *42*, 136–148.

Cattell, R. B. *Abilities: Their structure, growth and action.* Boston: Houghton Mifflin, 1971.

Cattell, R. B. *A new morality from science: Beyondism.* New York: Pergamon, 1972.

Cavalli-Sforza, L. L., and Bodmer, W. F. *The genetics of human populations.* San Francisco: W. H. Freeman, 1971.

Champakam, S., Srikantia, S. G., and Gopalan C. Kwashiorkor and mental development. *American Journal of Clinical Nutrition*, 1968, *21*, 844–852.

Chase, H. P. The effects of intrauterine and postnatal undernutrition on normal brain development. *Annals of the New York Academy of Sciences*, 1973, *205*, 231–244.

Chase, H. P., and Martin, H. P. Undernutrition and child development. *New England Journal of Medicine*, 1970, *282*, 933–939.

Christiansen, T., and Livermore, G. A comparison of Anglo-American and Spanish-American children on the WISC. *Journal of Social Psychology*, 1970, *81*, 9–14.

Citizens' Board of Inquiry into Hunger and Malnutrition in the United States. *Hunger USA 1968.* Washington: New Community Press, 1968.

Clark, G. M., Zamenhof, S., Van Marthens, E., Grauel, L., and Kruger, L. The effect of prenatal malnutrition on dimensions of cerebral cortex. *Brain Research*, 1973, *54*, 397–402.

Clark, W. E. LeG. *The fossil evidence for human evolution.* (2nd ed.) Chicago: University of Chicago Press, 1964.

Clayton, G. A., Morris, J. A., and Robertson, A. An experimental check on quantitative genetical theory. I. Short-term responses to selection. *Journal of Genetics*, 1957, *55*, 131–151.

Cleary, T. A. Test bias: Prediction of grades of Negro and white students in integrated colleges. *Journal of Educational Measurement*, 1968, *5*, 115–124.

Cody, M. A general theory of clutch size. *Evolution*, 1966, *20*, 174–184.

Cohen, R. A. Conceptual styles, culture conflict, and nonverbal tests of intelligence. *American Anthropologist*, 1969, *71*, 828–856.

Cole, M., and Bruner, J. S. Cultural differences and inferences about psychological processes. *American Psychologist*, 1971, *26*, 867–876.

Coleman, J. S., et al. *Equality of educational opportunity*. Washington, D.C.: U.S. Office of Education, 1966.

Conel, J. C. *The postnatal development of the human cerebral cortex*, 8 vols. Cambridge: Harvard University Press, 1939–1967.

Cook, G. C. Lactase activity in newborn and infant Baganda. *British Medical Journal*, 1967, *1*, 527–530.

Coon, C. S. *The origin of races*. New York: Knopf, 1962.

Coursin, D. B. Undernutrition and brain function. *Borden's Review of Nutrition Research*, 1965, *26*, 1–16.

Cravioto, J. Nutritional deficiencies and mental performance in childhood. *In* D. C. Glass (Ed.), *Environmental influences*. New York: Rockefeller University Press, 1968. Pp. 3–51.

Cravioto, J. Infant malnutrition and later learning. *Progress in Human Nutrition*, 1971, *1*, 80–96. (Westport, Conn.: AVI Publishing Co.)

Cravioto, J., and DeLicardie, E. R. Nutrition and behavior and learning. *World Review of Nutrition and Dietetics*, 1973, *16*, 80–96.

Cravioto, J., Gaona, C. E., and Birch, H. G. Early malnutrition and auditory-visual integration in school-age children. *Journal of Special Education*, 1967, *2*, 75–82.

Crow, J. F. Dominance and overdominance. *In* J. W. Gowen (Ed.), *Heterosis*. Ames, Iowa: Iowa State College Press, 1952. Pp. 282–297.

Dahlberg, G. An analysis of the conception of race and a new method of distinguishing races. *Human Biology*, 1942, *14*, 372–385. (a)

Dahlberg, G. *Race, reason and rubbish: A primer for the plain man*. London: Allen and Unwin, 1942. (b)

Dahlberg, G. Mathematical models for population genetics. New York: Interscience, 1948.

Damon, A. Stature increase among Italian-Americans: Environmental, genetic, or both? *American Journal of Physical Anthropology*, 1965, *23*, 401–408.

Damon, A. Race, ethnic group, and disease. *Social Biology*, 1969, *16*, 69–80.

Dancis, J. Nutritional management of hereditary disorders. *Medical Clinics of North America*, 1970, *54*, 1431–1448.

Darlington, R. B. Another look at "cultural fairness." *Journal of Educational Measurement*, 1971, *8*, 71–82.

Darwin, C. *On the origin of species by means of natural selection, or the preservation of favoured races in the struggle of life*. London: Murray, 1859.

Darwin, C. *The descent of man and selection in relation to sex*. London: Murray, 1871.

Dasen, P. R. Cross-cultural Piagetian research: A summary. *Journal of Cross-Cultural Psychology*, 1972, *3*, 23–40. (a)

Dasen, P. R. The development of conservation in aboriginal children: A replication study. *International Journal of Psychology*, 1972, *7*, 75–85. (b)

Davenport, C. B. Degeneration, albinism and inbreeding. *Science*, 1908, *28*, 454–455.

Davenport, R. K. Implications of military selection and classification in relation to universal military training. *Journal of Negro Education*, 1946, *15*, 585–594.

Davidson, S., and Passmore, R. *Human nutrition and dietetics*. (4th ed.) Edinburgh: E. & S. Livingstone, 1969.

Davis, T. R. A., Gershoff, S. N., and Gamble, D. F. Review of studies of vitamin and mineral nutrition in the United States (1950–1968). *Journal of Nutrition Education*, 1969, *1* (2, supplement), 41–57.

Davison, A. N., and Dobbing, J. The developing brain. *In* A. N. Davison and J. Dobbing (Eds.), *Applied neurochemistry*. Oxford: Blackwell Scientific Publications, 1968. Pp. 287–316.

Dawes, R. M. Technical comment. *Science*, 1972, *178*, 229–230.

De Crinis, M. *Aufbau und Abbau der Grosshirnleistungen und ihre anatomischen Gründe*. Berlin: Karger, 1934.

DeFries, J. C. Quantitative aspects of genetics and environment in the determination of behavior. *In* L. Ehrman, G. S. Omenn, and E. Caspari (Eds.) *Genetics, environment, and behavior*. New York: Academic Press, 1972. Pp. 5–16.

DeFries, J. C., et al. Near identity of cognitive structure in two ethnic groups. *Science*, 1974, *183*, 338–339.

DeLemos, M. M. The development of the concept of conservation in Australian Aboriginal children. Unpublished Ph.D. Thesis, Australian National University, Canberra, 1966.

DeLemos, M. M. The development of conservation in Aboriginal children. *International Journal of Psychology*, 1969, *4*, 255–269.

Dennis, W. Animism and related tendencies in Hopi children. *Journal of Abnormal and Social Psychology*, 1943, *38*, 21–36.

Dingwall, W. O., and Whitaker, H. A. Neurolinguistics. *Annual Review of Anthropology*, 1974, *3*, 323–356.

Dobbing, J. Effects of experimental undernutrition on development of the nervous system. *In* N. S. Scrimshaw and J. E. Gordon (Eds.), *Malnutrition, learning, and behavior*. Cambridge: M.I.T. Press, 1968. Pp. 181–202. (a)

Dobbing, J. Vulnerable periods in developing brain. *In* A. N. Davison and J. Dobbing (Eds.), *Applied neurochemistry*. Oxford: Blackwell Scientific Publications, 1968. Pp. 287–316. (b)

Dobbing, J. Undernutrition and the developing brain. *In* W. A. Himwich (Ed.), *Developmental neurobiology*. Springfield, Ill.: Thomas, 1970. Pp. 241–261. (a)

Dobbing, J. Undernutrition and the developing brain: The relevance of animal models to the human problem. *American Journal of Diseases of Children*, 1970, *120*, 411–415. (b)

Dobbing, J. Nutrition and the developing brain. *Lancet*, 1973, *1*, 48.

Dobbing, J. The later development of the brain and its vulnerability. *In* J. A. Davis and J. Dobbing (Eds.), *Scientific foundations of paediatrics.* Philadelphia: Saunders, 1974. Pp. 565–577.

Dobbing, J., and Sands, J. Timing of neuroblast multiplication in developing human brain. *Nature*, 1970, *226*, 639–640.

Dobzhansky, Th. Nature and origin of heterosis. *In* J. W. Gowen (Ed.), *Heterosis.* Ames, Iowa: Iowa State College Press, 1952. Pp. 218–223.

Dobzhansky, Th. *Mankind evolving: The evolution of the human species.* New Haven: Yale University Press, 1962.

Dobzhansky, Th. *Genetics of the evolutionary process.* New York: Columbia University Press, 1970.

Donald, H. P. Evidence from twins on variation in growth and production of cattle. *Proceedings Xth International Congress of Genetics*, Vol. 1. Toronto: University of Toronto Press, 1959. Pp. 225–235.

Dreger, R. M., and Miller, K. S. Comparative psychological studies of Negroes and whites in the United States. *Psychological Bulletin*, 1960, *57*, 361–402.

Dreger, R. M., and Miller, K. S. Comparative psychological studies of Negroes and whites in the United States: 1959–1965. *Psychological Bulletin Monograph Supplement*, 1968, *70*(3, pt. 2).

DuBois, P. H. A test standardized on Pueblo Indian children. *Psychological Bulletin*, 1939, *36*, 523. (Abstract)

Duncan, O. D. Ability and achievement. *Eugenics Quarterly*, 1968, *15*, 1–11.

Duncan, O. D., Featherman, D. L., and Duncan, B. *Socioeconomic background and achievement.* New York: Seminar Press, 1972.

Durnin, J. V. G. A., Edholm, O. G., Miller, D. S., and Waterlow, J. C. How much food does man require? *Nature*, 1973, *242*, 418.

Dwyer, R. C., Elligett, J. K., and Brost, M. A. Evaluation of the effectiveness of a problem-based preschool compensatory program. *Journal of Educational Research*, 1972, *66*, 153–156.

East, E. M. Inbreeding in corn. *Reports of the Connecticut Agricultural Experiment Station*, 1907, 419–428.

Eaves, L. J. Computer simulation of sample size and experimental design in human psychogenetics. *Psychological Bulletin*, 1972, *77*, 144–152.

Eaves, L. J., and Jinks, J. L. Insignificance of evidence for differences in heritability of IQ between races and social classes. *Nature*, 1972, *240*, 84–88.

Eckland, B. K. Genetics and sociology: A reconsideration. *American Sociological Review*, 1967, *32*, 173–194.

Elley, W. B. Changes in mental ability in New Zealand school children, 1936–1968. *New Zealand Journal of Educational Studies*, 1969, *4*, 140–155.

Emmett, W. G. The trend of intelligence in certain districts of England. *Population Studies*, 1950, *3*, 324–337.

Erlenmeyer-Kimling, L. Gene-environment interactions and the variability of behavior. *In* L. Ehrman, G. S. Omenn, and E. Caspari (Eds), *Genetics, environment, and behavior*. New York: Academic Press, 1972. Pp. 181–208.

Erlenmeyer-Kimling, L., and Stern, S. E. Technical comment, *Science*, 1973, *182*, 1044–1045.

Evans, D. E., Moodie, A. D., and Hansen, J. D. L. Kwashiorkor and intellectual development. *South African Medical Journal*, 1971, *45*, 1413–1426.

Evans-Pritchard, E. E. Forward. *In* L. Lévy-Bruhl, *The 'soul' of the primitive*. New York: Praeger, 1966.

Eyerich, G., and Loewenfeld, L. *Über die Beziehungen des Kopfumfangs zur Körperlänge und zur Geistigen Entwicklung*. Wiesbaden: J. F. Bergmann, 1905.

Eyferth, K. Eine Untersuchung der Neger-Mischlingskinder in Westdeutschland. *Vita Humana*, 1959, *2*, 102–114.

Eyferth, K. Leistungen verschiedener Gruppen von Besatzungskindern in Hamburg-Wechsler Intelligenztest für Kinder (HAWIK). *Archiv für die gesamte Psychologie*, 1961, *113*, 222–241.

Eyferth, K., Brandt, U., and Hawel, W. *Farbige Kinder in Deutschland*. Munich: Juventa Verlag, 1960.

Eysenck, H. J. *The IQ argument: Race, intelligence and education*. New York: Library Press, 1971.

Falconer, D. S. *Introduction to quantitative genetics*. Edinburgh: Oliver and Boyd, 1960.

Falk, L. A comparative study of transracial and inracial adoptions. *Child Welfare*, 1970, *49*, 82–88.

Fanshel, D. *Far from the reservation*. Metuchen, N.J.: Scarecrow Press, 1972.

Farley, R. Indications of recent demographic change among blacks. *Social Biology*, 1971, *18*, 341–358.

Feldman, D. Problems in the analysis of patterns of abilities. *Child Development*, 1973, *44*, 12–18.

Ferák, V., Lichardová, Z., and Bojnová, V. Endogamy, exogamy and stature. *Eugenics Quarterly*, 1968, *15*, 273–276.

Fisher, R. A. The correlation between relatives on the supposition of Mendelian inheritance. *Transactions of the Royal Society, Edinburgh*, 1918, *52*, 399–433.

Fisher, R. A. *The genetical theory of natural selection*. Oxford: Clarendon, 1930.

Fishman, M. A., Prensky, A. L., and Dodge, P. R. Low content of cerebral lipids in infants suffering from malnutrition. *Nature*, 1969, *221*, 552–553.

Flaugher, R. L. *The new definitions of test fairness in selection: Developments and implications.* GRE Board Research Report GREB No. 72–4R. Princeton, N. J.: Educational Testing Service, 1974.

Flaugher, R. L., and Rock, D. A. Patterns of ability factors among four ethnic groups. *Proceedings of the 80th Annual Convention of the American Psychological Association,* 1972, *7,* 27–28.

Flavell, J. H. *The developmental psychology of Jean Piaget.* Princeton, N.J.: Van Nostrand, 1963.

Folch-Pi, J. Composition of the brain in relation to maturation. *In* H. Waelsch (Ed.), *Biochemistry of the developing nervous system: Proceedings of the First International Neurochemical Symposium.* New York: Academic Press, 1955. Pp. 121–136.

Folkmar, D., and Folkmar, E. C. *Dictionary of races and peoples.* Reports of the Immigration Commission, Vol. 43. Washington, D.C.: U.S. Government Printing Office, 1911.

Franzblau, R. N. Race differences in mental and physical traits: Studied in different environments. *Archives of Psychology,* 1935, No. 177.

Freedman, D. G. An evolutionary approach to research on the life cycle. *Human Development,* 1971, *14,* 87–99.

Freeman, F. N., Holzinger, K. J., and Mitchell, B. C. The influence of environment on the intelligence, school achievement, and conduct of foster children. *27th Yearbook of the National Society for the Study of Education,* 1928, Part I, 103–217.

French, J. W., The description of aptitude and achievement tests in terms of rotated factors. *Psychometric Monographs,* 1951, No. 5.

Fulker, D. W. A biometrical genetic approach to intelligence and schizophrenia. *Social Biology,* 1973, *20,* 266–275.

Furth, H. G. *Piaget and knowledge.* Englewood Cliffs, N.J.: Prentice-Hall, 1969.

Galton, F. *Hereditary genius: An inquiry into its laws and consequences.* London: Macmillan, 1869.

Galton, F. *Natural inheritance.* London: Macmillan, 1889.

Garn, S. M. *Human races.* (3rd ed.) Springfield, Ill.: Thomas, 1971.

Garrison, R. J., Anderson, V. E., and Reed, S. C. Assortative marriage. *Eugenics Quarterly,* 1968, *15,* 113–127.

Garrow, J. S. Total body-potassium in kwashiorkor and marasmus. *Lancet,* 1965, *2,* 455–458.

Garrow, J. S. Loss of brain potassium in kwashiorkor. *Lancet,* 1967, *2,* 643–645.

Garth, T. R. *Race psychology: A study of racial mental differences.* New York: McGraw-Hill, 1931.

Géber, M., and Dean, R. F. A. The psychological changes accompanying kwashiorkor. *Courrier,* 1956, *6,* 3–14.

Genovés, S. De nuevo el aumento secular: Una revisión general muestra que existen muchas dudas e interrogantes. *Anales de Antropología*, 1970, *7*, 25–42.

Gershoff, S. N. Childhood malnutrition in the United States. *Progress in Human Nutrition*, 1971, *1*, 68–74.

Gibson, J. B. Biological aspects of a high socio-economic group. I. IQ, education and social mobility. *Journal of Biosocial Science*, 1970, *2*, 1–16.

Ginsburg, H., and Opper, S. *Piaget's theory of intellectual development: An introduction*. Englewood Cliffs, N.J.: Prentice-Hall, 1969.

Glick, P. C. Intermarriage among ethnic groups in the United States. *Social Biology*, 1970, *17*, 292–298.

Goffeney, B., Henderson, N. B., and Butler, B. V. Negro-white, male-female eight-month developmental scores compared with seven-year WISC and Bender test scores. *Child Development*, 1971, *42*, 595–604.

Golden, M., Birns, B., Bridger, W., and Moss, A. Social-class differentiation in cognitive development among black preschool children. *Child Development*, 1971, *42*, 37–45.

Goldhamer, H. Letter. *Science*, 1971, *172*, 10.

Goodenough, F. L. *Measurement of intelligence by drawings*. Yonkers-on-Hudson, N.Y.: World Book, 1926.

Goodnow, J. J. A test of milieu effects with some of Piaget's tasks. *Psychological Monographs*, 1962, *76* (Whole No. 555).

Goodnow, J. J. Problems in research on culture and thought. *In* D. Elkind and J. H. Flavell (Eds.), *Studies in cognitive development*. New York: Oxford University Press, 1969. Pp. 439–462.

Gossett, T. F. *Race: The history of an idea in America*. Dallas: Southern Methodist University Press, 1963.

Gottesman, I. Genetic aspects of intelligent behavior. *In* N. R. Ellis (Ed.), *Handbook of mental deficiency*. New York: McGraw-Hill, 1963. Pp. 253–296.

Gottesman, I. I. Biogenetics of race and class. *In* M. Deutsch, I. Katz, and A. R. Jensen (Eds.), *Social class, race, and psychological development*. New York: Holt, Rinehart and Winston, 1968. Pp. 11–51.

Gottfried, N. W. Effects of early intervention programs. *In* K. S. Miller and R. M. Dreger (Eds.), *Comparative studies of blacks and whites in the United States*. New York: Seminar Press, 1973. Pp. 273–293.

Gray, S. W., and Klaus, R. A. The early training project: A seventh-year report. *Child Development*, 1970, *41*, 909–924.

Griggs, et al. v. Duke Power Company, U.S. Supreme Court, March 8, 1971.

Gruenwald, P., et al. Influence of environmental factors on foetal growth in man. *Lancet*, 1967, *1*, 1026–1029.

Guilford, J. P. *The nature of human intelligence*. New York: McGraw-Hill, 1967.

Haddon, A. C. *History of anthropology*. New York: Putnam, 1910.

Haldane, J. B. S. *The causes of evolution*. London: Longmans, Green, 1932.

Hall, W. S., and Freedle, R. O. A developmental investigation of standard and nonstandard English among black and white children. *Human Development*, 1973, *16*, 440–464.

Hamy, E. T. Cited in P. Broca, Les cranes de la Caverne de l'Homme-Mort (Lozère). *Revue D'Anthropologie*, 1873, *2*, 1–53.

Hansen, J. D. L., Freesemann, C., Moodie, A. D., and Evans, D. E. What does nutritional growth retardation imply? *Pediatrics*, 1971, *47*, 299–313.

Harper, P. A., Fischer, L. K., and Rider, R. V. Neurological and intellectual status of prematures at three to five years of age. *Journal of Pediatrics*, 1959, *55*, 679–690.

Harper, P. A., and Wiener, G. Sequelae of low birthweight. *Annual Review of Medicine*, 1965, *16*, 405–420.

Harrell, R. F. Further effects of added thiamin on learning and other processes. *Teachers College, Columbia University, Contributions to Education*. 1947, No. 928.

Harrell, R. F., Woodyard, E. R., and Gates, A. I. The influence of vitamin supplementation of the diets of pregnant and lactating women on the intelligence of their offspring. *Metabolism*, 1956, *5*, 555–562.

Harris, A. J., and Lovinger, R. J. Quelques données longitudinales sur les modifications de QI dans l'intelligence d'adolescents noirs. *Enfance*, 1967, *20*, 171–174.

Hartlage, L. C. Sex-linked inheritance of spatial ability. *Perceptual and Motor Skills*, 1970, *31*, 610.

Haug, H. *Quantitative Untersuchungen an der Sehrinde*. Stuttgart: Thieme, 1958.

Hays, W. *Statistics for psychologists*. New York: Holt, Rinehart and Winston, 1963.

Heber, R., Dever, R., and Conry, J. The influence of environmental and genetic variables on intellectual development. *In* H. J. Prehm, L. A. Hamerlynck, and J. E. Crosson (Eds.), *Behavioral research in mental retardation*. Eugene, Ore.: University of Oregon Press, 1968. Pp. 1–23.

Heber, R., and Garber, H. An experiment in the prevention of cultural-familial mental retardation. Paper presented at the Second Congress of the International Association for the Scientific Study of Mental Deficiency, Warsaw, Poland, August 25–September 2, 1970.

Heber, R., Garber, H., Harrington, S., Hoffman, C., and Falender, C. Rehabilitation of families at risk for mental retardation. Progress Report, Rehabilitation research and training center in mental retardation. University of Wisconsin, Madison, 1972.

Hellmuth, J. (Ed.) *Disadvantaged child*. Vol. 3. *Compensatory Education: A national debate*. New York: Brunner/Mazel, 1970.

Henderson, N. D. Letter, *Science*, 1971, *172*, 8–10.

Hendricks, C. H. Delivery patterns and reproductive efficiency among groups of differing socioeconomic status and ethnic origins. *American Journal of Obstetrics and Gynecology*, 1967, *97*, 608–619.

Herrnstein, R. I.Q. *The Atlantic*, 1971, *228* (3), 43–64.

Herrnstein, R. J. *I.Q. in the meritocracy.* Boston: Little, Brown, 1973.

Herskovits, M. J. On the relation between Negro-white mixture and standing in intelligence tests. *Pedagogical Seminary and Journal of Genetic Psychology*, 1926, *33*, 30–42.

Herskovits, M. J. *The anthropometry of the American Negro.* New York: Columbia University Press, 1930.

Hertzig, M. E., Birch, H. G., Richardson, S. A., and Tizard, J. Intellectual levels of school children severely malnourished during the first two years of life. *Pediatrics*, 1972, *49*, 814–824.

Higgins, J. V., Reed, E. W., and Reed, S. C. Intelligence and family size: A paradox resolved. *Eugenics Quarterly*, 1962, *9*, 84–90.

Hirsch, J. Behavior-genetic analysis and its biosocial consequences. *Seminars in Psychiatry*, 1970, *2*, 89–105.

Holm, E. Myopia from the point of view of heredity. *Acta Ophthalmologica, Kopenhagen*, 1926, *3*, 335–347.

Holt, L. E., Jr., and Snyderman, S. E. The amino acid requirements of infants. *Journal of the American Medical Association*, 1961, *175*, 100–103.

Holtzman, N. A. Dietary treatment of inborn errors of metabolism. *Annual Review of Medicine*, 1970, *21*, 335–356.

Hooton, E. A. Methods of racial analysis. *Science*, 1926, *63*, 75–81.

Hooton, E. A. *The Indians of Pecos Pueblo: A study of their skeletal remains.* New Haven: Yale University Press, 1930.

Horton, C. P., and Crump, E. P. Growth and development XI. Descriptive analysis of the backgrounds of 76 Negro children whose scores are above or below average on the Merrill-Palmer scale of mental tests at three years of age. *Journal of Genetic Psychology*, 1962, *100*, 255–265.

Howells, W. *Evolution of the genus Homo.* Reading, Mass.: Addison-Wesley, 1973.

Hulse, F. S. Migration and cultural selection in human genetics. *Anthropologist*, 1969, special volume, 1–21.

Hultkrantz, J. V. Über die Zunahme der Körpergrösse in Schweden in den Jahren 1840–1926. *Nova Acta Regiae Societatis Scientiarum Upsaliensis*, Series 4, extra volume, 1927, 1–54.

Humphreys, L. G. Statistical definitions of test validity for minority groups. *Journal of Applied Psychology*, 1973, *58*, 1–4. (a)

Humphreys, L. G. Implications of group differences for test interpretation. *Proceedings of the 1972 Invitational Conference on Testing Problems—Assessment in a Pluralistic Society.* Princeton, N.J.: Educational Testing Service, 1973. Pp. 56–71. (b)

Humphreys, L. G., and Taber, T. Ability factors as a function of advantaged and disadvantaged groups. *Journal of Educational Measurement*, 1973, *10*, 107–115.

Husén, T. *Psychological twin research*. Stockholm: Almqvist & Wiksell, 1959.

Insel, P. Family similarities in personality, intelligence and social attitudes. Unpublished doctoral dissertation, University of London, 1971.

Jahoda, G. Child animism: I. A critical survey of cross-cultural research. *Journal of Social Psychology*, 1958, *47*, 197–212.

Jarvik, L. F., and Erlenmeyer-Kimling, L. Survey of familial correlations in measured intellectual functions. *In* J. Zubin and G. A. Jervis (Eds.), *Psychopathology of mental development*. New York: Grune and Stratton, 1967. Pp. 447–459.

Jencks, C., et al. *Inequality: A reassessment of the effect of family and schooling in America*. New York: Basic Books, 1972.

Jensen, A. R. Estimation of the limits of heritability of traits by comparison of monozygotic and dizygotic twins. *Proceedings of the National Academy of Sciences*, 1967, *58*, 149–156.

Jensen, A. R. Social class, race, and genetics: Implications for education. *American Educational Research Journal*, 1968, *5*, 1–42.

Jensen, A. R. How much can we boost IQ and scholastic achievement? *Harvard Educational Review*, 1969, *39*, 1–123.

Jensen, A. R. Hierarchical theories of mental ability. *In* W. B. Dockrell (Ed.), *On intelligence*. London: Methuen, 1970. Pp. 119–190. (a)

Jensen, A. R. IQ's of identical twins reared apart. *Behavior Genetics*, 1970, *1*, 133–148. (b)

Jensen, A. R. The race × sex × ability interaction. *In* R. Cancro (Ed.), *Intelligence: Genetic and environmental influences*. New York: Grune and Stratton, 1971. Pp. 107–161.

Jensen, A. R. *Genetics and Education*. New York: Harper and Row, 1972. (a)

Jensen, A. R. A two-factor theory of familial mental retardation. *Human genetics: Proceedings of the Fourth International Congress of Human Genetics, Paris, September 1971*. Amsterdam: Excerpta Medica, 1972. Pp. 263–271. (b)

Jensen, A. R. Comment. *In* L. Ehrman, G. S. Omenn, and E. Caspari (Eds.), *Genetics, environment, and behavior*. New York: Academic Press, 1972. Pp. 23–24. (c)

Jensen, A. R. *Educability and group differences*. New York: Harper and Row, 1973. (a)

Jensen, A. R. The differences are real. *Psychology Today*, 1973, *7*, 80–86. (b)

Jensen, A. R. Level I and level II abilities in three ethnic groups. *American Educational Research Journal*, 1973, *10*, 263–276. (c)

Jensen, A. R. Kinship correlations reported by Sir Cyril Burt. *Behavior Genetics*, 1974, *4*, 1–28, (a)

Jensen, A. R. Interaction of level I and level II abilities with race and socio-economic status. *Journal of Educational Psychology*, 1974, *66*, 99–111. (b)

Jensen, A. R. How biased are culture-loaded tests? *Genetic Psychology Monographs* (in press).

Jensen, A. R., and Frederiksen, J. Free recall of categorized and uncategorized lists: A test of the Jensen hypothesis. *Journal of Educational Psychology*, 1973, *65*, 304–312.

Jerison, H. J. *Evolution of the brain and intelligence*. New York: Academic Press, 1973.

Jinks, J. L., and Fulker, D. W. Comparison of the biometrical genetical, MAVA, and classical approaches to the analysis of human behavior. *Psychological Bulletin*, 1970, *73*, 311–349.

Johnston, R. F., and Selander, R. K. House sparrows: Rapid evolution of races in North America. *Science*, 1964, *144*, 548–550.

Jolly, A. *The evolution of primate behavior*. New York: Macmillan, 1972.

Juel-Nielsen, N. Individual and environment: A psychiatric-psychological investigation of monozygous twins reared apart. *Acta Psychiatrica et Neurologica Scandinavica*, 1965 (Suppl. 183).

Kallen, D. J. (Ed.) *Nutrition, development and social behavior*. Washington, D.C.: U.S. Department of Health, Education, and Welfare, 1973.

Kamin, L. Heredity, intelligence, politics and psychology. Paper presented at the Annual Meeting of the Eastern Psychological Association, Washington, D.C., May 1973. To be published *in* N. J. Block and G. Dworkin (Eds.), *The IQ controversy: Critical readings*. New York: Pantheon.

Kaplan, B. J. Malnutrition and mental deficiency. *Psychological Bulletin*, 1972, *78*, 321–334.

Karnes, M. B., Hodgins, A., and Teska, J. A. An evaluation of two preschool programs for disadvantaged children: A traditional and a highly structured experimental preschool. *Exceptional Children*, 1968, *34*, 667–676.

Karpinos, B. D. The mental test qualification of American youths for military service and its relationship to educational attainment. *Proceedings of the 126th Annual Meeting of the American Statistical Association*, 1966, 92–111.

Kelly, M. R. Some aspects of conservation of quantity and length in Papua and New Guinea in relation to language, sex and years at school. *Territory of Papua and New Guinea Journal of Education*, 1970, 55–60.

Kennedy, W. A. A follow-up normative study of Negro intelligence and achievement. *Monographs of the Society for Research in Child Development*, 1969, *34*, No. 126.

Kennedy, W. A., Van De Riet, V., and White, J. C., Jr. A normative sample of intelligence and achievement of Negro elementary school children in the Southeastern United States. *Monographs of the Society for Research in Child Development*, 1963, *28*, No. 90.

Kimura, K. A consideration of the secular trend in Japanese for height and weight by a graphic method. *American Journal of Physical Anthropology*, 1967, *27*, 89–94.

Kind. Ueber das Längenwachstum der Idioten. *Archiv für Psychiatrie*, 1876, *6*, 447–472.

Klaus, R. A., and Gray, S. W. The early training project for disadvantaged children: A report after five years. *Monographs of the Society for Research in Child Development*, 1968, *33*, No. 120.

Klein, R. E., Freeman, H. E., Kagan, J., Yarbrough, C., and Habicht, J. P. Is big smart? *Journal of Health and Social Behavior*, 1972, *13*, 219–225.

Klineberg, O. An experimental study of speed and other factors in "racial" differences. *Archives of Psychology*, 1928, *15*, No. 93.

Klineberg, O. (Ed.) *Characteristics of the American Negro*. New York: Harper and Brothers, 1944.

Klineberg, O. *Social psychology*. (2nd ed.) New York: Holt, 1954.

Klineberg, O. Negro-white differences in intelligence test performance: A new look at an old problem. *American Psychologist*, 1963, *18*, 198–203.

Knobloch, H., Rider, R., Harper, P., and Pasamanick, B. Neuropsychiatric sequelae of prematurity. *Journal of the American Medical Association*, 1956, *161*, 581–585.

Koppitz, E. M. *The Bender Gestalt Test for young children*. New York: Grune and Stratton, 1964.

Kotelmann, L. Die Augen von 22 Kalmücken. *Zeitschrift für Ethnologie*, 1884, *16*, 77–84.

Kreze, A., Zelina, M., Juhás, J., and Garbara M. Relationship between intelligence and relative prevalence of obesity. *Human Biology*, 1974, *46*, 109–113.

Kroeber, A. L. *Anthropology: Race, language, culture, psychology, prehistory*. (2nd ed.) New York: Harcourt, Brace and World, 1948.

Kroeber, A. L., and Kluckhohn, C. *Culture: A critical review of concepts and definitions. New York: Vintage Books, 1952.*

Krogman, W. M. Growth in man. *Tabulae Biologicae*, 1941, *20*, 1–967.

Krogman, W. M. *The human skeleton in forensic medicine*. Springfield, Ill.: Thomas, 1962.

Kubala, A. L., and Katz, M. M. Nutritional factors in psychological test behavior. *Journal of Genetic Psychology*, 1960, *96*, 343–352.

Kugelmass, I. N., Poull, L. E., and Samuel, E. L. Nutritional improvement of child mentality. *American Journal of the Medical Sciences*, 1944, *208*, 631–633.

Labov, W. The logic of non-standard English. *In* F. Williams (Ed.), *Language and poverty*. Chicago: Markham Press, 1970.

Layzer, D. Heritability analyses of IQ scores: Science or numerology? *Science*, 1974, *183*, 1259–1266.

Leahy, A. M. Nature-nurture and intelligence. *Genetic Psychology Mono-graphs*, 1935, *17*, 235–308.

Lee, A., Lewenz, M. A., and Pearson, K. On the correlation of the mental and physical characters in man. Part II. *Proceedings of the Royal Society, London*, 1903, *71*, 106–114.

Lee, E. S. Negro intelligence and selective migration: a Philadelphia test of the Klineberg hypothesis. *American Sociological Review*, 1951, *16*, 227–233.

Lehninger, A. L. *Biochemistry*. New York: Worth, 1970.

Leifer, A. Ethnic patterns in cognitive tasks. *Proceedings of the 80th Annual Convention of the American Psychological Association*, 1972, *7*, 73–74.

Lenneberg, E. H. *Biological foundations of language*. New York: Wiley, 1967.

Lesser, G. S. Problems in the analysis of patterns of abilities: A reply. *Child Development*, 1973, *44*, 19–20.

Lesser, G. S., Fifer, G., and Clark, D. H. Mental abilities of children from different social-class and cultural groups. *Monographs of the Society for Research in Child Development*, 1965, *30*, No. 4.

Levitsky, D. A., and Barnes, R. H. Nutritional and environmental inter-actions in the behavioral development of the rat: Long-term effects. *Science*, 1972, *176*, 68–71.

Levitt, E. A., Rosenbaum, A. L., Willerman, L., and Levitt, M. Intelligence of retinoblastoma patients and their siblings. *Child Development*, 1972, *43*, 939–948.

Lévy-Bruhl, L. *La mentalité primitive*. Paris: Félix Alcan, 1922.

Lévy-Bruhl, L. *Les carnets de Lucien Lévy-Bruhl*. Paris: Presses Universitaires de France, 1949.

Lewontin, R. C. Race and intelligence. *Bulletin of the Atomic Scientists*, 1970, *26* (3), 2–8.

Lewontin, R. C. The apportionment of human diversity. *In* Th. Dobzhansky, M. K. Hecht, and W. C. Steere (Eds.), *Evolutionary biology*. Vol. 6, New York: Appleton-Century-Crofts, 1972. Pp. 381–398.

Lewontin, R. C. The analysis of variance and the analysis of causes. *American Journal of Human Genetics*, 1974, *26*, 400–411.

Lindzey, G., Loehlin, J., Manosevitz, M., and Thiessen, D. Behavioral genetics, *Annual Review of Psychology*, 1971, *22*, 39–94.

Livingstone, F. B. On the non-existence of human races. *Current Anthro-pology*, 1962, *3*, 279.

Loehlin, J. C., Vandenberg, S. G., and Osborne, R. T. Blood group genes and Negro-white ability differences. *Behavior Genetics*, 1973, *3*, 263–270.

Lowie, R. H. *The history of ethnological theory*. New York: Farrar and Rinehart, 1937.

MacLean, C. J., and Workman, P. L. Genetic studies on hybrid populations. I. Individual estimates of ancestry and their relation to quantitative traits. *Annals of Human Genetics*, 1973, *36*, 341–351.

Malina, R. M. Biological substrata. *In* K. S. Miller and R. M. Dreger (Eds.), *Comparative studies of blacks and whites in the United States.* New York: Seminar Press, 1973. Pp. 53–123.

Marjoribanks, K. Ethnic and environmental influences on mental abilities. *American Journal of Sociology*, 1972, *78*, 323–337.

Marr, J. W. Individual dietary surveys: Purposes and methods. *World Review of Nutrition and Dietetics*, 1971, *13*, 105–164.

Martin, R., and Saller, K. *Lehrbuch der Anthropologie.* Vol. 2. Stuttgart, Germany: Fischer, 1958.

Mayer, J. Food habits and nutrition status of American Negroes. *Postgraduate Medicine*, 1965, *37*, A 110–115.

Mayeske, G. W., et al. *A study of our nation's schools.* DHEW Publication No. (OE) 72-142. Washington, D.C.: U.S. Government Printing Office, 1972.

Mayeske, G. W., et al. *A study of the achievement of our nation's students.* DHEW Publication No. (OE) 72-131. Washington, D.C.: U.S. Government Printing Office, 1973.

Mayr, E. *Animal species and evolution.* Cambridge: Harvard University Press, 1963. (a)

Mayr, E. The taxonomic evaluation of fossil hominids. *In* S. L. Washburn (Ed.) *Classification and human evolution.* Chicago: Aldine, 1963, Pp. 332–346. (b)

McCall, R. B., Hogarty, P. S., and Hurlburt, N. Transitions in infant sensorimotor development and the prediction of childhood IQ. *American Psychologist*, 1972, *27*, 728–748.

McCollum, E. V. Diet and nutrition. *In* E. M. East (Ed.), *Biology in human affairs.* New York: McGraw-Hill, 1931. Pp. 364-383.

McDougall, W. *The group mind.* London: Putnams, 1920.

McNemar, Q. *Psychological statistics.* (4th ed.) New York: Wiley, 1969.

Mead, M. An investigation of the thought of primitive children, with special reference to animism. *Journal of the Royal Anthropological Institute, London*, 1932, *62*, 173–190.

Mehrotra, S. N., and Maxwell, J. The intelligence of twins. A comparative study of eleven-year-old twins. *Population Studies*, 1949, *3*, 295–302.

Mendel, G. J. Versuche über Pflanzen-Hybriden. *Verhandlungen des Natur-forschunden Vereines in Brünn*, 1866, *4*, 3–47.

Mercer, J. R. Pluralistic diagnosis in the evaluation of Black and Chicano children: A procedure for taking sociocultural variables into account in clinical assessment. Paper presented at the Annual Meeting of the American Psychological Association, Washington, D.C., September 1971.

Michael, W. B. Factor analysis of tests and criteria: A comparative study of two AAF pilot populations. *Psychological Monographs*, 1949, *63* (whole No. 298).

Mitra, S. Education and fertility in the United States. *Eugenics Quarterly*, 1966, *13*, 214–222.

Mönckeberg, F. Effect of early marasmic malnutrition on subsequent physical and psychological development. *In* N. S. Scrimshaw and J. E. Gordon (Eds.), *Malnutrition, learning, and behavior*. Cambridge: M. I. T. Press, 1968. Pp. 269–278.

Montagu, M. F. A. *Man's most dangerous myth: The fallacy of race*. (4th ed.) Cleveland: World, 1964.

Montagu, M. F. A. *The idea of race*. Lincoln: University of Nebraska Press, 1965.

Montagu, M. F. A. *The concept of race*. New York: Collier, 1969.

Moore, W. M., Silverberg, M. M., and Read, M. S. (Eds.) *Nutrition, growth and development of North American Indian children*. DHEW Publication No. (NIH) 72-26. Washington, D.C.: U.S. Government Printing Office, 1972.

Morton, N. E. Human behavioral genetics. *In* L. Ehrman, G. S. Omenn, and E. Caspari (Eds.), *Genetics, environment, and behavior*. New York: Academic Press, 1972. Pp. 247–265.

Morton, N. E. Analysis of family resemblance. I. Introduction. *American Journal of Human Genetics*, 1974, *26*, 318–330.

Mosier, H. D., Grossman, H. J., and Dingman, H. F. Physical growth in mental defectives. *Pediatrics*, 1965, *36*, 465–519.

Mosteller, F., and Moynihan, D. P. *On equality of educational opportunity*. New York: Vintage Books, 1972.

Murdock, G. P. *Social structure*. New York: Macmillan, 1949.

Murray, S. L., Ellison, R. L., and Fox, D. G. Racial fairness of biographical predictors of academic performance. *Proceedings of the 81st Annual Convention of the American Psychological Association*, 1973, *8*, 35–36.

Myers, C. S. Hearing. *In* A. C. Haddon (Ed.), *Reports of the Cambridge Anthropological Expedition to Torres Straits*. Vol. 2, part 2. Cambridge: Cambridge University Press, 1903. Pp. 141–168.

Myrdal, G. *An American dilemma: The Negro problem and modern democracy*. New York: Harper, 1944.

National Academy of Sciences. A statement by the Council of the Academy. *Proceedings of the National Academy of Sciences*, 1968, *59*, 651–654.

National Academy of Sciences. *Technology: Processes of assessment and choice*. Washington, D.C.: U.S. Government Printing Office, 1969.

National Academy of Sciences. Recommendations with respect to the behavioral and social aspects of human genetics. *Proceedings of the National Academy of Sciences*, 1972, *69*, 1–3.

Naylor, A. F., and Myrianthopoulos, N. C. The relation of ethnic and selected socio-economic factors to human birth-weight. *Annals of Human Genetics*, 1967, *31*, 71–83.

Nei, M., and Roychoudhury, A. K. Gene differences between Caucasian, Negro, and Japanese populations. *Science*, 1972, *177*, 434–436.

Nei, M., and Roychoudhury, A. K. Genic variation within and between the three major races of man, Caucasoids, Negroids and Mongoloids. *American Journal of Human Genetics*, 1974, *26*, 421–443.

Nellhaus, G. Head circumference from birth to eighteen years. *Pediatrics*, 1968, *41*, 106–114.

Newman, H. H., Freeman, F. N., and Holzinger, K. J. *Twins: A study of heredity and environment*. Chicago: University of Chicago Press, 1937.

Newman, R. W. The body sizes of tomorrow's young men. *In* E. Bennet, J. Degan, and J. Spiegel (Eds.), *Human factors in technology*. New York: McGraw-Hill, 1963. Pp. 149–157.

Nichols, P. L. The effects of heredity and environment on intelligence test performance in 4 and 7 year white and Negro sibling pairs. (Doctoral dissertation, University of Minnesota) Ann Arbor, Mich.: University Microfilms, 1970, No. 71-18,874.

Nichols, P. L., and Anderson, V. E. Intellectual performance, race, and socioeconomic status. *Social Biology*, 1973, *20*, 367–374.

Nichols, P. L., and Broman, S. H. Familial factors associated with IQ at 4 years. Paper presented at Behavior Genetics Association annual meeting, Chapel Hill, N.C., April, 1973.

Nichols, P. L., and Broman, S. H. Familial resemblance in infant mental development. *Developmental Psychology*, 1974, *10*, 442–446.

Niswander, K. R., and Gordon, M. *The women and their pregnancies: The collaborative perinatal study of the National Institute of Neurological Diseases and Stroke*. Philadelphia: Saunders, 1972.

Nitowsky, H. M. Nutrition. *In* R. E. Cooke and S. Levin (Eds.), *The biologic basis of pediatric practice*. New York: McGraw Hill, 1968. Pp. 891–918.

Nixon, J. C., and Glorig, A. Noise-induced permanent threshold shift at 2000 cps and 4000 cps. *Journal of the Acoustical Society of America*, 1961, 33, 904–908.

Norman, R. D. Intelligence tests and the personal world. *New Mexico Quarterly*, 1963, *33*, 153–184.

O'Connell, E. J., Feldt, R. H., and Stickler, G. B. Head circumference, mental retardation, and growth failure. *Pediatrics*, 1965, *36*, 62–66.

Open Door Society, Inc. *Mixed Race Adoptions*. Montreal, 1970.

Orshansky, M. The shape of poverty in 1966. *Social Security Bulletin*, 1968, 31(3), 3–32.

Osborne, R. T. Racial differences in mental growth and school achievement: A longitudinal study. *Psychological Reports*, 1960, *7*, 233–239.

Osborne, R. T. Stability of factor structure of the WISC for normal Negro children from pre-school level to first grade. *Psychological Reports*, 1966, *18*, 655–664.

Osborne, R. T., and Gregor, A. J. Racial differences in heritability estimates for tests of spatial ability. *Perceptual and Motor Skills*, 1968, *27*, 735–739.

Osborne, R. T., Gregor, A. J., and Miele, F. Heritability of Factor V: Verbal comprehension. *Perceptual and Motor Skills*, 1968, *26*, 191–202.

Osborne, R. T., and Miele, F. Racial differences in environmental influences on numerical ability as determined by heritability estimates. *Perceptual and Motor Skills*, 1969, *28*, 535–538.

Osborne, R. T., and Suddick, D. E. Blood type gene frequency and mental ability. *Psychological Reports*, 1971, *29*, 1243–1249.

Page, E. B. Miracle in Milwaukee: Raising the IQ. *Educational Researcher*, 1972, *1*(10), 8–16.

Palmer, F. H. Socioeconomic status and intellective performance among Negro preschool boys. *Developmental Psychology*, 1970, *3*, 1–9.

Payne, P. R., and Wheeler, E. F. Comparative nutrition in pregnancy. *Nature*, 1967, *215*, 1134–1136.

Pearl, R. On the correlation between intelligence and the size of the head. *Journal of Comparative Neurology and Psychology*, 1906, *16*, 189–199.

Pearl, R. *Studies in human biology*. Baltimore: Williams and Wilkins, 1924.

Pearson, C. Intelligence of Honolulu preschool children in relation to parent's education. *Child Development*, 1969, *40*, 647–650.

Pearson, K. On the correlation of intellectual ability with the size and shape of the head. *Proceedings of the Royal Society*, London, 1902, *69*, 333–342.

Pearson, K. On a generalized theory of alternative inheritance, with special reference to Mendel's laws. *Philosophical Transactions of the Royal Society*, *A*, 1904, *203*, 53–86.

Pearson, K., and Lee, A. On the laws of inheritance in man. I. Inheritance of physical characters. *Biometrika*, 1903, *2*, 357–462.

Penrose, L. S. Review of Dunn and Dobzhansky, *Heredity, race, and society*. *Annals of Eugenics*, 1952, *17*, 252.

Penrose, L. S. Some recent trends in human genetics. *Proceedings IXth International Congress of Genetics, Carylogia*, 1954, 6 (Suppl.), 521–530.

Pesé, E. G. Letter. *American Journal of Diseases of Children*, 1966, *112*, 608.

Peterson, J. *Early conceptions and tests of intelligence*. Yonkers-on-Hudson, N.Y.: World Book, 1925.

Peterson, J., and Lanier, L. H. Studies in the comparative abilities of whites and Negroes. *Mental Measurement Monographs*, 1929, No. 5.

Pettigrew, T. F. *A profile of the Negro American*. Princeton, N.J.: Van Nostrand, 1964.

Piaget, J. *The child's conception of the world*. New York: Harcourt, Brace and World, 1929.

Piaget, J. *The psychology of intelligence*. London: Routledge and Kegan Paul, 1950.

Piaget, J., and Inhelder, B. *The psychology of the child*. New York: Basic Books, 1969.

Platt, B. S., and Stewart, R. J. C. Reversible and irreversible effects of protein-calorie deficiency on the central nervous system of animals and man. *World Review of Nutrition and Dietetics*, 1971, *13*, 43–85.

Pollitt, E. Ecology, malnutrition, and mental development. *Psychosomatic Medicine*, 1969, *31*, 193–200.

Pollitt, E., and Granoff, D. Mental and motor development of Peruvian children treated for severe malnutrition. *Revista Interamericana Psicologia*, 1967, *1*, 93–102.

Pollitt, E., and Ricciuti, H. Biological and social correlates of stature among children in the slums of Lima, Peru. *American Journal of Orthopsychiatry*, 1969, *39*, 735–747.

Post, R. H. Population differences in vision acuity: A review, with speculative notes on selection relaxation. *Eugenics Quarterly*, 1962, *9*, 189–212.

Poull, E. The effect of improvement in nutrition on the mental capacity of young children. *Child Development*, 1938, *9*, 123–126.

Priddy, D., and Kirgan, D. Characteristics of white couples who adopt black/white children. *Social Work*, 1971, *16*, 105–107.

Prince, J. R. Science concepts in New Guinean and European children. *Australian Journal of Education*, 1968, *12*, 81–89.

Prince, J. R. *Science concepts in a Pacific culture*. Sydney: Angus and Robertson, 1969.

Prosser, C. L. *Comparative animal physiology*. (3rd ed.) Philadelphia: Saunders, 1973.

Provine, W. B. Geneticists and the biology of race crossing. *Science*, 1973, *182*, 790–796.

Pryor, H. B., and Thelander, H. Abnormally small head size and intellect in children. *Journal of Pediatrics*, 1968, *73*, 593–598.

Quatrefages de Breáu, J. L. A. de. *Unité de l'espèce humaine*. Paris: Hachatte, 1861.

Quay, L. C. Language dialect, reinforcement, and the intelligence-test performance of Negro children. *Child Development*, 1971, *42*, 5–15.

Rajalakshmi, R., Deodhar, A. D., and Ramakrishnan, C. V. Vitamin C secretion during lactation. *Acta Paediatrica Scandinavica*, 1965, *54*, 375–382.

Rajalakshmi, R., and Ramakrishnan, C. V. Nutrition and brain function. *World Review of Nutrition and Dietetics*, 1972, *15*, 35–85.

Rajalakshmi, R., Subbulakshmi, G., Ramakrishnan, C. V., Joshi, S. K., and Bhatt, R. V. Biosynthesis of ascorbic acid in human placenta. *Current Science*, 1967, *36*, 45–46.

Rao, D. C., Morton, N. E., and Yee, S. Analysis of family resemblance. II. A linear model for familial correlation. *American Journal of Human Genetics*, 1974, *26*, 331–359.

Record, R. G., McKeown, T., and Edwards, J. H. An investigation of the difference in measured intelligence between twins and single births. *Annals of Human Genetics*, 1970, *34*, 11–20.

Reed, E. W., and Reed, S. C. *Mental retardation: A family study*. Philadelphia: Saunders, 1965.

Reed, T. E. Caucasian genes in American Negroes. *Science*, 1969, *165*, 762–768.

Reed, T. E. Number of gene loci required for accurate estimation of ancestral population proportions in individual human hybrids. *Nature*, 1973, *244*, 575–576.

Rhoads, T. F., Rapoport, M., Kennedy, R., and Stokes, J., Jr. Studies on the growth and development of male children receiving evaporated milk. *Journal of Pediatrics*, 1945, *26*, 415–454.

Richardson, S. A., Birch, H. G., and Hertzig, M. E. School performance of children who were severely malnourished in infancy. *American Journal of Mental Deficiency*, 1973, *77*, 623–632.

Rivers, W. H. R. Vision. *In* A. C. Haddon (Ed.), *Reports of the Cambridge Anthropological Expedition to Torres Straits*. Vol. 2, part 1. Cambridge: Cambridge University Press, 1901. Pp. 8–140.

Roberts, D. F. Anthropological genetics: Problems and pitfalls. *In* M. H. Crawford and P. L. Workman (Eds.), *Methods and theories of anthropological genetics*. Albuquerque: University of New Mexico Press, 1973, Pp. 1–17.

Roberts, J. *Intellectual development of children as measured by the Wechsler Intelligence Scale for Children*. DHEW Publication No. (HSM) 72-1004. Washington, D.C.: U.S. Department of Health, Education, and Welfare, 1971.

Robinow, M. Field measurement of growth and development. *In* N. S. Scrimshaw and J. E. Gordon (Eds.), *Malnutrition, learning, and behavior*. Cambridge: M.I.T. Press, 1968. Pp. 409–424.

Rosenfeld, M., and Hilton, T. L. Negro-white differences in adolescent educational growth. *American Educational Research Journal*, 1971, *8*, 267–283.

Rosensweig, N. S., Huang, S.-S., and Bayless, T. M. Transmission of lactose intolerance. *Lancet*, 1967, *2*, 777.

Saldanha, P. H. The genetic effects of immigration in a rural community of Sao Paulo. *Acta Geneticae Medicae et Gemellologiae*, 1962, *11*, 158–223.

Sandon, F. The relative numbers and abilities of some ten-year-old twins. *Journal of the Royal Statistical Society, Series A*, 1957, *120*, 440–450.

Sarason, S. B. Jewishness, blackishness, and the nature-nurture controversy. *American Psychologist*, 1973, *28*, 926–971.

Scarborough, B. B. Some mental characteristics of Southern colored and white venereal disease patients as measured by the Wechsler-Bellevue test. *Journal of Social Psychology*, 1956, *43*, 313–321.

Scarr, S. Effects of birth weight on later intelligence. *Social Biology*, 1969, *16*, 249–256.

Scarr, S. Race, social class, and intelligence: A study of individual and group variability. Unpublished report, University of Minnesota, 1971.

Scarr-Salapatek, S. Race, social class, and IQ. *Science*, 1971, *174*, 1285–1295. (a)

Scarr-Salapatek, S. Review of *Environment, heredity, and intelligence;* H. J. Eysenck, *The IQ Argument;* and R. Herrnstein, *IQ. Science*, 1971, *174*, 1223–1228. (b)

Scarr-Salapatek, S. Reply. *Science*, 1972, *178*, 235–240.

Scarr-Salapatek, S. Reply. *Science*, 1973, *182*, 1045–1047.

Schadé, J. P., and van Groenigen, W. B. Structural organization of the human cerebral cortex: 1. Maturation of the middle frontal gyrus. *Acta Anatomica*, 1961, *47*, 74–111.

Schaie, K. W. Generational vs. ontogenetic components of change: A second follow-up. Paper presented at the 79th Annual Convention of the American Psychological Association, Washington, D.C., September, 1971.

Schaie, K. W., and Strother, C. R. The effect of time and cohort differences on the interpretation of age changes in cognitive behavior. *Multivariate Behavioral Research*, 1968, *3*, 259–293.

Schmidt, F. L., and Hunter, J. E. Racial and ethnic bias in psychological tests: Divergent implications of two definitions of test bias. *American Psychologist*, 1974, *29*, 1–8.

Schroeder, H. A., Balassa, J. J., and Tipton, I. H. Abnormal trace metals in man: Tin. *Journal of Chronic Diseases*, 1964, *17*, 483–502.

Schull, W. J., and Neel, J. V. *The effects of inbreeding on Japanese children.* New York: Harper and Row, 1965.

Schwartz, M., and Schwartz, J. Evidence against a genetical component to performance on IQ tests. *Nature*, 1974, *248*, 84–85.

Schwarz, K. Tin as an essential growth factor in rats. *In* W. Mertz and W. E. Cornatzer (Eds.), *Newer trace elements in nutrition.* New York: Marcel Dekker, 1971. Pp. 313–326.

Schwarz, K., Milne, D. B., and Vinyard, E. Growth effects of tin compounds in rats maintained in a trace element-controlled environment. *Biochemical and Biophysical Research Communications*, 1970, *40*, 22–29.

Scottish Council for Research in Education. *The trend of Scottish intelligence: A comparison of the 1947 and 1932 surveys of the intelligence of eleven-year-old pupils.* London: University of London Press, 1949.

Scrimshaw, N. S. Early malnutrition and central nervous system functioning. *Merrill-Palmer Quarterly*, 1969, *15*, 375–388.

Scrimshaw, N. S., and Gordon, J. E. (Eds.), *Malnutrition, learning, and behavior.* Cambridge: M.I.T. Press, 1968.

Scrofani, P. J. Effects of pretraining on the conceptual functions of children at different levels of socioeconomic status, IQ, and cognitive development. *Proceedings of the 80th Annual Convention of the American Psychological Association*, 1972, *7*, 427–428.

Seashore, H., Wesman, A., and Doppelt, J. The standardization of the Wechsler Intelligence Scale for Children. *Journal of Consulting Psychology*, 1950, *14*, 99–110.

Seltzer, C. C., and Mayer, J. A simple criterion of obesity. *Postgraduate Medicine*, 1965, *38*, A101–107.

Semler, I. J., and Iscoe, I. Comparative and developmental study of the learning abilities of Negro and white children under four conditions. *Journal of Educational Psychology*, 1963, *54*, 38–44.

Semler, I. J., and Iscoe, I. Structure of intelligence in Negro and white children. *Journal of Educational Psychology*, 1966, *57*, 326–336.

Sewell, W. H., Haller, A. O., and Ohlendorf, G. W. The educational and early occupational status attainment process: Replication and revision. *American Sociological Review*, 1970, *35*, 1014–1027.

Shields, J. *Monozygotic twins*. London: Oxford University Press, 1962.

Shimberg, M. E. An investigation into the validity of norms with special reference to urban and rural groups. *Archives of Psychology*, 1929, No. 104. (Columbia University.)

Shockley, W. Dysgenics, geneticity, raceology: A challenge to the intellectual responsibility of educators. *Phi Delta Kappan*, 1972, *53*, 297–307.

Shockley, W. Deviations from Hardy-Weinberg frequencies caused by assortative mating in hybrid populations. *Proceedings of the National Academy of Sciences*, 1973, *70*, 732–736.

Shuey, A. M. *The testing of Negro intelligence*. (2nd ed.) New York: Social Science Press, 1966. (1st ed., Lynchburg, Va.: J. P. Bell, 1958.)

Shull, G. H. The composition of a field of maize. *Reports of American Breeders' Association*, 1908, *4*, 296–301.

Simpson, G. G. *The major features of evolution*. New York: Columbia University Press, 1953.

Simpson, G. G. *Principles of animal taxonomy*. New York: Columbia University Press, 1961.

Simpson, G. G. *Biology and man*. New York: Harcourt Brace Jovanovich, 1969.

Sitkei, E. G., and Meyers, C. E. Comparative structure of intellect in middle- and lower-class four-year-olds of two ethnic groups. *Developmental Psychology*, 1969, *1*, 592–604.

Skodak, M., and Skeels, H. M. A final follow-up study of one hundred adopted children. *Journal of Genetic Psychology*, 1949, *75*, 85–125.

Smart, M. S. Letter. *American Psychologist*, 1963, *18*, 621.

Smith, C. A. Effects of maternal undernutrition upon the newborn infant in Holland (1944–1945). *Journal of Pediatrics*, 1947, *30*, 229–243.

Smith, S. Language and non-verbal test performance of racial groups in Honolulu before and after a fourteen-year interval. *Journal of General Psychology*, 1942, *26*, 51–93.

Snyder, R. T., Holowenzak, S. P., and Hoffman, N. A cross-cultural item-analysis of Bender-Gestalt protocols administered to ghetto and suburban children. *Perceptual and Motor Skills*, 1971, *33*, 791–796.

Spuhler, J. N., and Lindzey, G. Racial differences in behavior. *In* J. Hirsch (Ed.), *Behavior-genetic analysis*. New York: McGraw-Hill, 1967. Pp. 366–414.

Stafford, R. E. Sex differences in spatial visualization as evidence of sex-linked inheritance. *Perceptual and Motor Skills*, 1961, *13*, 428.

Stanley, J. C. (Ed.) *Preschool programs for the disadvantaged: Five experimental approaches to early childhood education*. Baltimore: Johns Hopkins University Press, 1972.

Statistical Abstract of the United States. Washington, D.C.: U.S. Government Printing Office, 1953.

Stein, Z. A., and Kassab, H. Nutrition. *Mental Retardation: An Annual Review*, 1970, *2*, 92–116.

Stein, Z., Susser, M., Saenger, G., and Marolla, F. Nutrition and mental performance. *Science*, 1972, *178*, 708–713.

Sterling, E. B. Health studies of Negro children. II. The physical status of the urban Negro child: A study of 5170 Negro school children in Atlanta, Ga. *Public Health Reports*, 1928, *43*, 2713–2774.

Stern, C. *Principles of human genetics*. (3rd ed.) San Francisco: W. H. Freeman, 1973.

Stewart, R. J. C. Maternal diet and perinatal death. *Proceedings of the Royal Society of Medicine, London*, 1968, *61*, 1292–1295.

Stewart, W. A. Towards a history of American Negro dialect. *In* F. Williams (Ed.), *Language and Poverty*. Chicago: Markham Press, 1970.

Stoch, M. B., and Smythe, P. M. Does undernutrition during infancy inhibit brain growth and subsequent intellectual development? *Archives of Disease in Childhood*, 1963, *38*, 546–552.

Stoch, M. B., and Smythe, P. M. The effect of undernutrition during infancy on subsequent brain growth and intellectual development. *South African Medical Journal*, 1967, *41*, 1027–1030.

Stoch, M. B., and Smythe, P. M. Undernutrition during infancy, and subsequent brain growth and intellectual development. *In* N. S. Scrimshaw and J. E. Gordon (Eds.), *Malnutrition, learning, and behavior*. Cambridge: M.I.T. Press, 1968. Pp. 278–288.

Stodolsky, S. S., and Lesser, G. Learning patterns in the disadvantaged. *Harvard Educational Review*, 1967, *37*, 546–593.

Stunkard, A., d'Aquili, E., Fox, S., and Filion, R. D. L. Influence of social class on obesity and thinness in children. *Journal of the American Medical Association*, 1972, *221*, 579–584.

Sullivan, L. R. The pygmy races of man. *Natural History*, 1919, *19*, 687–695.

Sumner, W. G. *Folkways*. Boston: Ginn, 1906.

Tabah, L., and Sutter, J. Le niveau intellectuel des enfants d'une même famille, *Annals of Human Genetics*, 1954, *19*, 120–150.

Tanner, J. M. *Growth at adolescence*. (2nd ed.) Oxford: Blackwell, 1962.

Tanser, H. A. *The settlement of Negroes in Kent County, Ontario, and a study of the mental capacity of their descendants*. Chatham, Ont.: Shepherd, 1939.

Tanser, H. A. Intelligence of Negroes of mixed blood in Canada. *Journal of Negro Education*, 1941, *10*, 650–652.

Taylor, G. D., and Williams, E. Acoustic trauma in the sports hunter. *Laryngoscope*, 1966, *76*, 863–879.

Taylor, W., Pearson, J., Mair, A., and Burns, W. Study of noise and hearing in jute weaving. *Journal of the Acoustical Society of America*, 1965, *38*, 113–120.

Ten-State Nutrition Survey 1968–1970. See U.S. Department of Health, Education, and Welfare, Ten-State Nutrition Survey.

Terman, L. M. *The measurement of intelligence*. Boston: Houghton Mifflin, 1916.

Terman, L. M., and Merrill, M. A. *Measuring intelligence: A guide to the administration of the new revised Stanford-Binet tests of intelligence*. Boston: Houghton Mifflin, 1937.

Thelander, H. E., and Goebel, G. Microcephalia as a complication of pneumococcic meningitis. *American Journal of Diseases of Children*, 1949, *77*, 642–646.

Thelander, H. E., and Pryor, H. B. Abnormal patterns of growth and development in mongolism. *Clinical Pediatrics*, 1966, *5*, 493–501.

Thieme, F. P. (Measuring and analysis of data) *In* W. E. Martin, *The functional body measurements of school age children*. Chicago: National School Service Institute, 1954.

Thorndike, R. L. Concepts of culture-fairness. *Journal of Educational Measurement*, 1971, *8*, 63–70.

Thurstone, L. L. Primary mental abilities. *Psychometric Monographs*, 1938, No. 1.

Tizard, B. IQ and race. *Nature*, 1974, *247*, 316.

Tomlinson, H. Differences between pre-school Negro children and their older siblings on the Stanford-Binet scales. *Journal of Negro Education*, 1944, *13*, 474–479.

Trevor, J. C. Race crossing in Man: The analysis of metrical characters. *Eugenics Laboratory Memoirs*, 1953, No. 36.

Tuddenham, R. D. Soldier intelligence in World Wars I and II. *American Psychologist*, 1948, *3*, 54–56.

Tuddenham, R. D. A "Piagetian" test of cognitive development. *In* W. B. Dockrell (Ed.), *On intelligence*. London: Methuen, 1970. Pp. 49–70.

Tulkin, S. R. Race, class, family, and school achievement. *Journal of Personality and Social Psychology*, 1968, *9*, 31–37.

Tupes, E. C., and Shaycoft, M. F. *Normative distributions of AQE Aptitude Indexes for high-school-age boys.* Technical Documentary Report PRL-TDR-64-17, Office of Technical Services, U.S. Department of Commerce, Washington, D.C., 1964.

Tyler, L. E. *The psychology of human differences.* (2nd ed.) New York: Appleton-Century-Crofts, 1956.

Tyler, L. E. Human abilities. *Annual Review of Psychology*, 1972, *23*, 177–206.

Tylor, E. B. *Primitive culture: Researches into the development of mythology, philosophy, religion, language, art and custom.* Vol. 1. London: Murray, 1871.

Ucko, P. J., and Rosenfeld, A. *Palaeolithic cave art.* New York: McGraw-Hill, 1967.

Udry, J. R., Bauman, K. E., and Chase, C. Skin color, status, and mate selection. *American Journal of Sociology*, 1971, *76*, 722–733.

Underwood, E. J. The history and philosophy of trace element research. *In* W. Mertz and W. E. Cornatzer (Eds.), *Newer trace elements in nutrition.* New York: Marcel Dekker, 1971. Pp. 1–18.

United Kingdom, Department of Health and Social Security. *Recommended intakes of nutrients for the United Kingdom.* London: Her Majesty's Stationery Office, 1969.

United States v. Georgia Power Company, et al. U.S. Court of Appeals, Fifth Circuit (New Orleans). February 14, 1973.

U.S. Department of Health, Education, and Welfare. *Ten-state nutrition survey 1968–1970.* Vols. I–V. DHEW Publications Nos. (HSM) 72-8130-34. Washington, D.C.: U.S. Government Printing Office, 1972.

U.S. National Research Council, Food and Nutrition Board. *Recommended dietary allowances.* (7th ed.) NAS Publication No. 1694. Washington, D.C.: National Academy of Sciences, 1968.

Vallois, H. V. Neandertals and Praesapiens. *Journal of the Royal Anthropological Institute*, 1954, *84*, 111–130.

Vandenberg, S. G. (Ed.) *Methods and goals in human behavior genetics.* New York: Academic Press, 1965.

Vandenberg, S. G. Contributions of twin research to psychology. *Psychological Bulletin*, 1966, *66*, 327–352.

Vandenberg, S. G. (Ed.) *Progress in human behavior genetics: Recent reports on genetic syndromes, twin studies, and statistical advances.* Baltimore: Johns Hopkins University Press, 1968.

Vandenberg, S. G. A twin study of spatial ability. *Multivariate Behavioral Research*, 1969, *4*, 273–294.

Vandenberg, S. G. A comparison of heritability estimates of U.S. Negro and white high school students. *Acta Geneticae Medicae et Gemellologiae*, 1970, *19*, 280–284.

Vandenberg, S. G. What do we know today about the inheritance of intelligence and how do we know it? *In* R. Cancro (Ed.), *Intelligence: Genetic and environmental influences.* New York: Grune and Stratton, 1971. Pp. 182–218.

Van Duzen, J., Carter, J. P., Secondi, J., and Federspiel, C. Protein and calorie malnutrition among preschool Navajo Indian children. *American Journal of Clinical Nutrition*, 1969, *22*, 1362–1370.

Vernon, P. E. Ability factors and environmental influences. *American Psychologist*, 1965, *20*, 723–733.

Viteri, F. E., and Arroyave, G. Protein-calorie malnutrition. *In* R. S. Goodhart and M. E. Shils (Eds.), *Modern nutrition in health and disease.* (5th ed.) Philadelphia: Lea and Febiger, 1973. Pp. 604–624.

Waardenburg, P. J. *Genetics and ophthalmology.* Vol. II. *Neuro-ophthalmological part.* Springfield, Ill.: Thomas, 1963.

Wahlund, S. Zusammensetzung von Populationen und Korrelationserscheinungen vom Standpunkt der Vererbungslehre aus betrachtet. *Hereditas*, 1928, *11*, 65–106.

Waller, J. H. Achievement and social mobility: Relationships among IQ score, education, and occupation in two generations. *Social Biology*, 1971, *18*, 252–259.

Warren, N. Malnutrition and mental development. *Psychological Bulletin*, 1973, *80*, 324–328.

Watson, E. H., and Lowrey, G. H. *Growth and development of children.* Chicago: Year Book Publishers, 1951.

Watson, J. B. What the nursery has to say about instincts. *In* C. Murchison (Ed.), *Psychologies of 1925.* Worcester, Mass.: Clark University Press, 1926. Pp. 1–35.

Weidenreich, F. *Apes, giants, and man.* Chicago: University of Chicago Press, 1946.

Weikart, D. P. Relationship of curriculum, teaching, and learning in preschool education. *In* J. C. Stanley (Ed.), *Preschool programs for the disadvantaged.* Baltimore: Johns Hopkins University Press, 1972. Pp. 22–66.

Werner, E. E., Bierman, J. M., and French, F. E. *The children of Kauai: A longitudinal study from the prenatal period to age ten.* Honolulu: University of Hawaii Press, 1971.

Werner, E. E., Simonian, K., and Smith, R. S. Ethnic and socioeconomic status differences in abilities and achievement among preschool and school-age children in Hawaii. *Journal of Social Psychology*, 1968, *75*, 43–59.

Wheeler, L. R. A comparative study of the intelligence of East Tennessee mountain children. *Journal of Educational Psychology*, 1942, *33*, 321–334.

White, L. A. *The science of culture.* New York: Farrar, Straus, 1949.

Whitelaw, A. G. L. The association of social class and sibling number with skinfold thickness in London schoolboys. *Human Biology*, 1971, *43*, 414–420.

Whiteman, M., and Deutsch, M. Social disadvantage as related to intellective and language development. *In* M. Deutsch, I. Katz, and A. R. Jensen (Eds.), *Social class, race, and psychological development.* New York: Holt, Rinehart, and Winston, 1968. Pp. 86–114.

Wiener, G. Psychologic correlates of premature birth: A review. *Journal of Nervous and Mental Disease,* 1962, *134,* 129–144.

Wiener, G. Scholastic achievement at age 12–13 of prematurely born infants. *Journal of Special Education,* 1968, *2,* 237–250.

Wiener, G., Rider, R. V., Oppel, W. C., Fischer, L. K., and Harper, P. A. Correlates of low birth weight: Psychological status at six to seven years of age. *Pediatrics,* 1965, *35,* 434–444.

Wiener, G., Rider, R. V., Oppel, W. C., and Harper, P. A. Correlates of low birth weight: Psychological status at eight to ten years of age. *Pediatric Research,* 1968, *2,* 110–118.

Willerman, L. Review of H. J. Eysenck, *The IQ Argument. Contemporary Psychology,* 1972, *17,* 585–586.

Willerman, L., Broman, S. H., and Fiedler, M. Infant development, preschool IQ, and social class. *Child Development,* 1970, *41,* 69–77.

Willerman, L., and Churchill, J. A. Intelligence and birthweight in identical twins. *Child Development,* 1967, *38,* 623–629.

Willerman, L., Naylor, A. F., and Myrianthopoulos, N. C. Intellectual development of children from interracial matings. *Science,* 1970, *170,* 1329–1331.

Willerman, L., Naylor, A. F., and Myrianthopoulos, N. C. Reply. *Science,* 1971, *172,* 11.

Willerman, L., Naylor, A. F., and Myrianthopoulos, N. C. Intellectual development of children from interracial matings: performance in infancy and at 4 years. *Behavior Genetics,* 1974, *4,* 83–90.

Williams, M. Superior intelligence of children blinded from retinoblastoma. *Archives of Disease in Childhood,* 1968, *43,* 204–210.

Williams, R. L. The BITCH-100: A culture-specific test. Paper presented at the 80th Annual Convention of the American Psychological Association, Honolulu, September, 1972.

Wilson, A. B. Educational consequences of segregation in a California community. In report of U.S. Commission on Civil Rights *Racial isolation in the public schools.* Vol. 2, Appendices. Washington, D.C.: U.S. Government Printing Office, 1967.

Wilson, E. B. *The cell in development and heredity.* (3rd ed.) New York: Macmillan, 1928.

Winick, M. Nucleic acid and protein content during growth of human brain. *Pediatric Research,* 1968, *2,* 352–355. (a)

Winick, M. Nutrition and cell growth. *Nutrition Reviews,* 1968, *26,* 195–197. (b)

Winick, M. Biological correlations. *American Journal of Diseases of Children*, 1970, *120*, 416–418.

Winick, M., and Noble, A. Cellular response in rats during malnutrition at various ages. *Journal of Nutrition*, 1966, *89*, 300–306.

Winick, M., and Rosso, P. Head circumference and cellular growth of the brain in normal and marasmic children. *Journal of Pediatrics*, 1969, *74*, 774–778.

Wirth, L., and Goldhamer, H. The hybrid and the problem of miscegenation. *In* O. Klineberg (Ed.), *Characteristics of the American Negro*, New York: Harper, 1944, Pp. 249–369.

Witty, P. A., and Jenkins, M. D. Intra-race testing and Negro intelligence. *Journal of Psychology*, 1936, *1*, 179–192.

Woodworth, R. S. Heredity and environment: A critical survey of recently published material on twins and foster children. *Social Science Research Council Bulletin*, 1941, No. 47.

Wright, S. Evolution in Mendelian populations. *Genetics*, 1931, *16*, 97–159.

Wright, S. *Evolution and the genetics of populations*. Vol. 1. *Genetic and biometric foundations*. Chicago: University of Chicago Press, 1968.

Wright, S. *Evolution and the genetics of populations*. Vol. 2. *The theory of gene frequencies*. Chicago: University of Chicago Press, 1969.

Wysocki, B. A., and Wysocki, A. C. Cultural differences as reflected in Wechsler-Bellevue Intelligence (WBII) Test. *Psychological Reports*, 1969, *25*, 95–101.

Yerkes, R. M. Psychological examining in the United States Army. *Memoirs of the National Academy of Sciences*, 1921, Vol. 15.

Young, F. M., and Bright, H. A. Results of testing 81 Negro rural juveniles with the Wechsler Intelligence Scale for Children. *Journal of Social Psychology*, 1954, *39*, 219–226.

Young, F. M., and Collins, J. J. Results of testing Negro contact-syphilitics with the Wechsler-Bellevue Intelligence Scale. *Journal of Social Psychology*, 1954, *39*, 93–98.

Young, F. M., and Pitts, V. A. The performance of congenital syphilitics on the Wechsler Intelligence Scale for Children. *Journal of Consulting Psychology*, 1951, *15*, 239–242.

Young, M., and Gibson, J. In search of an explanation of social mobility. *British Journal of Statistical Psychology*, 1963, *16*, 27–36.

Yule, G. U. On the theory of inheritance of quantitative compound characters on the basis of Mendel's law—a preliminary note. *Report of the 3rd International Congress of Genetics*, 1906, 140–142.

Zamenhof, S., Van Marthens, E., and Margolis, F. L. DNA (cell number) and protein in neonatal brain: Alteration by maternal dietary protein restriction. *Science*, 1968, *160*, 322–323.

Zee, P., and Kafatos, A. G. Nutrition and Federal Food-assistance Programs:

A survey of impoverished preschool blacks in Memphis, Tennessee. *Federation Proceedings*, 1973, *32*, 926. (Abstract)

Zee, P., Walters, T., and Mitchell, C. Nutrition and poverty in preschool children. *Journal of the American Medical Association*, 1970, *213*, 739–742.

Zimmerman, R. R., Strobel, D. A., Steere, P., and Geist, C. R. Behavior and malnutrition in the rhesus monkey. *In* L. Rosenblum (Ed.), *Primate behavior*, Vol. 4. New York: Academic Press, 1974.

AUTHOR INDEX

SUBJECT INDEX